Urban Achievement in Early Modern Europe
Golden Ages in Antwerp, Amsterdam and London

This innovative work in comparative urban history explores why out-standing achievements in material and intellectual culture in early modern Europe tended to cluster in certain maritime cities. Patrick O'Brien and his co-editors have assembled a team of eighteen distin-guished historians from Belgium, the Netherlands, Britain and North America, who have collaborated to make detailed comparisons of economic, architectural, artistic, publishing and scientific achievements in three renowned mercantile and imperial cities during their golden ages: Antwerp (c. 1492–1585), Amsterdam (c. 1585–1659) and London (c. 1660–1730). The book examines growth and fluctuations in the for-tunes of all three cities in the context of broader trends in the growing urbanization of Europe's populations, cultures, societies and economies. The study is located in the histories of politics, warfare and culture in early modern Europe and offers fascinating insights to scholars and stu-dents of economic, social and cultural history.

PATRICK O'BRIEN is Centennial Professor of Economic History at the London School of Economics and Political Science, and Convenor of the Programme in Global History at the Institute of Historical Research, University of London. His books include *The Revolution in Egypt's Economic System*, *The New Economic History of the Railways*, *Economic Growth in Britain and France 1789–1914*, and *The Economic Effects of the American Civil War*.

DEREK KEENE is Director of the Centre of Metropolitan History at the Institute of Historical Research, University of London. He has pub-lished extensively on cities, metropolises and their hinterlands between the seventh and nineteenth centuries.

MARJOLEIN 'T HART is Lecturer in Social and Economic History at the University of Amsterdam. Her recent publications include *The Making of a Bourgeois State. War, Politics and Finance during the Dutch Revolt* and *A Financial History of the Netherlands*.

BARON HERMAN VAN DER WEE is Emeritus Professor of Social and Economic History at the Katholieke Universiteit Leuven in Belgium. His numerous publications cover the social and economic history of the Low Countries during the late Middle Ages and early modern times, the history of European banking and the world economy.

Urban Achievement in Early Modern Europe

Golden Ages in Antwerp, Amsterdam and London

Edited by

Patrick O'Brien
London School of Economics and Political Science

Derek Keene
Centre for Metropolitan History, University of London

Marjolein 't Hart
Universiteit van Amsterdam

Herman van der Wee
Katholieke Universiteit, Leuven, Belgium

CAMBRIDGE
UNIVERSITY PRESS

PUBLISHED BY THE PRESS SYNDICATE OF THE UNIVERSITY OF CAMBRIDGE
The Pitt Building, Trumpington Street, Cambridge, United Kingdom

CAMBRIDGE UNIVERSITY PRESS
The Edinburgh Building, Cambridge CB2 2RU, UK
40 West 20th Street, New York, NY 10011-4211, USA
10 Stamford Road, Oakleigh, VIC 3166, Australia
Ruiz de Alarcón 13, 28014 Madrid, Spain
Dock House, The Waterfront, Cape Town 8001, South Africa

http://www.cambridge.org

First published 2001

Printed in the United Kingdom at the University Press, Cambridge

Typeface Plantin 10/12   *System* QuarkXPress™   [SE]

A catalogue record for this book is available from the British Library

ISBN 0 521 59408 1 hardback

Contents

For
Gerry Martin
Inventor, Entrepreneur, Patron and Scholar

Figures

Tables

Contributors

Marten Jan Bok studied economic and social history at Utrecht University and wrote a dissertation on the economic history of painting in the Northern Netherlands in the seventeenth century (1994). He has worked as a researcher for the Utrecht Centraal Museum, the Provenance Index of the J. Paul Getty Art History Information Program, the J. Paul Getty Center for the History of Art and the Humanities, the Amsterdam Rijksmuseum and the Dutch Postgraduate School for Art History. Among his publications are monographs on the painters Pieter Saenredam (with Gary Schwartz, 1990) and Abraham Bloemaert (with Marcel Roethlisberger, 1993), as well as various contributions to exhibition catalogues in the field of Dutch painting.

Karel Davids studied history at Leiden and is Professor of Economic and Social History at Vrije Universiteit, Amsterdam. His books include *Zeewezen en wetenschap. De wetenschap en de ontwikkeling van navigatietechniek in Nederland tussen 1585 en 1815* (Amsterdam, 1986), *The Dutch Economy in the Golden Age: Nine Studies* (co-edited with Leo Noordegraaf, Amsterdam, 1993) and *The Dutch Republic in European Perspective* (co-edited with Jan Lucassen, Cambridge, 1995).

Peter Earle is Emeritus Reader in Economic History at the University of London. He is the author of several books including *A City Full of People: Men and Women of London, 1650–1750* (London, 1994) and *The Making of the English Middle Class: Business, Society and Family Life in London, 1660–1730* (London, 1989).

Paul Hoftijzer teaches the history of the book at the universities of Leiden and Amsterdam. He has written extensively on the history of publishing and bookselling in the Dutch Republic and on early modern histories of the Anglo-Dutch book trade. Among his publications are *Engelse boekverkopers bij de Beurs. De geschiedenis van de Amsterdamse boekhandels Bruyning en Swart, 1637–1724* (Amsterdam/Maarssen, 1987) and a study of the Leiden academic publisher and bookseller Pieter van der Aa (1659–1733) (Hilversum, 1999).

Adrian Johns is currently Professor of Sociology at the University of California, San Diego. Previous positions include Caltech and the University of Kent at Canterbury. He is a PhD in history and philosophy of science from the University of Cambridge, where he was a research fellow at Downing College, and then Munby fellow in bibliography at the University Library. He is the author of *The Nature of the Book: Print and Knowledge in the Making* (University of Chicago Press, 1998), which has won the Jon Ben Snow Prize, the Leo Gershoy Prize, the Louis Gottschalk Prize and the SHARP (Society for the History of Authorship, Reading, and Publishing) Prize. He is currently working on a long-term history of intellectual piracy.

Derek Keene is Director of the Centre of Metropolitan History at the University of London's Institute of Historical Research. He has published extensively on cities, metropolises and their hinterlands between the seventeenth and nineteenth centuries, with an emphasis on material conditions, environment and the interaction between the economy and the social order. That work includes studies of the organization of manufactures and technological innovation in the medieval period.

Clé Lesger is a lecturer in Economic and Social History at the University of Amsterdam. His current research includes entrepreneurship and the organization of early modern trade, the spatial structure of early modern cities and the history of migration. He is the author of *Hoorn als stedelijk knooppunt. Stedensystemen tijdens de late middeleeuwen en vroegmoderne tijd* (1990) and he co-edited *Entrepreneurs and Entrepreneurship in Early Modern Times. Merchants and Industrialists within the Orbit of the Dutch Staple Market* (1995).

Michael Limberger graduated in history from the University of Vienna. He is currently Assistant at the University of Antwerp where he is preparing a doctoral thesis on the economic changes in the rural environs of Antwerp in the sixteenth century. His publications include articles on urban networks, on the spread of merchant capitalism and on markets and consumption.

Judi Loach is a Senior Lecturer in the Welsh School of Architecture, Cardiff University, where she lectures on history of architecture and town planning. She has worked extensively on the relationship between theology, liturgy and architecture. Recent papers include a comparison of Primitivism in Gallicanism and in Anglicanism in the seventeenth and early eighteenth centuries.

Piet Lombaerde is a civil engineer who is Professor of the History and Theory of Architecture and Urbanism and of Garden History at the Higher Institute for Architectural Sciences (Antwerp). His research is focused on the history of towns and especially their fortifications in the Low Countries, from the sixteenth to the nineteenth century. His PhD thesis on urban planning in history was followed by several articles on historical gardens and architecture; he edited *Vesting Antwerpen* (Ghent and Antwerp, 1997).

Patrick O'Brien, formerly Director of the Institute of Historical Research, University of London, is currently Centennial Professor of Economic History at the London School of Economics and Political Science and Convenor of the Programme in Global History at the Institute. His books include *The Revolution in Egypt's Economic System* (1966), *The New Economic History of the Railways* (1977), *Economic Growth in Britain and France 1789–1914* (1978), and *The Economic Effects of the American Civil War* (1988). He has edited books on Industrialization (1998), Imperialism (1998), the Industrial Revolution in Europe (1994), Railways (1983) and Productivity Levels in Western Europe (1983). He is currently engaged in writing a history of world trade in the long run and European traditions in writing on the history of material progress.

David Ormrod studied at the London School of Economics before completing a doctorate at Christ's College, Cambridge. He has taught economic and social history at the University of Kent since 1970, and is author of *English Grain Exports and Agrarian Capitalism* (1985), *The Rise of Commercial Empires, 1650–1770* (forthcoming) and numerous essays and articles on English commercial and cultural history. Since the early 1990s, as a Visiting Fellow at the Institute of Historical Research, he has been researching into the history of the London art market. He is currently associated with the Luce Art and Economics Program based at Duke University, North Carolina. He is editor, with Michael North, of *Art Markets in Europe, 1400–1800* (1998).

Larry Stewart is a Professor of History at the University of Saskatchewan, Canada. He specializes in the history of science and has published widely on the interrelation of science, technology and culture in the eighteenth century. He is the author of *The Rise of Public Science. Rhetoric, Technology, and Natural Philoshophy in Newtonian Britain, 1660–1750* (Cambridge University Press, 1992).

Marjolein 't Hart lectures in Economic and Social History at the University of Amsterdam. Apart from her major book *The Making of a Bourgeois State. War, Politics and Finance during the Dutch Revolt* (1993) 't Hart co-edited *A Financial History of the Netherlands* (1995) and has written articles on urban and institutional history and on collective violence. Presently she is writing a monograph on the social and economic consequences of warfare in the early modern Netherlands.

Geert Vanpaemel teaches the History of Science at the Universities of Leuven and Nijmegen. His research concentrates on the national history of science in the Low Countries since 1500, with particular emphasis on the relations between science and society. He is the author of *Echo's van een wetenschappelijke revolutie* (Brussels, 1986) and of *Een standbeeld voor Stevin* (Nijmegen, 1995).

Hans Vlieghe is Professor of Art History at the Katholieke Universiteit, Leuven. He is Research Director of the Fonds Voor Wetenschappelyk Onderzoek Vlaanderen and Editor of *Pictura Nova. Studies in Sixteenth and Seventeenth Century Flemish Painting and Drawing.* His books include *Contributions to the Corpus Rubenianum Ludwig Burchard* (vols. 8 and 19) and *Monographic Studies on Rubens and Gaspar De Crayer*, and he has recently published *Flemish Art and Architecture 1585–1700* (Pelican History of Art, Yale University Press, 1998).

Werner Waterschoot teaches older Dutch literature at Ghent University. His major publications include editions of sixteenth-century authors: Lucas D'Heere, *Den Hof en Boomgaerd der Poësien* (1969), Jan van der Noot, *Stammbuch* (1971) and *De Poetische Werken* (1975, 3 vols.), and Karel van Mander, *Ter liefde der Const. Uit het Schilder-Boeck* (1983). His articles deal with, among others, analytical bibliography and emblematic literature.

Baron Herman van der Wee is Emeritus Professor of Social and Economic History at the Katholieke Universiteit Leuven, and has also taught at several European and American universities. His numerous publications cover the social and economic history of the Low Countries during the late Middle Ages and early modern times, European banking history from the Middle Ages to the present day, the world economy 1945–1990 and the reconstruction of Belgium's national accounts 1715–1900.

Part 1

Early modern cities as sources and sites
for achievement

1 Reflections and mediations on Antwerp, Amsterdam and London in their golden ages

Patrick O'Brien

In 1990 the Renaissance Trust, under the benign leadership of its chairman (Mr Gerry Martin), set up an Academic Committee to recruit and organize networks of scholars to engage in an ongoing series of conferences, meetings, seminars and conversations focused upon 'Achievement in Intellectual and Material Culture in Early Modern Europe'.[1] Apart from Gerry Martin, the Steering Committee of the Achievement Project (as it came to be called) comprised two historians of science, Robert Fox of Oxford and Simon Schaffer of Cambridge University; a cultural historian, Penelope Gouk of the University of Manchester; an economic historian, Patrick O'Brien, University of London; a sociologist, Steven Shapin of the University of California at San Diego; and a psychologist, Margaret Boden of Sussex University.

The Trust's programme of academic research, discussions and publications convened by the Steering Committee was summarized in the Achievement Project's successive newsletters (Oxford, 1991–1995), which are included in a Final Report edited by its Administrative Director, Penelope Gouk, in 1996.[2] Two collections of historical and theoretical essays concerned with Achievement are already in print, and a final book on the skilled workforce in early modern London is scheduled to appear in 2001–2002.[3]

---

[1] The first Achievement Project *Newsletter* (1, 1, Spring 1991) stated in its opening editorial that the focus of the project had been set on intellectual and material culture in *modern* Europe (circa 1500 to the present), with an emphasis on technological and scientific achievement. As the programme unfurled, the histories of achievements investigated were in practice located mainly in the early modern period.

[2] P. Gouk (ed.), *The Achievement Project, 1990–95* (Oxford, 1996). Copies of newsletters and the Report can be obtained from Dr P. Gouk, History Department, Manchester University.

[3] The published volumes are M. Boden (ed.), *Dimensions of Creativity* (Cambridge, Mass., and London, 1994) and P. Gouk (ed.), *Wellsprings of Achievement* (Aldershot, 1995). The final volume is D. Keene (ed.), *The Skilled Workforce in Early Modern London* (University of Massachusetts Press, forthcoming, 2001–2002).

All four related publications represent the outcomes of 'collaborative' intellectual endeavours that are common in the sciences, are visible in the social sciences, but remain rare in history and the humanities. 'Collaborative' means that the academics, recruited both to write and to offer introductions and responses to pre-circulated essays, participated in an ongoing discourse about 'Achievement'. More specifically, they agreed to locate their contributions to the project within a sub-theme or agenda, selected by the Steering Committee for a particular publication, meeting or conference.

As the five-year programme evolved, the Steering Committee widened its network in order to involve a 'core group' of scholars from several disciplines who participated on and off in the activities of the programme. Jim Bennett, University of Oxford; Michael Berlin, London; François Crouzet, Sorbonne; Peter Earle, London; Rob Iliffe, London; Ian Inkster, Nottingham Trent; Robert Kargon, Johns Hopkins; Derek Keene, London; Judi Loach, Cardiff; Lien Luu, Chichester; Alan Macfarlane, Cambridge; David Mitchell, London; David Ormrod, Kent; Graham Richards, London; Larry Stewart, Saskatchewan; and Joan Thirsk, formerly of the University of Oxford. Their contributions, formal and informal, written and conversational, provided an expanding basis for the selection, reception and syntheses of papers and comments delivered at annual symposia and other meetings organized by the Steering Committee.

My introduction (which has been influenced in all kinds of ways through interactions with this community of scholars from several disciplines) draws heavily on a range of papers, and commentaries upon them, submitted for two conferences held at Amsterdam in March 1994 and at Antwerp in May 1995. Several substantive essays commissioned as introductions and responses to pre-circulated papers and the taped record of those conferences could not alas be published as part of this volume.[4] Yet the authors would wish me to acknowledge the manifold intellectual contributions that all participants at the Amsterdam and Antwerp conferences made to the construction of this book. As I write, I am also conscious how much my attempt to produce some kind of coherent intro-

---

[4] The unpublished papers include illuminating contributions from the following: Marie-Claire Banquart, Sorbonne; Peter Burke, Cambridge; François Caron, Sorbonne; François Crouzet, Sorbonne; Philippe Dagen, Sorbonne; Jan de Vries, Berkeley; Herman Diederiks, Leiden; Penelope Gouk, Manchester; Ian Inkster, Nottingham Trent; Derek Keene, London; Jan Lucassen, Amsterdam; Alan Macfarlane, Cambridge; Jean-Luc Pinol, Strasbourg; Jean-Pierre Poussou, Sorbonne; Girolamo Ramonni, Paris; Pat Rogers, Florida; Simon Schaffer, Cambrige; Ed Taverne, Groningen; and Charles van den Heuvel, The Hague.

duction to this volume owes to regular contact with my distinguished friends on the Steering Committee, as well as to numerous other scholars (not all mentioned above) who participated in the Achievement Project between 1990 and 1995.

Fortunately my survey and mediation was also read, corrected and much improved by my co-editors (Derek Keene, Marjolein 't Hart and Herman van der Wee). I am pleased to thank Cathrine Delano-Smith for helping me select the book's cover and two maps for my introduction and Philip Hunt for his meticulous work on the index. Cassy O'Brien's interventions and suggestions have raised my own entirely limited knowledge and understandings of European art to a passable level. Of course mistakes, misapprehensions and rash syntheses are mine alone. Any illumination that comes across from this exercise in comparative urban history is (like most forms of academic history) another cooperative and disciplined achievement.

For the construction of this book everyone involved agreed to address a meta question, posed as usual with clarity and deceptive simplicity by Gerry Martin. 'Why', he enquired, 'do recognized and celebrated achievements, across several fields of endeavour, tend to cluster within cities over relatively short periods of time?' His question picks up on familiar perceptions of 'golden ages', 'belles époques', 'renaissances', 'restorations' and other 'cycles of time' which have dominated the published histories of many famous European cities right through from Rome to the post-1989 reconstruction of Berlin. Indeed histories of the rise, decline and revival of cities as diverse as Genoa, Venice, Bruges, Florence, Milan, Antwerp, Amsterdam, Brussels, Hamburg, Bordeaux, Paris and London are as common in early modern urban history as they are pervasive in the massive bibliography covering the histories of nation-states.[5]

Furthermore, many urban historians connect their deeply researched 'case studies' of particular towns and cities to less spatially and chronologically confined grand narratives concerned, for example, with urbanization and economic growth in national, continental and global contexts; with connections between cities and the formation of states; with the role of cities in geopolitical conflicts; and with urban networks and their links to national cultures. Alas, several important social themes that have not found a place in the urban achievements pursued in depth and detail in this project include the health, security, education and welfare that the

---

[5] Excellent bibliographies and reviews can be read in *Urban History Yearbook* (Leicester, 1974– to date).

governments of Antwerp, Amsterdam and London offered to their strat-
ified communities during their golden ages.[6]

Explicitly or implicitly all the chapters do, however, address broader histories of politics, warfare and culture in early modern Europe. They
connect above all with metanarratives concerned with material progress,
because the growth and fluctuations in the fortunes of all three cities are
part of broader European (and possibly global) trends in the urbanization
of populations, cultures, societies and economies that had been proceeding
since the early Middle Ages.[7] Indeed, the data suggest that, after a century
or more of stagnation following the Black Death, the share of Europe's
population residing in towns and cities probably rose again at a somewhat
faster rate, at the same time as the locus of urbanization shifted from
Mediterranean and central Europe to north-western regions of the continent – where Europeans began to concentrate in larger maritime and/or
capital cities, and particularly in Antwerp, Amsterdam and London.[8]

All observed 'trends' intensified during the seventeenth and eighteenth
centuries and continued after 1800 when Europe's urban network
widened to include an array of medium-sized industrial towns.[9]
Meanwhile, for the post-medieval period, Antwerp, Amsterdam and
London can be represented as prime examples of mercantile imperial
cities, actively engaged in intra-European and intercontinental trade, and
as 'central places' closely linked to productive agrarian hinterlands and
networked into hierarchies of smaller towns within their regions.
Simplified depictions of towns and cities are usually contested by historians, who are more impressed with the heterogeneity and uniqueness of
the places they study, and are often resistant to taxonomies that provide
for the analysis of processes as complex as urbanization. Agreed, all towns
are multifunctional and multifaceted. Nevertheless, significant common
features of Antwerp, Amsterdam and London are captured by the 'labels'
outlined above, which happen to be features they shared with other
famous maritime cities of that era, including Genoa, Venice, Bruges,
Lisbon, Hamburg, Marseilles, Bordeaux, Naples, Barcelona, Copenhagen
and other places of comparable scale and density.[10]

---

[6] For critical surveys of social welfare accorded by towns to their inhabitants, see C.R.
Friedrich's *The Early Modern City 1450–1750* (London, 1995) and C. Lis and H. Soly,
Poverty and Capitalism in Pre-industrial Europe (Brighton, 1979).

[7] P. Bairoch, 'Urbanization and the Economy in Pre-industrial Societies', *Journal of
European Economic History* 2 (1989), pp. 234–90. A.M. van der Woude et al. (eds.),
Urbanization in History (Oxford, 1990).

[8] J. de Vries, *European Urbanization 1500–1800* (Cambridge, 1984).

[9] P. Bairoch and G. Goetz, 'Factors of Urbanization in Nineteenth Century Developed
Countries', *Urban Studies*, 4 (1986), pp. 285–305.

[10] P. Hohenberg and L.H. Lees, *The Making of Urban Europe* (London, 1985).

Yet London clearly differed in significant respects from the two other cities considered here. With a long heritage as a national capital and a history of medieval growth and diversification behind it, throughout the early modern period London remained a much larger city, and economically and politically more dominant in relation to the countryside and towns of England than Antwerp and Amsterdam ever became within the Low Countries or north-western Europe.[11] Furthermore, London's prosperity depended in many varied and significant respects upon its status as the capital of a state actively engaged in the attainment of external security against any conceivable threat from powers on the mainland, in annexing the largest occidental empire since Rome, and in achieving a position of primacy in a centuries-old and violent struggle for the gains from intercontinental trade in commodities and services.[12]

Inseparable interconnections between European cities and the territorial empires, states and seignorial domains in which they were located have led historians to reconfigure their early modern histories in 'mercantilist' terms.[13] Such histories (following Braudel) are written within the parameters set by geopolitical competition for economic hegemony, backed by armed forces, among a succession of European states and cities experiencing their own particular long cycles of rise, decline and revival.[14] As it happens, Braudel's own model posits a succession whereby hegemony moved from Antwerp to Amsterdam and over to London, which was preceded by earlier (late medieval) cycles of polynuclear expansion dominated by the rise and decline (or 'recentering' to use Braudel's term) among other major mercantile cities, including the well-studied examples of Florence, Venice, Genoa and Bruges.[15]

Currently the geopolitical histories of these and other European cities are being incorporated into even larger metanarratives in historical sociology concerned with the rise and success of capitalism on the western promontory of the Eurasian landmass.[16] Global histories of the wealth and poverty of nations have recycled and elaborated further upon

---

[11] M. Reed, 'London and Its Hinterland 1600–1800' in P. Clark and B. Lepetit (eds.), *Capital Cities and Their Hinterlands in Early Modern Europe* (Aldershot, 1996), pp. 51–83; and D. Keene, 'Medieval London and Its Region', *London Journal* 14 (1989), pp. 99–111.

[12] P.K. O'Brien, 'Inseparable Connections: Trade Economy, Fiscal States and the Expansion of Empire 1688–1815' in P. Marshall (ed.), *History of the British Empire*, vol. II, *The Eighteenth Century* (Oxford, 1998), pp. 53–77.

[13] F. Braudel, *Civilization and Capitalism*, vol.III, *The Perspective of the World* (London, 1984).

[14] H.J. Nitz (ed.), *The Early Modern World System in Geographical Perspective* (Stuttgart, 1993).   [15] C.P. Kindleberger, *World Economic Primacy, 1500–1990* (Oxford, 1996).

[16] G. Arrighi, *The Long Twentieth Century* (London, 1994).

hypotheses outlined several decades ago by Max Weber and Henri Pirenne, who suggested the triumph of capitalism in the West depended 'significantly' upon the autonomies acquired by merchants and maritime cities within Europe's peculiar system of competing nation-states.[17] Although the contrast with Asia is being contested, nothing like the same degree of security, protection, encouragement and freedom seems to have been available to private enterprise in the maritime cities of the Chinese, Indian and Ottoman empires.[18] Europe's economic advance (and the contingent retardation of Asia, which became discernible during the seventeenth and eighteenth centuries and clear in the nineteenth century) has been connected by global historians to favourable outcomes from competition, including warfare, among an 'interconnected system' of European states and cities.[19]

European material progress has also been linked (following Weber) to the powers acquired by successful European cities vis-à-vis monarchies and aristocratic oligarchies as they attempted to assert fiscal, judicial and political sovereignty over the populations, towns and assets within their territories and domains.[20] Even in Europe, no city enjoyed anything like security from external aggression or freedom from state and seigneurial controls for long periods of early modern history.[21] As our comparisons between Antwerp, Amsterdam and London will show, their political and geopolitical positions differed and fluctuated in ways that clearly conditioned the timing, the prolongation and, indeed, the nature of their respective golden ages.[22]

Comparative history goes back at least to the Enlightenment and is exemplified in the writings of a line of distinguished scholars, including Montesquieu, Voltaire, Toqueville, Weber, Schmoller, Bloch and Braudel. All history that wishes to depart from cataloguing or narrating (or, as postmodernists recommend, recovering the meanings of past events for those alive at the time) must become comparative. Comparative history

---

[17] M. Weber, *General Economic History* (New York, 1961), pp. 233–58; and H. Pirenne, *Social and Economic History of Europe* (London, 1976), pp. 40–58.

[18] Dissenting views are elaborated by J. Blaut, *The Colonizers Model of the World* (New York, 1993); and A. Gunder-Frank, *ReOrient: Global Economy in the Asian Age* (London, 1998).

[19] E.L. Jones, *European Miracle* (Cambridge, 1981); and D. Landes, *The Wealth and Poverty of Nations* (London, 1998).

[20] C.Tilly and W. Blockmans (eds.), *Cities and the Rise of States in Europe* (Oxford, 1994).

[21] A. Cowan, *Urban Europe* (London, 1998).

[22] B. Pullan (ed.), *Crisis and Change in the Venetian Economy in the 16th and 17th Centuries* (London, 1965); H. van der Wee, *The Growth of the Antwerp Market and the European Economy* (The Hague, 1963); A.L. Beir and R. Findlay (eds.), *London 1500–1700: The Making of the Metropolis* (London, 1986); J. Israel, *Dutch Primacy in World Trade 1585–1740* (Oxford, 1989).

attempts to impose order, to escape from the complexity and diversity of local detail, and to persuade us that it can offer coherent and sensitive interpretations of past achievements that historians select for intensive study.

Successfully conducted, the comparative method should be persuasive, but it can never be as conclusive as the theories 'tested' by the natural or, according to their practitioners, by the more pretentious of social sciences! Nevertheless, not one of the chapters included in this collaborative work in European history is devoid of theory. Indeed, several authors made self-conscious use of economic, cultural and other theories. But, as usual among historians, the discovery that the significance of any particular variable for a specified outcome differed across space and time dominates most narratives and has constrained our initial aspiration to arrive at anything more than a limited range of generalizations about the origins of achievements that emerged in Antwerp, Amsterdam and London.

Indeed, the exercise exposed the ingrained and commendable working practices common to all professional historians, who worry deeply about facts, chronology and contextual integrity. As historians they remain committed to detail, to locality and to contingency. Several papers revel in paradox and seem more inclined to destroy than to deploy theory. Despite our predilection in favour of total history, we all found it difficult to grasp and to connect achievements within, or to compare them across, such complex social entities as Antwerp, Amsterdam and London. Perhaps that occurred because most of the scholars who agreed to participate in this collaborative endeavour were trained in a single national tradition, normally converse in their native languages and remained acutely aware of the effort required to make a research reputation in two, let alone three, national histories. European football looks easy enough to organize. Intellectual discourse at this level is both rare and daunting.

Nevertheless, teams of historians from three major European cities concentrated upon well-defined outcomes (achievements) emanating from locatable and already well-researched environments, which exhibited comparable but, more importantly, dissimilar economic, geographical, political, social, cultural, geopolitical and other characteristics and conditions.[23] They anticipated (as Marc Bloch suggested decades ago) that 'the comparative method can elicit from the chaotic multiplicity of circumstances those which were generally effective – the real causes'. He also told us that the main purpose of comparative history would reside in the elaboration of contrasts. As Bloch put it, 'correctly understand the

[23] W. Sewell, 'Marc Bloch and the Logic of Comparative History', *History and Theory* 6 (1967), pp. 208–18.

primary interest of the comparative method is . . . the observation of differences'.[24] Some, but by no means all, of the conditions for the formation of a book in comparative history are now present in the form of chapters dealing with economic, architectural, artistic and scientific achievements in Antwerp, Amsterdam and London during their golden ages. As the editor responsible for writing an introduction, I read all the chapters and listened to recordings of our discussions at the Amsterdam and Antwerp conferences with the questions about the clustering of achievement in mind. Several epistemological and conceptual problems appeared and constrained our aspiration to theorize or generalize. Yet they are still heuristic to contemplate.

First, several papers explored the uncertainty (and even the antipathy) that surrounds the notion of achievement.[25] Is achievement perhaps another Eurocentric, gendered or politically incorrect agenda for historians to pursue? Why did the Steering Committee fail to make space for the consideration of social welfare? After all, generations of critics of urban life have depicted cities as environments that undermine the health, morals and well-being of their inhabitants.[26] Were we talking about the peaks or plateaux of achievement? What are the overlaps with creativity, innovation and mere convergence to already known practices and techniques?[27] Our 'encompassing question' referred to 'celebrated achievements', but celebrated when, by whom and for how long?

Achievement turned out to be a more amorphous label than many other outcomes (such as the emergence of urban elites, cycles of collective violence, the low status of women, episodes of religious fervour, high rates of crime, and rising productivity, as well as other explicandum) investigated by historians using comparative methods. Furthermore, the delineation of upswings in levels of output or economic activity clearly proved less problematical for economic historians than for historians of other domains to measure. The former habitually deploy quantifiable indicators of success, such as incomes per capita, real wages, production and efficiency. If data are available they can at least locate discontinuities in rates of change as marking the possible onset of golden ages. Levels of achievement (however defined) for other areas of endeavour emerged as

---

[24] M. Bloch, 'Pour une histoire comparée des sociétés européenes', *Revue de Synthèse Historique* 46 (1925), pp. 15–50.

[25] The contested meanings and potential range of inferences surrounding the concept of achievement are rigorously explored in Gouk, *Wellsprings of Achievement*.

[26] A. Lees, *Cities Perceived: Urban Society in European and American Thought 1820–1940* (New York, 1985).

[27] Connections between creativity and achievement are analysed in Boden, *Dimensions of Creativity*, and between achievement and innovation in R. Fox (ed.), *Technological Change* (Amsterdam, 1996).

far more difficult to aggregate, pinpoint and weight. This meant that golden ages in the sciences, arts and architecture are contestable perceptions about the significance historians accord to different periods in the history of a city.

Finally, the widely debated problem about the appropriate spatial units for the analysis of different types of historical problem came to the foreground of discussion.[28] Are cities perhaps only the centres of much wider contexts required for fully elaborated comparisons and explanations for achievements?[29] It is a good question because, for more than two generations, urban historians have tried to settle upon an agreed definition of the perimeters and parameters of cities.[30] For some activities (such as the exploitation, diffusion and improvement of scientific knowledge), microspaces or nodes for interpersonal communication within larger towns are presented as more illuminating spaces for analysis.[31] As economies and even as locations for the production of innovative and high-quality works of art, architecture and design, Antwerp, Amsterdam and London (as well as Florence, Bruges and Venice before them) are recognized as 'embedded' in urban networks and in connections with productive agrarian hinterlands and, above all, as dominant entrepôts for transnational and intercontinental systems of trade, commerce and capital flows and for the exchange of information and novel ideas.[32]

Social and cultural historians conceive of cities as complexes generating fluid, open and adaptive cultures. They represent them as focal points for encounters between innovative or entrepreneurial individuals and receptive communities. In early modern Europe, cultural achievements generally (but not invariably) appeared and were first developed in cities. Nevertheless, the basis of or even the stimulus to all kinds of achievement (loosely ascribed to urbanization and concentrations of people in towns) may in some structuralist sense be imputed to those wider rural, urban, national and international networks within which Antwerp, Amsterdam, London and other famous cities became embedded long before the beginnings of their golden ages. Even the initial stimulus to an observed upswing might well, on examination, have emanated from changes in conditions beyond their boundaries, for example in declining food prices, booms in global trade or the unpredicted decline of rival towns during those centuries of dynastic, religious and destructive warfare.

---

[28] R.A. Dodgson, *The European Past. Social Evolution and Spatial Order* (London, 1987).
[29] A. Gunder-Frank and B.K. Gills (eds.), *The World System* (London, 1993).
[30] P. Abrams and E.A. Wrigley, *Towns in Societies, Essays in Economic History and Historical Sociology* (Cambridge, 1978).   [31] S. Shapin, *Scientific Revolution* (Chicago, 1996).
[32] J. Favier, *Gold and Spices. The Rise of Commerce in the Middle Ages* (London 1998).

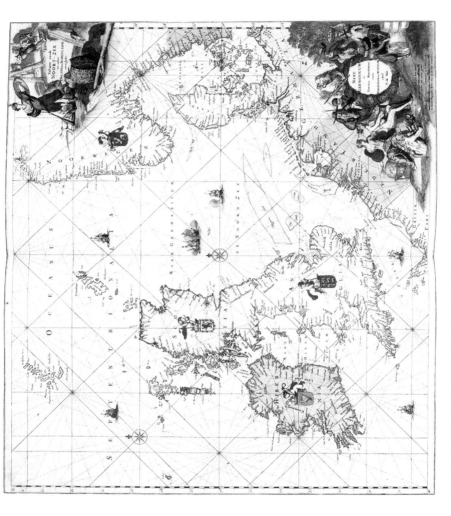

1.1 England and the Netherlands, 1680 (Source: *Frederick de Wits Atlas of the World*, London, 1680)

Urban historians seek to understand and to generalize about the significance of towns. Their fame, their continuous visual presence and the ready availability of urban records have led to some reification of their significance for European history.[33] In what ways and how far did the scale, concentration, density and heterogeneity of populations resident upon certain favourably located sites really matter for Europe's celebrated economic, scientific, artistic and architectural achievements? In what respects and to what degree did 'geographical space affect', as Braudel asserts, 'all historical realities, all spatially defined phenomena: states, societies, cultures and economies'?[34] Except implicitly in the number of pages he allocated to cities in a three-volume history of capitalism and material life, the great historian is rather noncommittal.[35]

Cities were usually the 'sites', but the question of how far they can be represented as the inspiration, basis or source of Europe's economic, political, artistic, architectural and other achievements remains to be carefully specified. We all hoped that some tentative answers might flow from exercises in comparative history of the kind recommended long ago by Marc Bloch.[36]

Largely because serious conceptual and contextual problems attended our collaborative attempt to juxtapose histories of Antwerp, Amsterdam and London during their golden ages, conclusions and firm generalizations are not to be inferred without care and qualification from the fifteen scholarly papers that make up this book. Nevertheless, professional historians from three European countries and North America, with wide ranges of expertise, did communicate with each other. Their research and reflections show that achievements across five domains of human endeavour during golden ages can be connected in some ways to each other and more clearly to the urban settings and historical chronologies from which they emerged.

Alas clouds can obscure the whole notion of golden ages. When do golden ages begin? What brings them to a close? Are they distinctive enough as periods or cycles in the development of cities? If they are to be

---

[33] V. Barbour, *Capitalism in Amsterdam in the 17th Century* (Ann Arbor, 1963); and see: P. Clark, *Small Towns in Early Modern Europe* (Cambridge, 1995).
[34] Braudel, *The Perspective of the World*, p. 21.
[35] Braudel's followers: Arrighi, *The Long Twentieth Century*, and Kindleberger, *World Economic Primacy*, are much less cautious.
[36] But alas, as Peter Burke observed (in the second edition of his famous study of 1974), undertaken all too infrequently by historians – P. Burke, *Venice and Amsterdam. A Study of Seventeenth Century Elites* (2nd edn, 1994), p. xiii. But see P. Hall, *Cities in Civilization: Culture, Innovation and Urban Order* (London, 1999), and M. G. Hansen (ed.), *A Comparative Study of Thirty City-State Cultures* (Historisk-filosofiske Skrifter 21 of Royal Danish Academy of Science and Letters, Copenhagen, 2000).

used as something other than nostalgic constructs, stages in history should be demarcated from preceding and succeeding periods and defended in terms of the forces for change that carried cities from one plateau to another. Golden ages start from a certain base of capacities, evolve into something 'better', and the new situation at some end point should help us to determine the meaning of what has happened before. Belgian and Dutch historians have less trouble with the selection of a golden age for Antwerp and Amsterdam than British (and French historians) do for their capital cities. Antwerp's and Amsterdam's histories certainly exemplified more of the characteristics required for unified and coherent stages than the shorter époque selected for golden decades from 1660 to 1713 that followed the restoration of a monarchical regime in London. Indeed London (and Paris) seem to have evolved through several golden ages.

As a prelude, perhaps the obvious point to make is that, well before the early years of the periods demarcated to represent golden ages, all three cities had accumulated considerable endowments of physical capital, human skills and organizational capacities. Antwerp's system of fairs by, say, 1450, Amsterdam's port linked to Antwerp by 1550 and London (connected to the staple markets of Amsterdam) by the mid-seventeenth century had crossed thresholds of scale, in terms of population size, supplies of skilled and professional manpower as well as stocks of social overhead and directly productive capital. Furthermore, the cities had for some time operated within frameworks of laws, institutions and property rights required to promote the individual effort and investments necessary for success in several domains of human endeavour.

Favourably located on seas, rivers and artificial waterways, their expanding populations could be fed and their workforces supplied with raw materials from agrarian hinterlands or, whenever necessary, from more distant sources of supply through intra-European and international trade.[37] Well-functioning markets and networks of transportation had long connected all three cities into regional, national and international trade. They possessed facilities – docks, ships and warehouses and working capital in the form of inventories of goods – as well as the craft, nautical, professional, mercantile and embryo banking skills necessary to produce, or to acquire, the commodities to engage actively in the expansion of regional, European and intercontinental commerce, underway by the mid-fifteenth century.

[37] For an exemplary study of 'feeding cities' see B.M.S. Campbell et al., *A Medieval Capital and Its Grain Supply: Agrarian Production and Distribution in the London Region* (London, 1993).

Finally, all three cities entered their golden ages with civic/patrician elites experienced in managing the political and administrative institutions established to cope with the normal problems (and even the occasional disasters) of urban existence, such as subsistence crises, plagues, fire, crime, disorder, high mortality rates and the debilitating morbidity that afflicted densely concentrated populations in early modern Europe.[38] Of course, all these problems remained acute but they never became serious enough to depress the cities' potential for continuing and even extraordinary rates of 'progress' when opportunities arose.

Omnipresent and potentially crippling political and geopolitical challenges, which for decades they managed to evade and resist, also threatened their security as viable and functioning economies and communities. Although Antwerp's golden age came to a close before the end of the sixteenth century, somehow, even after the Spanish Fury of 1576 and its sack and forcible reincorporation into the Habsburg empire in 1585, the city recovered to enjoy an Indian summer of stability and more modest prosperity down to the Treaty of Münster in 1648.[39] Amsterdam revived again and again, war after war, despite the power and depredations of three formidable and envious nation states – Spain, France and England. That city's clear and unequivocal decline into a satellite of London occurred only after thirty-four years of internal revolution and geopolitical turmoil (1781–1815), which witnessed Holland's incorporation into the Napoleonic empire in 1806 and the destruction of its foreign trade and conquest of its colonies in Asia, Africa and the Americas by British naval power.[40]

To sum up, given their medieval histories and with infrastructures and institutions in place, Antwerp, Amsterdam and London seem more likely to have sustained booms in the sixteenth, seventeenth and eighteenth centuries than, say, Madrid, Naples and Vienna.[41] However, our exercise in urban history made no attempt to pose the counterfactual and systematically compare their histories with another trio of cities, where anticipated development and achievement somehow failed to materialize.[42]

Furthermore, the political crises and dangers confronted by Antwerp,

[38] H. Diederiks et al. (eds.), *Economic Policy in Europe since the late Middle Ages. The Visible Hand and the Fortune of Cities* (Leicester, 1992).
[39] F. Suykens et al., *Antwerp. A Port for All Seasons* (Antwerp, 1986).
[40] J. Israel, *The Dutch Republic. Its Rise, Greatness and Fall* (Oxford, 1995).
[41] G. Rozman, *Urban Networks in Russia 1750–1800 and Premodern Periodization* (Princeton, 1976), D. Ringrose, *Madrid and the Spanish Economy 1560–1850* (Berkeley, 1983) and B. Marin, 'Naples: Capital of the Enlightenment' in Clark and Lepetit, *Capital Cities*, pp. 143–67.
[42] An implicit counterfactual is however at play in F. Braudel, *Civilisation and Capitalism 15th–18th Centuries. The Structure of Everyday Life* (London, 1981), pp. 479–558.

Amsterdam and London just prior to and over initial and later years of their golden ages can be represented positively as moments of 'cultural reordering', when their citizens responded collectively and with unusual zeal to potentially disastrous threats to their autonomy, as well as to less serious ecological crises such as fire, plague and the influx of refugees fleeing from religious persecution.

For example, the adroit diplomacy pursued by noble and mercantile patricians of Antwerp in backing Habsburg claimants to the Burgundian dominions during the long succession of diplomatic and military struggles over the fifteenth century turned out to be percipient.[43] Antwerp merchants also appear to have been more aggressive than their established rivals, operating out of Bruges, in developing comparative advantages in handling commerce in new ways and in a range of 'new' and expanding products – including English woollens, fustians, German silver and copper and tropical groceries carried to Europe by the Portuguese from recently established connections in Africa and Asia. The comfortably ensconced merchants of Bruges perceived no particular reason to diversify and adjust their ways. Inertia was built into that city's already successful economy before the port began to be afflicted by locational disadvantages compared with Antwerp as well as the silting of its harbours on the Swin.[44] By the time of the Habsburg regency of Maximillian, Antwerp had matured into a 'commercial capital' of the Netherlands.[45] Entrepreneurial vigour and political acumen stimulated by the persistent and intense competition between these two cities helped Antwerp hold onto that top position within the Low Countries and north-western Europe as a whole until Spanish armies and Dutch naval power destroyed a large part of its physical capital and locational advantages and killed and dispersed much of its skilled and professional workforce during the Revolt against Spain, 1572–1600.

Amsterdam then gained enormously from Antwerp's political misfortunes and the 'step' migration northward to Holland of Antwerp's craftsmen and key capitalists at the head of hierarchical systems of control over Europe's trade, craft and proto-industrial regions.[46] Nevertheless, Amsterdam's culture, vitality and identity were surely consolidated by coming late but moving rapidly to the centre of Holland's long and bitter struggle for survival in the revolt against Spain and the forces of Counter-Reformation.[47]

---

[43] W. Prevenier and W. Blockmans, *The Burgundian Netherlands* (Cambridge, 1986), pp. 52–80.

[44] On inertia see R.A. Dodgshon, *Society in Time and Space* (Cambridge, 1998).

[45] Suykens, *Antwerp*, pp. 43–79.   [46] Israel, *The Dutch Republic*, pp. 307–27.

[47] S. Schama, *The Embarrassment of Riches* (London, 1987), pp. 53–93.

In London, memories of more than a decade of unprofitable instability and the destructive violence of civil war encouraged England's restored monarchial and aristocratic elite to cooperate with the capital's merchants, proto-bankers and businessmen in the reconstruction of a viable political regime. After a republican interregnum, England's 'gentlemanly capitalists' designed and consolidated a powerful fiscal military state that proved capable of checking Louis XIV and later Bourbon and Napoleonic pretensions to dominate Europe. The restored state lent effective support to London's merchants, financiers, industrialists and craftsmen as they engaged for more than a century in mercantilist competition for trade and empire with Holland, Spain and above all France.[48]

Golden ages in all three cities seem, therefore, to have been preceded and accompanied by 'cultural reordering' connected to successful resistance to political threats to their stability, security and prosperity as central places and entrepôts in Europe's drive to profit from the expansion of global trade.[49] Cultural reordering followed most obviously from the circulation of elites when and wherever 'reformers' superseded 'establishments'. But it also manifested itself in intense rivalries and quests for identities along all the 'frontiers' of artistic, architectural, scientific as well as economic endeavour that divided Protestant from Catholic communities throughout post-Reformation Europe. Geopolitical and religious (and their contingent cultural) rivalries that marked the three centuries before the French Revolution reinforced centripetal tendencies towards cooperation within cities and centrifugal tendencies towards competition among European cities.[50]

Thus, on examination, golden ages turn out to be 'path dependent'. They came to cities well endowed by location; prepared by histories of physical and human capital accumulation, actively engaged in regional, international and intercontinental trade, and enjoying some degree of autonomy from potentially coercive and predatory states. Upswings in achievement were sustained by cultures forged in adversity, which fostered cooperation among their citizens and a vigorously competitive and mercantilist stance towards rival cities.

When they came on stream, the booms in economic, scientific, artistic and constructional activities in Antwerp, Amsterdam and London included rather more comparable than contrasting features. First of all their historians noticed the rapid growth of city populations, basically

---

[48] P.K. O'Brien, 'Political Preconditions for the Industrial Revolution' in P.K. O'Brien and R. Quinault (eds.), *The Industrial Revolution and British Society* (Cambrige, 1993), pp. 124–56.

[49] J.D. Tracy (ed.), *The Rise of Merchant Empires, 1350–1750* (Cambridge, 1990).

[50] C. Tilly, *Coercion, Capital and European States AD 990–1990* (Cambridge, Mass., 1990).

through very high rates of net immigration – quite extraordinary in the case of Amsterdam, remarkable for London, and very important for Antwerp.[51] Many immigrants, particularly women, children, the unhealthy and the unskilled, brought difficulties as well as cheap labour into cities. The impoverished lived in squalid conditions and experienced the highest rates of death and disease. Somehow all three cities coped with the problems of good order, public morals and morbidity associated with high-density settlement and overcrowding. For centuries the condition of a large urban underclass can only be represented as the dark side of urban achievement. Welcomed immigrants included men who added to the stocks of capital and artisanal skills and possessed the status, knowhow and connections required to link cities into networks of trade, communication and credit around and beyond Europe.

All three cities promoted personal and social patterns of behaviour required to cooperate with and to assimilate communities of otherwise alien merchants, bankers and craftsmen from all over Europe, regardless of ethnic and religious differences. Falteringly, and with different degrees of success, they evolved and maintained enduring and profitable cultures of 'tolerance'.[52]

Successive waves of 'betterment migrants', who came either to settle or to locate temporarily in Antwerp, Amsterdam and London, carried wealth, knowledge, information, contacts and the entrepreneurial drives of 'outsiders' with them. As young people, immigrants from wherever they came also brought distinctive and attractive patterns of consumption into cities. They interacted with indigenous communities to generate another common feature of golden age booms, namely transformations in consumer behaviour. For all kinds of reasons, households in towns matured into experimental buyers of housing, foodstuffs, clothing, furnishings, fine and decorative arts, books, plays and music. When their collective incomes rose or prices fell, cities became unusually open and flexible markets for novel products, new experiences and innovative designs.[53] With more money to spend, their citizens entered into productive dialogues with merchants, shopkeepers, craftsmen, painters, publishers, actors and musicians, which in turn produced higher levels of traded

---

[51] All participants at the Amsterdam conference were educated by reading two exemplary unpublished   surveys on population growth and internal migration: J. Lucassen, 'Amsterdam. A Golden Age, Based on Immigration' (Internationaal Instituut voor Sociale Geschiedenis, Amsterdam, March 1996), and D. Keene, 'London's Population at the End of the Seventeenth Century' (Centre for Metropolitan History, Institute of Historical Research, University of London, March 1996).

[52] O.C. Cox, *Foundations of Capitalism* (New York, 1959), part I, deals with these cultural attributes of Italian and north European cities.

[53] J. Brewer and R. Porter (eds.), *Consumption and the World of Goods* (London, 1993).

output and stimulated more specialized and variegated patterns of production, design and performance across a range of artefacts and activities.

Markets in all three cities offered all kinds of profitable opportunities for producers (of food, clothing, furnishings, household wares, paintings, ornaments, books, newspapers, musical instruments, and theatrical and musical performances) to expand and diversify their activities. For manufacturers and traders, cities were peculiarly hospitable social and cultural spaces. In towns, information about what 'others' were enjoying could be more easily conveyed, not simply in the form of advertising by merchants and shopkeepers in newspapers and windows but also through 'social mingling' among and across classes, living as neighbours in confined or traversable spaces. Detached from families and local communities, city dwellers became 'free' to adopt 'modern' values, to engage in self-fashioning and to display their identities through 'material culture' in the form of dwellings, diet, dress, furnishings, decorations, ornaments and the pursuit of civilizing and sexually gratifying pleasures available in towns.[54] Demonstration effects brought about higher and more diverse propensities to consume and transformed these cities into markets for everything and anything brought in from their hinterlands, urban networks and far-flung trading connections around the world.

Cities often look so ideal as markets for consumers, producers, merchants and innovators of all kinds that some historians have been tempted to explain the observed booms of their golden ages with reference to the 'rise of material culture' or 'revolutions in consumer behaviour' initiated and promoted by the concentration of people in cities such as Antwerp, Amsterdam and London.[55] Unfortunately, this now fashionable reification of markets, consumers and cities leads to grossly underspecified models of early modern economic growth – models that cannot moreover distinguish between factors initiating from factors sustaining upswings in economic activity.[56]

The three chapters on the economies of the three cities, presented in part 2, certainly recognize their real significance as markets and as European and global entrepôts. But the chapters are rounded to include perspectives on their long histories as sites of production and of interactions with agrarian hinterlands and urban networks, as well as their complex relations with territorial states and empires. Communities of

---

[54] A. Bermingham and J. Brewer (eds.), *The Construction of Culture, Image, Object, Text* (London, 1995).

[55] N. McKendrick et al. (eds.), *The Birth of Consumer Society* (London, 1982).

[56] J. Mokyr, 'Demand versus Supply in the Industrial Revolution', *Journal of Economic History* 37 (1977), pp. 981–1008, and L. Tiersten, 'Redefining Consumer Culture: Recent Literature on Consumption and the Bourgeoisie in Western Europe', *Bolletino del diciannovesimo* 5 (1996), pp. 5–20.

1.2 Maritime Europe, 1585 (Source: *Teerste deel vande Spieghel der Zeevaerdt, etc.* Leyden, Christoffel Plantijn, 1585)

consumers, merchants and shopkeepers concentrated in these cities were not groups apart; they resided alongside diverse ranges of manufacturing industry, transportation networks, financial services, facilities and personnel for training and education as well as systems for the transmission of useful knowledge and commercial intelligence. They operated within established legal and governmental institutions. All cities derived externalities from agglomeration and concentration of these activities within defined contexts and regulated spaces.[57] Each city displayed particular competitive advantages in industry, transportation, construction, finance and other sectors of economic activity, as well as unique political positions in Europe's mercantilist order.[58] For example, from the time of Cromwell, London enjoyed prolonged and unrivalled protection and support from the English state. Braudel's thesis, which posits a succession of hegemonic cities moving from Antwerp (in the sixteenth century) to Amsterdam (a century later), and on to London after 1688, can be explained largely in these geopolitical terms.[59]

Interconnections between investment in private houses and public buildings and other forms of urban infrastructure on the one hand, and upswings in economic growth on the other, are commonplace in analyses of cycles of economic growth. Thus, evidence of increased allocations by monarchs, aristocrats and municipal authorities (from taxes and rents) and of expenditures by merchants, bankers, industrialists, lawyers, guild masters and other rich citizens, designed to replace, maintain, improve and extend the buildings and built environments of Antwerp, Amsterdam and London, was hardly remarkable.[60] It would be interesting to measure the relatively high but presumably different proportions of their revenues and incomes that the governing authorities and affluent citizens of the three cities allocated to the construction of residences, churches, civic buildings, monuments, hospitals, alms houses, factories, warehouses, offices and fortifications. These structures and their arrangements in space, which represent achievements in the domain of architecture and urban planning, are often pleasingly preserved as visible and central manifestations of golden ages.

Clearly the scale and nature of accomplishments in this sphere can be linked to the quantity and quality of resources mobilized for construction and reconstruction. Although actual investments cannot be quantified, it

[57] P. Bairoch, *Cities and Economic Development* (Chicago, 1990).   [58] See pp. 39–86.

[59] Although Braudel is inclined to neglect the geopolitical context (Braudel, *The Perspective of the World*, pp. 92–276), that omission is redressed by several essays in J.D. Tracy (ed.), *The Political Economy of Merchant Empires* (Cambridge, 1991).

[60] J.W. Konwitz, *The Urban Millennium: The City Building Process from the Early Middle Ages to the Present* (Carbondale, 1985).

does seem as if elites in Antwerp, Amsterdam and London found the money, motivation and spaces required to redesign rather considerable areas of their cities.

In Antwerp, apart from investments by the city authorities in protective fortifications (the Spanish walls and citadel) and its impressive Town Hall, urban developments were financed, planned and managed by merchants, entrepreneurs and bankers operating within a lose framework of municipal regulation.[61]

Apparently the municipal government of Amsterdam took a stronger lead in funding and shaping the built environment and overall appearance of that city than did the authorities of Antwerp or London. Nevertheless, no overall masterplan guided the gradual construction of houses, canals and fortifications and the incorporation of new areas into the boundaries of Amsterdam. As the city grew and prospered, its Regents actively mediated between conflicting military, economic, demographic, social and cultural demands. Like their precursors in Venice, they assumed responsibilities for canals, sewerage, street lighting and fortifications.[62] Public investment flowed into Admiralty House, a huge warehouse in Oostenburg, churches, hospitals, alms houses, prisons, the Bourse, a theatre, an opera house, a hotel, the Athenaeum Illustre, and the famous Town Hall, which included the Amsterdam Bank of Exchange which 'radiated the image of Amsterdam as a world metropolis'. Housing, commercial districts, luxury shops and churches were 'zoned' in order to facilitate efficiency as well as the residential comfort and aesthetic ideas of a self-confident mercantile elite.[63]

London's Great Fire of 1666, which succeeded the City's last outbreak of plague and a long interregnum of republican government, presented the Crown, Parliament and the City Fathers with an almost unique opportunity to execute some kind of overall plan for the reconstruction of England's devastated and rundown medieval capital. In the event, the powers (or more likely the resources) of the recently 'restored' Stuart monarchy proved to be insufficient to rebuild London as a royal capital city, on the verge of its long eighteenth century (1660–1815) of commercial, industrial and imperial expansion. Wren formulated plans that still look exciting.

[61] See pp. 99–127.
[62] S.Ciriacono, 'Venise et la Hollande pays de l'eau' (XVe–XVIIIe siecle), *Revue historique*, 175, 2 (1995), pp. 295–320.
[63] pp. 128–50. Participants at the Amsterdam conference read a scholarly paper by E. Taverne, '"Mercator Sapiens". The extension of Amsterdam of 1613 viewed in the context of humanist ideas about the city and the merchant' (unpublished paper, Groningen, 1994), published in Dutch as 'Mercator sapiens. De Amsterdamse stadsuitleg (1613) in het licht van humanistische oprattingen over stad en koopman', *De Zevententiende Eeuw* 6 (1990), pp. 1–6.

Nevertheless, no Renaissance city emerged from the ashes, despite the cultivated ambitions of successive Stuart monarchs to impose order, symbolic as well as physical, upon a potentially unruly capital. Instead, London's developers, merchants, bankers, guildsmen and city councillors got on with the job. Operating within the framework of a revised and tighter set of building regulations, in a desperate hurry to revive the City they put up their residences, constructed housing for the lower orders, offices, warehouses, shops and livery halls and repaired the grandiose Guildhall in ways and styles that suited the needs and aspirations of businessmen.[64]

Unlike Antwerp and Amsterdam, London was a capital city but, after the fire, investment in its reconstruction, layout and design appears to have been spread out over several decades and confined to the construction of a large number of new parish churches – including the magnificent St Paul's Cathedral – most, but not all, designed and supervised by Wren and his pupil Hawksmoor.[65]

All three cities recruited the craftsmen (bricklayers, carpenters, joiners, plasterers and masons) employed to execute the demands and designs of private clients and public patrons, largely from local and regional supplies of skilled labour. Entrepôts are places for cultural encounters for the exchange of ideas, as well as goods and commercial services. Thus the architects, engineers and designers (who negotiated with patrons and who formulated and supervised plans for the construction and reconstruction of the buildings and urban spaces in Antwerp, Amsterdam and London) called upon pools of classical, Renaissance and more up-to-date bodies of printed texts and tacit knowledge for their purposes.[66] They drew, moreover, from the experience of technical success and visual appeal of other towns: Antwerp from Bruges and Florence; Amsterdam from Antwerp, Venice, London and Rome, and above all from other Dutch towns in its own urban network; London emulated Rome and Paris and copied from Amsterdam.

Alas, this domain posed peculiarly difficult problems for comparative history. Were Antwerp before the sack, Amsterdam in 1648 and London by the Peace of Utrecht, 1713, better designed, more aesthetically pleasing and habitable cities than they had been at the start of their golden ages?[67] Each city produced buildings, monuments and layouts that can be represented as local compromises, mediations and innovations to

[64] A.L. Beier and R. Findlay (eds.), *London 1500–1700. The Making of the Metropolis* (London, 1986); and D. Keene, '333 Years after the Great Fire' (unpublished paper, Centre for Metropolitan History, Institute of Historical Research, 1999).
[65] See pp. 151–69. The Royal Military Hospital at Chelsea and the Royal Naval Hospital (later College) at Greenwich are, of course, included among Wren's distinguished buildings.
[66] H. Roseneau, *The Ideal City* (London, 1974) surveys the canonical texts of the period.
[67] W. Braunfels, *Urban Design in Western Europe, Regime and Architecture 900–1900* (Chicago, 1988).

established classical and Gothic ideals. Thus Antwerp's *stadhuis* merges both styles. Van Campen and Vingboons adapted Palladian ideals to the tastes and demands for comfort of grand Amsterdam merchants. St Paul's displays unorthodox but functional geometries, representing Wren's interpretation of the ambitions of an Anglican confessional state to identify itself with an early Christendom that predated the hegemony of Roman Catholicism.[68]

Similar links between the patronage of monarchs, aristocrats, court officials, municipal oligarchies, lawyers, bankers, merchants and other businessmen, on the one hand, and the production of fine and decorative arts, on the other, are elaborated upon by the three chapters in part 4. Since the authors' concerns are with expensive paintings, engravings, sculpture, ornaments, tapestries, furniture, glassware and majolica, produced by highly skilled artisans, they connected the diverse artefacts and crafts they studied to underlying movements in the economies of all three cities.[69] Again, the increased production of luxuries and semi-luxuries (sold to landowners receiving rents in towns, to municipal oligarchies allocating local revenues, to merchants, bankers, lawyers, industrialists and artisans spending extra money upon the decoration of their homes, churches, civic buildings, fraternities, favoured alms houses, hospitals and other charities) can be connected (more or less rigorously) to economic trends, short cycles and exogenous shocks such as wars and to upswings in urban construction.[70]

During their respective golden ages, all three cities witnessed an extension in demand for 'luxuries' (and artefacts moving into categories now labelled as quasi or semi-luxuries). Markets widened to include non-traditional clients with sufficient purchasing power to fashion their households in the styles of princes, aristocrats and wealthy patricians or, occasionally, in new 'bourgeois' ways. At the same time the cities also exemplified a European-wide tendency for secular institutions (municipalities, guilds, livery companies, charities, etc.) to supplement and, in places, to replace court and ecclesiastical patronage. Both tendencies were, for several reasons, taken much further in Amsterdam than in London. Although they had appeared to a discernible extent several decades earlier in Antwerp. By the mid-sixteenth century wealthy businessmen of Antwerp already dealt with specialized dealers in works of art

---

[68] See pp. 99–169.
[69] R. Fox and A. Turner (eds.), *Luxury Trades and Consumerism in Ancien Régime Paris* (Aldershot, 1998); and G. Crossick (ed.), *The Artisan and the European Town 1500–1900* (Aldershot, 1997).
[70] M. North and D. Ormrod (eds.), *Art Markets in Europe* (Aldershot, 1998). The most rigorous attempt at connection is made in this volume in chapter 9 by Bok.

and other luxuries, purchased for their own residences in towns and on behalf of clients in Iberia, New Spain, England, Scandinavia and other towns in their European commercial networks. The city's artists and craftsmen produced and exported an increasingly diverse range of paintings, dominated by religious images but broadening out to include portraits, landscapes and moralizing pictures that appealed to the self-importance, experience and cultural aspirations of successful men of commerce, industry, government and the law. Artisans modified their styles in painting, sculpture and other fine arts to embody Renaissance techniques and approaches in art and design imported from Italy. Although they shifted increasingly towards a non-commissioned market for art, most of the art and crafts produced in Antwerp continued to be made for a well-defined body of discerning and knowledgeable clients, both at home and abroad.[71]

After 1585 the painters and artisans resident in Amsterdam extended their range, cheapened their outputs and adapted their methods of production in order to sell on the early modern equivalent of a 'mass market'. 'Dutch' paintings and prints, produced (and/or sold through specialized dealers) in Amsterdam, widened to include all known genres and dealt with every conceivable subject: portraits, still lives, domestic and church interiors, flowers, foodstuffs, fish, meat, animals, battle scenes, histories, town-, village-, sea- and landscapes, scenes of debauchery and pornography; as well as a plethora of visual narratives, printed and painted in order to elevate private and public morals and to substitute for Catholic images that reformed churches sought to banish from Protestant cultures.

Dutch art represents a massive breakthrough in the scale and scope of European painting which can, to some considerable extent, be accounted for in economic terms. Clearly, and as measured, the increased flows of expenditures by households and public authorities of Amsterdam upon art, prints and luxury artefacts can be convincingly linked to successive cycles of prosperity experienced by the Dutch Republic (including Amsterdam) for more than a century after 1585, and connected to the increasing diversity, falling prices and changing qualities of the luxuries and quasi-luxuries on offer in Amsterdam and other Dutch towns, distributing local products through that great mart. The numbers of artists and craftsmen working in the city went up and up – sharply at first when hundreds of refugees with scarce skills fled from persecution in Antwerp and the Southern Netherlands. Thereafter, Amsterdam's endowment of skill continued to rise year after year as trained artisans migrated in from neighbouring towns within the city's network and orbit. Refined special-

---

[71] See pp. 173–85.

ization, batch production and differentiation for niche markets (for example, the representation of fish or popular emblems of morality) followed from intensified competition and from the steady flow of apprentices from established masters, workshops, studios and schools, entering Amsterdam's rapidly expanding arts and crafts workshops.[72]

Although rising incomes, falling prices, product differentiation and improvements in the dexterity and productivity of the urban workforce all clearly mattered, the scale, scope and speed of the expansion in the production of fine and decorative arts in (and around) Amsterdam do seem to require a deeper investigation into Dutch traditions, religion and geopolitical experience as well as a likely cultural reordering of tastes and propensities to consume in the Southern Netherlands (and somewhat later in the Northern Netherlands) in the wake of the Reformation and the Revolt against Spain. In short, the explanation for achievement in the fine and decorative arts in Amsterdam could be widened and taken further than the 'proximate determinants' that satisfy economists. After all (and responding to comparable economic incentives), luxury industries in Antwerp and London could counterfactually have proceeded to grow at a similar speed in roughly the same diverse directions; particularly as the artists and craftsmen in Antwerp, Amsterdam and London all tapped into the same pools of classical, Italian and German knowledge to inform their techniques and styles. Each city also gained considerably from the influx of skilled migrants: Antwerp less than London, but perhaps Amsterdam most of all from waves of refugees fleeing from Spanish, French and pervasive Catholic intolerance towards Protestants and Jews.

We must, however, recall that Antwerp's promising trajectory had been violently interrupted by Spanish power and Dutch blockades, while in London the evolution of the fine and decorative arts (already visible during the reigns of Elizabeth and the early Stuarts) clearly suffered from the Civil War – an interregnum of 'democratic' disdain for monarchical and aristocratic luxury – and from Puritan antipathies to a 'papist' culture and of religious images and icons.[73] Yet English republicanism and protestantism did not celebrate the triumph of Parliament with anything approaching the exuberance vividly displayed by Dutch burghers for their victories over Spain and the forces of counter-reformation.[74] The 'restoration' of fine and decorative arts and architecture in London, depended heavily upon older traditions of court and aristocratic patronage, classical ideals, French taste and the importation of foreign artefacts

---

[72] See pp. 186–209.
[73] R. Strong, *Lost Treasures of Britain. Five Centuries of Creation and Destruction* (London, 1990).   [74] J. Brewer, *The Pleasure of the Imagination* (London 1997), pp. 3–20.

as well as the City's attraction for German, Flemish, Italian and Dutch painters and craftsmen. Despite 'English' resentment towards the capital's dependence on foreign craftsmen and the aristocracy's preference for continental (particularly French) artefacts, art and design, the substitution of native production for imported luxuries took more than a century to achieve.[75] London apparently required an articulated Whig programme of cultural nationalism, fulminations from Hogarth as well as high tariffs and an aggressive stance in foreign policy to begin to rival Amsterdam's success in the fine and decorative arts.[76]

Holland's and Amsterdam's achievements cannot, moreover, be fully comprehended without reference to the relatively high levels of literacy and urbanization that characterized social and economic life in the Low Countries for more than a century before the rise of Antwerp and Amsterdam. Even smallish towns in the Burgundian dominions supported painters and printers, who catered for an established and widespread demand for 'images' (spiritual, realistic and secular) engraved or woodcut into simple prints or embodied as illustrations in Books of Hours and other printed religious books, designed largely to instruct and edify the laity.[77] The prior accumulation of skills in engraving, woodcutting, printing, painting in oils, carving in wood and sculpting in stone for homes as well as churches made the 'visual culture' of townspeople in the Low Countries (and the Rhineland) as rich if not richer than the culture of urban societies in Italy before and during the Renaissance.[78] This Netherlandish tradition was drawn upon, revived and extended to cater for a widespread demand among all ranks of Dutch society to celebrate themselves, their religion, their possessions, their landscape, their victories over Spain, their material success, their virtues and even their vices.

From a comfortable base and secure local market in the mercantile and cosmopolitan city of Antwerp, craftsmen and artists transmitted the high culture of the Northern and Italian Renaissance to discerning clients all over Europe and in the Iberian colonies overseas.[79] London's restored monarchical regime and aristocracy preferred, for several decades, to patronize the most expensive and refined of European art and design in order to proclaim their power and to reconfigure their culture after a democratic, republican and provincial challenge to noble authority and identity.[80] Of

---

[75] D.Ormrod, 'Art and Its Markets', *Economic History Review* 52 (1999), pp. 544–51.
[76] See pp. 210–30.
[77] U. Mayr-Harting, *Early Netherlandish Engraving* (Oxford, 1997); and W. Blockmanns, 'The Social and Economic Context of Investment in Art in Flanders' in M. Smeyers and B. Cardon (eds.), *Flanders in European Perspective* (Leuven, 1995), pp. 711–19.
[78] A. Châtelet, *Early Dutch Painting* (Seacaucus, 1986).
[79] J. Snyder, *Northern Renaissance Art* (New York, 1985), pp. 399–419.
[80] B. Denvir, *The Eighteenth Century Art, Design and Society* (London, 1983), pp. 1–24.

course, in some degree the artisans and artists of Amsterdam elaborated and mediated their way through European forms and traditions, but their achievement resides, above all, in innovating and extending a heritage of Burgundian, Brabantine and Flemish culture in order to celebrate themselves and transmit representations and images of Dutch success to their envious enemies and rivals in Iberia, France and England.[81]

All three authors whose chapters are grouped in part 5 suggest that the urban domain of printing and publishing can also be analysed in illuminating ways as a composite industry, employing capital and skilled labour (including authors, publishers, printers, illustrators, translators, type founders, punch cutters, merchants, retailers and other distributors). This industry printed texts for a European market that was already expanding rapidly by the closing decades of the fifteenth century.

For centuries, books and prototype books had been produced expensively by scribes and in limited volumes by means of wood block printing (xylography).[82] Typographical methods of reproduction (utilizing movable type) appeared in Europe around 1450 and cut the costs of textual reproduction sharply at a time when the spread of education and literacy (particularly in Italy and the Low Countries) increased demands for reading matter of all kinds.[83] The innovation of movable type diffused rapidly. In 1480 more than a hundred European towns housed printing presses and by 1500 that number had more than doubled. Books ceased to be rare and the total numbers printed may have multiplied seven to ten times over the sixteenth century.[84]

Favourable local and urban conditions encouraged printing and publishing to concentrate in Antwerp, Amsterdam and London (as well as all other major European towns). For example, the workforces of all three cities contained an increasing proportion and widening range of skilled and professional men (and women) with demands for didactic books and manuals in order to raise their capacities to operate efficiently as clerics, lawyers, teachers, officials, accountants, merchants, mariners, pharmacologists, cartographers, midwives, surgeons, musicians, etc. Cities supported a plethora of municipal and private institutions accumulating libraries for purposes of education and training. The literate citizens of towns also read books for pleasure and for spiritual edification and religious instruction. They purchased a dominant proportion of the books,

[81] D. Freeberg and J. de Vries (eds.), *Art History, History in Art: Studies in Seventeenth Century Dutch Culture* (Santa Monica, 1991); and B. Haak, *The golden age of Dutch Painting of the Seventeenth Century* (London, 1984).
[82] G. Basalla, *The Evolution of Technology* (Cambridge, 1988), pp. 193–5.
[83] C. Cipolla, *Literacy and Development in the West* (London, 1969), pp. 44–60.
[84] Braudel, *The Structures of Everyday Life*, p. 400; and A. Pacey, *The Maze of Ingenuity* (London, 1994), p. 58.

pamphlets and other printed matter coming onto the market in order to understand and participate in the great theological and political controversies of their time.[85] Thus, the Reformation and Counter-Reformation began and continued to be a 'battle of books', long after the Peace of Westphalia (1648) when princes, prelates and republican oligarchies virtually ceased to mobilize armies to defend or propagate Catholic and Protestant doctrines.[86] Although the data are not yet available, it would be interesting to discover when the proportion of books published that could be somehow classified as religious really declined.[87] Meanwhile and during the early modern centuries of religious conflict, when authors, printers and publishers could be severely punished for heresy and treason, political authorities who either tolerated or were lax in enforcing censorship against the writing, production and distribution of prohibited books could attract and retain this politically dangerous industry in their cities. Yet in no city in Europe did the political, municipal and ecclesiastical authorities tolerate anything like the free publication of what they defined as heretical and treasonable reading material.[88] In Antwerp, authors, printers and sellers of books suffered from intermittent bouts of persecution throughout the sixteenth century. After the reabsorption of the Southern Netherlands into the Habsburg Empire, Antwerp virtually ceased to publish non-Catholic religious texts.[89]

That substantial market passed to Amsterdam, a city that retained a record (albeit imperfect) and a reputation for tolerance in this domain, perhaps second to none in Europe. Catholics, Jews and other political and religious minorities produced and sold books in Amsterdam that contravened legal codes and certainly challenged the dominant Dutch conventions of religious, moral and political behaviour in ways that were not open to minorities and outsiders in London before the very end of the seventeenth century.[90]

Clearly the religious and political conditions promoting or constraining the long-term development of printing and publishing in particular cities varied from place to place and through time, but economic factors were also at work. For example, loans and credit could be raised cheaply in Antwerp, Amsterdam and London to fund the buildings, machinery and inventories of books required to set up and sustain a relatively capital-intensive industry. Paper could either be made within their environs or imported by water. If and when political conditions became tolerable, the cities could attract writers, printers and booksellers to locate

---

[85] Cowan, *Urban Europe*, pp. 93–120.   [86] See pp. 233–63.
[87] R. Chartier, *The Order of Books* (Cambridge, 1994).
[88] D. Nicholas, *The Later Medieval City* (London, 1996).
[89] See pp. 233–48.   [90] See pp. 264–83 and Israel, *The Dutch Republic*, pp. 361–98.

in entrepôts already networked into regional, European and intercontinental markets.[91]

For some two to three centuries after the diffusion of movable type (an
innovation associated with Gutenberg of Mainz on the Rhine and/or
Coster of Haarlem), Antwerp between 1585 and 1650 and Amsterdam
after 1585 enjoyed several competitive advantages over London as
regards the commissioning, printing, publishing and distribution of
books. First of all, the Low Countries possessed longer traditions and
wider markets for the production and distribution of illustrated (largely
religious and moral) texts, using xylographic techniques for printing and
engraving.[92] Secondly, their mercantile networks and political connections across northern, central and southern Europe provided markets for
books and access to the linguistic skills (in Latin, Hebrew as well as the
vernacular) required to publish in a variety of European languages.[93]
Antwerp's role as a bastion of the Counter-Reformation gave its printing
industry a Catholic market for most of the seventeenth century. These
long-standing competitive advantages did not wane until the London-
based industry served English-speaking imperial and American markets.
Finally, and although censorship proved increasingly difficult to enforce
in Tudor and Stuart London, English toleration, flexibility and freedom
to publish may have remained less liberal than in Amsterdam and other
rival cities on the continent until quite late.[94]

In no other domain did the boundaries of the three cities and the nature
of achievement become more problematical than for the historians of
early modern science who wrote (or commented upon) submissions for
the conferences at Amsterdam and Antwerp.[95] Names of famous, and not
so famous, botanists, pharmacologists, herbalists, anatomists, physicians,
engineers, mathematicians, cartographers, opticians and instrument
makers who lived and worked or who merely visited Antwerp,
Amsterdam and London are carefully cited in all three presentations in
part 6.[96] Their individual achievements as 'proto-scientists' are not
however ranked, weighted and explained in ways favoured by the 'inter-
nalist' accounts that have dominated more traditional histories of the sciences.[97] Clear-cut definitions of breakthroughs or even incremental
additions to the progress of European science turned out to be

---

[91] See pp. 233–83.   [92] Snyder, *Northern Renaissance Art*, pp. 271–92.
[93] See pp. 233–63.
[94] But see D. Zaret, 'Printing and the Invention of Public Opinion in Seventeenth Century
England' in Gouk, *Wellsprings of Achievement*, pp. 180–201; and O. Grell et al. (eds.), *From
Persecution to Toleration. The Glorious Revolution and Religion in England* (Oxford, 1991).
[95] The reasons are analysed in a brilliant paper by Simon Schaffer, 'Making up Discovery'
in Boden, *Dimensions of Creativity*, pp. 13–48.
[96] See pp. 287–344.   [97] A.R. Hall, *The Scientific Revolution 1500–1800* (Boston, 1962).

contestable and our discussion preferred to remain focused upon the cultures, economic conditions and urban networks in north-western Europe (including the Netherlands and England) that promoted the production and diffusion of flows of 'reliable and useful knowledge'.[98] That focus and definition pushed our research and discussion towards a consideration of the 'investment' of time, skill and energies (located both within and around the three cities) into detailed investigations of specific natural phenomena and away from natural philosophies and philosophers engaged with the reformulation of cosmologies, universal laws and grand theories.[99] However, none of the contributors (or respondents) would subscribe to the notion that scholarly investigation of contexts tells us enough about how scientific achievements actually emerged or to the related view that progress in the sciences depended in some direct and predictable sense upon socio-economic change and the concentration of populations in large cities.[100]

Meanwhile, the three contributions to part 6 elaborate in scholarly ways on the urban contexts within which flows of reliable and useful knowledge emerged in Antwerp, Amsterdam and London. As mercantile cities in process of rapid expansion, their leading commercial sectors demanded potentially exploitable knowledge for sustained engagement in long-distance trade by sea. Merchants (and their peers running city governments) invested in urban schools, colleges and libraries for the training of labour. They patronized institutions within and beyond the walls of their cities that produced knowledge about shipbuilding, navigation, cartography, mathematics, optics, instrument making, hydraulics, surveying and engineering of potential relevance to their concerns as businessmen. They congregated in clubs, societies, coffee-houses, taverns and other public 'spheres' where new knowledge might be demonstrated, communicated and debated.[101]

Interestingly, not one of the three cities founded universities to develop and propagate potentially useful forms of academic knowledge. Antwerp relied heavily on links with the neighbouring and distinguished University of Leuven, established in 1425.[102] Amsterdam (along with many other Dutch towns) established its own Athenaeum Illustre in 1632. Nevertheless Leiden retained its position as Holland's (and possibly Europe's) leading university in the sciences. With Leiden and several other modern universities nearby, the businessmen of Amsterdam could buy the

[98] This handy Baconian label and satisfying substitute for 'Science' was suggested to us by Gerry Martin.
[99] A.C. Crombie, *Styles of Scientific Thinking in the European Tradition*, vol. I (London, 1994), pp. 3–92.   [100] Shapin, *Scientific Revolution*.   [101] See pp. 287–344.
[102] See pp. 287–304.

information and professional experience required from institutions of higher education located within the city's extensive urban network in the Republic and also call upon their own wider channels of communication with Italian, German and other nodes of learning throughout Europe.[103]

Likewise, London could recruit talent from that tiny group of very high-quality polymaths residing in Oxford and Cambridge to work on problems of national importance as defined and taken up by the ministers of the Crown.[104] Yet the sense that some institution (preferably with monarchical and aristocratic patronage) was still needed to promote 'science' led to the foundation of a Royal Society in 1662. Its proclaimed mission was 'to improve the knowledge of natural things, and all useful arts, Manufactures, Mechanic practices, Engynes and inventions by experiment.' In the words of Thomas Sprat, the Society's work was 'for the use of cities and not for the refinement of schools'.[105]

No doubt the stress upon utility and Baconian styles of experimentation, which stuck to facts and evaded doctrines, theologies and cosmologies, helped to make science and scientists acceptable in Restoration London.[106] Nothing like a Royal Society seems to have been needed in Amsterdam (or Antwerp) to promote and regularize the activities of institutions and scholars devoted to the production of reliable knowledge about the natural world.[107] In the rival towns, decentralized political authority and competitive theological doctrines of the Low Countries, experimentally derived knowledge about the body and nature could be represented and generally accepted as revealing God's ways to mankind.[108] Across the North Sea and after a long interregnum of civil dispute and violence over religious doctrine and political authority, the rediscovery and restoration of the latitudinarian traditions of the English reformation forged a compromise with natural philosophy which turned into a tolerant and hospitable culture for the promotion and diffusion of experimental science.[109] As a clearing house for new theories, as a prose-

---

[103] See pp. 305–25.

[104] O.J. Henry, 'The Scientific Revolution in England' in R. Porter and M. Teich (eds.), *The Scientific Revolution in National Contexts* (Cambridge, 1994), pp. 182–90.

[105] T. Sprat, *History of the Royal Society* (London, 1667), cited by P. Mathias, 'Who Unbound Prometheus? Science and Technical Change 1600–1800' in J. Hoppit and E.A. Wrigley (eds.), *The Industrial Revolution in Britain* (Oxford, 1994), pp. 149–54.

[106] M. Hunter, *Establishing the New Science: The Experience of the Early Royal Society* (Woodbridge, Suffolk, 1989).   [107] See pp. 326–44.

[108] H.J. Cook, 'The New Philosophy in the Low Countries' in Porter and Teich (eds.), *The Scientific Revolution in National Context*, pp. 115–49.

[109] Henry, 'The Scientific Revolution' in Porter and Teich (eds.), *The Scientific Revolution in National Contexts*, pp. 178–209; as exemplified in the career of the inventor of the power loom – see P. O 'Brien, 'The Micro Foundations of Macro Invention: the Case of the Reverend Edmund Cartwright', *Textile History*, 28 (1997).

lytizer for experimental knowledge and as the public face of politically neutral and theologically acceptable science, the Royal Society helped to reorder metropolitan and provincial culture in Britain after the Restoration.[110]

Nevertheless the chapters on Antwerp, Amsterdam and London emphasize just how much reliable knowledge that came on stream in those cities flowed from fruitful and mutually profitable connections at mundane and practical levels between merchants and proto-scientists. Commerce within and beyond Europe brought the agricultural produce, trees, plants, animals, fish and insects of the world into the cities for botanical observation, pharmacological transfer and chemical analysis. Mercantile and municipal investment in public libraries and private collections of 'curiosities' provided the material basis for potentially useful experiments and reflection. Employment and markets for their knowledge attracted natural philosophers and educated craftsmen to migrate and to locate in or near prospering maritime cities. Once in situ and from a multiplicity of regular economic and intellectual interactions in hospitable spaces and tolerant cultures, reliable knowledge emerged. Over time, specialized scientific disciplines devoted to the routinized investigation of nature and biological phenomena grew up in the matrix of such cities.[111]

In their wisdom, the syndics of Cambridge University Press perceived that the readership for this volume of papers might come largely from historians of early modern European towns. Nevertheless, the book originated and remains the product of a collective, interdisciplinary enterprise, designed to explain why celebrated and interconnected achievements across a variety of domains of endeavour tended to cluster within cities over finite spans of time. All the authors and the respondents to their papers engaged in a collegial discourse. From a basis of expertise about a particular localized domain of urban activity, academics attempted to deploy their scholarship in order to generalize about the nature of achievement in economic, architectural, artistic and scientific endeavours in Antwerp, Amsterdam and London in their golden ages. For this exercise in comparative history the Steering Committee did not commission close analyses dealing with the innovations, creations and

---

[110] Some of its direct but tenuous links to technology are explored in A. Pacey, *The Maze of Ingenuity* (Cambridge, 1992), pp. 90, 127 and 138.

[111] L. Stewart, *The Rise of Public Science. Rhetoric, Technology and Natural Philosophy in Newtonian Britain 1660–1750* (Cambridge, 1992). But, for a more elevated view of 'high' European Science and its connections to economic change, see M. Jacob, *Scientific Culture and the Making of the Industrial West* (Oxford, 1997).

discoveries of canonical figures (such as Plantin in Antwerp, Rembrandt in Amsterdam, or Newton in London), because they anticipated that the prospects for generalization based upon biography (or prospography) are problematical and limited to a vocabulary of psychological depiction that many historians (despite postmodern admonitions) continue to find superficial.[112] Rather, the Committee preferred to preconfigure achievement as something that emerged within and emanated from the complex geographies, economies, societies and cultures of cities and set up conversation to explore why that occurred.

With inescapable relevance, the prelude to our discussions became concerned with the contested nature, narrow range and also, paradoxically, the broadly defined sectors of achievement selected for investigation. In order to proceed we simply agreed that achievement consists of culturally ascribed qualities preselected for esteem; and that our focus on economies, built environments, art and design, printing and publishing and the sciences could be represented as both too broad and too narrow. Of course we also recognized that generalizations inferred from the histories of these 'domains' could be qualified and perhaps invalidated by micro research into particular artefacts, designs, genres and ideas. The conversation then continued.

Golden ages and their trajectories into decline turned out to be difficult to date. Furthermore, the boundaries of maritime, centrally placed cities as sites of achievement are, for many purposes, porous. Cities have long histories and the relevant geographies of Antwerp, Amsterdam and, above all, London certainly included their agrarian hinterlands and their European and intercontinental networks for the exchange of commodities, people, information and ideas. Most historians (committed as they are to the exploration of local contexts, particular circumstances and, above all, the contingencies surrounding the events and outcomes that they attempt to explain) resist widening urban spaces and societies taken as boundaries for their narratives. Nevertheless, this particular group of historians certainly recognized that the maritime locations of Antwerp, Amsterdam and London, and their positions of 'primacy' during golden ages as entrepôts in intra-European and intercontinental commerce, provided a large part of the economic basis and a great deal of the proximate stimulus for ostensibly 'local' achievements in the arts, publishing, architecture and the accumulation of useful knowledge.

Material life envelops all and a reading of the research and reflection included in this volume suggests that the familiar range of connections to

[112] But see M. Boden, *The Creative Mind* (London, 1990) and Boden, *Dimensions of Creativity.*

an established economic base (and to cycles of prosperity) remains, as canonical social scientists suggested long ago, the most plausible way to account for the achievements from these three maritime cities.[113] For example, commerce brought into their ports the raw materials, artefacts and data upon which production in luxury industries and wider reflection on the purposes, adaptation and improvement of imports could be based. These cities continued for decades to attract merchants, entrepreneurs and skilled artisans into the security, tolerance and opportunities provided within their environs. Their young, experimental, relatively affluent and discriminating populations formed dense and accessible markets for everything and anything – particularly novelties, luxuries and new knowledge. Cities acted as arenas for competition, emulation and the diffusion of commercial intelligence and reliable knowledge within their boundaries. Easy and productive connections could be formed across domains of expertise and among neighbours, often promoted by polymaths and brokers, celebrated as remarkable citizens of Antwerp, Amsterdam and London. Printers and authors, architects and engineers, painters and engravers, artisans and scientists mingled with each other and with merchants. They shaped and reordered urban cultures from which clusters of achievements and, from time to time, peaks of excellence and innovation appeared.

Urban historians have also reminded us that not all European cities can be represented in the progressive light that shines through this book. The dark side of 'city-scapes' includes histories of political repression and social neglect which afflicted the majority of citizens before Victorian times.[114] Some major cities of the early modern era continue to be represented by historians as 'parasitic' rather than 'generative' – an entirely traditional dichotomy in the perception of urban civilization.[115]

As a last word, I must qualify any impression of 'economic reductionism' conveyed by my introductory survey and mediation. All the scholars who contributed to this volume remained completely aware that achievements attributed to the three cities might have been dramatically curtailed and permanently constrained by unfavourable turns in their geopolitical circumstances. Thus London's prolonged succession of golden ages could be attributed basically to its position as the capital city of an island kingdom, provided for centuries by a powerful territorial and imperial state with unrivalled security against external aggression. Neither Antwerp nor Amsterdam could depend on that kind of political and armed support. In early modern Europe, cities lived and died, rose and declined in the shadow of swords and the wake of battleships.

[113] J. Appleby et al. (eds.), *Knowledge and Postmodernism in Historical Perspective* (London, 1996).

[114] H.J. Dyos and M. Wolff (eds.), *The Victorian City. Images and Realities* (London, 1973).

[115] R. Williams, *The Country and the City* (London, 1973).

Part 2

Economic growth and demographic change

2 'No town in the world provides more advantages': economies of agglomeration and the golden age of Antwerp

Michael Limberger

For readers not familiar with the economic or cultural history of early modern Europe, the choice of Antwerp as one of the three cities of this comparative study may be somewhat surprising. At present, despite possessing one of the largest harbours in the world, Antwerp is of only secondary importance in comparison with Amsterdam and London. In terms of economic history however, the choice is easy to understand. During a great part of the sixteenth century, Antwerp was the major commercial and financial centre of western Europe, a metropolis which impressed contemporaries with its modernity and its international character. The Florentine Ludovico Guicciardini, for instance, dedicated a considerable part of his *Descrittione di tutti i Paesi Bassi* to a description of the town and its business life; the Augsburg artist Jost Amman chose Antwerp to form the background for his well-known *Allegory of Trade* (1585); and the Londoner Thomas More situated his encounter with a Portuguese seafarer, during which the latter tells him about the existence of *Utopia*, in the heart of Antwerp.[1]

Antwerp, Amsterdam and London in their golden ages had some important features in common. They all were port towns situated on a major inland waterway with easy access to the sea. They all were major centres of European trade and finance. And, finally, they also played a role as leading cultural centres during their period of economic prosperity. As commercial centres, they took, in turn, the leading role in the same international trade network and were, in this context, successors of each other. This makes the three success stories part of the same long-term development and they are therefore especially interesting for a comparative study. The aim of this contribution is, first, to provide a short synthesis of the economic background of Antwerp's golden age, and especially its role as a major centre of the European economy during the sixteenth

---

[1] L.Guicciardini, *Descrittione di tutti i Paesi Bassi, altrimenti detti Germania Inferiore* (Antwerp, 1567); Jost Amman, *Allegory of Trade* (Royal Library Albert Ist, Brussels, Prentenkabinet s. II. 4990); T. Morus, *Libellus de optimo reip. stato deque nova insula Utopia* (Leuven, 1516), reprinted St. T. Morus, *Utopia: 1516* (Menston, 1971).

century. We will then discuss to what extent Antwerp was a place of economic innovation, and the economic logic behind it. From this discussion we finally hope to be able to deduce some more general hypotheses about the problematic of to what extent a commercial metropolis, or urban pole, such as Antwerp was privileged to become a focus of economic achievements.

The expansion of long-distance trade around 1500 has been assigned great importance in European history. This expansion was a question not only of discovering new continents, but also of 'a new permanence, a regularization of contacts, and the development of a technology capable of sustaining wider geographical and economic probes'.[2] The idea of an intensifying European trade network that was also beginning to incorporate great parts of the world into a 'European world economy', via the great discoveries, has become an explanatory model commonly accepted by economic historians.[3] The changes within this network of European trade, with its different regions and urban centres, have been described most convincingly by Fernand Braudel. His concept of an *économique monde européenne*, the world of international, predominantly urban, capitalism, forms the highest level of economic activity within a three-tiered model of material life; the intermediate level is formed by the world of trade and daily life forms its basis. This world economy worked on the basis of a division of labour between the core areas in western Europe, where manufacturing production prevailed, and a periphery, which contributed raw materials and agrarian products. One of the central aspects of Braudel's concept of the *économie monde* is that its economic activities concentrate and culminate in one dominating place, a so-called urban pole, where the streams of commerce accumulate and transactions are coordinated. This role is held by a series of cities, which each dominated a period of European long-distance trade and finance.[4]

The origins of the European world economy go back into the Middle Ages. At that stage, it was characterized by a bipolar structure, with the Mediterranean as one focus and north-western Europe the other. Accordingly, there were also two cities which formed the urban poles of this network. The powerful city-state and merchant empire[5] of Venice was

---

[2] H.A. Miskimin, *The Economy of Later Renaissance Europe. 1460–1600* (Cambridge, 1977), p. 123.

[3] Although there have been severe criticisms of one of the major theoretical concepts concerning this rising world economy: I. Wallerstein, *The Modern World System*, 3 vols. (New York, 1974–1989).

[4] F. Braudel, *Le temps du monde, Civilisation matérielle, économie et capitalisme, XVe–XVIIIe siècle*, vol. III (Paris, 1979), pp. 17–24.

[5] On the term 'merchant empire', see J.D. Tracy (ed.), *The Rise of Merchant Empires. Long Distance Trade in the Early Modern World 1350–1750* (Cambridge, 1990)

the dominating place in the south while, in the north, Bruges fulfilled the function of gateway for north-western Europe to this network, as well as a link with the Baltic trade. The link between the two areas had been formed by the Champagne fairs in central France until the 13th century. After their decline during the fourteenth century, two alternative routes gained importance: the direct maritime route between Italy and Bruges, through the Straits of Gibraltar and along the Atlantic coast, and the inland route via the Alps.[6]

At the end of the fifteenth century, however, Antwerp took over the position of urban pole from Bruges, and to some extent also from Venice. By shipping spices along the African coast, and erecting a monopoly in Antwerp, the Portuguese provided serious competition to the Venetian and Genoese spice trade. This victory of the Atlantic over the Mediterranean was only temporary, as we will see later on. For a little over half a century, however, it made Antwerp the major node of the dynamic expansion of West European trade.

After this short period of commercial primacy with its ups and downs, Antwerp had to make way for another *pole urbain*. Braudel still keeps to the duality of the early *économie monde*. It was not Amsterdam that becomes the successor of Antwerp; at least for the financial world, this position was partly taken over by Genoa. Only later did Amsterdam set off an era of Dutch supremacy in the world economy and was in its turn replaced by London in the eighteenth century. Braudel's presentation of changing supremacy between Venice and Bruges, Antwerp and later Genoa, and finally Amsterdam can be criticized as being a rather simplistic view of the interactions between the different centres of the European world economy. Venice remained one of the leading European commercial centres during the sixteenth century. Only in the seventeenth century did it start to decline.[7] What is remarkable, however, with regard to the success story of Antwerp are the dimensions which its metropolitan position reached during the short period comprising its rise and decline. The latter made the town rise in economic importance above cities such as Venice, Bruges and Amsterdam. To arrive at a better understanding of this economic boom, the stages of Antwerp's rise and fall as a commercial metropolis will be sketched.

When the Portuguese factor settled in Antwerp in 1498 and the town

[6] J. Bernard, 'Trade and Finance in the Middle Ages, 900–1500', in C.M. Cipolla (ed.), *The Fontana Economic History, Vol. I: The Middle Ages* (Hassocks, 1976), p. 275.
[7] S. Ciriacono, 'The Venetian Economy and Its Place in the World Economy of the 17th and 18th Centuries. A Comparison with the Low Countries' in H.J. Nitz (ed.), *The Early-modern World-System in Geographical Perspective* (Stuttgart, 1993), pp. 120–35, 120–1; see also R.T. Rapp, *Industry and Economic Decline in Seventeenth Century Venice* (Cambridge, Mass., 1977).

on the Scheldt 'awoke at the visible top of the world', the fact hardly surprised the economic world of the period.[8] Antwerp had been preparing for its leading role for more than a century. At an early stage of development, in the late thirteenth and early fourteenth centuries, the fairs of Antwerp and Bergen op Zoom served as a link between a young expanding Brabantine cloth industry and English wool imports, and also for interregional exchanges with merchants from the Rhineland. Then, during a period of about half a century (1356–1406) under Flemish dominance, the so-called Brabantine fairs came into contact with the international trading world of Bruges. It is true, however, that Antwerp had remained rather small until then: in the second half of the fourteenth century its population is estimated between 7,000 and 12,000 inhabitants. At this time, Bruges had 46,000 and Ghent as many as 64,000 inhabitants and within the duchy of Brabant there were four towns with more people than Antwerp.[9] In the fifteenth century, however, Antwerp's population and economic importance both grew rapidly. Already in 1437, the population had increased to 20,000 inhabitants; in 1480, it was as high as 33,000 (figure 2.1).[10] The Brabantine fairs increasingly attracted merchants from England, from different parts of Germany, from the Northern and Southern Netherlands, including the duchy of Brabant, and also from southern European countries such as Portugal, Spain and Italy.

A crucial role in this commercial development was played by England. Until the fourteenth century it had been the main supplier of wool and therefore an important trading partner for the Low Countries. After becoming more and more a producer of cloth itself, its role turned into that of a serious competitor. Although the Flemish towns tried repeatedly to ban English cloth from the Low Countries, the fairs of Brabant remained open to English imports. Neither Antwerp nor Bergen op Zoom was strong in textile production in comparison with other Flemish and Brabantine towns. Trade and the finishing and dyeing of English cloth were therefore more profitable for them than protecting their own textile production, which was only marginal in the fourteenth century. English exports were not primarily oriented towards the Low Countries, where cloth was present in

---

[8] Braudel, *Le temps du monde*, p. 122.
[9] Brussels, Mechlin, Louvain and Den Bosch; compare P.M.M. Klep, *Bevolking en arbeid in transformatie. Een onderzoek in Brabant 1700–1900* (Nijmegen, 1981), p. 354; for Den Bosch: W.P. Blockmans, G. Pieters, W. Prevenier and A.W. van Schaik, 'Tussen crisis en welvaart: sociale veranderingen 1300–1500', in D.P. Blok et al. (eds.), *Algemene Geschiedenis der Nederlanden*, 2nd edn (Haarlem, 1977–1983), vol. IV, pp. 42–86, at 51.
[10] Klep, *Bevolking en arbeid*, p. 354; in the hierarchy of the Brabantine cities, Antwerp rose from fifth to second position, behind Brussels (39,000).

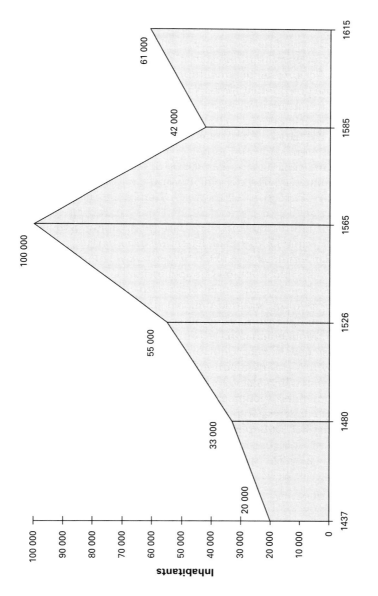

2.1 Population of Antwerp, 1437–1615 (Based on estimates by Klep, *Bevolking en arbeid*, p. 354)

abundance, but rather towards continental Europe, especially western and central Germany. In the early fifteenth century, merchants from the German Rhineland, dominated by the citizens of Cologne, were the most active in this trade. Around 1450, however, southern Germans appeared increasingly and added an important product to the Antwerp market, that is, precious metals such as copper and silver from central Europe. It was precisely these precious metals that attracted a third group of merchants of major importance, the Portuguese. For their rising colonial trade, they were in need of copper, which was in high demand in western Africa, and of silver, which was the primary means of payment for their Asian spice trade. The convergence of these products formed the main pillars in Antwerp's first stage of commercial predominance.[11]

When Antwerp finally took over the pole position from Bruges, the transition was influenced by both political and structural factors. Economic factors played a role especially in the long term. The production of high-quality cloth had been the economic basis of the prosperity of the Flemish towns and of the rise of Bruges. The difficulties facing Flemish cloth production from rising competition from England, Brabant and secondary centres in Flanders itself had threatened the position of Bruges since the fourteenth century, but especially during the fifteenth century.[12] Also Bruges' unfavourable situation in respect to the increasingly important markets of central and southern Germany and its limited accessibility to bigger ships were negative factors in comparison with the Brabant fairs. Nevertheless, Bruges remained the dominant commercial centre until the 1480s. The political factors, on the other hand, had a more immediate impact on Bruges' position. The situation of the late fifteenth century was dominated by conflicts between the Flemish, but also many Brabantine, towns and the rule of Maximilian of Habsburg. During this conflict, Antwerp was one of the few towns that took the side of Maximilian, who thanked the town by conferring on it important monopolies and even instructing the foreign merchant communities to move to Antwerp. According to an article by R. van Uytven, Bruges was so exhausted by the political tensions, the blockades and the political measures of Maximilian

[11] W. Brulez, 'Bruges and Antwerp in the 15th and 16th Centuries: An Antithesis?' *Acta historiae Neerlandica*, 6 (1973), pp. 1–26, at 2.
[12] H. van der Wee, 'Structural Changes and Specialization in the industry of the Southern Netherlands 1100–1600', *Economic History Review*, 28 (1975), pp. 203–21, at 216, and H. van der Wee, 'Industrial Dynamics and the Process of Urbanisation and De-Urbanisation in the Low Countries from the Late Middle Ages to the Eighteenth Century. A Synthesis', in H. van der Wee (ed.), *The Rise and Decline of Urban Industries in Italy and in the Low Countries (Late Middle-Ages – Early Modern Times)* (Leuven, 1988), pp. 307–81, at 329–32.

against the town that many foreign merchants left for Antwerp because of increasing taxes and the limited accessibility to the town.[13] But the political circumstances were favourable for Antwerp also in more general terms. As early as the fifteenth century, the political centre of the Burgundian Netherlands had been clearly transferred to the duchy of Brabant. Brussels and the enclosure of Malines became the major residences of the Burgundian court and the administrative centres of the Low Countries, and in Leuven, another Brabantine town, the famous university was founded in 1425. The rising demand for high-quality products in these towns, as well as in Antwerp itself, stimulated the rise of their local industries, as well as the latter's role as a centre of provision.[14] Both, political reasons and the economic situation hence played a role, and they were closely interrelated. The Flemish revolt was the culmination of these tensions, causing the major groups of merchants to decide to move to Antwerp, which had gradually widened its opportunities during the fifteenth century.[15]

After this initial phase of development, when Antwerp accumulated commercial contacts at the time of the fairs but was still a city of secondary importance in comparison with Bruges, the 1490s marked the actual beginning of the period of Antwerp's metropolitan position, which lasted until about 1565. It was during this short period of some seventy years that Antwerp can be called the urban pole of the European economy. Nevertheless, the actual decline of Antwerp's economic activity took place only after the beginning of the Dutch Revolt, at the latest in 1585, following the closure of the river Scheldt. During the first half of the seventeenth century, Antwerp continued to play an important role as a commercial centre, although one not comparable to the dimensions of Amsterdam or even its own glorious past.[16]

The 'metropolitan period' of Antwerp was interrupted by a period of

[13] R. van Uytven, 'Stages of Economic Decline: Late Medieval Bruges', in J.M. Duvosquel and E. Thoen (eds.), *Peasants & Townsmen in Medieval Europe. Studia in honorem Adriaan Verhulst* (Ghent,1995), pp. 259–69, at 267–9.

[14] R. van Uytven, 'Brabantse en Antwerpse centrale plaatsen (14de–19de eeuw)', in *Het stedelijk netwerk in België in historisch perspectief (1350–1850). Een statistische en dynamische benadering / Le reseau urbain en Belgique dans une perspective historique (1350–1850), une approche statistique et dynamique* (Handelingen 15de Internationaal Colloquium /Actes 15e Colloque International, Spa, 4–6 September 1990) (Brussels, 1992), pp. 29–79, at 37–8.

[15] Compare Myrdal's concept of cumulative causation, referred to in chapter 3 by Lesger on Amsterdam, which contains the argument that it was especially in moments of crisis that the advantages of a metropolis are undermined, and that other places, where the situation is more favourable, are able to replace the dominant centre.

[16] See W. Brulez, 'Anvers de 1585 à 1650', *Vierteljahrsschrifte für Sozial- und Wirtschaftsgeschichte*, 53 (1967), 75–99; and R. Baetens, *De nazomer van Antwerpens welvaart. De diaspora en het handelshuis De Groote tijdens de eerste helft der 17e eeuw* (Brussels, 1976), 2 vols.

difficulties in the 1520s, which divided it into two distinct stages of
growth marked by profound differences in function and dynamic. The
crucial importance of the triangle formed by English, southern German
and Portuguese at the Brabantine fairs has already been mentioned.
Apart from them however, traders from many other countries participated in the markets of Antwerp and Bergen op Zoom. Germans from
the Rhine area formed the most numerous group, but there were also
many Italians, French and Spaniards, and a great number of Dutch,
Flemings and Brabanders.[17] The role of Antwerp in this international
trade was mainly that of a transit market. The English cloth staple was
the main distribution centre for continental Europe, as was the case for
the Portuguese spice staple, which was installed in 1501 as a monopoly
for Europe north of the Alps and the Pyrenees. Traders from the southern Netherlands were present both as exporters of high-quality manufactures and as sellers of raw materials. Italian merchants would therefore
come to purchase English cloth to resell in the Levant, bringing, in their
turn, silk, which was processed by the local silk industry.[18] During the
first decades of the sixteenth century, the system of periodic fairs was still
maintained. This rhythm was also well suited to craftspeople from
Brabantine and Flemish towns, because market activity was concentrated during the short periods of the fairs. This allowed them to participate actively in a world market during a limited period. During this first
phase of commercial predominance, Antwerp witnessed an economic
boom which also stimulated industrial production in other Brabantine
cities. Apart from the merchants, from all over Europe, many local
people were active in retail trade, transport and different service sectors.
Furthermore, local industry, led by textile finishing, offered employment
to thousands of people. The population of the town increased to about
55,000 inhabitants in 1526, more than twice the size it had been in
1437.[19]

Already in the 1520s, political difficulties brought about a temporary
decline. The wars between Charles V and Francis I of France and a conflict
between Germany and Denmark formed serious obstacles to trade along
the Atlantic coast and to traffic towards the Baltic. In central Europe, economic life was hampered by the German Peasant Wars. Furthermore, the

---

[17] R. Doehaerd, *Etudes anversoises. Documents sur le commerce international à Anvers,
1488–1514* (Paris, 1962–3), vol. I, pp. 31–9.
[18] A.K.L. Thijs, 'Een ongeziene commerciële bloei', in K. van Isacker and R. van Uytven
(eds.), *Antwerpen. Twaalf eeuwen geschiedenis en cultuur* (Antwerp, 1986), pp. 93–102, at
93–4.
[19] Klep, *Bevolking en arbeid*, p. 413. Klep's estimates are based on the Brabant household
counts, edited by J. Cuvelier, *Les dénombrements de foyers en Brabant (XIVe–XVIe siècle)*
(Brussels, 1912).

commercial situation changed during that decade. The Portuguese spice monopoly was bypassed by the Venetians, who, after a period of absolute Portuguese predominance, reappeared on the European spice market by 1515, following renewed trade concessions from the Mamluk sultan. The Portuguese were able to maintain their leading position in the northern European spice trade until the 1530s, but Portuguese spices no longer formed the 'moteur sans égal'[20] of Antwerp's importance.[21]

During the second stage of Antwerp's metropolitan period, between the 1530s and 1566, the role of transit trade was less important than during the first two decades of the century. Instead, imports to and exports from the Low Countries gained considerable importance. At the international level, the Italian commercial revival around 1540 as well as the growing imports of American silver by the Spanish were the most dynamic factors. Italian trade with the Levant recovered after a treaty with the Turks in 1540 and influenced the Antwerp market positively via massive imports of silk on the one hand and by the purchase of English cloth as well as manufactures from the Low Countries for re-export to the Levant.[22] According to Braudel, however, it was mainly Spanish silver which dominated the second phase of Antwerp's predominance. For the exploitation of the American colonies, the Spaniards needed raw materials, ships and shipping equipment and grain which they bought to a considerable extent in Antwerp. The Spanish products that they offered in exchange, such as wine, wool, oil and fruit, were not sufficient to pay for these goods. To compensate the negative balance, they paid with huge amounts of silver.[23] Besides these foreign factors, the Southern Low Countries themselves played an important part in the economic development of the mid-sixteenth century, especially through high-quality manufactures and luxury industries, which formed a major export product of the Low Countries at that time. The favourable commercial situation helped to create an international market for tapestries, expensive clothes, jewellery and paintings from Brussels, Malines and Antwerp itself. It was especially these bigger towns which had acquired the skills and traditions necessary for the production of luxury goods, and now found international sales prospects.[24] During the industrial and commercial boom of

---

[20] The term 'moteur sans égal' is quoted from Braudel, *Le temps du monde*, p. 124.
[21] H. van der Wee, 'Structural Changes in European Long-distance Trade, and Particularly in the Re-export Trade from South to North, 1350–1750' in Tracy, *Merchant Empires*, pp. 14–33, at 29–30, referring to F. Braudel, *La Méditerranée et le monde méditerranéen à l'époque de Philippe II*, 2nd edn (Paris, 1966), vol. II, pp. 495–7.
[22] Van der Wee, 'Long Distance Trade', p. 31, F.C. Lane, *Venice, a Maritime Republic* (Baltimore, Md., 1973), p. 297.   [23] Braudel, *Le temps du monde*, p. 125.
[24] H. Soly and A.K.L. Thijs, 'Nijverheid in de Zuidelijke Nederlanden' in Blok et al., *Algemene Geschiedenis der Nederlanden*, vol. VI, pp. 27–57, at 29.

this period, Antwerp achieved its demographic peak. Around 1565, the city reached a size of about 100,000 inhabitants, which made it not only the largest city of the Low Countries, but also one of the largest in Western Europe. This considerable size indicates the exceptional economic potential during this period.

At the same time, Antwerp became one of the leading financial centres of Europe. At the beginning of the century, financial activity was predominantly concentrated on trade. Political finance only gained importance after 1515, when Charles V increasingly took up short-term loans, and the bad commercial situation as well as the rising demand for political funding in the 1520s made public loans an interesting alternative. Based on the financial potential of German banking houses such as the Fugger, Antwerp integrated itself into the financial network supporting the Habsburg empire, together with Lyons, the Castilian fairs and, after 1528, Genoa.[25] It is to a greater extent due to its role in this financial network, and not so much because of its commercial importance, that Antwerp occupies such a central place in the works of Braudel and Wallerstein.[26] The Spanish bankruptcy in 1557 therefore formed a turning point for Antwerp's role as an *urban pole*. Even though Antwerp was able to maintain its economic predominance until the 1560s, the diminishing importance of the German financiers weakened Antwerp's financial market considerably and reduced the town's international attractiveness.

The Revolt of the Netherlands marked the end to the period of economic boom. The political situation that had helped Antwerp to take over predominance from Bruges, during the revolt against Maximilian around 1480, now turned to Antwerp's disadvantage. Owing to a rigid fiscal policy, military interventions, blockades and other obstacles, Antwerp ceased to be the advantageous international market-place it had been until then. The golden age of Antwerp as well as its position as an urban pole of the European economy came to an end during the Revolt. This also had demographic effects. After the famous blockade of the river Scheldt in 1585, the population of the city decreased from its peak of 100,000 inhabitants in 1565 to a mere 42,000. This does not mean that the town lost all of its economic importance after that date.

[25] H. van der Wee, *The Growth of the Antwerp Market and the European Economy (Fourteenth–Sixteenth Centuries)* (The Hague, 1963), vol. II, p. 201.
[26] Wallerstein even considers it as the place where Charles V's attempt to create a world empire on the foundations of the rising European world economy failed, finally, in 1557, because capitalist forces proved stronger than the political designs of empire. See Wallerstein, *Modern World System*, vol. I, p. 177.

Recent historiography has built the first half of the seventeenth century into the success story of Antwerp. In this period of Antwerp's 'Indian summer', the town continued to play a role as a commercial centre at the border of the Spanish empire, where important international transactions were settled. Although transit trade had lost its importance, the Southern Low Countries continued to export considerable quantities of textiles and high-quality manufactures to the Iberian peninsula and to the New World.[27] As a centre of the Catholic Counter-Reformation, Antwerp also continued to play a major role as an artistic and cultural metropolis where famous personalities such as Rubens and Van Dijk were active.[28] At the level of the European economy, however, Antwerp had ceded its primacy to Amsterdam. In this transition, we can find parallels to what had happened a hundred years earlier to Bruges. The relative advantage of the dominant commercial centre, which had slowly diminished during several decades, was suddenly lost within a few years. In both cases, political crisis formed the turning point, when the balance changed abruptly.

The question of economic achievement is a central theme in the historiography on Antwerp. Although there are still discussions about the social benefits of the golden age, it is commonly accepted that, with the quantitative growth of the Antwerp market, important qualitative improvements in organization and infrastructure also took place.[29] Various authors have drawn up long lists of achievements that, allegedly, occurred in Antwerp during its golden age: the spread and improvement of organization forms in trade and finance (such as share-companies, trade on commission and commercial bills), the opening of an exchange, improvements in commercial insurance, the settlement of new industries and important improvements in urban infrastructure and communication. In this section we will deal with these improvements and innovations in more detail, considering to what extent they were accomplishments of

---

[27] See, for example, H. van der Wee and J. Materné, 'Antwerp as a World Market in the Sixteenth and Seventeenth Centuries' in J. van der Stock (ed.), *Antwerp, Story of a Metropolis*, exhibition catalogue, Antwerp, Hessenhuis, 25 June – 10 October 1993 (Ghent, 1993), pp. 19–32; syntheses on the period between 1585 and 1650 are to be found in Brulez, 'Anvers', and Baetens, '*Nazomer*'.

[28] A. Balis, 'Antwerp, Foster-mother of the Arts: Its contribution to the Artistic Culture of Europe in the Seventeenth Century' in van der Stock, *Story of a Metropolis*, pp. 115–27, at 116.

[29] See especially H. Soly, 'De dominantnie van het handelskapitalisme: stad en platteland' in E. Witte (ed.), *Geschiedenis van Vlaanderen. Van de oorsprong tot heden* (Brussels, 1983), pp. 105–78. and H. Soly, 'Social Relations in Antwerp in the Sixteenth and Seventeenth Centuries' in van der Stock, *Story of a Metropolis*, pp. 37–48.

Antwerp and at their economic impact in the long term. Finally, we will try to investigate the economic logic behind the clustering of such achievements in metropoles such as Antwerp by referring to the economic concept of 'advantages of agglomeration'.

The sector that originally dominated the economy of Antwerp was certainly international trade. The increasing volume of transit trade at the beginning of the sixteenth century and the contacts between merchants from all over Europe led to major improvements in the organization of trade. The development of share-companies, based on participation in someone else's enterprise made it possible for merchants with less capital also to participate in the commercial expansion.[30] Another form of organization that became increasingly popular was trade on commission, that is, a merchant paying a local partner or agent in a remote place for selling or purchasing merchandise for him, in order not to have to employ a factor, as the big firms used to do. Together with other developments, such as improvements in the field of commercial insurance, the spread and refinement of these techniques favoured a democratization of long-distance trade. This was a central feature of sixteenth-century commerce which resulted in a huge increase of petty merchants participating in international trade. In fact, Guicciardini remarked in 1567 that 'nowadays everybody is busy with trade'.[31] According to more recent calculations, about 2,000 merchants were active in international trade around 1550 in Antwerp, of whom 400–500 were from the Southern Low Countries.[32] Another technical innovation in the field of commerce was the general spread of double-entry bookkeeping. Originally an Italian invention, it became a common practice in western Europe and a necessary tool for managing the complex international transactions which characterized the commercial expansion of the sixteenth century.[33]

Closely linked to the development of trade were the improvements in financial technique. Here the spread of commercial bills was one of the major developments. The traditional instrument of credit at the Brabantine fairs, the letter obligatory payable to bearer was improved by guaranteeing increasing legal as well as financial security to its holder, and as a result made it a negotiable trade paper. At the same time, the letter of exchange (until then mainly used in the south) spread across the commercial networks of western Europe. Via assignment, both letters

---

[30] See W. Brulez, *De firma Della Faille en de internationale handel van Vlaamse firma's in de 16e eeuw* (Brussels, Koninklijke Vlaamse Academie voor Wetenschappen, Letteren en Schone Kunsten van België, 1959), pp. 432–4; and the comments by van der Wee, *Growth*, vol. II, p. 326, n 91.   [31] Brulez, *Della Faille*, pp. 368–70.
[32] Van der Wee and Materné, 'World Market', p. 23.
[33] Van der Wee, *Growth*, II, p. 331.

obligatory and letters of exchange became very popular forms of commercial bill, which were exchanged between merchants. They formed a means of short-term commercial loans, and also a form of payment that was quicker and safer than payment in cash.[34] The diffusion of these techniques, in and beyond the city, was sustained by bookkeeping manuals in different languages which were published in great numbers in Antwerp.[35] Through these technical improvements, which were partly the combination of different traditions, and through the massive influx of precious metals first from central Europe and later from America, the money market of Antwerp not only adapted to the demands of expanding trade, but also served as the major market for public loans. The Antwerp exchange, although not the first in history, had nevertheless introduced new dimensions and forms of organization, which were further applied, later on, in Amsterdam and London.[36]

Finally, considerable developments took place in the industrial sector. Through influence from Italian towns, especially Venice, luxury industries such as glass production, the majolica industry, silk weaving and sugar refining were introduced to Antwerp. They formed only a part of the broad spectrum of luxury crafts settled in the city, which included tapestry, woodcarving, goldsmithing, diamond-cutting and fur-processing. While the demand for luxury products was originally mainly met by imports from Italy, the larger urban centres of the Low Countries, led by Bruges, set up their own production from the fifteenth century onwards by means of Italian immigrants. During the sixteenth century, Antwerp and Brussels, the economic and the political centre of the Low Countries, had particularly wealthy elites and a large middle class who stimulated the local luxury and fashion industries.[37] Also here, many new industries were introduced by Italians such as the Venetian mirror-maker J.M. Cornachini or the glass-maker Ciacomo Pasquetti from Breschia,[38] and throughout

[34] Van der Wee, 'Antwerp and the New Financial Methods of the 16th and 17th Centuries' in *The Low Countries in the Early Modern World* (Aldershot, 1993), pp. 145–66, at 149–53.

[35] Van der Wee and Materné, 'World Market', p. 24.

[36] This impact of the Antwerp exchange can be illustrated by the fact that the exchange buildings of Amsterdam, London and Copenhagen are built in a style very similar to that of the Antwerp 'Beurs'. See R. van Uytven, Antwerpen: Steuerungszentrum des europäischen Handels und Metropole der Niederlande im 16. Jahrhundert' in B. Sicken (ed.), *Herrschaft und Verfassungsstrukturen im Nordwesten des Reiches. Beiträge zum Zeitalter Karls V. Franz Petri zum Gedächtais (1903–1993)* (Cologne, 1994), p. 10, and H. Baeyens, 'De Bouwmeesters' in *Flandria Nostra* (Antwerp, 1957), vol. II, pp. 47–54.

[37] H. van der Wee, 'Industrial Dynamics', pp. 329–38, and R. Lauwaert, 'Ambachten en nieuwe nijverheden' in W. Couvreur et al., *Antwerpen in de XVIde eeuw* (Antwerp, 1975), pp. 143–59.

[38] J.A. Goris, *Etude sur les colonies marchandes méridionales (portugais, espagnols, italiens) à Anvers de 1488 à 1567. Contribution à l'histoire des débuts du capitalisme moderne* (Louvain, 1925), pp. 429–35.

the sixteenth century it was Italians that remained dominant in them. Antwerp's position as a commercial metropolis helped the town to become a leading export centre for luxury industries, through its easy access to raw materials and the great skill of its artisans, as well as through the presence of foreign merchants actively seeking products to purchase. Luxury products made in Antwerp, worked from precious raw materials such as silk, gold, silver, pearls and diamonds, attained an international reputation and were amongst the most successful products of the Southern Low Countries' export industries during the sixteenth and early seventeenth centuries.[39]

Among all these economic achievements, those in commercial and financial organization were especially important. Together, they were the preconditions for the development of modern world trade. European trade was only able to cope with the complexity and scale of the expanding world economy on the basis of enhanced technical skills and innovations. This appears equally from the account of N. Rosenberg and L. E. Birdzell with respect to *the economic transformation of the industrial world*. According to them, bills of exchange and banking, insurance, economic associations without kinship and double-entry bookkeeping count among the major points of institutional innovations allowing the growth of an autonomous merchant class during the modern period.[40] On a closer view however, these innovations in commercial technique are not really Antwerp inventions, since in many cases there are foreign influences, especially from Italy. Concerning trade, W. Brulez even states 'that there was no creative contribution in commercial technique originating in Antwerp,'[41] only the spread of techniques that were already known. The real achievement that took place in Antwerp was the application and adaptation of numerous new techniques, forms of organization and products and their effective combination within the new context of an international commercial network. This applies to the field of finance and commerce as well as to the industrial sector. Hence, it was not inventions that constituted the crucial aspect of Antwerp's innovative character, but rather the application or diffusion of existing information to new uses.[42] Paradoxically, it was the decline of Antwerp that helped to spread throughout Europe the know-how that was achieved during the golden

[39] A.K.L. Thijs, 'Antwerp's Luxury Industries: the Pursuit of Profit and Artistic Sensitivity' in van der Stock, *Story of a Metropolis*, pp. 105–13.
[40] N. Rosenberg and L.E. Birdzell, *How the West Grew Rich. The Economic Transformation of the Industrial World* (London, 1986), pp. 113–15, and chapter 4 passim.
[41] W. Brulez, 'De handel' in Couvreur et al., *Antwerpen in de XVIe eeuw*, pp. 109–41, at 125.
[42] Compare J. Mokyr, *The Lever of Riches. Technological Creativity and Economic Progress* (Oxford, 1990), p. 6, and N. Rosenberg, *Inside the Black Box: Technology and Economics* (Cambridge, 1982), p. 143.

age. The thousands of merchants, artisans and workers who left Antwerp during the Revolt took their skills and new techniques with them and passed them on to commercial centres of a new generation, like Amsterdam, Hamburg and London.[43]

Although the nature of economic achievement in Antwerp can therefore be summarized as the diffusion and adaptation of know-how, the reason for their clustering in particular urban centres remains to be explained. An explanatory model for this question has been established by spatial economists with the concept of economies of agglomeration.[44] They discern three types of advantage of urban agglomeration: (a) *internal* advantages in terms of economies of scale, (b) *external* advantages in terms of localization economies, and (c) advantages of *urbanization* as such. We will bypass internal economies of scale, with the size of individual firms and advantages resulting from a higher volume of production, and concentrate on the so-called external advantages, which relate to the advantages of agglomeration at a specific place. H. W. Richardson sums up various aspects of these external advantages, such as the common use of transport facilities, so-called labour market economies (larger pools of and more varied skills, a greater elasticity in labour supply, superior training facilities); a larger supply of managerial and professional talent and the presence of facilities likely to attract these, opportunities for specialization offered by the large urban market, access to sources of capital, communication and information economies – especially face-to-face contact, or greater adaptability and flexibility of fixed investments.[45] These factors form important economic advantages of big cities. They are to be found within specific sectors, in the form of economies of localisation and, for the economic activity within a city in general, are called economies of urbanization.

In Antwerp, a sector where the impact of localisation economies can be shown very clearly is the cloth-finishing and dyeing industry. Finishing and dyeing cloth was already an important industry in Antwerp in the fifteenth century; and became one of the largest industrial sectors in the sixteenth century, where more than 1,600 people were employed.[46] One advantage in terms of transport costs was the fact that Antwerp was not

[43] See, for example, van der Wee, 'New Financial Methods', pp. 145–66, Brulez, 'De handel', pp. 131–6, van Uytven, 'Steuerungszentrum', p. 10.
[44] The concept of economies of agglomeration has been applied to sixteenth-century Antwerp by B. Blondé, 'Antwerpen: metropool van het noorden', in J.M.E. Worms et al., *Orientatiecursus cultuurwetenschappen 1, De Bouergondisch–Habsburgische Nederlanden* (Heerlen, 1992), pp. 43–61, at 52.
[45] H.W. Richardson, *The Economics of Urban Size* (Farnborough, 1973), p. 39.
[46] A.K.L. Thijs, *Van "werkwinkel" tot "fabriek". De textielnijverheid te Antwerpen (einde 15de – begin 19de eeuw)* (Brussels, 1987), p. 71. Some documents even declare that the number was as high as 5,000–6,000 masters and journeymen before 1584.

only the centre of distribution of English cloth on the continent, but also a big interregional market for dyeing materials. Thus, by locating the dyeing industry in Antwerp, the import costs of these raw materials were minimized. The English Merchant Adventurers had an advantage in shipping unfinished cloth over the Channel instead of finished and dyed fabric. In this way, the risks of loss or damage by sea water during overseas export were considerably reduced. Furthermore, the location of the finishing industry in Antwerp, instead of England, made it possible for clients to choose the colour and design of the final product and even the artisan of their preference. At the same time, it gave them the chance to control not only the process of finishing and dyeing, but also the quality of the *unfinished* cloth, which facilitated its replacement on complaint. As a consequence, the concentration of the finishing industry in Antwerp gave rise to strong competition among the artisans, and therefore helped to maintain competitive price level and to increase quality standards, which had already been on a very high level in the fifteenth century.[47]

Similar factors were responsible for Antwerp's position as a centre of luxury industry. The town offered a combination of raw materials, highly skilled labour force and a high demand for local consumption as well as for export. This led to important economies of scale through specialization and, to a certain degree, even through division of labour.[48] Furthermore, the quality and variety of production were continuously improved by introducing new techniques and expertise and by combining them with local know-how.

Antwerp was not only the location of specific branches of industry. Its particular appeal lay in its multifunctional character. As a commercial and financial as well as industrial centre, it offered the advantages of urbanization to a high extent, and contemporaries were fully aware of it. A very good example of this awareness can be found in a seventeenth-century textbook for merchants which made the advantages of urban concentration the subject of a fictitious discourse between two merchants in sixteenth-century Antwerp.[49]

A foreign merchant: 'La ville d'Anvers a ceste commodité par dessus toutes autres villes de ce Pais bas, que l'on y trouve ordinairement Postes, Mesagers, à cheval et à pied, chartiers et mariniers, quasi de tous autres

[47] Ibid., pp. 63–9. The great problem of the Antwerp finishing industry, however, was the strong dependence on English imports, which were the object of a centralized commercial policy by the Merchant Adventurers. When the political situation in the 1560s interrupted commercial contacts between England and the Low Countries, the role of this industry was definitely undermined.

[48] Van der Wee, 'Industrial Dynamics', p. 340.

[49] G. de Vivre, *Dialogues Flamen–Françoys traictants du fait de la marchandise* (Delft, 1642), cited in Goris, *Colonies marchandes*, p. 133.

endroicts du monde tant l'Angleterre, de France, d'Espaigne, des Indes, de l'Italie, de l'Alemaigne commme de Danemarc, du pais de Levant et plusieurs autres royaumes et Provinces.' A Flemish merchant: 'Vous dites vray, c'est aussi la cause que tant de Nations se trouvent ici communé-ment, pource que non seulement ilz ont moyen d'entendre nouvelles de leurs païs, mais aussi de mener train et traffique de plusieurs sortes de marchandises, lesquelles de ce lieu ci l'on transporte par toute l'Europe.'

This high praise of the economic location of Antwerp contains several references to economies of agglomeration. First, it is possible to deal with different sorts of products which are transported to the rest of Europe from there. This summarizes the town's basic function as a major European transit market. The aspect of 'mener train et traffique' includes the coordination of international traffic, a strategic function which is very much dependent on face-to-face communication even in the business world of the late twentieth century.[50] Communication and transport facil-ities constitute the second central argument in the discussion of the two merchants. In a period when travelling over longer distances was ham-pered by the technical possibilities, the existence of an effective system of transport and communication was crucial for the success of commercial activity. The availability of 'post services, messengers on foot and on horseback, carters and mariners', to use the words of the seventeenth-century author, was very high in Antwerp. The official post service of the Milan family de Tassis, which was centred on Brussels from 1505, also had an important office in Antwerp. By the middle of the sixteenth century, the de Tassis post service, which had been founded exclusively for official correspondence, was available to individuals and protected by a monopoly.[51] Other means of communication that were common in Antwerp were printed price lists and *tijdingen*, an early form of news-papers which were published, although still not regularly. They contained information on wars, trials or other important events, such as the arrival of the bullion fleets from the New World.[52] Transport organization in Antwerp was also very favourable for international trade. During the six-teenth century, numerous merchants specialized in long-distance over-land transport. This specialization had its advantages in an establishment of fixed tariffs and the possibility of payment at the route's destination

[50] Richardson, *Economics of Urban Size*, p. 39, and P. Dicken and P.E. Lloyd, *Modern Western Society. A Geographical Perspective on Work, Home and Well-being* (London, 1981), p. 71.
[51] Goris, *Colonies marchandes*, p. 134.
[52] L. Voet, 'De typografische bedrijvigheid te Antwerpen in de 16e eeuw' in Couvreur et al., *Antwerpen in de XVIde eeuw*, p. 242. See also R. Pieper, 'Informationszentren im Vergleich. Die Stellung Venedigs und Antwerpens im 16. Jahrhundert' in M. North (ed.), *Kommunikationsrevolutionen. Die neuen Medien des 16. und 19. Jahrhunderts* (Cologne and Vienna, 1995), pp. 45–60.

instead of having to pay all the different carriers and tolls separately along the way.[53] Together with the spread of transport insurance, these services helped to obtain a faster, safer and more regular exchange of goods and merchandise. In Antwerp, merchants could rely on these long-distance expediters as well as on hundreds of local carriers to load and unload their ships and transport merchandise within the town. The town magistrate intervened repeatedly against the increasing corporatism of the carriers' guilds in order to safeguard the functioning of local transport. A first step was made by increasing the members of the carriers' guilds and, after complaints against corporatist monopolies in 1538, even ordering that merchants were free to choose carriers for loading and unloading their ships.[54] This is only one example of the crucial importance of municipal policy for the economic attractiveness of the town. Around the middle of the century, many initiatives were taken to improve the commercial infrastructure of the town. Some of the most remarkable results were the construction of the New Exchange, the 'Nieuwe Beurs', in 1531 (figure 2.2) and the 'Hessenhuis', a commercial building for merchants and carters from Hessen in central Germany, in 1564, and especially the urbanistic activities of Gilbert van Schoonbeke in the 1540s, including an important amplification of the port to the north of the town.[55]

A third central point in the dialogue of the two merchants is the attraction of the city to foreign traders. The presence of facilities likely to attract professional talent is one of the essential features for the potential of innovation of a big city mentioned by Richardson. If we see achievements as a result of individual creativity, the increase of a city's human capital, and therefore the attraction of qualified immigrants, is a vital precondition for the clustering of innovations. The dramatic increase in Antwerp's population during the sixteenth century up to about 100,000 inhabitants around 1565 was largely based on immigration. Natural reproduction was not sufficient to increase urban population and would even have caused a negative balance. The great mass of Antwerp immigrants came from the surrounding countryside, especially from the duchy of Brabant (see figure 2.3). Yet, there were also many new citizens from other towns within the Low Countries, such as Brussels, Malines, Bruges, Ghent or Lille (see table 2.1), and from other European countries, especially from Germany, France, England, Italy and Spain (figure 2.3).[56]

[53] Brulez, *Della Faille*, p. 408.
[54] G. Asaert (ed.), *De Antwerpse Naties* (Tielt, 1993), pp. 24–6.
[55] See H. Soly, *Urbanisme en kapitalisme te Antwerpen in de 16e eeuw. De stedebouwkundige en industriële ondernemingen van Gilbert van Schoonbeke* (Brussels, 1977).
[56] M. Limberger, 'Die Metropolenstellung Antwerpens im 16. Jahrhundert. Aspekte der Antwerpener Zentralität auf verschiedenen Wirtschaftsebenen: Weltwirtschaft, nationaler und regionaler Markt' (unpublished MA thesis, University of Vienna, 1990), pp. 92–109.

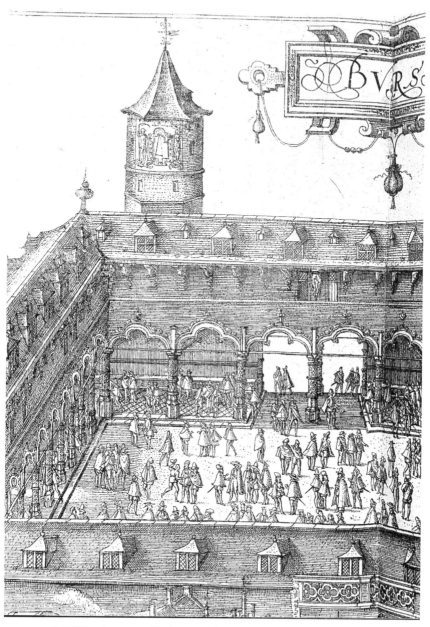

2.2 The Antwerp Exchange (detail) (Source: Lodovico Guicciardini, 'La description de tous les Pais-Bas, autrement appellés la Germaine inférieure, ou Basse Allemagne', Antwerp, 1582)

Table 2.1 *Towns of origin of new Antwerp citizens, 1554–5*

Brabant	No.	Flanders	No.	Others (selection)	No.
Leuven	21	Bruges	13	Namur	12
Malines	14	Oudenaarde	6	Cologne	6
Brussels	10	Aalst	4	Liège	5
Lier	8	Kortrijk	3	Valkenburg	5
Den Bosch	7	Ghent	3	Lille	3
Turnhout	6	Dendermonde	2	Valenciennes	3
Bergen op Zoom	4	Ieper	2	Delft	2
Breda	4			Utrecht	2
Diest	9			Cambrai	2
Tienen	4			Münster	2
Herentals	3			Aachen	2
Zoutleeuw	3			Amsterdam	1

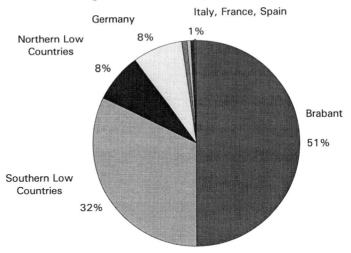

2.3 Countries of origin of new Antwerp citizens, 1554–1555 (Source: Stadsarchief Antwerpen, *Antwerpse poortersboeken 1533–1608*, Antwerp, 1988, vol. I)

Among the foreigners who emigrated to Antwerp we find mainly merchants, but also highly qualified artisans, such as the Italian silk weavers, mirror-makers and glass-blowers mentioned above.[57] Some of them ranked among the most dynamic as well as wealthy personalities of sixteenth-century Antwerp, for example, the Germans Erasmus Schetz and Lazarus Tucher, and the Frenchman Christophe Plantin, who established later one of the biggest publishing houses in Europe.[58] In a letter to Pope Gregory XIII, Plantin explains why he had chosen to move to Antwerp:

I chose to settle down in Belgium and in this town of Antwerp in particular. What made me decide this was the fact that, in my opinion, *no town in the world provides more advantages for the profession I wanted to pursue*. It is easy to get there, one sees different countries get together at the market; one also finds all the raw materials which are indispensable for my craft; for all professions, there is no problem in finding labourers who can be instructed within a short time.[59]

In a modern and analytical way, Plantin sums up the economies of agglomeration he expected and found in Antwerp. This is striking, and shows what a pole of attraction the Brabantine metropolis was for contemporaries.

The economic prospects in the metropolis hence attracted, among others, many qualified and ambitious immigrants who contributed to the city's human capital. In Antwerp, they found advantageous conditions to apply their skills and to develop them further through professional contacts and training. As far as professional contacts are concerned, a commercial and financial metropolis such as Antwerp scored extremely well. Not only all countries but all the major European business firms were represented by a factor or commissioner. The Antwerp exchange and the English exchange were therefore *the* place to be for getting into contact with potential business partners or to receive information from all parts of the known world. Training, finally, a major multiplier of professional skills and new techniques, was also an ace of Antwerp. The quality of teaching was very high. There were numerous schools – according to some authors 150–200[60] – including private schools for children belonging to the merchant class. It was there that languages, calculating and commercial techniques were taught, not only

---

[57] Stadsarchief Antwerpen, *Antwerpse Poortersboeken, 1533–1608* (Antwerp: 1977), 3 vols.

[58] L. Voet, *De gouden eeuw van Antwerpen. Bloei en uitstraling van de Metropool in de zestiende eeuw* (Antwerp, 1973), p. 301.

[59] Cited in M. Sabbe, *De meesters van den Gulden Passer* (Amsterdam, 1937), p. 14; my translation.

[60] H.L.V. de Groote, 'De zestiende-eeuwse Antwerpse schoolmeesters', *Bijdragen tot de Geschiedenis*, 50 (1967), pp. 179–318, at 186–7.

to boys but also to girls.[61] Another source of information were the great number of textbooks on bookkeeping, trade or banking which were published in several languages by Antwerp printers. They helped to transmit the latest commercial and financial know-how within the city and throughout Europe.[62] Finally, Antwerp was a 'practical school of commerce'[63] itself. Many a young merchant from the Low Countries came to the commercial metropolis as an apprentice, to learn his profession and to get in touch with the world of international commerce. This was the case, for example, for the 16-year-old Herman Pottey, who later worked as factor for the wealthy merchant Jan Della Faille, and for the 18-year-old Pieter Seghers from Ghent.[64] Young artisans could also obtain a very good training in the workshops of skilled master from Antwerp or from abroad. In fact, many specialists were attracted to 'bring in new crafts and teach them to the city's children'.[65]

Economies of agglomeration and the impulse for innovation are, however, not the only effects of urban concentration. Against these advantages, there stand also negative effects. Great cities tend to have a very high price and wage level, which, from a certain point, can turn into a disadvantage of agglomeration. From this point of view, sixteenth-century Antwerp was no exception. Other negative aspects of big urban agglomerations, such as a lack of hygiene and a high degree of violence and criminality, were also well known to the metropolis's inhabitants.[66] The increasing concentration and attraction to the economic pole generally has a polarizing effect on the surrounding regional economy. Sixteenth-century Antwerp also developed such a tendency of polarization. Research has shown that the regional economy of the Southern Low

[61] J. de Wolf, 'Het meisjesonderwijs te Antwerpen, 16de–18de eeuw' (unpublished MA thesis, Rijksuniversiteit Gent, 1989). R. Baetens, 'Le rôle d'Anvers dans la transmission de valeurs culturelles au temps de son apogée (1500–1650)', in *Cities and the Transmission of Cultural Values in the Late Middle Ages and Early Modern Period* (Seventeenth International Colloquium, Spa, 16–19 May 1994) (Brussels, 1996), pp. 37–72, at 57–8.

[62] H. van der Wee, 'Das Phänomen des Wachstums und der Stagnation im Lichte der Antwerpener und südniederländischen Wirtschaft des 16. Jahrhunderts', *Vierteljahrsschrifte für Sozial- und Wirtschaftsgeschichte*, 54 (1967), pp. 203–49, at 205, and the literature referred to in footnote.

[63] Brulez, *Della Faille*, p. 500.

[64] K. Degryse, *Pieter Seghers. een koopmansleven in troebele tijden* (Antwerp, 1990), pp. 17, 110; De mémoires van Herman Pottey, factor van Jan Della Faille' in Brulez, *Della Faille*, appendix XVIII, pp. 559–67, at 560.

[65] From the Antwerp city accounts, cited by Thijs, 'Luxury Industries', p. 108.

[66] Blondé, 'Metropool van het noorden', p. 52. On prices and wages, see van der Wee, *Growth*, and E. Scholliers, *Loonarbeid en honger. De levensstandaard in de XVe en XVIe eeuw te Antwerpen* (Antwerp, 1960). On the hygiene situation, see P. Poulussen, *Van burenlast tot milieuhinder. Het stedelijk leefmilieu 1500–1800* (Kapellen, 1987), and P. Maclot et al., (eds.), *'N Propere tijd!? (On)leefbaar Antwerpen thuis en op straat (1500–1800)* (Antwerp, 1988).

Countries suffered such a process in various sectors. The industrial sector of the smaller towns of Brabant for instance, had to deal with difficulties arising from the superior competition from Antwerp and other big towns on the one hand, and from the declining importance of the Brabant fairs on the other.[67] Similar problems arose in the secondary commercial centres, for example Bergen op Zoom, the second place where the Brabant fairs took place. Here, Guicciardini remarked in 1567: 'Nowadays, only little trade is being done here, because the neighbourhood and the great power of Antwerp attracts the surrounding countries.'[68] For the rural economy there are indications that its development depended strongly on the economic situation of respective local centres.[69]

Finally, even in Antwerp itself the benefits of economic success were not equally shared. The group of wealthy merchants, bankers and artisans who gained from the economic boom, stood against thousands of poor people whose economic situation was very insecure and dependent on favourable conjunctures.[70]

Taking into account these polarizing effects of Antwerp's economic growth, it is difficult to make an overall assessment of Antwerp's golden age, or even to call the economic growth of the metropolis as an achievement in itself. We hope however to have shown that the extraordinary economic concentration strongly favoured the spread and application of technical as well as organizational innovations. Antwerp's potential of clustering innovation or achievements was based on the concentration of the staple market for various products and raw materials and of highly specialized industries, as well as on a favourable situation in terms of demand markets especially with respect to the Low Countries but also further into the continental interior. A second precondition was the highly developed infrastructure, including transport facilities, means of communication and commercial services. Finally, the exceptional

---

[67] Van der Wee, 'Industrial Dynamics', pp. 338–41.

[68] L.Guicciardini, *Descrittione di tutti i Paesi Bassi*, 1588 edn, pp. 178–9, cited in this context in B. Blondé, *De sociale structuren en economische dynamiek van 'S-Hertogenbosch 1500–1550*, Bijdragen tot de geschiedenis van het zuiden van Nederland 74 (Tilburg, Stichting Zuidelijk Historisch Contact, 1987), p. 141.

[69] For the surroundings of Louvain, see R. van Uytven, 'In de schaduwen van de Antwerpse groei: het Hageland in de zestiende eeuw', *Bijdragen tot de Geschiedenis*, 57 (1974), pp. 171–88. For the surroundings of Antwerp, I am currently doing research for my PhD dissertation. First results are in 'Merchant Capitalism and the Countryside: Antwerp and the West of the Duchy of Brabant (XVth–XVIth Centuries)', in P. Hoppenbrouwers and J.L. van Zanden (eds.), *From Peasants to Farmers? The Transformation of the Rural Economy and Society in the Low Countries (Middle Ages – 19th Century) in the Light of the Brenner Debate* (Turnhout, in press).

[70] H. Soly, 'Social Relations' stresses the social and economic polarization in Antwerp; see also Scholliers, *Loonarbeid en honger*, and E. Scholliers, 'De lagere klassen', in Couvreur et al., *Antwerpen in de XVIe eeuw*, pp. 161–80.

concentration of human capital was reinforced by the increasing number of immigrants attracted from the rest of Europe and by the town's facilities for training and professional contacts. The economic achievements of Antwerp during its golden age in commercial, financial and industrial organization were thus due to the favourable circumstances for economic initiative which were typical of international commercial and financial centres such as Antwerp, Amsterdam or London. They helped to establish new forms of economic organization and infrastructure, which were necessary for the expansion of the international commercial network which forms, in many ways, a base of our modern world economy.

3 Clusters of achievement: the economy of Amsterdam in its golden age

Clé Lesger

From [the] chrysalis of economic simplicity Amsterdam emerged – somewhat abruptly, as it seemed to contemporaries – in the quarter-century covering the last fifteen years of the sixteenth century and the first decade of the seventeenth, to enter upon a metropolitan and cosmopolitan career.

Violet Barbour[1]

It was a period of unprecedented activity and achievement in many fields that launched Amsterdam on its 'metropolitan and cosmopolitan career'. Amsterdam not only became dominant in trade and shipping, it also took a leading role in the manufacture of luxury goods, in printing and publishing, in cartography, in science and technology, in learning and in the arts. Simultaneous advances in so many different areas suggest some common agent at work but, although the suggestion is obvious, much study of specific fields is needed to establish what exactly created the conditions for sustaining the boom and what exactly set it off. In this paper I shall restrict myself to the economic aspect of the process that brought about what Charles Wilson once described as 'explosions of collective and individual genius'.[2]

The rapid growth of Amsterdam's economy from 1585 coincides with the expansion of Amsterdam's trading network to include almost every corner of the then known world and the city's rise as an international commodity market and centre of finance. In its role as a major market and international clearing house, Amsterdam greatly contributed to the division of labour among nations, as well as providing a powerful impetus towards their economic cooperation. A contemporary observer wrote of Amsterdam as 'one of the cities with the greatest trade that there is in the world, whether by the amount of money remitted by its merchants and bankers to all foreign countries, or by the almost infinite number of commodities with which its warehouses are filled, and which come in and go

---

[1] V. Barbour, *Capitalism in Amsterdam in the 17th century* (Ann Arbor, 1963), p. 15.
[2] C. Wilson, *The Dutch Republic and the Civilisation of the 17th century* (London, 1968), p. 123.

out unceasingly in the commerce which she carries on, even to the ends of the earth'.[3]

In the following I will try to show that Amsterdam's commercial boom did not appear out of the blue but was rooted in the regional economy, while arguing that its position in this regional economy by itself cannot explain the city's rise to international prominence in the first half of the seventeenth century. It was only in the complex interaction between the often unique characteristics of the local and regional economy and the opportunities and restraints of the international context that Amsterdam's golden age came into being.[4]

What some contemporaries saw as Amsterdam's meteoric rise to prominence after 1585 was preceded by a lengthy period during which the city gradually came to dominate the spatial economy of Holland, the north-western region of the Netherlands. Until the middle of the fourteenth century Holland had been little more than a farming region served by small towns whose commerce and industry were geared strictly to regional needs. Politically and economically the towns were of little importance beyond their regional spheres. In the latter half of the four-teenth century the picture began to change. Profound changes in the region's physical geography and agricultural structure, combined with opportunities in international shipping and trade, started off the transfor-mation to a commercial, industrial and urbanized society.[5]

Within the compass of this paper I should like to focus on develop-ments in the service sector but we should be aware of the fact that these were intimately linked with developments in agriculture, fishing and industry. If we consider the position of Holland's ports relative to the sur-rounding regions, we can distinguish between the North Sea ports in the Rhine–Meuse delta and the ports that arose along the coast of Holland's inland sea, the Zuiderzee. The delta ports mainly served the flow of goods between the eastern hinterland and the sea in the west. Among these ports Dordrecht ranked first.[6] By their convenient situation at the junc-

---

[3] Cited in Barbour, *Capitalism in Amsterdam*, pp. 22–3.

[4] For a recent overview of the economic history of the Netherlands see J. de Vries and A. van der Woude, *Nederland 1500–1800. De eerste ronde van moderne economische groei* (Amsterdam, 1995); and see also C.P. Kindleberger, *World Economic Primacy 1500–1990* (New York, 1996), ch.6.

[5] H.P.H. Jansen, *Hollands Voorsprong* (Leiden, 1976) (inaugural lecture, also published in English in *Acta Historiae Neerlandicae* 10 (1978), pp. 1–19); D.E.H. de Boer, *Graaf en grafiek. Sociale en economische ontwikkelingen in het middeleeuwse 'Noordholland' tussen 1345 en 1415* (Leiden, 1978); C.M. Lesger, *Hoorn als stedelijk knooppunt. Stedensystemen tijdens de late middeleeuwen en vroegmoderne tijd* (Hilversum, 1990).

[6] W. Jappe Alberts and H.P.H. Jansen, *Welvaart in wording. Sociaal-economische geschiedenis van Nederland van de vroegste tijden tot het einde van de middeleeuwen* ('s-Gravenhage, 1977), pp. 46–8 and 197–202; J. Baart, 'De materiële stadscultuur', *De Hollandse stad in de dertiende eeuw* (Zutphen, 1988), pp. 93–112.

ture of trade routes from the German Rhineland and Meuse basin to Flanders, Brabant, Holland and the North Sea countries, the merchants and carriers of Dordrecht came to handle much of the trade that went on in both directions. Next to Dordrecht, the port towns of Schiedam, Delfshaven and Rotterdam pulled little weight.[7]

Whereas the delta ports linked the east and the west, the ports on Holland's Zuiderzee coast were intermediaries between the north and the south. First among them was Amsterdam. By the first quarter of the fourteenth century it was Holland's main gateway to the northern German ports and second in importance only to Dordrecht. Amsterdam had the advantage of a good, deep harbour in the river IJ and good transport links with an extensive hinterland. A network of navigable inland waters gave easy access to the agricultural regions in the north and the industrial towns of southern Holland, to the delta region, to Zeeland and to the densely populated and well-developed regions of Flanders and Brabant.

Although most of the goods handled by Amsterdam's port were still being shipped by foreign carriers, gradually its merchants began to expand their own business abroad.[8] After a fire in May 1452 had destroyed a large part of Amsterdam's warehouses, the Burgundian duke Philip the Good commented that the goods stored in them 'valoient plus sans comparison que les dites maisons', and he recommended that the town be quickly rebuilt and reinforced 'pour cause des marchans, qui affluent de toutes pars pour la notable port, qui y est, et que c'est la ville la plus marchande de tout nostre dit pays de Hollande.'[9] As a matter of fact, by 1450 Amsterdam had eclipsed the other ports on the Zuiderzee that traded with northern Germany and the Baltic states. Ports such as Hoorn, Enkhuizen, Medemblik and Edam, which served the thinly populated, largely agrarian part of Holland north of the IJ river, were less well located to function as gateways for southern Holland, Zeeland and the populous towns of Brabant and Flanders.

During the last quarter of the fifteenth and the first decade of the sixteenth century a deep crisis took hold of Holland and other parts of the Low Countries. In Holland it was brought on by a combination of adverse developments. A long-standing problem was the rising groundwater level

---

[7] Z.W. Sneller, 'Handel en verkeer in het Beneden-Maasgebied tot het eind der zestiende eeuw', *Nederlandsche Historiebladen* 2 (1939), pp. 341–73; Johan de Vries, *Amsterdam–Rotterdam. Rivaliteit in economisch-historisch perspectief* (Bussum, 1965).

[8] W.S. Unger, 'De Hollandsche graanhandel en graanhandelspolitiek in de middeleeuwen', *De Economist* (1916), pp. 243-69, 337-86, 461-507, F. Ketner, *Handel en scheepvaart van Amsterdam in de vijftiende eeuw* (Leiden, 1946); and N.W. Posthumus (ed.), *De Oosterse handel te Amsterdam; het oudst bewaarde koopmansboek van een Amsterdamse vennootschap betreffende de handel op de Oostzee, 1485-1490* (Leiden, 1953).

[9] Cited in Ketner, *Handel en scheepvaart*, p. 126.

and the intrusions of sea and rivers in frequent flooding, spoiling farmland and severely hampering farm production. It was also a time of political tension. After the death of Charles the Bold of Burgundy, a movement for regional independence arose and plunged the region into turmoil, aggravated by incursions of marauding bands from the regions of Sticht and Gelre. Constant warfare forced up the burden of taxation and piracy at sea was paralysing trade and fishing. To make matters worse, a harrowed and starving population was visited by epidemics of the plague. However, it was this long crisis that bred the processes that favoured Amsterdam's rise to supremacy in the region and its economic expansion after 1585.

One such process was the decline in agriculture, which forced Holland's rural population to look for additional sources of income. From a survey held in 1514 we know that small dairy farmers throughout northern Holland supplemented their income with what they could earn in a variety of other occupations. Lucassen demonstrated a correlation between these occupations and the annual cycle of farm work in Holland. In his view, the small farmers in Holland interspersed their farming with a succession of activities, such as hunting, inland fishing, navvying, mowing and haying, and going to sea with the herring fleet or as sailors on merchant vessels.[10] None of these activities by itself could provide them with enough income to support a family. The practice was not a new one, however, especially in the Waterland region just north of Amsterdam, where cargo shipping had long been an occupation supplementing farmers' incomes from the poor soil.[11]

In demographic terms, the population's ability to earn additional income in other occupations enabled them to raise larger families, principally by allowing them to marry younger.[12] Because a good portion of a man's income was earned not in farming but in other lines of work, a little plot of land would do for a young couple, who would otherwise have had to wait for a share of their parents' land. Because couples started families at an earlier age, they raised more children. Although detailed information on the occupational structure and marriage patterns of the rural population is not available for this period, the theory is backed by statistics showing a rapid increase in Holland's rural population throughout the

[10] J. Lucassen, 'Beschouwingen over seizoengebonden trekarbeid', *Tijdschrift voor Sociale Geschiedenis*, 8 (1982), especially fig. 1.
[11] J.J. Voskuil, 'Tussen Twisk en Matenesse. Faseverschillen in de verstening van de huizen op het platteland van Holland in de 16e eeuw', *Volkskundig Bulletin* 8 (1982), map 1.
[12] A. Knotter, 'De Amsterdamse scheepvaart en het Noordhollandse platteland in de 16e en 17e eeuw. Het probleem van de arbeidsmarkt', *Holland* 16 (1984), pp. 281–90; J.L. van Zanden, 'Op zoek naar de "missing link". Hypothesen over de opkomst van Holland in de late middeleeuwen en de vroeg-moderne tijd', *Tijdschrift voor Sociale Geschiedenis* 14 (1988), pp. 359–86.

sixteenth century. It was this growing reservoir of rural manpower that supplied the cheap labour for Holland's expanding merchant marine. Shipowners and merchants alike also benefited from technological innovations in shipbuilding. The superior caravels from the Iberian peninsula were first copied and later adapted to meet the requirements of the shallow waters in which they were to operate.

The second process stimulated by the crisis in Holland was the decline of some ports and the rise of others.[13] Most ports in Holland suffered severely from the economic and demographic setbacks of the crisis and from the decline in foreign trade. Many merchants saw their reserves dwindle through lack of earnings and cut-throat taxes, levied to pay for the unending wars that followed the death of Charles the Bold. In those wars material damage could be considerable: the records of the time speak of the loss of many ships and goods.[14] The impoverished merchants and shipowners could not replace the ships and goods they lost, and, as they lost their fleets and business, ports and towns went into decline. The few among them rich enough to start again left the declining ports to try their luck elsewhere. Records from 1494 and 1514 complain of this desertion and mention Amsterdam as a place where merchants and shipowners were still doing business.[15]

True enough, the crisis had not been as hard on Amsterdam as on the rest of Holland. In 1514 the local governors mourned the loss of many ships in recent years, but another record, adding up the rental of a crane, points to increasing activity in Amsterdam's port.[16] This evidence ties in with the fact that towards the end of the fifteenth century Amsterdam was the only town in Holland with a growing, not a declining, population.[17] For this exceptional development several explanations have been put forward. The most plausible one is that even before the crisis Amsterdam had outstripped the other towns as a cargo port and trading centre. Many of its merchants and shipowners were able to survive the crisis and even to benefit from the decline of the other ports. Amsterdam's port thrived when it came to handle virtually all imports of grain from the Baltic and most exports to this area as well. Records of shipments from the port of Danzig

[13] C. Lesger, 'Intraregional trade and the port system in Holland, 1400–1700', *Economic and Social History in the Netherlands* 4 (1992), pp. 186–217.

[14] R. Fruin (ed.), *Enqueste ende Informatie upt stuck van der reductie ende reformatie van den schiltaelen, voertijts getaxeert ende gestelt geweest over de landen van Hollant ende Vrieslant, gedaen in den jaere MCCCCXCIIII* (Leiden, 1876).

[15] Ibid., p. 16.

[16] L. Noordegraaf, *Hollands Welvaren? Levensstandaard in Holland 1450-1650* (Bergen, 1985), p. 81.

[17] See the number of hearths listed in R. Fruin (ed.), *Informacie up den staet faculteyt ende gelegentheyt van de steden ende dorpen van Hollant ende Vrieslant om daernae te regulieren de nyeuwe schiltaele, gedaen in den jaere MDXIV* (Leiden, 1866), pp. 629–38.

show a marked rise in grain exports to the Low Countries after 1475.[18] The swift advance of Baltic grain was linked to falling supplies from traditional grain-producing areas in the Netherlands and northern France. Crop failures through flooding, the ravages of war and French bans on grain exports reduced supplies to a trickle and what little came through was game for French pirates. Amsterdam at that time was already carrying on a lively trade with the Baltic ports and handled most of the goods imported from that area. So when the Low Countries began to import grain from the Baltic, Amsterdam's port was the chief beneficiary from this new trade. The major losers in the process were the ports of Dordrecht, Gouda, Delft and Schoonhoven, which had handled the grain imports from France and now found themselves out of business. In Gouda, for instance, it was reported that around 1477 grain was imported from France in thirty boyers and that the number of vessels in 1494 had dropped to five or six.[19] The already mentioned circumstance that many wealthy merchants and shipowners took their business to Amsterdam no doubt speeded up this process of selective growth within Holland's port system.

During the sixteenth century, competing ports such as Antwerp and Middelburg tried to get a hold on the expanding trade in Baltic grains, but to no avail. By offering fiscal advantages the magistrate of Amsterdam was able to make the city the most attractive grain staple in the Netherlands, thereby promoting its export trade as well. During the sixteenth century Amsterdam clearly became the major gateway in Holland, exporting most of its agricultural produce, herring and industrial output and virtually monopolizing the overseas trade. From the 1530s onwards Amsterdam also became a transit port for grain destined for Spain and Portugal. However, compared with Antwerp and the Zeeland ports, Amsterdam's trade and shipping to the Iberian peninsula pulled little weight. It was only towards the end of the century that Amsterdam evolved from a transit port for grain to a true intermediary between northern and southern Europe.

The changes wrought by the late-medieval crisis are best understood in their relation to developments in the wider European context. During what is conveniently set apart as the 'long sixteenth century', i.e. the period between 1450 and 1650, that wider European context was marked by population growth, increasing volumes of trade and expansion of the European trade system.

---

[18] Jan de Vries, *The Dutch Rural Economy in the Golden Age, 1500-1700* (New Haven, Conn., 1974), p. 71; R. van Uytven, 'Politiek en economie: de crisis van de late XVe eeuw in de Nederlanden', *Belgisch Tijdschrift voor Filologie en Geschiedenis* 53 (1975), pp. 1111–25; M. van Tielhof, *De Hollandse graanhandel, 1470–1570. Koren op de Amsterdamse molen* (The Hague, 1995).   [19] Fruin, *Enqueste ende Informatie*, p. 178.

The growth of Europe's population was anything but evenly distributed in time and space. The period between 1500 and 1600 was marked by general demographic expansion. In a hundred years the population of Europe increased from 61.6 to 78 million.[20] Of this growing population, an increasing part came to live in the towns. Urbanization in Europe went from 5.6 per cent in 1500 to 7.6 per cent in 1600. In the first half of the seventeenth century the picture becomes more contrasting. Population and urbanization continued to rise in northern and western Europe, but population numbers dropped in other parts. In southern Europe, where the towns suffered more from a loss of population than the countryside, urbanization went down as well. In Europe as a whole, however, the proportion of people living in towns went up from 7.6 per cent in 1600 to 8.3 per cent in 1650.

As Europe's population grew and became more and more urbanized, so did the demand for all sorts of commodities. For the sake of my argument it is important to note that increasing demand not only swelled the flow of goods from suppliers to markets, but also widened the distance between the two. Domestic production still supplied people's first needs, but some of the larger population centres were already importing basic supplies from abroad.

A case in point is the supply of grain. In medieval and early modern times grain was Europe's staple food and a basic necessity. Urban populations in southern Europe and the Low Countries soon came to depend on foreign imports for part of their grain. As populations and urbanization continued to grow, however, the traditional production areas saw their surplus stocks for export dwindle and the regions that had depended on their supplies were forced to look for grain elsewhere. The Dutch, with their long history of trading with the Baltic states, began to import grain from there. Population centres in southern Europe also suffered shortages of grain and in the course of the sixteenth century had to resort to markets further afield – even as far as Turkey. From the second quarter of the sixteenth century the port of Antwerp was handling shipments of Baltic grain destined for the Mediterranean, but in the long run it was Amsterdam that benefited most from the growing demand for Baltic grain.[21]

A similar pattern occurred in the trade in such bulk goods as timber, and it was not restricted to bulk goods. The same growth in volume and distance marks the flow of luxury goods from western and southern

[20] Jan de Vries, *European Urbanization 1500-1800* (London, 1984), ch. 3 and pp. 19–21 for an account of the territory defined as Europe.
[21] K. Glamann, 'The Changing Patterns of Trade', *Cambridge Economic History of Europe*, vol. V (Cambridge, 1977), pp. 222–3, and F. Braudel, *Civilization and Capitalism 15th-18th century, vol. III, The Perspective of the World* (London, 1985), p. 207.

Europe to prospering landlords in the Baltic region. When trade began to expand beyond Europe the process gained momentum. The geographic expansion of Europe's trade network, the increasing demand for goods and the inability of regions to satisfy the needs of their own populations began to create a situation in which Europe's separate regions became more or less dependent on each other's produce. This mutual dependence was not to the advantage of all but benefited a number of regions by creating a division of labour on a scale so far unknown.

As Limberger has pointed out, in this network of trade, fast growing in size and capacity, the port of Antwerp played a central role during most of the sixteenth century. It was served by a system of outports, the most important of which were ranged along the coast of the island of Walcheren in Zeeland. Antwerp's sphere of influence, however, went far beyond this cluster of outports in the Zeeland delta. It encompassed all of Holland, and, indeed, Holland's economy and especially its cargo trade could not have grown as they did without the Antwerp market on the doorstep. Antwerp and the other ports in the Southern Netherlands had only small merchant fleets, but they needed large numbers of ships to carry their booming trade. The port towns and, as we have explained, the countryside of Holland had a large reservoir of manpower as well as a maritime tradition to offer. It was a deal that benefited both sides and Holland's cargo ships became the main carriers of Antwerp's trade. By the middle of the sixteenth century they completely dominated the cargo trade to southern Europe.[22]

The Antwerp cargo market and the opportunities it offered were one of the factors that prevented a situation of Malthusian overpopulation developing in rural Holland and it helped to build up the region's economy. The expanding cargo trade stimulated the industries of shipbuilding and ship maintenance and a wide range of ancillary industries. Of the materials used in these industries (e.g. timber, hemp, pitch and tar) many had to be brought in from the Baltic region and so contributed to the growth of Holland's shipping and trade. The relation between capital from Antwerp and Dutch shipping is illustrated by the fact that Antwerp merchants financed a number of Dutch expeditions to northern Russia to explore trade opportunities there.[23] In this case also, the Dutch acted as carriers in the service of Antwerp entrepreneurs.

In this period all Holland's ports south of the river IJ were – at least in

---

[22] J.A. Goris, *Etude sur les colonies marchandes à Anvers de 1488 à 1567* (Leuven, 1925), pp. 158–61.

[23] T.S. Jansma, 'Olivier Brunel te Dordrecht. De Noordoostelijke doorvaart en het Westeuropeesch–Russisch contact in de zestiende eeuw', *Tijdschrift voor Geschiedenis* 59 (1946), pp. 337–62.

part – outports of the Scheldt metropolis, with Amsterdam as the north-ernmost. For centuries Amsterdam had served as a gateway to Holland's inland waterways to the south. Among Antwerp's satellite ports Amsterdam was the one most specialized in trading with the Baltic states. Antwerp's shipments to the Baltic were largely handled by Amsterdam and it may be assumed that considerable quantities of grain, timber and other 'Eastern wares' were handled the other way. So, although Amsterdam benefited more than other towns in Holland from the oppor-tunities offered in domestic and international trade and came to handle most of the trade that went on between Holland and the rest of the world, in a wider context the city's position as a centre of trade was still a secon-dary one. Within the European trade network, dominated by Antwerp, Amsterdam's only prominent role was that of an import and tranship-ment centre in the Baltic trade.

The final years of the sixteenth century saw a profound change in the structure of international trade and finance. Antwerp and the Southern Netherlands as a whole went into stagnation and decline. The process of the international division of labour and economic integration of which Antwerp had been the centre, however, did not decline with it. In the first decades of the seventeenth century it became clear that the young Dutch Republic was in many ways the heir and successor of the Southern Netherlands and that Amsterdam had inherited Antwerp's important position in international trade and finance.

As has been pointed out by Limberger, the position of Antwerp as a centre of international trade and finance was undermined by the growing importance of maritime trade, for which Antwerp was not very well equipped, and by the financial problems of the Habsburg empire around the mid-sixteenth century. Because the Habsburg empire was no longer able to meet its financial obligations, the ruling elite set out on a powerful drive towards centralization which could prepare the ground for a uniform and effective taxation system guaranteeing a constant flow of revenue to the state. This centralist drive inevitably clashed with established regional interests. In the Netherlands it generated strong political resistance at a time when high taxes, grain shortages and infla-tion were causing hardship for the greater part of the population. When the central government set out to crush the religious reform movements that had long served as an outlet for popular discontent, the Netherlands rose against the oppressor in an open rebellion that plunged the country into political and economic chaos for decades on end.

This period of political and economic instability constituted the kind of situation that Braudel labelled a phase of de-centring, in which established structures begin to fall apart.[24] As the economy of the Southern Netherlands entered a period of contraction, which by itself dealt a blow to Antwerp's trade, the city also lost the leading position it had held in international trade and finance for most of the sixteenth century. When Spanish troops conquered Antwerp in 1585 and the Scheldt river was closed by the rebellious North, the city's cosmopolitan merchant community, facing economic hardship and religious persecution, left the city in droves. By the end of the century Antwerp's commercial role was back to that of a regional centre.

The political and economic chaos and the imminent restoration of a central government that many had come to reject not only drove the Antwerp merchants away but forced many in the Southern Netherlands to emigrate to surrounding countries.[25] Thousands of textile workers settled in the North and – especially in Leiden and Haarlem – revived the declining woollen industry, while others introduced silk weaving, mainly in Amsterdam.[26] For the purpose of this paper, however, we will focus on what Brulez calls 'the diaspora of Antwerp's merchants'. The cosmopolitan merchant community of Antwerp dispersed to all parts of Europe. They went to live in London, Hamburg, Cologne, Frankfurt, Middelburg, Amsterdam, Seville and Cadiz, or Paris, the French Atlantic ports, Italy and the Baltic region.[27]

As Westermann points out, most of them did not intend to settle permanently in their new residences, but planned to return to Antwerp as soon as the Spanish occupation was over.[28] This explains why initially so many of them were content to stop at the nearby town of Middelburg in Zeeland rather than move on to a bigger city such as Amsterdam. It was not until the mid-1590s, when it became clear that Antwerp would remain Spanish and the Scheldt river closed, that many began to look for

[24] F. Braudel, *Afterthoughts on Material Civilization and Capitalism* (Baltimore, Md., 1977), p. 85.
[25] J.A. van Houtte, 'Het economisch verval van het Zuiden', *Algemene Geschiedenis der Nederlanden*, vol. V (1952), pp. 174–209; T.S. Jansma, 'De economische opbloei van het Noorden', *Algemene Geschiedenis der Nederlanden*, vol. V (1952), pp. 210–44; J.G.C.A. Briels, *De Zuidnederlandse immigratie te Amsterdam en Haarlem omstreeks 1572–1630* (n.p., 1976) and Briels, *Zuidnederlanders in de Republiek 1572–1630; Een demografische en cultuurhistorische studie* (Sint Niklaas, 1985).
[26] L. Lucassen and B. de Vries, 'Leiden als middelpunt van een Westeuropees textielmigratiesysteem, 1586–1650', *Tijdschrift voor Sociale Geschiedenis* 22 (1996), pp. 138–67.
[27] W. Brulez, 'De diaspora der Antwerpse kooplui op het einde van de 16e eeuw', *Bijdragen voor de geschiedenis der Nederlanden* 15 (1960), pp. 279–306; and van Houtte, 'Het economisch verval van het Zuiden'.
[28] J.C. Westermann, 'Beschouwingen over de opkomst en den bloei des handels in de Gouden Eeuw', in A.E. D'Ailly (ed.), *Zeven Eeuwen Amsterdam, II. De zeventiende eeuw* (Amsterdam, n.d.), p. 72.

a place where they could set up their business for good. In that phase of 're-centring', to continue in Braudel's terms, the place that attracted more of Antwerp's dislodged merchants than any trading centre in Europe was Amsterdam. The general preference for Amsterdam was the sum of many individual choices, and we must therefore try to reconstruct the complex interplay of factors that contributed to these choices.

For the sake of my argument I need to distinguish between internal factors and external ones. The internal factors are specific to Amsterdam, while the external factors constitute the wider context with which the internal factors interacted. Principal among the internal factors were the location and physical properties of Amsterdam's harbour. Amsterdam's port was well placed to handle the swelling flow of trade between the north and south of Europe and much of the growing Atlantic trade as well. It was so located that Baltic grain of the year's harvest could reach it before the onset of winter, to be exchanged for colonial products from Lisbon, which arrived there at about the same time. The harbour itself, at the mouth of the river IJ, was, in sixteenth-century terms, spacious, deep and well protected. Another important internal factor was Amsterdam's leading position in the port system of Holland. Amsterdam at the end of the sixteenth century was by no means an insignificant trading port. Even if the better part of the commodities it handled were bulk goods from the Baltic region, its trade already far surpassed that of the other Holland ports in volume and variety. Amsterdam's established role in the Baltic trade, moreover, served it well at a time when southern demand for grain and other 'eastern' wares was rapidly growing. Specific to Amsterdam was also its command and cheap exploitation of a large merchant fleet manned by low-paid seasonal crews from rural North Holland.[29] Amsterdam's shipping capacity, large in itself, could be expanded at will by chartering ships from other ports, such as Hoorn. Finally, the comparatively few restrictions imposed on trade in the Netherlands at that time must have played a role. Unlike the crafts and the retail trade, Amsterdam's wholesale traders were subject to few limitations.[30] The spiritual climate was equally free. After the city took the side of the Revolt, it granted a considerable degree of religious freedom to its citizens.

Important though these internal factors may be, they do not adequately explain the migrants' preference for Amsterdam over ports such as

---

[29] Posthumus, *De Oosterse handel*, ch. 8.
[30] W. van Ravesteyn, *Onderzoekingen over de economische en sociale ontwikkeling van Amsterdam gedurende de 16de en het eerste kwart van de 17de eeuw* (Amsterdam, 1906), ch. 2.

London or Hamburg, where conditions towards the end of the sixteenth century were not much different from those in Amsterdam. Other, external factors were decisive. They constitute what Johan de Vries likes to call 'the favour of the times'.[31]

Firstly, there were the political and financial problems of the Habsburg empire. Its military designs on France and preparations to invade and subjugate the Protestant kingdom of England left it with insufficient resources to complete Parma's successful campaign against the rebellious Netherlands. This gave the Northern provinces the respite they needed to regain their military strength in the critical phase just after the fall of Antwerp. The routing of the Spanish Armada in 1588 made it clear that the Northern Netherlands were no longer in any immediate danger from the Spanish Crown. During the 1590s the new Dutch Republic grew in military strength and political confidence until in 1596 it signed the Triple Alliance with England and France, which thereby recognized it as a worthy ally against Spain. Now that Amsterdam was secure, many who had still found it unsafe to settle there in the early 1590s were ready to do so at last.[32]

Besides, there were few alternatives. In the course of the sixteenth century the old trade centres of the Mediterranean had gone into decline and so had the old Hanseatic ports. Lisbon had been conquered by the Spanish in 1580. Nor did Germany, France or England qualify as safe havens for trade. Germany was in the throes of internal turmoil, which came to a head in the 1618–1648 Thirty Years War. France, too, was torn by political and religious conflicts during the second half of the sixteenth century. England, though to a lesser degree, also had its share of internal trouble, and merchants from the Southern Netherlands who contemplated settling in London were further discouraged by England's economic policies, which before the Civil War were completely subordinate to the financial interests of the Crown.[33] English merchants were organized in numerous companies, each of which had to purchase a monopoly from the Crown for trading in a certain product or area. This system, which virtually excluded newcomers, and the knowledge that taxation in England was the prerogative of the monarch, who could raise taxes at will, held little attraction for migrants from the Southern Netherlands.

---

[31] J. de Vries, *De economische achteruitgang der Republiek in de achttiende eeuw* (Leiden, 1968), pp. 14 ff.   [32] Westermann, 'Beschouwingen over de opkomst', p. 72.

[33] H.C. Diferee, *De geschiedenis van den Nederlandschen handel tot den val der Republiek* (Amsterdam, 1908) pp. 298 ff.; R. Backhouse, *Economists and the Economy. The Evolution of Economic Ideas 1600 to the Present Day* (Oxford, 1988) p. 46; and R. Brenner, *Merchants and Revolution. Commercial Change, Political Conflict and London Overseas Traders, 1550–1653* (Cambridge, 1993), pp. 84–5 and 210.

The fact that Amsterdam benefited most from the 'diaspora' of Antwerp's merchants can probably best be seen as resulting from a fortunate combination of the specific qualities of its local and regional base and an international context in which there were at that time no serious competitors. It is not easy to assess the contribution of the 'Antwerp diaspora' to the changing spatial structure of international trade around 1600. Much depends on the question of whether or not the decline of Antwerp and the subsequent rise of Amsterdam were inevitable and part of the internal logic of international trade in the early modern period. This is still a matter for debate, but it is beyond doubt that the influx of merchants from the Southern Netherlands, and especially Antwerp, was very important for the development of trade and finance in Amsterdam. They were the entrepreneurs who took the lead in expanding Amsterdam's trade network to Italy and the Levant, to Russia, to North America and to the Spanish and Portuguese possessions in South America. They were also the driving force in the introduction of whaling. Research by van Roey shows that, in the capital procured for the Amsterdam chamber of the Dutch East India Company (VOC) in 1602, the merchants from the south took a bigger share than had formerly been assumed. Of the eighty-eight major shareholders, i.e. those who contributed 10,000 guilders or more, there were forty-two from the North, forty-one from the South, four from Germany and one from Italy. The forty-one Southerners between them put up 926,460 guilders, considerably more than the 672,500 put up by the Northern Dutch.[34] The business acumen and capital power of the immigrants also show from the fact that by 1620 more than half of the 320 major account-holders in Amsterdam's 'Wisselbank' (Exchange Bank) were immigrants from the Southern Netherlands.[35]

The immigrants brought not only their capital resources, but also their more advanced trading techniques, geographical knowledge and trade relations to Amsterdam. It was especially the latter which gave Amsterdam a great boost. Brulez points to the role the 'diaspora' played in this respect.[36] Before it, the merchants from the Southern Netherlands had their trade settlements abroad, but they were few and small in size. Most foreign trade was conducted from Antwerp through agents or

[34] J. van Roey, 'Enkele Antwerpse aantekeningen bij het oudste aandeelhoudersregister van de kamer Amsterdam der Oost-Indische Compagnie', *Liber Amicorum Jhr.Mr. C.C. van Valkenburg* ('s-Gravenhage, 1985), pp. 251–4, referring to J.G. van Dillen, *Het oudste aandeelhoudersregister van de Kamer Amsterdam der Oost-Indische Compagnie* ('s-Gravenhage, 1958).

[35] J.G. van Dillen, 'Geld en bankwezen in de zeventiende eeuw te Amsterdam', in D'Ailly, *Zeven Eeuwen Amsterdam*, pp. 121–48.

[36] Brulez, 'De diaspora der Antwerpse kooplui'.

brokers. In the 'diaspora', however, the Antwerp trading houses moved their seats to other parts of Europe and, as many families split up in different directions, they formed close-knit networks that spanned most of the Continent. Even after many trading houses had established their headquarters in Amsterdam, these networks continued to function, so that the 'new' Amsterdammers had the advantage of relatives and countrymen present in virtually all the major trading centres of Europe. This network also benefited Amsterdam's indigenous merchants, who were able to conduct their business through Flemish and Brabant agents abroad.

It was this comprehensive trading network, born in part from the 'diaspora', that boosted the expansion of Amsterdam's trade. From a port specialized in handling bulk shipments from northern and eastern Europe it became a major market, a place where commodities from all corners of the European trade network were available in marketable quantities. This 'worldwide' orientation also made Amsterdam the most suitable place to conduct international financial business, as Antwerp had been before 1585.

While recognizing the importance of Southern capital, know-how and international relations in Amsterdam's commercial expansion, we should not play down the role of the 'indigenous' element. On the contrary, it was the local merchant community which had given Amsterdam its position as Holland's leading port and trading centre and which after 1585 became, by their sheer numbers, the carrier and driving force of that expansion. However, the locational decisions of the dispersed Antwerp merchants were a major element in the complicated mixture of local, regional and international developments which gave Amsterdam a lead even over London and Hamburg as a centre of international trade and finance.

When the resources of local merchants and migrants from Antwerp came together in a city that had already developed a lively goods and carrier trade, the process that Myrdal described as cumulative causation was started.[37] Amsterdam's market attracted more and more merchants because supply and demand there were varied and plentiful. Not only could parties negotiate favourable deals, they could buy and sell a wide range of wares. This big and varied market also provided the shipping capacity to carry the goods all over Europe and even beyond, thus enabling merchants to trade on a truly international scale. Besides, freightage was relatively cheap, because the market was big enough to dispose of cargoes quickly and to find profitable return cargoes.

---

[37] G. Myrdal, *Economic Theory and Underdeveloped Regions* (London, 1957).

As more and more merchants, goods and ships converged on Amsterdam, the city was bound to become Europe's chief information centre in matters of trade, shipping and even politics. Price currents, i.e. lists of prices fixed on the Amsterdam market, were already being published in the late sixteenth century, and the early seventeenth century saw the emergence of a periodical press. Not public, but at least as important, was the business correspondence between merchants and the information exchanged on the Amsterdam Bourse. Amsterdam-based merchants and agents usually had first knowledge of the latest developments in all the markets, which gave them a competitive edge over their colleagues elsewhere. With the expansion of the commodity and cargo trade came the need for services such as brokerage and insurance. The above-mentioned Wisselbank was instituted in 1609 to try to establish some order in currency exchange rates, but it soon became a deposit bank through which merchants could safely settle their accounts. This, the use of bills of exchange and the rapidly declining interest rates greatly facilitated financial transactions and thereby helped the expansion of shipping and trade.

Despite the fact that Amsterdam during its golden age was a major European market and an international clearing house, it basically stuck to the well-known Italian and Antwerp ways of conducting trade. The Wisselbank, for instance, was copied from the famous Banco di Rialto in Venice and some of the more recent innovations in the Antwerp money market were altogether ignored. From chapter 4 it is clear that we have to turn to London in the 1690s for a real financial revolution to occur.[38] The most important contribution of Amsterdam to international trade was probably the fact that, in contrast to Bruges and Antwerp, trade was conducted in Amsterdam on a year-round basis. In western Europe the old system of periodic fairs was now definitely a thing of the past. Unlike in Antwerp, trade in Amsterdam was conducted by Amsterdam-based merchants and not by foreign nationals from offices where they stayed for only part of the year.[39]

The common denominator of the advantages offered by Amsterdam's market was: greater certainty and therefore less risk. Communications in early modern times were slow and erratic, and merchants could never be quite sure about their decisions or how they would work out. A large market and the institutions that developed there substantially reduced

---

[38] De Vries and van der Woude, *Nederland 1500–1815*, ch. 4; and J.A.F. Wallert, *Ontwikkelingslijnen in praktijk en theorie van de wisselbrief 1300–2000* (Amsterdam, 1996), ch.3.

[39] It should be noted, however, that from the mid-sixteenth century local Antwerp merchants were also engaged in more regular forms of trade.

that uncertainty and gave Amsterdam-based merchants an advantage over their competitors in lesser trade centres. This attracted more capital and enterprise to Amsterdam, fuelling further expansion. This trend could continue so long as the regional and international context remained favourable and so long as Amsterdam could offer its merchants a favourable economic, political, social and cultural environment. Until the middle of the seventeenth century, both conditions were being fulfilled.

One of the main arguments of this paper is that the economic development of Amsterdam cannot be detached from the regional economy of which it was part. Consequently, it is not easy to ascertain what may be regarded as achievements of its local economy. What might at first sight be regarded as such, were in fact intimately linked with regional developments. Amsterdam was able to become the international commodity market and financial centre it was during the seventeenth century, only because it was backed by high levels of productivity in agriculture, fishing and industry. However, at the same time the urban economy provided important stimuli for specialization and productivity gains throughout the region. Amsterdam did not suffocate the economy of other centres in the region, like Antwerp seems to have done. On the contrary, the growth of the Amsterdam commodity and money markets promoted the development of a spatially integrated regional economy where both town and countryside specialized and, in doing so, gained productivity levels that would otherwise not have been easily attained.

Given the small size of production and exchange in pre-modern economies, the fact that, for instance, Leiden concentrated on the production of cloth, Delft and Gouda on brewing, Haarlem on linen bleaching, and Enkhuizen on herring fishery was of the utmost importance because it promoted economies of scale and innovation. The advantages of spatial concentration did not escape the attention of a perceptive observer such as William Temple, who wrote in his *Observations upon the United Provinces* that the economic power of the Dutch Republic was also due to 'the custom of every Towns affecting some particular Commerce or Staple, valuing itself thereupon, and so improving it to the greatest heighth'.[40]

For such an integrated regional economy to develop and be successful, an extensive transport network was essential. From the sixteenth century onwards the numerous natural waterways were used to create a system of regular services. Within this system, Amsterdam clearly held a central position, linking cities and their regional and subregional transport

[40] W. Temple, *Observations upon the United Provinces of the Netherlands* (London, 1673; reprinted Oxford, 1972), p. 116.

networks. For the sake of passenger transportation this network was sup-plemented in the seventeenth century by man-made waterways on which numerous (towing) barges provided transport facilities.[41]

In exploiting the opportunities provided by the international economy some merchants were extremely successful. In late sixteenth-century Amsterdam, great wealth was a rare phenomenon. Within a few decades, however, large fortunes were being gathered. It took only two generations for the Poppen family to work its way up from very modest means to wealth and power. Whereas Jan Poppen, an immigrant from Holstein in present-day Germany, started his career in Amsterdam as a clerk to a grain merchant, his son Jacob ended up as a burgomaster and the wealthi-est Amsterdammer of his age, leaving an estate worth nearly 1 million Dutch guilders at his death in 1624. Lodewijk Trip, to name but one other example, invested 46,000 Dutch guilders in two family firms and within three decades managed to increase his capital to over 600,000 guilders.[42]

In order to accumulate such wealth, merchants reinvested much of their profits in trade. Still, there remained plenty of money for luxury items such as Venetian-style glassware, jewellery, silks and art. Small wonder, then, that from the end of the sixteenth century luxury industries in Amsterdam were rapidly expanding. Only The Hague, with the seat of the central government and the court of the *stadhouder*, could compete with Amsterdam in this branch of industry. The bent for luxury did not meet with approval from all. In particular, the migrants from the Southern Netherlands were blamed for introducing pomp and vanity in Amsterdam. The *Spaanschen Brabander* by the Amsterdam playwright and poet Bredero is the most famous expression of this view.

An effective brake on pomp and conspicuous consumption was prob-ably the successful performance of the economy itself. As long as invest-ments in trade, shipping, fishing, agriculture and industry proved worthwhile, profits were reinvested. From the mid-seventeenth century, however, Amsterdam's trade, and the regional economy in general, faced serious problems. Mercantilism, war and economic stagnation made wealthy merchants look for alternative investment opportunities and urban real estate seems to have been among them. The 1660s and early 1670s witnessed a building boom in the upper segment of the real estate market. In these years many of the spacious and richly decorated

[41] J. de Vries, 'Barges and Capitalism. Passenger Transportation in the Dutch Economy, 1632–1839', *AAG-Bijdragen* 21 (1978), pp. 33–398.
[42] De Vries and van der Woude, *Nederland 1500–1815*, pp. 768–9; and P.W. Klein, *De Trippen in de 17e eeuw. Een Studie over het ondernemersgedrag op de Hollandse staplelmarkt* (Assen, 1965).

'merchant palaces' along the Amsterdam canals were built and furnished.[43] The Amsterdam elite clearly began to distinguish itself from the
lower and middle classes.

Nevertheless, if we compare real incomes in Amsterdam (and Holland
in general) with those abroad, we cannot but conclude that the lower and
middle classes were relatively well off. The rapidly expanding regional
economy in which Amsterdam played such a prominent role created a
large demand for labour and lifted wages to a level high enough to compensate for rising prices. For almost half a century (1580–1620) real
incomes in Holland were rapidly rising, while those in the surrounding
countries fell dramatically. In this relatively short period, real incomes for
labour became the highest in Europe and they remained so at least until
the end of the seventeenth century. If we also take into account that the
rising nominal wages were paid at a time when the supply of labour in
Dutch cities was growing much more rapidly than elsewhere (through
migration, urbanization, an increasing number of working days and possibly natural population increase), this is all the more astonishing.[44] Being
rooted in the extraordinary achievements of the local and regional
economy, the wealth of the (merchant) elite and the rising real incomes
for the lower and middle classes substantially contributed to achievements in other fields of Dutch society and culture.

[43] A. Knotter, 'Bouwgolven in Amsterdam in de 17e eeuw', in P.M.M. Klep et al. (eds.),
Wonen in het verleden 17e-20e eeuw. Economie, politiek, volkshuisvesting, cultuur en bibliografie
(Amsterdam, 1987), pp. 25–37.
[44] De Vries and van der Woude, *Nederland 1500–1815*, ch. 12 and pp. 700–1; L.
Noordegraaf and J.L. van Zanden, 'Early Modern Economic Growth and the Standard
of Living: Did Labour Benefit from Holland's Golden Age?', in K. Davids and J. Lucassen
(eds.), *A Miracle Mirrored. The Dutch Republic in European Perspective* (Cambridge, 1995),
pp. 410–37.

4   The economy of London, 1660–1730

Peter Earle

Antwerp, Amsterdam, London – three cities which in turn became the commercial and financial centres of the European economy and so provided a focus for achievements in spheres well beyond the mere making of money. Few would argue, except in detail, about the dates of the golden ages of Antwerp and Amsterdam. The case of London, however, poses rather greater problems, since the city has at many times in its history played a leading role in the economy of Europe and indeed of the world. Medievalists might plump for the eleventh century, when London became one of the most important and dynamic cities of Latin Europe. Others might select the reign of Elizabeth, when London ceased to be a mere satellite of Antwerp and beginnings were made in a process of commercial, industrial and imperial expansion that was to continue for a very long time into the future. Still others might choose the culmination of this process in the late Victorian age, when London was in its heyday as a great imperial capital and the 'City' dominated world trade and finance as no other city has ever done before or since.

Here the focus is instead on the years 1660–1730, with a special emphasis on the later seventeenth century. This was the period when what the Elizabethans had initiated was achieved and London became the equal of Amsterdam as a trading centre. It was also when the institutions were established that eventually would make London the centre of world finance. And, finally, it was in these years that London became the capital of a great power and so foreshadowed the glories of its Victorian heyday. This was not so much a golden age in the sense that one can use the expression of Antwerp or Amsterdam, since London continued to be 'golden' for another two centuries. It was more a coming of age, the culmination of a century of achievement transforming London from the capital of an offshore island to a great world city.

This chapter will examine the economy of late seventeenth-century London. The focus will be on international trade, as in the chapters on Antwerp and Amsterdam, but also on the development of a demand-led growth fuelled by rising real incomes and changes in the propensity to consume. Attention will also be paid to the elastic and innovative response seen in the supply of both goods and services. But first some general characteristics of the London economy will be considered.

It is important to remember that London, unlike Amsterdam or Antwerp, was the capital of a major nation-state and so was the focus of activities far removed from those of a large urban economy or trading centre. London was also, unlike other European capitals, the only town of any size in the country.[1] In 1700, when London's population was more than half a million, the next two largest towns were Norwich and Bristol with populations of 30,000 and 20,000 respectively. This total dominance of England's urban hierarchy meant that, from an early stage, London had a national market for its manufactured goods and services. London, too, was likely to attract a high proportion of the talented, wealthy and ambitious, who had little choice but to make their way to the metropolis if they were to make their name and fortune. The impact of London then was felt not just in its surrounding region, as seems to have been the case for Paris, but throughout the entire country.

London, to use a metaphor much loved by Defoe,[2] was the heart which circulated England's blood, that is to say, its money, rent and taxes, which flowed into the city and were then pumped back into the country as payment for raw materials and food and as investment in agriculture, internal trade and provincial manufacturing. This circulation was mutually beneficial. Metropolitan dominance was often bitterly resented by provincial towns, but there is little doubt that London's early emergence as the one big city in England speeded the development both of the metropolis itself and of the country as a whole.

The reason for London's huge size relative to other English towns was that the metropolis had monopolized a wide variety of functions which in other countries were shared out between several different cities. Most importantly, London was not only the seat of government and the court but also by far the largest port, a combination found elsewhere in Europe only in Lisbon and in Italian states, such as Naples and Venice. London had gradually been accumulating a higher and higher proportion of English commerce and this process was at its peak in the late seventeenth century, by which time the city handled around two-thirds of all overseas trade and completely dominated the coastal trade, such dominance by a

[1] This chapter is based on research done for my two books *The Making of the English Middle Class: Business, Society and Family Life in London, 1660–1730* (London, 1989) and *A City Full of People: Men and Women in London, 1650–1750* (London, 1994). Full references can be found in these books and the notes here will be kept to a minimum.

[2] For example, Daniel Defoe, *The Complete English Tradesman* (London, 1726–7), vol. 2, pt. 2, p. 122.

single port being again virtually unknown elsewhere in Europe. The dual demands of government and foreign traders allowed London to develop as England's only financial market, while easy access to imported fuel and raw materials, the presence of a large, wealthy and concentrated market and the labour-intensive nature of contemporary industry also enabled London to become far and away the biggest manufacturing centre in the country. This combination of functions naturally acted as a magnet for other functions, such as conspicuous consumption, publishing and the practice of the professions.

This combination of social and economic functions was unique in Europe and it is no wonder that London continually got bigger. The city's population grew fastest in the second half of the sixteenth century and after 1750, with the period under consideration being one of comparatively modest growth, from somewhere between 400,000 and 500,000 in 1660 to about 600,000 in 1730.[3] But even this modest growth was remarkable in a period when few other great cities in Europe saw any growth at all and several declined in size. Even more remarkable was the fact that London was able to grow by some 50 per cent in this period, while the population of England hardly grew at all. As a result, London was to house more and more of the national population, about one in nine by 1700, a proportion matched by no city in any other European country except perhaps Naples.

London could grow only through migration, since there was considerable natural decrease within the city itself. Professor Wrigley has estimated that, for London to grow as it did between 1650 and 1750, a net figure of some 8,000 immigrants must have moved to the city every year.[4] These immigrants typically arrived in their teens or early twenties and they completely dominated the adult population of the city, with somewhere between two-thirds and three-quarters of all adult men and women in London being born outside the city.[5]

London, then, like most early modern cities, was a city of immigrants. Was this good or bad for the metropolitan economy? Chapters 2 and 3 stress the positive contribution made by immigrants to the development of the cities of Antwerp and Amsterdam. Many other continental writers, however, especially the French, treat migrants in a far less positive manner. They see them as inferior beings who came into the cities as

---

[3] For a recent survey see Vanessa Harding, 'The Population of London, 1550–1700: A Review of the Published Evidence', *London Journal* 15 (1990). See also E.A. Wrigley, 'A Simple Model of London's Importance in Changing English Society and Economy, 1650–1750' and, for London's growth relative to other European cities, Wrigley, 'Urban Growth and Agricultural Change: England and the Continent in the Early Modern Period', both republished in E.A. Wrigley, *People, Cities and Wealth* (Oxford, 1987).
[4] Wrigley, 'Simple model', p. 135.   [5] Earle, *City*, p. 47.

servants or menial workers and did not stay very long before returning to their rural origins. Their influence on the cities that briefly became their homes was thus fairly marginal. Migrants in early modern England are treated more positively by historians and are often analysed in terms of 'betterment' and 'subsistence' migrants, the former moving to towns with the aim of improving themselves, for example by apprenticeship or a good marriage, the latter moving simply to keep themselves alive from what charity, relief or casual employment the towns might offer.[6]

The 'subsistence' element was less dominant in our period than it had been in the late sixteenth and early seventeenth centuries, since the check to population growth after 1650 enabled real wages to improve throughout the country, while vagrancy ceased to be such a serious problem. Meanwhile, London acted as a positive attraction to migrants seeking 'betterment', a self-selecting group who included the most ambitious, skilful and enterprising of the various social strata from which they came. 'It is observed', wrote John Chamberlayne, 'that in most Families in England, if there be any Son or Daughter that excels the rest in Beauty, or Wit, or perhaps Courage, or Industry, or any other rare Quality, London is their North Star, and they are never at rest till they point directly thither.'[7] Signature evidence supports this view that migrants were the 'cream' of provincial society, both male and female migrants being far more likely to be able to sign their names than the average person in the areas from which they came. Migrants were also not usually the short-stay visitors typical of many continental towns, since they formed an even greater proportion of the more elderly cohorts of the city's population than they did of those in their twenties and thirties.[8]

Most immigrants to London came from the British Isles, but a significant minority came from European countries and some of these played a vital role in the economy by bringing with them large amounts of capital, both in money and in the human capital of skill, and by introducing new ideas, new technologies and even new industries. The French Huguenot influence on such industries as silk manufacture, paper, hatmaking and silver-smithing is very well known, but one needs to remember also the large numbers of foreigners – Germans, Dutch, Jews, Scandinavians and others – in the London mercantile and financial communities. Such people were drawn to London as foreigners were drawn to Michael Limberger's Antwerp by 'the presence of facilities likely to attract

---

[6] Peter Clark, 'The Migrant in Kentish Towns, 1580–1640' in Peter Clark and Paul Slack (eds.), *Crisis and Order in English Towns, 1500–1700* (London, 1972). For a discussion of continental writing on migration, see Earle, *City*, pp. 40–5.

[7] John Chamberlayne, *Angliae Notitia* (London, 1707), p. 352.

[8] Earle, *City*, pp. 36–7, 45.

professional talent'. Success in developing these facilities, which will be discussed later, thus made London a truly cosmopolitan community where foreign ideas and foreign money would play a major role in economic development.

The late Professor Fisher, in his articles on the London economy, identified two main sources of growth: overseas trade and the conspicuous consumption of the country gentry and aristocracy within the metropolis, which acted as a multiplier on the urban economy as a whole.[9] This combination highlights the duality of London's role as both major port and capital city. Overseas trade and the associated mercantile and financial community were clearly fundamental in the development of Antwerp and Amsterdam as well as London. Aristocratic spending was fundamental in the development of Paris and Madrid, but less so in Antwerp and hardly at all in Amsterdam, for even though the totality of luxury spending was large in the Low Countries it was spread between many different cities. Only in London did the stimuli to growth of both overseas trade and conspicuous consumption have their full impact.

In 1550, London had been a mere trading satellite of mighty Antwerp. By the early seventeenth century, this dependent relationship had come to an end, mainly as a result of Antwerp's own domestic problems, and Londoners had opened up a number of long-distance trading routes. However, London's commerce was still very much in the shadow of the now dominant Amsterdam. But, by 1690, London had become Amsterdam's equal as a trading city and would overtake it in the first half of the eighteenth century. Antwerp had been the one great market in the first half of the sixteenth century where products from the whole world known to Europeans were traded. By the end of the seventeenth century, there were two great markets which between them dominated the hugely expanded trade of Europe and, through Europe, of the world.

England's trading breakthrough occurred between 1650 and 1690 and especially in the 1670s and 1680s, the years of most rapid growth. This was to be halted by the outbreak of the French wars, and growth thereafter was to be comparatively modest until the great expansion of the mid-eighteenth century.[10] The most striking aspect of England's 'Commercial Revolution' in the second half of the seventeenth century was the very rapid growth of trade with distant regions of the world, with Asia, Africa,

[9] His articles are collected in F.J. Fisher, *London and the English Economy, 1500–1700* (London, 1990).
[10] Ralph Davis, 'English Foreign Trade, 1660–1700' in W.E. Minchinton (ed.), *The Growth of English Overseas Trade in the 17th and 18th centuries* (London, 1969); Phyllis Deane and W.A. Cole, *British Economic Growth, 1688–1959* (Cambridge, 1964), pp. 48–9.

the Mediterranean and, above all, the English colonies in the Americas. The Dutch had of course also developed such distant trades, with great success in Asia but less so in America and the West Indies where successful British colonization gave an advantage to the mother country. The 'rise of the Atlantic economy' shifted England and its dominant port, London, from a peripheral position in European trade to a central position in the new pattern of world trade. This emphasis on long-distance trade should not disguise the fact that England also did well in the 'peripheral' short-distance trades during this period, particularly the trade in the re-export of colonial products to Europe but also trade with northern Europe and the Baltic. Such success indicates that English shipping was now able to compete with the Dutch even in the carriage of low-value, high-bulk goods, partly through the acquisition of large numbers of Dutch ships during the Anglo-Dutch wars but also through the imitative building of Dutch-type bulk-carriers in English shipyards. More trade, together with the effective government policy which reserved as much trade as possible for English and colonial shipping, also meant a huge increase in the English merchant fleet from some 200,000 tons in 1660 to 340,000 tons in 1686, according to Ralph Davis.[11]

The metropolis clearly benefited most from this commercial boom, since some two-thirds of all English trade passed through the capital and London was particularly dominant in the dynamic long-distance and re-export trades. The impact was felt in many sectors of the city's economy. Shipbuilding, especially the building of large ships for the long-distance trades, flourished on the Thames. The ancillary trades, such as sail- and rope-making did even better since ships built in other ports were often fitted out or repaired on London's river. More trade also meant more work for many of London's manufacturing and processing industries, such as the cloth-finishing trades and sugar- and tobacco-refining.

The main beneficiary of the commercial boom was, however, the mercantile community, which grew to reach perhaps 1,000 full-time merchants by the 1690s, with probably as many again who occasionally dabbled in overseas trade.[12] Merchants owned between them much the biggest accumulation of wealth within the city and they seem to have been accumulating more as time went on, at least until the 1690s when the impact of war and heavy shipping losses made serious inroads into mercantile wealth.

---

[11] Ralph Davis, *The Rise of the English Shipping Industry in the 17th and 18th Centuries* (Newton Abbot, 1972), p. 15.

[12] D.W. Jones gives a total of 2,000, based on port-books, but these would include many small dealers who would not have been considered merchants. 'London Merchants and the Crisis of the 1690s' in Clark and Slack (eds.), *Crisis and Order*, p. 350, n. 30.

Growing merchant wealth was clearly an essential factor in the success of the London economy, enabling it to operate efficiently by continuous investment in shipping, finance and overseas trade, while at the same time providing a similar sort of consumption multiplier as the aristocracy and gentry did in the West End. Commercial success was also important in other ways. It attracted immigrant merchants from all over Europe who built up trading networks with their kinsmen and former fellow citizens, just as foreign merchants had done in sixteenth-century Antwerp. Such immigrants introduced or encouraged the development of commercial methods that had long been in use in continental trading centres, such as commission trading, double-entry book keeping and the use of bills of exchange and other credit instruments. Commercial development also stimulated the growth of infrastructure and financial institutions that had long existed in Antwerp and Amsterdam, such as a banking system, an efficient commercial intelligence service, a marine insurance market and, in the 1690s, a fully fledged stock market, though in none of these features of a major commercial centre was London as yet as sophisticated or efficient as Amsterdam. In all this, England and hence London were greatly assisted by a government and judiciary who firmly believed that commercial expansion was good for the country. English traders clearly benefited from the effective mercantilism of the Navigation Acts, which reserved for English shippers and merchants the profits to be made from colonial trade, much to the detriment of the Dutch. Less obviously, judicial decisions and legislation also enabled the development of such essential features of a mature financial centre as negotiability of bills and other financial paper and an effective system for collecting debts. In all these developments, London learned from Amsterdam, which in turn had learned from Antwerp, and Antwerp itself was in many ways the pupil of the Italian trading cities of the Middle Ages.

Although the growth of foreign trade was quite clearly a fundamental factor in the development of London's economy, the impact of aristocratic and gentry spending, with its obvious importance for the city's luxury service and manufacturing trades, is less clear cut. This was certainly of very great importance in the late sixteenth and early seventeenth centuries, a period of rising land prices and landed incomes. But conditions in the period 1660–1730 were very different. These decades were characterized for landowners by falling rents and growing arrears and this decline in their income as a class was exacerbated by the heavy taxation that fell on land, particularly during the wars against France between 1689 and 1713.

The gentry themselves were the first to bemoan their economic hardship and one would have thought that conspicuous spending in London would be unlikely to have had the dynamic impact that it had once had.

Such a hypothesis is, however, belied by the available evidence. For it is just in this period of falling rents that much of the West End was built and there is little doubt that the gentry population (together with their servants and other dependants) was growing faster than the population of London as a whole. This would have been particularly true of the reign of Charles II when much of St James's, Soho, Bloomsbury and the eastern part of Mayfair was first built up. There was for sure an almost complete lull in West End building during the French wars, but in the last fifteen years of our period the builders were once again at work.

Such work provided a great stimulus, not just for the building and luxury furnishing trades, but also for everyone else engaged in providing for the expensive tastes of the West End gentry – tailors and dressmakers, servants and seamstresses, jewellers and caterers, and a host of other trades. One has to conclude that aristocratic and gentry consumption remained a very important component of the urban economy and that members of the landed class almost certainly devoted an increasing proportion of their incomes to spending in London, especially during the first three decades of our period.

The West End was, however, not the only source of conspicuous spending in the London economy. The growing wealth of the merchant community has already been stressed and merchants, too, built fine houses and were prepared to put fine furniture into them, even if they were unlikely to spend as lavishly as their role models amongst the gentry of the West End. However, London had long had the lion's share of England's trade, and merchant wealth was as visible in Elizabethan London as it was in our period, even if the merchants of the late seventeenth century were on average richer and there were more of them.

What is perhaps more important is that merchants were to be joined in a rapidly expanding middle class by large numbers of other people who had little or nothing to do with overseas trade. Inland trade was also growing fast and the richer wholesalers, such as the big linen-drapers and ironmongers, could certainly compare in wealth with the average overseas trader. It was in this period, too, that shopkeeping really came of age and many a mercer or woollen-draper had the wealth and income to live a very comfortable middle-class life. Nor was manufacturing simply a matter of artisans working away in small workshops. Nearly every trade included wealthy men whose control of capital dominated the lives of a host of smaller masters and journeymen – the big hatmakers, leather-dressers and master pewterers for instance – while some branches of manufacturing such as brewing and sugar-refining were already operating in factory-type premises whose scale was sufficient to ensure that only men of considerable wealth could enter them.

The growth in London's commercial and manufacturing middle class was paralleled by a rise in the numbers and wealth of the city's professional middle class.[13] The most rapid period of growth in the number of London's lawyers was probably already over by 1650, but numbers continued to rise in our period while fee levels rose even faster. The law, like all professions, had a huge tail of struggling practitioners, but at the top and in the middling ranks there were large numbers of barristers and attorneys with a life-style similar to that of the West End gentry and with incomes that compared favourably with those in the commercial world. Similar comments could be made of the medical profession, whose numbers were increasing rapidly as surgeons and apothecaries successfully challenged the former medical monopoly of the physicians. At the same time, the numbers in newer professions such as surveying, architecture and accountancy were growing, while it was the later seventeenth century that saw the first flowering of a professional and permanent civil service, a group whose opportunities and numbers were very considerably swelled by the enormous increase in taxation and other government business during the French wars.

So far only about a quarter of the city's population has been considered, that quarter composed of the gentry and middle classes who possessed practically all of the accumulated wealth and must have enjoyed considerably more than half of all incomes accruing to Londoners. Analysis of the earnings of the great mass of poorer Londoners is fraught with difficulties since the only evidence we have is of wage rates in a few industries, mainly building, and there is no way to tell how well these rates reflect income. However, if wage rates do reflect income, then it is clear that the poor were getting a little richer.

The Phelps-Brown and Hopkins' data, for instance, show a rise in the money wages of building craftsmen from about 16 pence a day in 1650 to about 22 pence in 1730, while data on the annual wages of female domestic servants suggest that these may have doubled over the same period.[14] Nor were these gains eroded by inflation as they had been in the late sixteenth century. There were short periods of very high wheat and bread prices, as in the middle 1690s, but overall the long-term movement of such price series as are available was modestly downwards. Since artisans and the poor comprised some three-quarters of the city's population, this increase in spending power needs to be taken into consideration when

[13] See in general on this subject, Geoffrey Holmes, *Augustan England: Professions, State and Society, 1680–1730* (London, 1982).
[14] E.H. Phelps-Brown and Sheila V. Hopkins, 'Seven Centuries of Building Wages' in E.M. Carus-Wilson (ed.), *Essays in Economic History*, vol. II (London, 1962), pp. 177–8. On servants, see Earle, *City*, p. 125.

assessing London's economy. Increased consumption was a very important factor in the general growth of the urban economy and increased consumption by the poor would clearly have been of interest to, amongst others, butchers, brewers and distillers, haberdashers and other makers and purveyors of cheap clothing.

This chapter has so far concentrated on the three decades between 1660 and 1690, which seem to have been the period of most rapid growth in the city's economy. It would be useful, however, to make a more balanced assessment of the economic impact of the French wars on London. So far, it has been assumed that this was fairly negative since war brought an end to the commercial expansion of the 1670s and 1680s and the Land Tax caused a serious check to the growth of conspicuous consumption in the West End. It seems probable, too, that increases in the excise and its imposition on new articles of consumption would have had a negative impact on the spending of the poor.

However, the effects of the wars were not all negative. Taxes were spent as well as collected and much of the spending was done in the metropolis. The fairly high levels of unemployment or underemployment which were a normal feature of the peacetime economy were largely wiped out, at least for men, by the huge increase in demand for soldiers and sailors. Military and naval pay was hardly generous and was nearly always in arrears, but it was more than could be earned in London's large casual labour force and so would have added considerably to the earnings of the poor as a whole. War also created new civilian employment which may well have balanced the loss of jobs in the building trades and in many consumer-oriented industries. The demands of the navy and the losses of shipping to French privateers caused a boom in shipbuilding and in the other trades of the river, while wartime was clearly a good time for sword-cutlers and gunsmiths and others employed in London's large armaments industry.

Middling people, too, could find compensations for the decline in trading opportunities brought about by war. Sometimes it was simply a question of shifting capital and shipping from one trade to another, from the trades of southern Europe, which were seriously affected by privateers, to the trades of the North Sea for instance. Much merchant shipping was also moved into the government's transportation service, carrying soldiers and horses, food and weapons, back and forth between London and Flanders, Ireland or Spain. The provisioning and supply of the army and navy also created great opportunities for the enterprising, so that fortunes that might have been made in the Turkey trade in peacetime were made instead in the supply of bread to King William's army in Ireland. And, finally, we have to remember that it was the demands of war which created the conditions for the Financial Revolution of the 1690s. This not only brought about very important innovations in London's financial world, such as the establishment of a stock market and the creation of the Bank of England, but also provided tremendous opportunities for the wealthy to lend money to the government at very high rates of interest. War thus acted as a catalyst in the development of those aspects of financial infrastructure which have already been considered.

The French wars, then, were not disastrous for the London economy, though this might not have been too apparent during the crisis years of the middle 1690s. Many individuals did very well while, overall, resources were successfully shifted from peacetime to wartime demands. Nevertheless, one's impression is that London's economy grew faster in the 1670s and 1680s than it did in the two decades of war that followed. This growth, as has been seen, was fuelled by expansion of trade, by conspicuous consumption in the West End, by a growing middle class and by an improvement in the real wages of the poor. The emphasis here is on a demand-led growth as Londoners earned more and spent more and so created opportunities for other Londoners to produce the goods and services which were demanded.

Historians are increasingly getting the impression that there was a spending spree in the second half of the seventeenth century, the beginnings of what has been called the 'Consumer Revolution'.[15] People of all classes seem to have been relieved of previous restraints on consumption and so were prepared to spend a higher proportion of their incomes. Since these incomes were rising, the impact of this change in the propensity to consume was considerable.

Such a change might have had something to do with the moral relaxation associated with the Restoration and the decline of Puritanism. It was also almost certainly associated with a breakdown in social and class barriers which allowed greater social mobility within the city and encouraged imitative and competitive spending, so that London's middle classes could be found adopting gentry patterns of consumption with a lag of a few years. These psychological changes in attitudes towards consumption may well have been encouraged by a change in the way that both gentry and middling people in London held their money.

Hoarding and the retention of large and unproductive cash balances seem to have been a common feature in the portfolios of well-to-do people before the Civil War. But the rise of the goldsmith-bankers and

---

[15] On this concept, see Neil McKendrick, John Brewer and J.H. Plumb, *The Birth of a Consumer Society: the Commercialization of Eighteenth-century England* (London, 1982). I would date the consumer society rather earlier than they do.

improvements in the law relating to negotiable financial instruments and the recovery of debt made the holding of large cash balances seem increasingly unnecessary after 1650. The gradual elimination of the Earl of Bedford's 'money chest' in the 1660s, and its replacement by deposits with the goldsmith-bankers, was a sign of the times although, as Gladys Scott Thomson points out, 'the practice had been fairly common for some time' before the Earl and his receiver-general adopted it.[16] By the 1660s, it was certainly unusual for business people to keep large 'money chests'[17] and a man such as Samuel Pepys with a hoard buried in the garden was distinctly old-fashioned. This change in financial practice was of great importance. The money supply grew rapidly as bankers' receipts and notes circulated and as loans in excess of deposits were made to borrowers. Incomes were swelled by interest payments, and gentry and middling people found that they had more money both to invest and to spend.

The analysis of this increased spending is constrained by the availability of sources, which means that most attention has been paid to such durable items as are listed in inventories.[18] These show a very considerable improvement in amenity and comfort between 1660 and 1700 as artefacts once confined to the households of the very rich or fashionable became commonplace, while completely new items of expenditure were also introduced. It would be easy to draw up a formidable list of items that were rare or non-existent in middle-class homes of the 1660s but virtually ubiquitous by 1700. This would include window-curtains, clocks, easy chairs, looking-glasses, silk and cotton furnishing fabrics, chinaware, tea- and coffee-making equipment, cane and lacquerware, and many other attractive items. The focus was on comfort and a growing emphasis on sociability.

The acquisition of such durable objects can have taken up only a fairly small proportion of that part of income devoted to consumption, but determining what the rest was spent on is difficult since we very rarely have evidence of flows as opposed to stocks of expenditure. Entertainment was obviously important, especially drinking and eating in London's taverns and inns, alehouses, dramshops and coffee-houses, such establishments comprising one in every twelve houses in the metropolis by the 1690s, according to Gregory King.[19] Then there was

[16] Gladys Scott Thomson, *Life in a Noble Household, 1641–1700* (London, 1965), pp. 369–70.
[17] For the low proportion of assets held as cash by London businessmen, see Earle, *Making of Middle Class*, p. 121.
[18] This section is based on Lorna Weatherill, *Consumer Behaviour and Material Culture in Britain, 1660–1760* (London, 1988); Peter Thornton, *Seventeenth-century Interior Decoration in England, France and Holland* (New Haven, Conn., 1978); and my own research in *Making of Middle Class*, pp. 290–301.   [19] Public Record Office, T64/302.

the theatre, though the provision of seats did not expand much in the late seventeenth century and for some of the time there was only one theatre. Nevertheless there was something interesting going on in the world of the arts, as what had once been available only to the court and the connoisseur now began to 'trickle down' to the middle classes. Public concerts and art auctions began in the 1670s and 1680s, and large numbers of pictures and prints could be found in middle-class homes by the turn of the century, some of them 'bespoke' paintings of members of the family. The 'commercialization of art' as well as of everything else was under way.

Expenditure on entertainment would certainly have been eclipsed by the amount spent on clothes. Gregory King thought that rather more than a quarter of middle-class spending went on 'apparel'[20] and the evidence suggests that more and more was being spent on clothes, by all classes and by both men and women, as fashions changed faster and as being in fashion became increasingly imperative. The later seventeenth century also saw some major changes in the patterns of expenditure on food, with a rapid growth in imported groceries such as sugar, tea, coffee, rice and dried fruits, not to mention tobacco, this rise in demand being of course a major factor in the growth of colonial trade. There must also have been a considerable growth in the consumption of fruit and vegetables, since it has been estimated that there was a tenfold increase in the area of garden ground in the London area between 1660 and 1720.[21] Diarists and others who describe their diet very rarely mention vegetables, but they always make a great play of the amount of meat they ate and this was certainly increasing amongst all classes as agricultural improvement lowered the cost of this essential element in the Londoner's diet.

A long-term fall in the prices of imported and home-produced foodstuffs was clearly an important factor in their increased consumption. Measuring the changes in price of any other sorts of goods is, however, difficult since it is virtually impossible to compare like with like. Nevertheless, inventories are suggestive in this respect. If one compares the inventoried contents of houses belonging to people of similar social or wealth levels, there is a big difference between those listed in the 1660s or 1670s and those listed in the 1690s and 1700s. Not only does one find the introduction of all the new items mentioned above, but there were also far more of such standard things as brass and copperware, bedding and

[20] Earle, *Making of Middle Class*, p. 271; based on Greater London Record Office, JB/Gregory King f.210.
[21] Malcolm Thick, 'Market Gardening in England and Wales' in Joan Thirsk (ed.), *The Agrarian History of England and Wales*, vol. V, (Cambridge, 1985), p. 507.

kitchen equipment. And yet there was no increase in the average valuations given by assessors to the total contents of houses.[22]

The implication is that there had either been a considerable fall in price of a wide range of artefacts or that goods of higher value were being replaced by cheaper imitations. Both were in fact happening in the later seventeenth century. Veneers and stains were used to embellish cheap furniture, gunmetal was employed as an imitation of silver, ready-made clothes could make a reasonable imitation of the bespoke garments worn by the prosperous, while the scope for dressing up textiles to look better than they really were was virtually unlimited. At the same time, changes in supply were leading to a reduction in costs and making manufacturers more responsive to the changing demands of the market.

It is always difficult to disentangle supply and demand, but there can be no doubt that the supply side of the London economy was very elastic and was able to produce an increasing flow of goods, many of them completely new, at stable or falling prices. Exactly how this was done is difficult to say at the current stage of research, but there are enough hints to suggest that what was happening in London foreshadowed many aspects of what would later be called the Industrial Revolution.

London had long been the most important manufacturing centre in England, but the city's industrial base had grown enormously both in scale and in the range of goods produced ever since the late sixteenth century. By 1700, this development had reached its zenith and London was probably at its all-time peak as an industrial centre relative to the rest of the country. Much of this industrial growth reflected the expansion of traditional industries such as brewing, metal-working and the finishing of woollen cloth. But much was also due to import substitution as goods such as silk fabrics, hats, glassware or paper were increasingly made within or just outside the city rather than being brought in from overseas. Such developments were greatly assisted by foreign immigrants, but they also demonstrate a new confidence amongst the manufacturers and artisans of London.

Some of London's industries remained conservative and simply produced more of the same in the same way. But, in many others, the prevailing system of small workshops run by self-employed artisans was increasingly suborned by the power of capital. In some industries, small independent workshops became mere subcontractors to entrepreneurs who controlled the work of hundreds of small people. Elsewhere, small workshops became big workshops enjoying the bene-

---

[22] There is a general discussion of this phenomenon in Carole Shammas, 'Changes in English and Anglo-American Consumption from 1550 to 1800' in John Brewer and Roy Porter (eds.), *Consumption and the World of Goods* (London, 1993).

fits of better supervision and increasing division of labour. And, in a few industries, such as brewing and sugar-refining, the scale became such that one can describe them in terms of proto-factories rather than workshops.

Control by capitalist entrepreneurs, themselves often major distributors, meant that production was more easily attuned to the changing demands of the market and indeed was often able to pre-empt such changes by product innovation. Increases in scale reduced unit costs, sometimes dramatically, as in the brewing industry. Specialization and increased division of labour could have the same effect, as in the gunmaking and clock and watch industries, where increasingly each artisan produced only one part to be assembled on the premises of a big master. Such specialization was encouraged by the tendency of industries to cluster in particular parts of the city, a fact which also fostered the rapid assimilation of new ideas and techniques. These new techniques were often piecemeal and difficult for historians to observe, but sometimes the changes were substantial, as in the increasing use of machines and other labour-saving devices in the knitting, ribbon-weaving and silk-throwing industries for example. None of these changes was truly revolutionary but, collectively, they reduced costs, expanded the product range on offer and demonstrated that the supply side of the London economy was no longer chained by the conservatism of the past. Demand may have led the growth of the London economy in the later seventeenth century, but supply was always ready to foster that demand and channel it into new directions.

When one surveys the economy of late seventeenth-century London it is clear that a lot of interesting things were happening at around the same time; that there was indeed a 'cluster of achievements'. These achievements included fundamental economic changes such as the commercial and financial revolutions, the beginnings of the consumer revolution and the establishment of London as a cosmopolitan world city. They also included such comparatively trivial but interesting developments as the rise of the coffee-house, the concert hall, the newspaper and the three-piece suit. London was clearly a vibrant city, eager to experiment and innovate, eager to enjoy itself.

This paper argues that three main economic trends lay behind these achievements. In the first place, England, and London in particular, came of age as a trading nation in a commercial boom which enabled London to achieve parity with the once dominant Amsterdam. In the second place, all groups within the city enjoyed a rise in income in the second half of the seventeenth century, except the West End gentry, and they seem to have spent a larger proportion of their landed incomes in London than before the Civil War. Finally, there seems to have been a change in the mind-set of the middle classes. The aristocracy and the poor had always spent their money with abandon, if they had any money to spend. The middle classes, by contrast, were careful, saving, frugal people almost by definition. And yet, in the late seventeenth century they seem to have broken out of this miserly cocoon and to have learned the joys of spending, while not abandoning the careful attention to getting and keeping money that was the chief characteristic of their class.

There was little particularly original in the ways that they spent their money. Paris was the model for fashion in clothes, furniture and polite behaviour, while Amsterdam had long anticipated London as a city of middle-class spenders, as Simon Schama has shown.[23] But it was now the turn of London to enjoy itself and it is no surprise to find in the 1680s and 1690s the beginnings of the realization that luxury is a necessary vice if there is to be economic growth. 'Those who are guilty of Prodigality, Pride, Vanity, and Luxury, do cause more wealth to the Kingdom, than Loss to their own Estates,' wrote John Houghton.[24] There were many guilty of all these vices in London, and London benefited from them.

The emphasis in this paper on expanding foreign trade and on rising real incomes reflects very closely the experience of Amsterdam a century earlier, the Dutch city being virtually unique in the late sixteenth and early seventeenth centuries in enjoying rising real incomes when the rest of Europe was sinking deeper and deeper into misery. And indeed London's experience reflects that of both Antwerp and Amsterdam in many other ways, hardly surprisingly since much of what happened in London was simply a process of catching up with its mentors in the Low Countries. The creation of financial institutions and infrastructure, the development of commercial and information networks both within the city and with the wider trading world, innovations and technical ingenuity in industry – none of these would have seemed at all strange to the citizens of Antwerp or Amsterdam. London, too, was to experience the 'economies of agglomeration' discussed by Michael Limberger in chapter 2, though London in 1700 was five times larger than Antwerp at its peak and so such economies were likely to be greater. Where London does seem different was in the duality of its function as at once a great port city and the centre of government and court, a duality that enabled it to enjoy and eventually to exploit successfully the economic stimuli of both Paris and Amsterdam.

[23] Simon Schama, *The Embarrassment of Riches: an Interpretation of Dutch Culture in the Golden Age* (London, 1987); for Paris see Thornton, *Seventeenth-century Interior Decoration*.
[24] Quoted in Joyce Appleby, *Economic Thought and Ideology in seventeenth-century England* (Princeton, 1978), p. 171.

Part 3

Architecture and urban space

5 Antwerp in its golden age: 'one of the largest cities in the Low Countries' and 'one of the best fortified in Europe'

Piet Lombaerde

> So it is quite fair to say that Antwerp
> is now not only one of the largest cities
> in the Low Countries, but it is certainly
> also one of the best fortified in Europe.
>
> L. Guicciardini, Descrittione di tutti i
Paesi Bassi (Antwerp, 1567)

For sixty years from 1540 the city of Antwerp was the leading centre of Renaissance architecture, urban planning and fortifications in the Low Countries. During the first decades of the seventeenth century Antwerp lost that privileged position to Amsterdam, but then the stimulus of the Counter-Reformation in the Southern Netherlands made Antwerp – along with Brussels and cities such as Ghent, Leuven and Malines – again an important centre for architecture and a focus for the baroque style.

The extraordinary position which the port of Antwerp occupied in European trade from the early sixteenth century onwards made the city a prime meeting-point for many cultures and peoples. The Germans were the most important colony in Antwerp, but the Spaniards, the Portuguese, the French and the Italians also took part in its economic boom. Italian culture was the most influential, playing the role of trend-setter as the Renaissance spread through the Low Countries.[1]

The lack of an imperial or royal court in Antwerp did not hinder the spread of new ideas, models and practices. On the contrary, that took place almost simultaneously in various fields of science and the arts, due mainly to the efforts of innumerable traders, merchants and entrepreneurs. It was also encouraged by the many princes, governors, nobles and diplomats who stayed in Antwerp on several occasions, though

---

[1] H. van der Wee, *The Growth of the Antwerp Market and the European Economy (Fourteenth – Sixteenth Centuries)*, 3 vols. (The Hague, 1963); H. Soly, *Urbanisme en kapitalisme te Antwerpen in de 16de eeuw. De stedebouwkundige en industriële ondernemingen van Gilbert van Schoonbeke*, Historische Uitgaven Pro Civitate, 47 (Brussels, 1977); F. Braudel, *Civilisation matérielle, économie et capitalisme, XVe–XVIIIe siècle, vol. 1, Le Temps du Monde* (Paris, 1979), pp. 114–44.

sometimes only for short periods. However, Antwerp did not become a Renaissance city like Florence, where successive generations of the Medici family encouraged the new culture from the top. Nor was it a city like seventeenth-century London or Paris, where royal patronage supported the introduction of new cultural patterns.

The city administration, which was powerful and wealthy at that time, provided freedom and many opportunities for enterprising building contractors, traders, merchants and bankers. There was a high degree of tolerance towards new ideas and trade practices. The traditional privileges and rights of the guilds were not allowed to stand in the way of the new enterprise. Nevertheless, the municipal authority exercised little initiative of its own in the domain of urban planning or in the development of public space, except when such measures were imposed by the Spanish government for the military requirements of defence.

Achievements in building were very great in sixteenth-century Antwerp. Three different kinds of structures can be considered: private houses; public and private buildings for economic, religious or political activities; and military works. The huge increase in the city's population – a direct consequence of the economic boom – also led to large-scale land and building speculation. In 1437 Antwerp had a population of about 17,000 people, who occupied some 3,440 buildings; in 1526 there were some 42,000 inhabitants and 8,479 buildings, and in 1580 approximately 80,000 inhabitants and 11,000 buildings. By 1591, however, only six years after the capture of Antwerp by Spanish troops, the number of inhabitants had decreased to 46,123 and only 8,074 buildings were occupied. About 1,732 were empty and 2,520 were demolished or unified.[2] By 1612 the number of inhabitants had increased slightly to 53,918.

Certainly, the most important and expensive achievements were the military works. Following the inauguration in the Low Countries of the Habsburg emperor Charles V, a scheme emerged for adapting the late-medieval fortifications of Antwerp to the new threats from artillery. The medieval walls of European towns were no longer adequate for siege warfare. In 1519, while he was travelling in the Low Countries, Albrecht Dürer (1471–1528) was asked by the Antwerp municipality to draw up proposals for strengthening the old fortifications.[3] His suggestions involved the introduction of the *retirata* system for the walls and the

---

[2] For these data, see H. Soly, 'De megalopolis Antwerpen' in L. Voet, A. Verhulst et al., *De stad Antwerpen van de Romeinse tijd tot de 17de eeuw. Topografische studie rond het plan van Virgilius Bononiensis 1565* (Brussels, 1978), pp. 95–119.

[3] On Dürer and the Antwerp fortifications, see H. Wauwermans, 'Les fortifications d'Anvers au XVIe siècle à l'Exposition Universelle de 1894', *Annales de l'Académie d'Archéologie de Belgique, 8*, 4ème série (Antwerp, 1894), pp. 5–8.

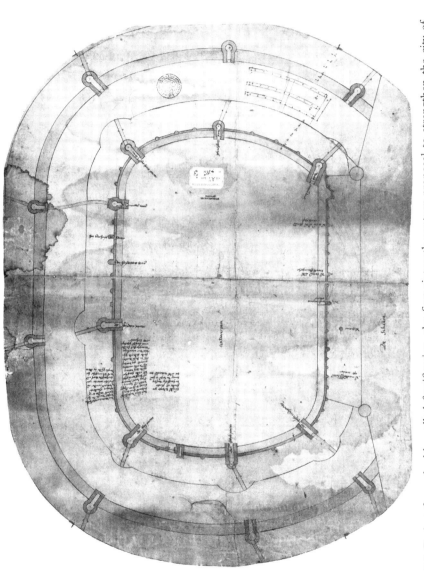

5.1 Project for a double-walled fortification, the first sixteenth-century proposal to strengthen the city of Antwerp. First quarter of the sixteenth century, Albrecht Dürer (?).

addition of casemated bastions to their lower part. It seems that soon after 1533 the rebuilding of the Blauwe toren (the Blue Tower), a strong circular tower, was inspired by his ideas. Constructional details, similar to those in the tower, can be found in his publication *Etliche underricht, zu befestigung der Stett, Schlosz, und flecken* (Nuremberg, 1527). German publications were well known in Antwerp, because merchants coming from Augsburg, Nuremberg, Frankfurt, Cologne and the Hanse cities distributed their books and prints in the Southern Netherlands. The German Hanse was at that time the most important trading association in Antwerp, and merchants from Nuremberg were responsible for a large share of Antwerp's export trade.[4] Young German engineers also came to Antwerp to study the new fortifications. Daniël Specklin, one of the most famous German engineers, was trained by Peter Frans, the city architect of Antwerp. Afterwards he published the chief German work on fortification: *Architectura von Festungen* (Strasbourg, 1589), containing several drawings of the Spanish walls and the citadel at Antwerp.

From this, we can conclude that, long before the Spanish walls were built, Antwerp was already a testing ground for modern ideas on fortification. On the other hand, both the Spanish walls, which replaced Antwerp's medieval walls, and the citadel were primarily the work of engineers who came from Italy.

Engineers could be craftsmen or artisans, artists or scientists. Their capacity for *innovation* was an essential condition. They were free and not bound by any statutory obligations to the guilds. Infrastructural and military works, reflecting the respective needs of peace and war, were both realized by engineers. This profile of the engineer-architect was totally new and was inspired by the Italian Renaissance.[5]

The building of the Spanish walls by Italian engineers was very significant in the Low Countries, as a large-scale example of the new type of fortification system by which artillery could provide flanking fire from protruding bastions. The project was begun in 1542 but not completed until 1562. At that time, according to plans made by the Italian engineer Donato Boni de Pellizuoli, the Spanish walls were the largest bastioned fortification work in Europe.[6] Their construction cost 2 million guilders. The work consisted of a polygonal wall with nine bastions and a half

[4] H. van der Wee and J. Materné, 'Antwerp as a World Market in the Sixteenth and Seventeenth Centuries', in J. van der Stock (ed.), *Antwerp. Story of a Metropolis 16th–17th century* (Ghent, 1993), pp. 19–31.

[5] Concerning the difference between the terms 'architect' and 'engineer', see U. Schütte, 'Architekt und Ingenieur' in *Architekt & Ingenieur. Baumeister in Krieg und Frieden* (Wolfenbüttel, 1984), pp. 18–31.

[6] E. Guidoni and A. Mariano, *Storia dell'urbanistica: Il Cinquecento* (Rome-Bari, 1982), pp. 400–7.

Architecture and urban space: Antwerp 103

bastion, all built of brick with an external face of hard white stone. The foundation for this enormous weight consisted of hundreds of wooden piles, sometimes up to 8 m deep. The total length of the walls was 6,000 m, with five monumental city gates decorated in Renaissance style. The walls and bastions were surrounded by a deep moat, and were cited as a model of perfection in many European treatises on military architecture. One of the best-known representations of them is the woodcut print by Virgilius Bononiensis,[7] which can be compared with the view of Amsterdam by Cornelis Anthonisz (1538), and with the general view of Venice by Jacopo de Barbari (c.1500). In these two representations, as in earlier views of Antwerp, the cities are seen from the riverside or the lagoon and were surrounded only by medieval fortifications. Such views attached great importance to the way in which the city and the walls were combined with a planned extension. A notable feature of the Bononiensis representation of Antwerp, however, is its new viewpoint from the east, emphasizing the strength of the new defensive circuit. From that time onwards this was to be the preferred viewpoint (see figure 5.2), replacing that from the river Scheldt. This representation served both as propaganda and as a means of attracting entrepreneurs, merchants and traders to a strongly defended site.

One may ask why the city council agreed to undertake and finance such spectacular fortifications. It is quite possible that the city, which had large amounts of capital, gave its approval to the new military structure for purely opportunistic reasons. After all, it projected an image of power, order, wealth, strength and safety – all conditions which would help to make the flow of commercial traffic both possible and attractive. Military reasons alone cannot have been sufficient to justify the investment, which was out of proportion to any possible threat. The brief siege by Maarten van Rossem in 1542 seems to have been used as an excuse to put into effect plans which had been drawn up from 1540 onwards by Italian engineers in the service of Emperor Charles V. The city architect Peter Frans himself put forward an alternative proposal.

Another much-praised aspect of the building of the Spanish walls was the simultaneous building of the so-called Nieuwstad by the contractor Gilbert van Schoonbeke (1519–1556), who was also responsible for the construction of the walls themselves. This new neighbourhood to the north of the old city was essentially a prototype for urban expansion according to a strict geometric pattern, and was commercial rather than purely residential in nature. Moreover, the pattern of streets did not correspond with the military arrangement of the surrounding bastions. The

---

[7] On the woodcut by Bononiensis, see especially Voet, Verhulst et al., *De stad Antwerpen*, pp. 133–46.

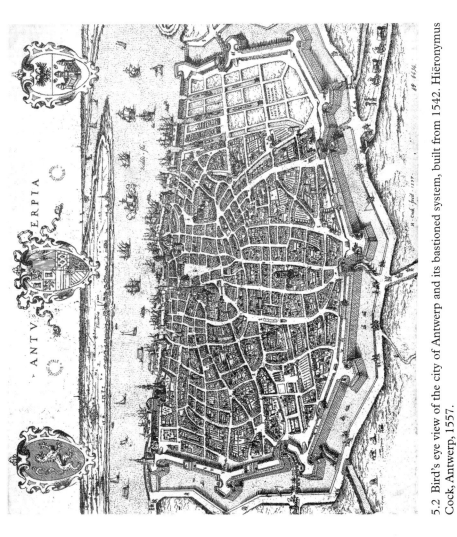

5.2 Bird's eye view of the city of Antwerp and its bastioned system, built from 1542. Hiëronymus Cock, Antwerp, 1557.

alignment of the rectangular building blocks was determined by three parallel canals perpendicular to the river Scheldt. That was where the new port of Antwerp was to be. The plots were intended to be filled with warehouses, storehouses, breweries and houses for merchants and traders.

The second important military achievement was the construction of the citadel to the south of the city in 1567, an event which for a second time attracted universal attention to Antwerp's defences. The Italian engineer Francesco Pacciotto (1521–1591) integrated the city, the Spanish walls and the citadel into a whole by means of a *joincte*, thus creating a new prototype for modern city defence and a ground plan which was copied by engineers throughout Europe.[8] In a period when the economic climate was weak, the construction of the citadel (800,000 guilders) and the *joincte* (142,000 guilders) was again welcomed by Antwerp contractors, who on this occasion were bankers and merchants rather than tradesmen as before.[9] Opportunism and self-interest made sure that there was little difficulty in financing the project, although the money required was five times more than was needed for the new Town Hall, which was identified as Antwerp's foremost Renaissance building.

Apart from these spectacular military structures, there was also a great deal of building activity in Antwerp involving real estate speculators and contractors, of whom van Schoonbeke was by far the most important. Van Schoonbeke's achievements were unparalleled at that time, especially by comparison with those of the many other property developers and real estate speculators active in Antwerp at the end of the fifteenth century.[10] The unique features of van Schoonbeke's real estate and building activities were their vast scale and the way in which he set up large organizational structures in a short time. Above all he was able to adapt his activities to changing economic circumstances. His achievements involved both the rebuilding of the public area in the old city centre (Vrijdagmarkt, Stadswaag, Arenbergstraat, etc.) and the development of the St Laurentius neighbourhood (Markgravelei, Haantjeslei), the first residential area outside the city walls. His way of working was always the same: acquiring different lots, bringing them together and dividing the ground, building an attractive (economic) centre and then selling the newly divided lots. At the end of his life, his fortune was estimated at 112,000 guilders.

[8] C. van den Heuvel, *'Papiere bolwercken'. De introductie van de Italiaanse stede- en vestingbouw in de Nederlanden (1540–1609) en het gebruik van tekeningen* (Alphen aan den Rijn, 1991); P. Lombaerde, 'The Southern Citadel of Antwerp' in J. van der Stock, *Antwerp*, p. 264.

[9] H. Soly, 'De bouw van de Antwerpse citadel (1567–1571) sociaal-economische aspecten', *Belgisch tijdschrift voor militaire geschiedenis* 21 (1976), pp. 549–78.

[10] Soly, *Urbanisme en kapitalisme*, pp. 109–28.

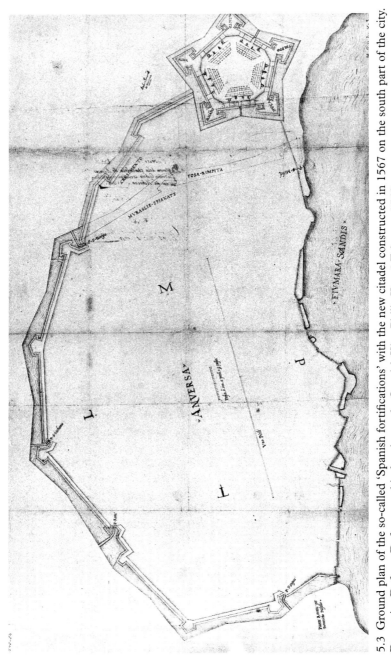

5.3 Ground plan of the so-called 'Spanish fortifications' with the new citadel constructed in 1567 on the south part of the city. Domenico Dafano; Dafano sent his drawing to the Spanish King Philip II on 2 February 1568.

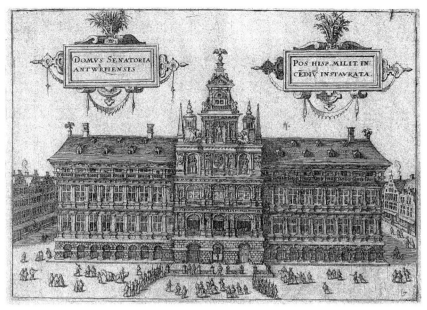

5.4 The new Town Hall of Antwerp. This Renaissance building was constructed between 1561 and 1565. It was the 'symbol of republican self-awareness of the city' as described by the Florentine Lodovico Guicciardini in 1567. Other town halls were inspired by this model, for example in Flushing (Northern Netherlands, 1594) and in Emden (North Germany, end sixteenth century); from L. Guicciardini, *Descrittione di tutti i Paesi Bassi*, Antwerp, 1581, pl. 7.

In the domain of architecture, new mercantile houses and warehouses were designed as Renaissance *palazzi*. The *Groot Oostershuys* (Oosterlingenhuis or Hanse House), built in 1564–8 for the German Hanse towns, can be considered as a prototype for other large store houses, designed around a large inner court, with a simple and rational ground plan, and decorated only on the main façade. Its designers were the city architect Peter Frans and the artist Cornelis Floris de Vriendt, who was at that time involved in the plans for the new Town Hall (see figure 5.4). In some respects, especially in its dimensions, this store house served as the model for the old arsenal of the Amsterdam Admiralty, build by the city architect Daniël Stalpaert in 1656. A typical example of a smaller store house is the *Coophuys* (Hessenhuis or Hessen House) built in 1563. The oldest of this group was the Tapissierspand, erected by van Schoonbeke in 1551–2. In the seventeenth century, there was an excess of store houses in Antwerp, and so those of the English nation were converted by Wenceslas Cobergher into Berg van Barmhartigheid, a pawnshop for poor people. This first example of public pawshops was very successful and Cobergher built similar groups of public pawnshops all over the Southern Netherlands between 1619 and 1633, in Brussels, Ghent, Kortrijk, Malines, Mons, Arras, etc.

In 1531 the municipality built a new exchange (the so-called Nieuwe Beurs). This large building had a spacious interior courtyard or *cortile*. Despite that Italian influence, the architectural decoration is reminiscent of late Gothic style with Moorish characteristics (the so-called *mudéjar* style). The surprising choice of site for this commercial building – near the *Meir* and so outside the traditional business centre of Antwerp – is to be explained by the advantages it offered for an easy flow of traffic. The clear structure of the ground plan, the multifunctional character of the building, the way of placing it in relation to the existing streets and the permanent multilateral trade in stocks made the Antwerp exchange the model for the new exchanges in London and Amsterdam. Sir Thomas Gresham, chief broker for English government finance at the Antwerp exchange from 1552 onwards, had the London exchange (in 1571 named the Royal Exchange) built by Antwerp firms between 1566 and 1569.[11] The new Amsterdam stock exchange, designed by Hendrick de Keyser, was built between 1608 and 1611.

The model of the *cortile* was also adopted for many private houses in conjunction with the building of watchtowers, a typical Antwerp feature which may also have been taken over from Italy. On the street side these houses were mostly soberly decorated with fillet gables, but behind were ornamental interior courtyards with arcades and houses lying further back. Splendid examples of these small Renaissance palaces include the Van Straelenhof, the Witte Arend, the Hof van Liere, the Hof van Plantin, the former Van Immerseelhof and the Gulden Ring (now the Rockoxhuis).[12]

These achievements did not necessarily involve innovations in Renaissance architecture or town planning taking place in Antwerp. The Spanish walls provide a fine example of the application of Renaissance ideas, which were not specific to Antwerp. Nevertheless, the combination of the walls with the city extension gave rise to a prototype of *modern* urban planning. The intermeshing of innovations with specific local

---

[11] J. Materné, 'Schoon ende bequaem tot versamelinghe der cooplieden' in G. de Clercq (ed.), *Ter beurze: geschiedenis van de aandelenhandel in België, 1300–1990* (Bruges, 1992), pp. 51–85; A. Saunders (ed.), *The Royal Exchange: Studies in the History of a London Institution* (London, 1997).

[12] L. De Barsée, 'De Bouwkunst', Genootschap voor Antwerpse Geschiedenis, *Antwerpen in de XVIde eeuw* (Antwerp, 1975), pp. 361–89.

interpretations and achievements created new models. These in turn generated new applications, which in some cases took place several decades
later and on a totally different scale. Thus, Antwerp was the model for
Amsterdam as the famous city of canals as it developed in the seventeenth
century. In both cities, extensions were determined by digging canals in
parallel lines around the existing settlement. In the case of Antwerp, the
work was limited to the area north of the city. There, in a single innovative
operation, land was reclaimed; the ground between the canals was par-
celled out; merchant houses and stores were erected; and between the
canals, which were lined with quays for handling goods, were created an
interconnecting system of small waterways and locks and a street system
separate from but running parallel to and across the canals. In 1566 this
model of town planning, combined with new fortifications, was adopted
on a large scale by the Dutch map-maker Christiaan s'Grooten in his
project for Amsterdam.[13] During the extensions planned after 1585 (the
year of the capture of Antwerp by Alessandro Farnese), the Amsterdam
project resulted in the creation of the famous city of canals.

New applications in architecture and urban planning led also to technological innovations. Breweries were at that time envisaged as technical
buildings to be equipped with machines. Following Italian and German
examples, there were experiments in Antwerp with the water supply to
the new city extension.[14] In order to provide the sixteen new breweries in
the Nieuwstad with water, van Schoonbeke from 1554 onwards elaborated a plan for obtaining fresh water from the moat by means of an
underground pipe. The water flowed to the *Waterhuys* (the Water House,
now the Brouwershuis), whence, by a network of four small canals, it supplied almost ten breweries.[15] Van Schoonbeke used a horse mill to lift the
water up to the small canals from the low-lying reservoirs into which it
flowed. The mill drove a cogwheel, which by means of wooden pins acti-
vated a chain-of-buckets pump. Almost forty iron buckets lifted the water
to an upper reservoir above ground level. At that time wood was still the
basic material for this kind of machine-construction, and such extensive
use of metal was exceptional. Nevertheless, Georg Bauer (alias Agricola,
1494–1555) in his *De re metallica, libri XII* (Basel, 1556) described a
similar chain-of-buckets pump which made extensive use of iron. Van
Schoonbeke's pump system is significant because it represented an
improvement on a well-known type of machine which was also discussed
in contemporary literature.

---

[13] E. Taverne, *In 't land van belofte: in de nieue stadt. Ideaal en werkelijkheid van de stadsuitleg in de Republiek 1580–1680* (Maarssen, 1978), pp. 127–9.

[14] P. Galluzzi, *Les ingénieurs de la Renaissance: de Brunelleschi à Léonard de Vinci* (Florence, 1995), pp. 136–40 and especially p. 177.   [15] Soly, *Urbanisme en kapitalisme*, pp. 288–98.

The combination of a horse mill, a cogwheel and a chain-of-buckets pump was in itself a technological innovation and provides a good example of applied hydraulics during the second half of the sixteenth century, when there was Europe-wide interest in the subject, culminating in Agostino Ramelli's *Le diverse et artificiose machine* (Paris, 1588). Earlier examples are known from Italy, where in the fifteenth century a similar water supply system was designed by the Siennese engineer Taccola (1381–c.1453).[16] Moreover, Vitruvius discussed problems of hydraulics in book eight of *De architectura libri decem*.

The construction of underground water pipes was one of the numerous applications of hydraulics at that time. During the last decades of the sixteenth century, the water for the new Antwerp breweries became unusable because seeds and leaves from the trees planted on the walls fell into the moat. In 1635 the city council decided to separate the water of the moat from that of the Herentals canal. This canal, carrying pure water, reached the moat near the Blauwe toren (see above). By means of an aqueduct 1,800 m long, starting at the end of the Herentals canal, fresh water was discharged into a reservoir near the Rodepoort, one of the gates giving access to the Nieuwstad, whence it reached the canals connected to the Water House.[17]

It seems that at the end of the sixteenth century and during the first decades of the seventeenth the Southern Netherlands were acknowledged as a place where important achievements in hydraulic theory took place. Just after his arrival from Italy in 1597, Archduke Albert visited the Antwerp Water House. At the same time, he asked the Italian engineer Pietro Sardi (1560 – after 1630) to make a detailed study of the possibilities for supplying fresh water to his palace on the Coudenberg in Brussels. The French engineer Salomon de Caus (1576–1621) was asked to devise several mechanical automata, involving applications of the laws of hydraulics and statics, for the parterres, fountains and grottos in the palace gardens. Some years later, de Caus published *Les raisons des forces mouvantes Auec diuerses Machines* (Frankfurt, 1615). In England in 1610 he undertook several waterworks in combination with a statue gallery in the gardens at Richmond for the Prince of Wales. He was described as 'Surveyor general', in the same manner as Inigo Jones who was the architect of the palace.[18] During this stay de Caus published *La Perspective*,

[16] Galluzi, *Les ingénieurs*, p. 177, cat. II.5a.16.
[17] P. Génard, *Quelques notes sur le canal d'Herentals, la maison hydraulique et les prises d'eau directes à l'aqueduc de la ville, connu sous le nom de Brouwershuis* (n.p., n.d.); W. van Craenenbroeck, 'Oorsprong en uitbouw van de watervoorziening in het Antwerpse Brouwerskwartier' in P. Maclot and W. Pottier (eds.), *'N Propere tijd!? (On)leefbaar Antwerpen thuis en op straat (1500–1800)* (Antwerp, 1988), pp. 65–92.
[18] C. Maks, *Salomon de Caus 1576–1626* (Paris, 1935), p. 12 ff.

avec la Raison des ombres et miroirs (London, 1612), the first book on perspective to be published in England. At that time, several engineers and
mathematicians went deeply into hydraulics and wrote down their knowledge and innovations in theoretical works. In the Northern Netherlands,
Simon Stevin (1548–1620) published *Nieuwe Maniere van Sterctebou door
Spilsluysen beschreven door Symon Stevin van Brugghe* (Rotterdam, 1617).
There were at that time in the Low Countries numerous practical projects
of this type, including the design for digging a drain basin at Ostend in
1604–5, and the reclamation of the Moeren in Flanders (1620–2), both
enterprises of Wenceslas Cobergher (1560–1634). These outstanding
applications promoted new empirical methods in science. New publications appeared containing the results of experimental research and critical discussions, which during the seventeenth century were considered to
be essential for the evolution of pure and applied science. Michael
Florentio van Langren (*c.*1600–1675), for example, proposed a method
of ridding Antwerp of its 'pestighe ende onghesonde Locht, komende uyt
de vuyle verrotte ende stinckende Ruyen' ('pestilent and unhealthy air,
coming from dirty, rotten and stinking canals').[19] He corresponded with
Constantijn Huygens, discussing Simon Stevin's innovation of *spilsluizen*
(pivoted sluice-locks).

Architects and engineers at that time commonly belonged to scientific
circles and societies: in England, Christopher Wren, primarily an astronomer and only secondly an architect, was a member of the Royal Society,
founded in 1662. At that time, however, Antwerp lacked a comparable
institution. In contrast to the English situation, the Antwerp St Luke's
guild in 1663 established an Academy of Arts, permitted by a decree of
Philip IV of Spain and modelled on the French Académie Royale de
Peinture et de Sculpture. The French Academy had been established in
Paris in 1648, and its programme gave prominence to geometry and perspective, as was also the case in Antwerp. London did not acquire its
Royal Academy of Arts until 1768, and it is noteworthy that the architect
William Chambers played an important part in its foundation and
designed the new Somerset House, where the Academy had rooms.[20]

Renaissance innovation in the form and ornament of architecture was
spread mainly by the new language of the classical orders. The Italian
journeys undertaken by many artists and architects and the spread of
numerous prints and books were also influential. The great number of

---

[19] P. Poulussen, 'Een wetenschappelijke oplossing voor de 17de-eeuwse stedelijke water-
verontreiniging' in Maclot and Pottier, *'N Propere tijd!?*, pp. 93–104.
[20] S.C. Hutchison, 'The Royal Academy of Arts in London: Its History and Activities' in A.
Boschloo et al. (eds.), *Academies of Art. Between Renaissance and Romanticism* (The
Hague, 1989), pp. 451–63.

trading and merchant firms coming from the Iberian Peninsula and Italy took an active part in the propagation of early Renaissance printed texts on architecture and ornament. For example, we can note the testament (dated 13 June 1617) of the widow of Emanuel Ximenez, a knight of the Portuguese firm, in which were mentioned books by Alberti (Paris, 1512, and Venice, 1601), Palladio (1601), Vignola (1596), Serlio (1600) and Vitruvius (1567).[21] The leading work, *Libri de re aedificatoria decem* (Paris, 1512) by Leon Baptista Alberti, was to be found both in the book collections of prominent merchants and traders and in the libraries of cloisters and convents, including that of the Beggaarden convent near the Meir.[22] Moreover, the edition of Vitruvius' *De Architectura Libri Decem* (Venice, 1497), illustrated by Fra Giocondo, circulated in Antwerp humanist society.[23] We can presume that thanks to several Spanish merchants the very early book about the classical orders *Medidas del Romano* (Toledo, 1526), written by Diego de Sagredo, was available in Antwerp. The German colony probably promoted the diffusion of such early printed books on antique orders and ornament as those edited by Hans Blum and Wendel Dietterlin, and also Walther Rivius' translation of Vitruvius (1548).

Interest in the new ornament of the Renaissance was evidently great in Antwerp from 1530 onwards, because several publications were edited in the vernacular after that date. In 1539 Pieter Coecke van Aelst (1502–1550), after his travels in Italy, published for the first time in the Low Countries a book on the classical orders, *Die inventie der colommen* (Antwerp, 1539). This was the so-called 'little Vitruvius' or *kleine metselrijboeksken* ('little book on masonry'). Coecke used for this work Cesariano's commentaries on Vitruvius, published in 1521.[24] It was not until 1563 that John Shute published the first English engravings of the orders in *The First and Chief Groundes of Architecture* (London). At that time, Antwerp exported more books and engravings to England than any other European city, especially those published by Hieronymus Cock

21 E. Duverger, *Antwerpse kunstinventarissen uit de zeventiende eeuw, Fontes Historiae Artis Neerlandicae. Bronnen voor de Kunstgeschiedenis van de Nederlanden* (Brussels, 1984), vol. I, 1, p. 438.
22 Actually, this specimen belongs to the public library of the city of Antwerp (SBA: preciosa H 5589/rek 8c). The conveyance took place as a result of the confiscation of ecclesiastical goods by the French revolutionaries in 1796.
23 H.-W. Kruft, *Geschichte der Architekturtheorie. Von der Antike bis zum Gegenwart* (Munich, 1985), pp. 72–9.
24 Ibid., p. 186. On this publication, see especially R. Rolf, *Pieter Coecke van Aelst en zijn architectuuruitgaven van 1539. Met reprint van zijn 'Die Inventie der Colommen' en 'Generale Reglen der Architecturen'* (Amsterdam, 1978); J. Offerhaus, 'Pieter Coecke et l'introduction des traités d'architecture aux Pays-Bas' in J. Guillaume (ed.), *Les Traités d'architecture de la Renaissance* (Paris, 1988), pp. 443–52.

(1510–1570).[25] By this means the so-called 'strap-work', a 'light-as-air architecture writhing and curvetting in space', influenced by early *cinquecento* decoration arrived in England from Antwerp.[26] Grotesque decoration, combined with strap-work cartouches designed by Cornelis Floris de Vriendt, Cornelius Bos, Pieter Coecke van Aelst, Jan Mone and Colyn van Utrecht, fascinated English people and helped them to rediscover Rome.[27] Production of *Die inventie der colommen* was remarkably high, and from 1542 Cornelius Bos sold 114 copies of this 'booklet'.[28]

The most widely distributed books on the classical orders of columns and pillars were the different editions and translations of Sebastiono Serlio's Fourth Book *Regole generali di architettura sopra le maniere degli edifici*. The first Italian edition appeared in September 1537 in Venice. Only two years later, Coecke translated it into Dutch – the so-called *groote metselrijboek* ('the great book on masonry'). Such books on the classical orders were specially produced for craftsmen and artisans, who made direct practical use of the clear and simple drawings and commentaries. Coecke's translation was very successful and had many editions. He delivered no fewer than 300 copies to Bos, who in two years sold seventy-nine of them, plus six copies of a German translation by Jacob Reichlinger, published in Antwerp in 1542.[29]

With these books, the idea and status of 'architect' were introduced to the Low Countries. The position of the architect was related to that of the engineer, who was totally free from guild regulations and was allowed freely to design military and infrastructural works, fortifications and works of water supply. Traditionally a clear demarcation was drawn between the competences of the different artisans involved with the building process – the joiners, carpenters, stonemasons and stonecutters, sculptors, plumbers, nailmakers, thatchers, slate-layers, locksmiths, tinfounders, sawyers and lime-carriers. Discussions concerning who could make designs, patterns or models led to a lawsuit at Utrecht in 1542. On the occasion of this quarrel, several testimonies were collected in Antwerp, especially concerning the content of the terms *ordoneren* (the use of the orders and good proportions in architecture) and *fatsoeneren* (making models and patterns).[30] The witnesses – Philips Lammekens,

[25] J. Summerson, *Architecture in Britain 1530–1830*, The Pelican History of Art (Harmondsworth, 1953), p. 23.   [26] Ibid., p. 24.

[27] On strap-work and the *grottesche* in the Netherlands, see especially H. Mielke, 'Antwerpener Graphik in der 2. Hälfte des 16.Jahrhunderts. Der Thesaurus veteris et novi Testamenti des Gerard de Jode (1585) und seine Künstler', *Zeitschrift für Kunstgeschichte* 38, 1 (1975), pp. 29–83.

[28] J. Cuvelier, 'Le graveur Corneille van den Bossche', *Bulletin de l'Institut Historique Belge de Rome* 20 (1939), pp. 1–49.   [29] Ibid., p. 10.

[30] S. Muller Fz, 'Getuigenverhoor te Antwerpen over het maken van ontwerpen van gebouwen in de 16de eeuw door schilders, goudsmeden, timmerlieden en metselaars', *Archief voor Nederlandsche Kunstgeschiedenis, 4 (1881–1882)* (Rotterdam, 1976), pp. 227–45; R.

master designer of the Antwerp cathedral, Peter Teels, carpenter at the same cathedral, chief mason Peter Frans and *cleynsteker* (stonemason-sculptor) Rombaut de Drijvere – all agreed that the construction of buildings was the privilege of masons and stonecutters, and eventually also of sculptors, whereas design was the sphere of artists and architects. During the examination, translated quotations from the writings of Vitruvius and Alberti were added to the evidence. One of those from Vitruvius was that 'all the arts are included under architecture'.[31]

Much later, the influence of Vitruvius was mentioned by Hans Vredeman de Vries in his *Architectura* (Antwerp, 1577, re-issued in 1581, 1597 and 1601) and in the manuscript by Charles de Beste from Bruges, *Architectura. Dat is Constelicke Bouwijnghen huijt die Antijcken Ende Modernen.*[32] Vredeman de Vries, however, was probably familiar with Vitruvius' writings many years earlier, for he appears in 1549 to have been in Antwerp, where he copied the writings of Vitruvius and Serlio as translated by Pieter Coecke.[33] The publications on architecture by de Vries were those most widely used in Elizabethan and Jacobean England, but it was not until Inigo Jones (1573–1652) drew directly on Italian sources that an English architect gave a new direction to English architecture.[34]

At the end of the sixteenth century the writings of Vitruvius thus came to be more precisely interpreted than before by considering in depth his commentaries on construction characteristics, the use of different materials, the choice of sites for building and the applications of mathematics. In view of this new interest in reading Vitruvius, it is important to note that there were manuscripts by Vitruvius in the monastic and archiepiscopal libraries in medieval England, where they seem to have been used by masons seeking practical guidance on the choice of site and building materials.[35]

During the reign of the Archdukes Albert and Isabella, the Counter-Reformation contributed to much new building, as different religious

footnote 30 (*cont.*)

Meischke, 'Het architectonische ontwerp in de Nederlanden', *Bulletin KNOB*, 6de serie, 5, 5 (15 December 1952), pp. 161–230; H. Miedema, 'Over de waardering van Architekt', *Oud-Holland* 94, 1 (1980), pp. 71–87; W. Kuyper, *The Triumphant Entry of Renaissance Architecture into the Netherlands*, 2 vols. (Alphen aan den Rijn, 1994), vol. I, pp. 305–11.

[31] Muller, 'Getuigenverhoor te Antwerpen', pp. 243–4.
[32] C. van den Heuvel, 'De Architectura (1599) van Charles De Beste', *Bulletin KNOB* 94, 1, (1995), pp. 11–23.
[33] C. van Mander, *Schilderboeck. Het leven der doorluchtighe Nederlandtsche en hooghduytsche schilders* (Haarlem, 1604), fo 266.
[34] J. Newman, 'Italian Treatise in Use: the Significance of Inigo Jones's Annotation' in Guillaume, *Les traités d'architecture*, pp. 435–40.
[35] M. Howard, 'The Ideal House and Healthy Life: the Origins of Architectural Theory in England' in Guillaume, *Les traités d'architecture*, pp. 425–33.

communities, including the Jesuits and the Dominican and Austin Friars, again settled in Antwerp, following their banishment under the Calvinist rule between 1577 and 1585. From this time, Antwerp became one of the most important centres of mannerism north of the Alps. Several new buildings were erected in a mannerist or pure baroque style, including the Augustin Friars' church, designed by Cobergher in 1615; the church of St Ignatius (now the St Charles Borromeo church) built according to several designs by the Jesuit François de Aguilón (1567–1617), the Jesuit brother Peter Huyssens (1577–1637) and the famous painter Peter Paul Rubens (1580–1640); the Sodality House designed by Huyssens; and the church of the convent of the Theresian Carmelites.[36] The Jesuit church (see figure 5.5) is especially interesting, since Aguilón at first designed several schemes for a centrally planned church with domes, and also designed a version with a polygonal ground plan. Cobergher's choice of a heptagonal plan for the church of Our Lady of Montaigu (1609) may have influenced Aguilón's preference for a nonagon. Possibly because of the troubles with the construction of a dome on the Jesuit church in Douai, where eventually in 1623 a flat ceiling was constructed, Aguilón changed his mind, and built the Antwerp church without a dome. Inspiration for this scheme came from several sources, including Vignola's *Il Gesù* and Serlio, but above all from Carlo Borromeo, *Instructionum Fabricae et Supellectilis Ecclesiae Libri II* (Milan, 1577).[37] The ensemble of the Jesuit church, the Sodality House and the sacristies remains a pure example of the marriage between Counter-Reformation and baroque architectural principles. The setting of the Jesuit church has been designed so that the attention of the onlooker is seized by the powerful religious images displayed on the baroque façade. There is a strong contrast between on the one hand the simplicity and regularity of the façades of the house of the professed Jesuits and of the Sodality House, and on the other the lively and elaborate west front of the church. Thus humanist education and Roman Catholic principles, with a complex renewal of iconography after the Council of Trent (1545–63), led to a very productive generation of new architectural achievements.

The designs for porches by the mannerist architect Jacques Francart (1583–1651) included in his *Premier Livre d'Architecture* (Brussels, 1617) referred to Michelangelo's and Vignola's published models and to existing Roman porches.[38] Designs inspired by Michelangelo's *Porta Pia* were

[36] J.H. Plantenga, *L'architecture religieuse du Brabant au XVIIe siècle* (The Hague, 1925).
[37] A. Ziggelaar S.J., *François de Aguilón S.J., Scientist and Architect* (Rome, 1983), pp. 13–27.
[38] Ibid., pp. 47–74; A. de Vos, 'Premier livre d'Architecture (1617) van Jaques Francart: een post-michelangelesk, maniëristisch traktaat', *Belgisch tijdschrift voor Oudheidkunde en kunstgeschiedenis* 63 (1994), pp. 73–90.

5.5 Façade of St Ignatius church in Antwerp, designed by François de Aguilón, Peter Huyssens and Peter Paul Rubens(?). Drawing *c.*1644.

especially successful and were on several occasions reproduced by architects and artists. This porch, known from J.B. Vignola's, *Regola delli cinque ordini d'architettura* (Rome,1607), also inspired Inigo Jones in his design for one of the gates built at Arundel House (1618). He owned a copy of the 1607 edition of Vignola's *Regola* (now at Oxford) in which an engraving of the Porta Pia was published.[39] The design of this porch was used by Rubens on several occasions, after he bought Vignola's *Regola* and, in

[39] J. Harris and G. Higgott, *Inigo Jones: Complete Architectural Drawings* (London, 1989), pp. 126–8.

1617, a copy of Francart's *Premier livre d'architecture*.[40] His design for the monumental porch of the inner court of his house on the Wapper (*c.* 1611, now known as the Rubens House) and for the window arches on the lower part of the tower of the St Ignatius church (the original scheme was designed by Peter Huyssens, *c.* 1615–21), and his drawings for the triumphal arch Mercurius Abituriens, erected in 1635 on the occasion of the *Pompa Introïtus* of prince-cardinal Ferdinand of Spain, all repeated the porch motif of the *Porta Pia*. But above all, Rubens' *Palazzi di Genova* (Antwerp, 1622, with new editions in 1652 and 1663) was very popular in the Netherlands and in England. His accurate engravings of different Genoese palaces and church façades provided fine examples of mannerism and baroque that influenced English architects and masons.[41] Even Inigo Jones' Whitehall designs bore a resemblance to parts of the turrets of the St Ignatius church.

With the introduction of the Renaissance in the Low Countries, particular attention was given to mathematics and especially to geometry. That discipline, one of the seven *artes liberales*, in its applied form made a fundamental contribution to the skills of stone-cutting, perspective drawing, shadow drawing and designing fortifications. Urban planning frequently employed its principles. Geometry and arithmetic were also essential tools for map-makers and land-surveyors. By about 1550, books on geometry were being published and used in connection with laying out buildings.[42] The famous treatise on land measurement by Gemma Frisius had been published in Antwerp in 1533. Twenty years later the widow of Pieter Coecke van Aelst published a Dutch translation of Serlio's First Book, dealing with geometry and perspective. The problems of fortifications and geometry were discussed in Marco Aurelio da Pasino's *Discours sur plusieurs poincts de l'architecture de guerre* (Antwerp, 1578). The mathematician Simon Stevin, who mentioned Pasino, can be regarded as the leading scholar in the Low Countries who considered the problems of mathematics, town planning, architecture and fortifications all together. Finally, from 1600 onwards lessons in the theory of surveying and mathematics were provided at Leiden University so as to educate the new engineers in the Dutch Republic. Two professors were originally responsible for the lectures: Symon van Merwen and Ludolph van Ceulen. The latter

[40] Concerning books about architecture in P.P. Rubens' private collection, see the document 'Grootboek 1610–1618' (AR 128, 129) conserved in the Archives of the Plantin Moretus Museum, Antwerp. The problem of Rubens as architect was superficially treated in O. van de Castyne, 'La question Rubens dans l'histoire de l'architecture', *Revue belge d'archéologie et d'histoire de l'art* 1, 2 (1931), pp. 103–19.

[41] Summerson, *Architecture in Britain 1530–1830*, p. 85.

[42] A. Meskens, *Wiskunde tussen Renaissance en Barok. Aspecten van wiskunde-beoefening te Antwerpen 1550–1620* (Antwerp, 1994), pp. 220–30.

stayed at Antwerp in 1575 and was in contact with the famous mathematician Michel Coignet, who was on several occasions involved with the Antwerp fortifications and with surveys of the city walls.[43] In 1615 de Aguilón founded a school for mathematics at Antwerp, which six years later moved to the University of Leuven.[44]

One of the most practical and important applications of geometry in the Renaissance was the use of perspective drawing in art and architecture. The knowledge of central perspective in architecture became common only some decades after the application of the classical orders. The model books and prints of Hans Vredeman de Vries (1526– after 1606) were of particular interest and were very popular at that time all over Europe. We need mention only *Architectura* (Antwerp, 1577, 1581), *Artis perspectivae plurium generum elegantissimae formulae* (Antwerp, c.1568), *Hortorum viridariorumque elegantes et multiplices formae* (Antwerp, 1583), *Variae Architecturae Formae* (Antwerp, c.1601) and *Perspective* (The Hague/Leiden, 1604 and 1605). Moreover, in 1580 Vredeman de Vries made drawings in connection with the completion of the link between the now partly dismantled citadel of Antwerp and the city walls which testify to a good knowledge of the laws of perspective (figure 5.6).[45]

Subsequently, representations in perspective were worked into panels, fronts, volets and screens for Triumphal Entries, such as those of Archduke Ernest in 1594 and Archdukes Albert and Isabella in 1599. Perspectival representations were also used in figurative wall decorations in the interiors of Renaissance buildings and houses. One undoubtedly beautiful drawing in central perspective was that produced by Vredeman de Vries for the new Antwerp Town Hall. Others were designed for the houses De Croone, Het Gulden Sweert and St.-Jacob in Galliciën.[46]

The idea of perspective as a way of interpreting city space was, however, current in Antwerp before such drawings were made. From 1540 onwards greater attention was paid to the façades of houses, which increasingly were decorated with Renaissance ornaments. Following a fire in the St.-Kathelijnevest, in which twenty-two wooden houses were reduced to ashes, the city administration ordered that from that time on new houses were to be built only in stone. It is noticeable that more and more attention was paid to houses on street corners or in the inside of

---

[43] F. Westra, *Nederlandse ingenieurs en de fortificatiewerken in het eerste tijdperk van de Tachtigjarige Oorlog, 1573–1604* (Alphen aan den Rijn, 1992), pp. 82–9.

[44] Ziggelaar, *François de Aguilón*, pp. 45–52.

[45] P. Lombaerde, 'Overzicht van de opzoekingen over de Antwerpse vestingbouw, de architectuur en het urbanisme' in Dirk Stoclet and Dirk Coutereels, *400 Jaar scheiding der Nederlanden, 1585–1985* (Antwerp, 1990), pp. 45–66.

[46] R. Fabri, 'De "inwendighe wooninghe" of de binnenhuisinrichting' in *Stad in Vlaanderen: cultuur en maatschappij 1477–1787* (Brussels, 1991), pp. 127–40.

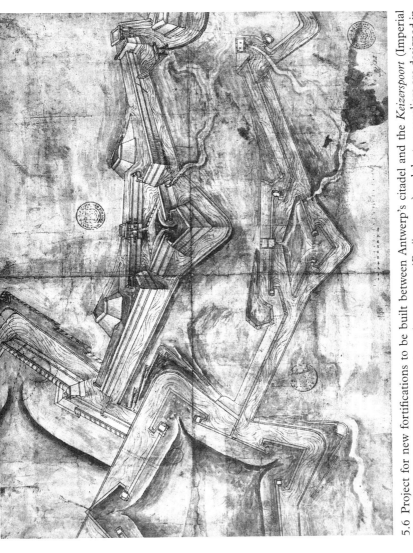

5.6 Project for new fortifications to be built between Antwerp's citadel and the *Keizerspoort* (Imperial Gate). The new bastions, the courtines, the new gate (*Begijnenpoort*) and the two cavaliers are designed in perspective. Hans Vredeman de Vries and Abraham Andriessen(?).

curving streets, on account of their high visibility. The visual relationship between the observer and the façade of the building was therefore becoming more important. Initially, this characteristic affected only the street façade of the building, because the traditional pattern by which land was divided into plots was largely maintained. On the other hand, the Hanse House, the Hessen House and the Stadswaag (Town Weigh-house) were buildings which could be observed from all sides. The Hanse House, for example, was surrounded by a spacious square and wide quays, and was easily visible from the Scheldt river and from the various canals in the Nieuwstad. The ornaments of the central part of its façade could also easily be seen from the Slijkpoort. The Town Weigh-house was surrounded by an open square 'in the middle of cross-streets'.[47]

The most remarkable example of perspectival criteria influencing the siting of a Renaissance building in Antwerp is the Town Hall on the Grote Markt (Market Square). In 1541 the block of houses on the south side of the Market Square, close to the Schepenhuis (Aldermen's House), was destroyed by fire. Rebuilding schemes were drawn up and the master mason of Antwerp cathedral, Domien de Waghemaker, was charged with erecting a new Town Hall. Originally it was planned to occupy the southern side of the Market Square, but the attacks by Maarten van Rossem in 1542 delayed the project. On the occasion of Prince Philip of Spain's Antwerp Entry of 1549, many Renaissance-style decorations and temporary structures were erected. The city clerk Cornelius Grapheus (alias Scribonius) devised the iconographical programme. In *Spectaculorum in Susceptione Philippi Hisp. Princ. Antverpiae aeditorum mirificus apparatus* (Antwerp, 1550) he provided an extensive description, illustrated with woodcuts attributed to Pieter Coecke van Aelst.[48] On this special occasion, the Market Square was transformed for a few days into an Italian *piazza*,[49] and to disguise the irregular triangular space several wooden constructions were erected. The entrance to the square was marked by a triumphal arch, provided by the English merchants and inspired by the Arch of Constantine. Lambert van Noort (1520–1571) designed a classical arch for the exit from the square to the Hoogstraat (High Street), along which the procession was to pass. The western, southern and northern sides were occupied by the impressive Aula Temporaria, a temporary Town Hall.[50]

[47]   Soly, *Urbanisme en kapitalisme*, p. 167.
[48]   I. von Roeder-Baumbach and H.G. Evers, *Versieringen bij Blijde Inkomsten gedrukt in de Zuidelijke Nederlanden gedurende de 16de en 17de eeuw* (Antwerp, 1943), pp. 12–14, 46–64.
[49]   Kuyper, *The Triumphant Entry*, vol. I, pp. 7–78.
[50]   Z. van Ruyven-Zeman, *Lambert van Noort Inventor, Verhandelingen van de Koninklijke Academie voor Wetenschappen, Letteren en Schone Kunsten van België, Klasse der Schone Kunsten, 57, 1995, n°61* (Brussels, 1995), pp. 74–7.

The wooden hall, put up in 1549, set the precedent for the siting of
the permanent new Town Hall, which from 1561 onwards was erected
on the western side of the Market Square, reducing its area. The shift
from the south side of the square may have been suggested by two
factors: first the desire to create a free-standing building that could be
seen from all sides, and secondly the wish to accentuate a visual axis
pointing towards the central section of the main façade. The observer
who enters the Market Square from the Kaasrui (Cheese Quay) sees on
this axis only the vertical central part of the façade *en saillie* decorated
with classical orders and terms in the local style, designed by Cornelis
Floris de Vriendt.[51] That central part was late Gothic in terms of its
stepped gable structure and composition, contrasting with the two side
wings of the new building, which were inspired by Renaissance *palazzi*
and have a horizontal composition. As the observer moves into the
Market Square, he or she finally perceives the entire building in successive visual stages.

In the Dutch Republic, similar principles were applied to the siting of
the new Town Hall of Amsterdam, designed by Jacob van Campen in
1648.[52] Hendrick de Keyser's Town Hall at Delft (1618–19) displays the
same concern to elevate a separate building with four decorated
façades.[53]

This degree of attention to the siting of the façades of new buildings
was already common in the fifteenth century. A typical example is the
Cathedral in the new square in Pienza, designed by Bernardo Rossellino
between 1459 and 1462.[54] Standing underneath the arcade of the Palazzo
del Pretorio the visitor has a vantage point from which to look out over the
piazza and see the façade of the cathedral in all its glory. Van Schoonbeke
put this possibility into words with his recommendation that commercial
buildings in market squares be constructed with arcades of columns on
the ground floor, in order to enlarge the public space and allow the square
to be seen in its entirety. On the occasion of the laying out of Antwerp's
Vrijdagmarkt (Friday Market) he suggested that the municipality build
arcades around the square, so as to enlarge its surface. The houses were to
be constructed 'op pillerren, sulcx dat se doorluchtich zijn zellen ende
alsoo men de ghantse merckt sal moghen oversien' ('on columns so they

51 A. Huysmans, J. van Damme et al., *Cornelis Floris 1514–1575, beeldhouwer, architect, ontwerper* (Brussels, 1996), pp. 115–20.
52 K. Ottenheym, 'Architectuur' in J. Huisken, K. Ottenheym and G. Schwarz (eds.), *Jacob
van Campen. Het klassieke ideaal in de Gouden Eeuw* (Amsterdam, 1995), pp. 155–99.
53 Kuyper, *The Triumphant Entry*, vol. I, p. 289.
54 P. Lombaerde, 'Verschuivingen binnen het planningsdenken over de ruimte: van een per-
spectivische naar een semiologische benaderingswijze' (Leuven, unpublished doctoral
thesis, 1982), pp. 130–46.

are transparent and one can see the whole market').[55] This wish to make public spaces more transparent reflects growing interest in the visual qualities of the urban landscape. Above all, Hans Vredeman de Vries set great store by using the laws of central perspective for interpreting the city environment in his principal publication *Perspective*, which contained striking engravings. In the preface he defined perspective as follows: 'De Perspective is een inschynende oft deursiende ghesichte der oogen' ('perspective is an in-shining and through-seeing sight from the eyes').[56]

Another important feature was the move towards the identical treatment of façades along streets. In this regard, the burning of the new Town Hall and the surrounding streets during the Spanish Fury of 1576 was a critical moment for Antwerp, for it was stipulated that, when the houses were rebuilt, the façades should be the same and should conform to a predetermined model. The model provided for shops on the ground floor, where the façades were to be divided into three bays, with rounded arches in hard blue stone (see figure 5.7). On the upper stories the house fronts were to be clad with white sandstone and to have large square windows, while at the top was to be a stepped gable with a three-paned window. Façades were allowed to be decorated with ornament in the typical Antwerp strap-work and grotesque style. At the same time as this plan for rebuilding the houses, the building lines of the surrounding streets were made as straight as possible.

Streets that followed straight lines were also very popular under the Calvinist city administration (1577–85). In 1578 the regime stipulated that the property of the monasteries and convents was to be secularized,[57] an action with far-reaching consequences in the Northern Netherlands, among other things for the extension of the city of Amsterdam. In Antwerp, work on a systematic inventory of the properties, sites and buildings of the religious orders began in 1579, and on 18 May 1581 the city administration confiscated their holdings. Apart from religious motives, there were two reasons for the measure. One was pragmatic and utilitarian: land and building materials were sold in order to finance new military works. The second reflected an interest in urban planning: the possibility of constructing new streets to form short and direct links between specific neighbourhoods of the city, improving the appearance of the city, and profiting from new plots of land. Several of the schemes and

[55] Soly, *Urbanisme en kapitalisme*, p. 184; R. Fabri, 'Het Vlaamse stadsbeeld in de 16de en 17de eeuw' in E. Taverne and I. Visser, *Stedebouw. De geschiedenis van de stad in de Nederlanden van 1500 tot heden* (Heerlen/Nijmegen, 1993), pp. 72–7.

[56] P. Karstkarel, *Hans Vredeman de Vries Perspective, part I (1604) and part II (1605)* (Mijndrecht, 1979).

[57] F. Prims, *De kolonellen van de 'Burgensche Wacht' te Antwerpen (december 1577-augustus 1585)*, Reeks van historische monografieën 16 (Antwerp, 1942).

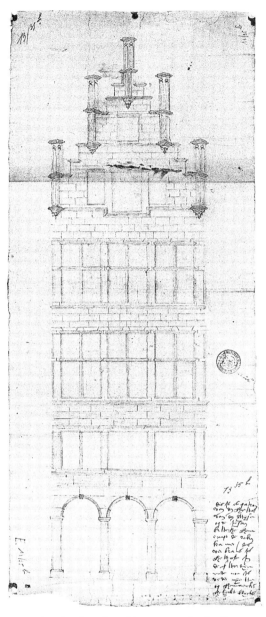

5.7 Model for the façade of houses to be built near Antwerp's new Town Hall, *c*.1577

plans associated with these measures use the terms *profijt* (in the sense of providing gain for the inhabitants), *commiteit* ('propriety', more subtle than useful) and *sierraet* ('beauty'), adopting the notions of *utilitas, commoditas* and *voluptas* as employed by Vitruvius and Alberti in relation to architecture.[58]

In concrete terms the main purpose of these measures was to improve the functioning of the network of streets in the old city, where the large monastic precincts were a major barrier to movement. Moreover, the high density of population in the city made the open land within the precincts especially valuable for building. After the city was captured by the Spaniards in 1585, some of the new streets that had been laid out across the precincts remained (e.g. the Beggaardenstraat through the convent of the Beggaarden) and new short-cuts were proposed, even as late as 1610 when a new street was built between the Huidevetterstraat and the Wapper, right through the Carmelite monastery of Our Lady.

Under the Calvinist administration an attempt was made to expand the city further to the south into a new neighbourhood called Nieuwe Suytstad (New Southern City). This development was made possible by dismantling part of the citadel: curtain 1–5 and the Hernando bastion which pointed towards the city. The pentagonal ground plan of the citadel influenced proposals for laying out the new settlement, the first deliberate town planning schemes for land to the south of the city. The city administration wished to create a direct link between the old city centre and the new commercial area being planned for inside the citadel. The discussion concerning the pattern of streets within its walls can be compared with the problem of how to fit the best possible street network within the polygonal circuit of city walls. The problem was typical of those that faced urban planners during the High Renaissance in Italy and during the mannerist and early baroque periods in the Low Countries. Books by Pietro Cataneo (1554, 1564), Daniël Specklin (1589), Jean Errard de Bar-le-Duc (1594, 1600), Claude Flamand (1597), Giorgio Vasari il Giovanni (1598), Francesco de Marchi (1599), Samuel Marolois (1615) and Simon Stevin (1594, 1649) and others all discussed the advantages and disadvantages of the grid pattern and the radial-concentric pattern within polygonal city walls.[59] Similar works on fortification and town planning were published very early in Antwerp. One example is *Maniere, Reigle, moyen & façon, de bien bastir, edifier, & munir Chasteaux, Forteresses, Villes, & autres Places* . . . (Antwerp, 1573), probably written by the engineer Hans van Schille

---

[58] Lombaerde, 'Overzicht van de opzoekingen over de Antwerpse vestingbouw', pp. 49–52.
[59] *Architekt & Ingenieur*, pp. 166–70; A. Biral and P. Morachiello, *Immagini dell'ingegnere tra Quattro e Settecento. Filosofo, soldato, politecnico* (Milan, 1985).

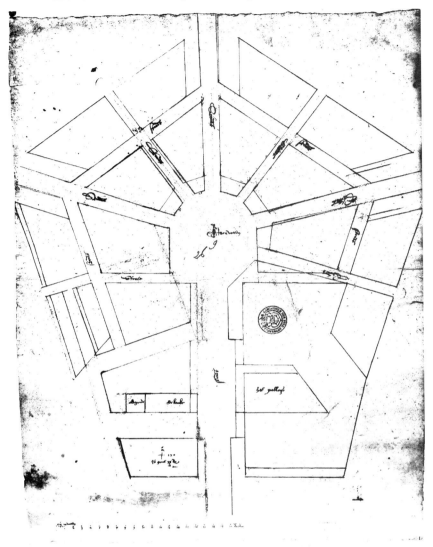

5.8 Project for a radial-concentric ground plan for the inner part of
Antwerp's partly demolished citadel, c.1580

using some copies of original designs by Francesco de Marchi. This famous Italian engineer was consulted on many occasions by Margaret of Parma, for instance for the siting of the Antwerp citadel. Van Schille was very productive at that time, and two years later he published *Le livre des cinq ordres* in Antwerp.

Nevertheless, some of these ideas concerning town planning had already been implemented in the Southern Netherlands before these books appeared: the new rectilinear city of Mariembourg was designed by Donato de Boni and built in 1546; the new pentagonal town of Philippeville was built in 1555; and in 1604 Wenceslas Cobergher designed a ground plan on a regular heptagon for the city of Montaigu.[60] In the drawings for Antwerp's Nieuwe Suytstad, a geometric pattern following a radial-concentric ground plan had already been proposed in the 1580s. This polygonal pattern favoured the opening up of a new centrally situated square, with surrounding blocks of houses and a new street leading to the old city centre. In *Fortification ou Architecture Militaire tant offensive que défensive* (The Hague, 1614–15), Samuel Marolois recommended that the central market square should have the same shape as the polygonal city walls, in order to solve the problem of connecting streets and city gates with the central square in the simplest possible way. But this theoretical statement came several decades after the proposals had been formulated on the site itself. Although the proposal for Antwerp's southern extension on a geometrical concentric model was not implemented, it articulated in a practical fashion ideas concerning fortifications and town planning before they were discussed more theoretically in treatises published in the Low Countries. The same observation is relevant to the application of the laws of perspective. In this sense one might even claim that Antwerp provided a unique site for the practical expression of many of the ideas typical of Renaissance, mannerist and early baroque architecture and town planning. Moreover, in the field of building regulation Antwerp at the end of the sixteenth century took an interesting initiative. Until then building regulations had been based on medieval tradition, by which the private owners of adjoining plots had to make agreements between themselves. The new orders dealt with such matters as exposure to the sun, outlook, property boundaries and all kinds of easements. From 1546 onwards, these 'rights, privileges, customs, uses and ancient traditions of the city of Antwerp' were assembled in a manuscript version. Later they were published by Carel Fabri (misprinted as Gabri) and Philips van Mallery, both lawyers, and by Adriaen vanden Bossche, a boundary official, as *Rechten ende*

---

[60] Lombaerde, 'Verschuivingen binnen het planningsdenken', pp. 168–93.

Costumen van Antwerpen (Antwerp, 1582). Because of their value as an exemplar, they were later also published in Amsterdam (1612 and 1639) and Roermond (1620).[61]

The city of Antwerp thus played a dual role in terms of its achievements during the period 1540–1640. First, it was a key site for the implementation of important principles in the areas of fortification, architecture and urban planning which had already in part been theoretically elaborated and then applied in Italy. Treatises and writings from Italy (which were published and distributed widely, either in translation or otherwise) and the direct involvement of Italian engineers and architects both contributed to this process. At this level we find certain practical achievements which were made possible thanks to the capital that was available and the dynamism of traders, merchants and bankers in Antwerp during its golden age. These achievements mainly took place during the period 1540–76. Secondly, at the experimental or empirical level, a number of proposals were formulated during the last quarter of the sixteenth century, and these were also implemented to a limited extent. At that time Antwerp was seen as a kind of laboratory for new interpretations of Renaissance, mannerist and early baroque ideas specific to the situation of the Low Countries. The use of models, the principle of uniformity in street profiles and a rethinking of existing traffic outlets are some examples of this. Several important theorists such as Albrecht Dürer, Daniël Specklin, Francesco de Marchi, Ludolph van Ceulen and Simon Stevin spent varying periods of time in Antwerp, and they may have seen these experiments in the city as a practical training-ground for their later more theoretical work in their own countries.

[61] R. Tijs, *Crowning the City. Vernacular Architecture in Antwerp from the Middle Ages to the Present Day* (Antwerp, 1993), pp. 129–30 and especially pp. 425–34.

6   The glorious city: monumentalism and public space in seventeenth-century Amsterdam

Marjolein 't Hart

> Were the Netherlands a ring you, O city, would be the diamond stone
> (Reinier Anslo, in a poem dedicated to the burgomasters of Amsterdam
> on the occasion of the laying of the foundation stone in 1648)[1]

Cities are concentrations of wealth and power. Fortified walls, fine decorated town halls, spacious squares with bustling markets impressed and still impress the visitor. In order to render the town an attractive residence for the rich and skilled, municipal governments strove to improve urban fronts and façades. This paper considers the attempts to present Amsterdam as a glorious city. Town planning, churches, secular public buildings and house façades are assessed as attempts to create an attractive city for the elite, skilled workers, scholars and artists alike. Following the structure of this volume, comparisons with Antwerp and London in their respective golden ages are to be found throughout the chapter.

Amsterdam had specific reasons to distinguish itself from its numerous urban neighbours. During the sixteenth century, the city was by no means the highest-ranking town of the urban network. Naval blockades checked the metropolis of Antwerp after 1585, but the possibility that it would recuperate lingered on. Dordrecht was still classified first in all urban political representations of the North. Neighbouring Haarlem and Leiden, both quite populous, were far stronger as industrial centres than Amsterdam.[2] The rising industries of the nearby rural Zaanstreek should not be ignored either. As for the sciences, Leiden gained a monopoly as

We are grateful to Ed Taverne and Charles van den Heuvel for their personal communications to the conferences of the Achievement Project. They were most helpful with suggestions for this paper as well. Further, I would like to thank Marten Jan Bok, Karel Davids, Penelope Gouk, Derek Keene, Piet Lombaerde, Marijke Spies and Herman van der Wee for their constructive comments.

[1] Quoted by Katharine Fremantle, *The Baroque Town Hall of Amsterdam* (Utrecht, 1959), p. 5.

[2] On the rivalry between Haarlem, Leiden and Amsterdam and the consequences thereof for the writing of topographical works, see Henk van Nierop, 'How to Honour One's City: Samuel Ampzing's Vision of the History of Haarlem', *Theoretische Geschiedenis* 20 (1993), 273–4.

Holland's only university town. During the seventeenth century, more-over, other urban centres were on the rise: The Hague, with its depart-ments of central government, and Rotterdam with its expanding trade. Furthermore, each of the eighteen constituent cities of Holland held an equal vote in the government of Holland. In the States General itself, Holland's vote was equal to that of each of the other six constituent prov-inces of the Dutch Republic. Amsterdam may have been an important city, but constitutionally the 2,000 inhabitants of nearby Purmerend enjoyed the same power.[3]

Still, within the setting of the federal republic that rose from the Revolt, Amsterdam's municipal autonomy was substantial. From the earliest beginnings, Amsterdam had always enjoyed more autonomy than most other urban centres. The governing body (numbering four burgomasters annually) was not elected by the city council, nor was it subject to approval by the sovereign as in most other cities, but was chosen by former burgomasters and magistrates. The elitist burgomasters, fre-quently re-elected, exercised a supreme power over city affairs. Their advisory board, the thirty-six-member city council, was elected by co-option. As a result, outside interference with local politics was extremely low.[4]

In 1578, the municipality shifted in favour of the Revolt and the House of Orange, a move labelled the Alteration (*Alteratie*). Taking advantage of the Reformation, the city government appropriated revenues from church properties. In addition, Amsterdam claimed specific privileges from the wording of the Alteration, which, among other things, allowed Catholic magistrates to remain in office and increased the city's control over church funds.[5] Thereafter, Amsterdam soon achieved the position of the foremost financial and economic centre of the Northern Netherlands, partly at the expense of Antwerp.[6]

By the end of the sixteenth century, any visitor could tell that concen-trated within this city was a significant portion of Europe's most wealthy families. Following the examples in Antwerp, 'the capital of the baroque', the Holland Renaissance style of building had come into full bloom with its leading architect Hendrick de Keyser, the Amsterdam town sculptor and stonemason. The houses were colourful and decorated with many ornaments such as cartouches, garlands and masks. Red brick with stone

[3] Marjolein 't Hart, *The Making of a Bourgeois State. War, Finance and Politics during the Dutch Revolt* (Manchester, 1993).

[4] R. Fruin, 'Bijdrage tot de geschiedenis van het burgemeesterschap van Amsterdam ten tijde van de Republiek', *Verspreide Geschriften* 4 (1901), p. 306.

[5] J.F. van Beeck Calkoen, *Onderzoek naar de rechtstoestand der geestelijke en kerkelijke goederen in Holland na de reformatie* (Amsterdam, 1910), pp. 89–91, 145–6, 262–9.

[6] See chapter 3 by Clé Lesger in this volume.

bands and quoins dominated. Foreigners praised the joyous elegance and luxury of merchant houses and archways. Cloisters, chapels and other religious structures abounded.[7]

Following the Alteration, several Roman Catholic structures were converted for new and public purposes. Convents, monasteries and chapels were transformed into orphanages, almshouses, hospitals, an old men's home, a customs house and workshops for new industries of immigrant entrepreneurs.[8] A comparable change in the use of religious buildings occurred in Antwerp, during its Calvinist period. Moreover, in both Amsterdam and Antwerp some church land was employed to improve connections to the inner city.[9]

However, Amsterdam's works and buildings were still modest. Within the fortifications, which partly dated from the 1480s, houses and workshops jostled for space. The town hall was housed in an unassertive building at the Dam, the central but cramped market square. The whole aspect of the town was essentially small in scale. Extensions were deemed necessary, not least because of the rapid increase in the number of inhabitants, following massive immigration in the 1580s.

The Alteration of 1578 allowed for a major enlargement of the city in the direction of the harbour area to the east, the Lastage. The inclusion of this area had long been a subject for debate: the wharves and industries there were unprotected from enemy attack. For a long time the burgomasters were reluctant to include in the city the illegal housing and trading activities of this district. Several of the newly elected councillors in the city government, many of whom had interests in the area, now voted for a solution to this pressing problem.[10] In the 1590s, the extension was enlarged, allowing for the application of a strict geometrical plan, inspired by the erudite burgomaster Mr Willem Baerdesen among others. Streets were wider than before and bridges were improved. With these plans, industry, in particular shipbuilding, obtained a secure site in a well-ordered neighbourhood within the city.[11]

[7] H.J. Zantkuijl, 'De eeuw van de verbeelding. De renaissance in de Amsterdamse architectuur' in Renée Kistemaker and Michiel Jonker (eds.), *De smaak van de elite* (Amsterdam, 1996), pp. 93–107.
[8] Ed Taverne, *In 't land van belofte: in de nieue stad. Ideaal en werkelijkheid van de stadsuitleg in de Republiek 1580–1680* (Maarssen, 1978), p. 141.
[9] Piet Lombaerde, 'Overzicht van opzoekingen over de Antwerpse vestingbouw, de architectuur en het urbanisme' in Dirk Stoclet and Dirk Coutereels (eds.), *400 Jaar scheiding der Nederlanden, 1585–1985* (Antwerp, 1990), pp. 53–6.
[10] Taverne, *In 't land*, p. 130. The reluctance of the City authorities to include this neighbourhood can be compared to the city of London's refusal to incorporate its suburbs: T.F. Reddaway, *The Rebuilding of London after the Great Fire* (London, 1943), p. 44.
[11] C.P. Burger, 'Amsterdam aan het einde der zestiende eeuw: studie bij uitgaaf van den grooten plattegrond van 1597', *Jaarboek Amstelodamum* 16 (1918), pp. 41–2; Taverne, *In 't land*, pp. 136–7.

In this extension, Amsterdam built on planning innovations already accomplished in Antwerp. In its utilitarian approach the project was comparable to those of the Antwerp entrepreneur Gilbert van Schoonbeke in 1549–52. Similar geometric schemes were employed in Antwerp planning during its Calvinist period in the 1580s.[12] During the seventeenth century, the geometrical trend was apparent in other European cities, as in proposals for rebuilding London after the Great Fire.[13]

Finance and trade, in the meantime, lacked a permanent location. The merchants met at a specific spot in the open air, or in the event of rain in a church or chapel. In 1607, however, when it became clear that Antwerp would remain blockaded and that the leaders of the financial community expected to stay in Amsterdam, the city council decided to erect a bourse next to the central Dam Square. Houses were torn down in order to allow for a worthy entrance on all sides. Hendrick de Keyser modelled the structure on the Royal Exchange of London, which, in turn, had been closely modelled upon Antwerp's Bourse of 1531–2. The Bourse symbolized the new status of the city as a leading international centre for finance and trade.[14]

The location was well chosen, as the inner city constituted the social and economic hub.[15] Many stores for luxury products, such as booksellers and art dealers, were located there. Within a minute's walk of the Town Hall (which housed the famous Bank of Exchange) were the Bourse, the Corn Exchange, the Weigh-house, several market-places and a multitude of shipping connections. No more than five or ten minutes away, one could meet renowned painters and other artists in their workshops, get a drink at the Doelen (the inns of the militia with shooting ranges, where performances were staged too), go out shopping for maps or curiosities, visit the (public) theatre or look up some books in the public library. As well as being the centre for information exchange, the Dam was the site for major festivities, including the annual parades of the militia. These colourful processions, accompanied by music and

<hr>

12 Hugo Soly, *Urbanisme en kapitalisme te Antwerpen in de 16e eeuw* (Brussels, 1977), p. 453; Ria Fabri, 'Het Vlaamse stadsbeeld in de 16de en 17de eeuw' in Ed Taverne and Irmin Visser (eds.), *Stedebouw. De geschiedenis van de stad in de Nederlanden van 1500 tot heden* (Nijmegen, 1993), p. 73. See also chapter 5 by Piet Lombaerde in this volume.
13 See chapter 7 by Judi Loach in this volume.
14 Peter Spufford, 'Access to Credit and Capital in the Commercial Centres of Europe' in Karel Davids and Jan Lucassen (eds.), *A Miracle Mirrored. The Dutch Republic in European Perspective* (Cambridge, 1995), p. 309.
15 Herman Diederiks, 'Bankers, Banks, and Other Financial Institutions in the Urban Landscape of Amsterdam' in H. Diederiks and D. Reeder (eds.), *Cities of Finance* (Amsterdam, 1996), p. 252. Cf. the elevated level of information exchange in London's financial district: D. Keene, 'The Financial District of the City of London: Continuity and Change, 1300–1871' in ibid., p. 288.

military shows, presented an idealized image of the past, of urban independence and of internal harmony. In the other cities of Holland these annual processions lasted just one day, but in Amsterdam they extended over several Sundays.[16]

Even when the Bourse had been completed (1611), Amsterdam remained a city of small scale. New opportunities were created with the comprehensive enlargement of 1613. Basic economic needs were met by the creation of another harbour district, now to the west of the city, and by the construction of living quarters for the middle and lower classes (the Jordaan) to relieve the population pressure in the old town. In addition to these traditional devices for housing and industry, a new exclusive inner area was designated for the elite: the *grachtengordel* (the canal girdle).

Whether or not the canal girdle was the result of an ambitious plan from the start has become the subject of debate.[17] One point is certain: there was no single concept for the whole city. The new ring of fortifications was designed first and the plan for the land contained within them was considered separately. The new bulwarks showed parallels with the ideal models of Vitruvius and Speckle, and their concentric shape was regarded as highly advantageous.[18] Within, the new street system was laid out in a strict geometric style. In sharp contrast to the Jordaan extension, the area of the canal girdle was evidently intended as something special. First, the three main canals forming the girdle ignored all existing property boundaries. Secondly, the building lots were larger than in the old city and were sold subject to covenants intended to promote the construction of impressive residences. Thirdly, the neighbourhood was planned as a residential area, which constituted something new as hitherto most merchant residences had incorporated warehouses. Fourthly, the area itself displayed a hierarchy: the innermost canal was to house the leaders of the upper class, the second canal was for the upper middle

[16] At least up to 1648: Paul Knevel, *Burgers in het geweer. De schutterijen in Holland, 1550–1700* (Hilversum, 1994) pp. 133, 273–78. See also R.E. Kistemaker, 'Het gebruik van de openbare ruimte in Amsterdam vóór 1800' in G. van der Plas (ed.), *De openbare ruimte van de stad* (Amsterdam, 1991), p. 54. By comparison with its rival in the South, however, Antwerp's festive pageants must have overshadowed all of Amsterdam's processions. Werner Waterschoot, 'Renaissance feesten en intochten' in R.L. Erenstein (ed.), *Een theatergeschiedenis der Nederlanden. Tien eeuwen drama en theater in Nederland en Vlaanderen* (Amsterdam, 1996), p. 191.

[17] E.R.M. Taverne, 'Stedelijk mecenaat. De Amsterdamse koopman als opdrachtgever en ontwerper van het stedelijk milieu (1613)' in A.H. Huussen Jr and B. Kempers (eds.), *In opdracht van de staat* (Groningen, 1994), p. 103; B. Bakker, 'De stadsuitleg van 1610 en het ideaal van de volkomen stad', *Jaarboek Amstelodamum* 87 (1995), p. 94.

[18] Bakker, 'De stadsuitleg', p. 88; Casper van der Hoeven and Jos Louwe, *Amsterdam als stedelijk bouwwerk* (Nijmegen, 1985), p. 56.

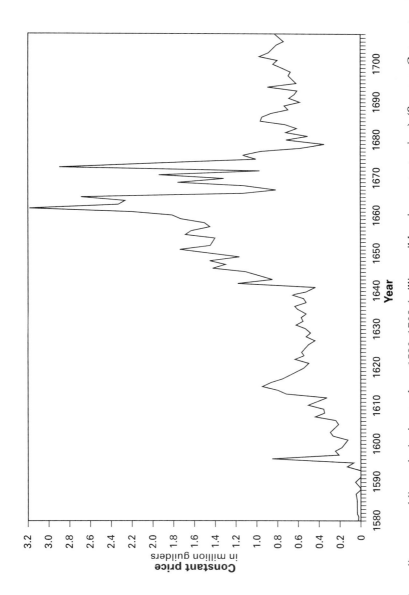

6.1 Expenditure on public works in Amsterdam, 1580–1708 (million guilders in constant prices) (Sources: Gemeentearchief Amsterdam, Archief Thesaurieren Ordinaris 5039, Memorialen)

class, whereas the third canal was allowed some business or storage.[19] This unique area provided accommodation for the new class of magistrates and directors of trading/banking houses, allowing them to live in a style representative of their status.

The whole extension proved extremely costly, resulting in a first peak in Amsterdam's expenditure on public works after the Lastage project during the 1610s (see figure 6.1).[20] Profiteering in land values added significantly to the expense. Among others, the burgomasters Oetgens and Cromhout had bought parcels needed for the extension, which they then sold to the city, enriching themselves out of public funds.[21] Still, the canal girdle represented Amsterdam's first step on its route to a more monumental appearance.

Specific arrangements were made for new churches. Around the Oude Kerk and the Nieuwe Kerk in the centre, six Protestant churches were to emerge in a circle: Zuiderkerk, Oosterkerk, Noorderkerk, Westerkerk, Eilandskerk and Amstelkerk. The Noorderkerk (1620–3), with a pulpit that could be seen from all corners, was a specific Dutch innovation in the most advanced Calvinist style, and for several decades the Westerkerk (1620–31) was actually the largest Protestant church to have been built in Europe.[22]

A further step is represented by the adoption of a new Palladian style for both public and private building. A fine example of this development is the Coymans House (1625), a double house for the prosperous merchant brothers Balthasar and Johan Coymans (see figure 6.2). Its architect, Jacob van Campen (1596–1657), almost immediately became widely known. In his design, he followed the classicist models of the Italian Renaissance architects Andrea Palladio and Vincenzo Scamozzi.[23]

---

[19] On the first two canals, moreover, the building lots were not to be subdivided, whereas this was allowed occasionally for the third one. Taverne, *In 't land*, pp. 152–4. The major canals were lined with trees and were regarded as an embellishment of the town; a disadvantage, however, was the smell, particularly in a warm summer.

[20] Public works are defined here as the expenditure of the *Fabriek*, which entailed the maintenance of public buildings, streets and bridges, fortifications and the like. On the organization and workings of the *Fabriek*, see the introduction to H.W. Werkman, *Inventaris van het archief van het stadsfabrieksambt* (Amsterdam, 1991). The figures, in three-year moving averages, are deflated by the price indices of Hubert Nusteling, *Welvaart en werkgelegenheid in Amsterdam 1540–1860* (Amsterdam, 1985), p. 260.

[21] See the embitterment expressed by Hooft, one of the more virtuous burgomasters: H.A. Enno van Gelder, *De levensbeschouwing van Cornelis Pieterszoon Hooft, burgemeester van Amsterdam 1547–1626* (Utrecht, 1982), pp. 13–14. Earlier extensions had not been free from speculation either. Taverne, *In 't land*, p. 125.

[22] W. Kuyper, *Dutch Classicist Architecture. Gardens and Anglo-Dutch Architectural Relations from 1625 to 1700* (Delft, 1980), pp. 10, 205; van der Hoeven and Louwe, *Amsterdam als stedelijk bouwwerk*, p. 69.

[23] However, another building in Amsterdam could actually claim the position of the first truly Palladian structure in the Netherlands: the Zeerecht, a watch-house for soldiers

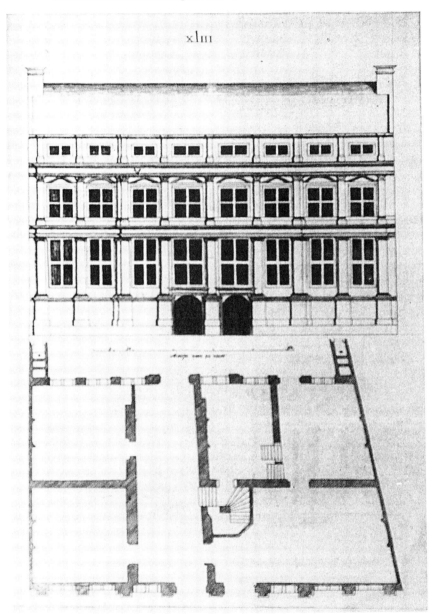

6.2 The Coymans House in Amsterdam (1625), designed by Jacob van Campen; from Salomon de Bray, *Architectura moderna ofte Bouwinge van onsen tyt bestaende in verscheyde soorten van gebouwen . . .*, Amsterdam, 1631

The design was symmetric and monochrome and had clear ratios, the length of the façade being twice the height and so on. In its sobriety, the Coymans House was revolutionary. Instead of a traditional gable, the roof was rectilinear.[24]

The style, in particular concerning the orders of the columns and the frontons above the windows, was remarkably similar to that of the Banqueting House in London (1619–22), designed by Inigo Jones, with which van Campen may have been familiar. Jones constructed several buildings in a Palladian style, far ahead of his time in Britain. His exemplary work, based on ideals of symmetry, harmony and proportion, had to wait until the second half of the century before it was followed on a wide scale by other British architects.[25]

The impact of the Coymans House upon Dutch architecture, however, was more immediate and widespread. Its characteristics became the new standard for Dutch building. The pace was set for a new architecture which developed rapidly, stimulated by the building booms following the extensions, which were to last until around 1670.[26] One of the most famous architects was Philips Vingboons (1607–78), the versatile Amsterdam artist, who had worked probably as a draughtsman for van Campen. Like van Campen, Vingboons was both painter and architect, which was regarded as an ideal combination.[27] Vingboons' books, which entailed adaptations of the Palladian ideal for narrow frontages (columns, for example, require a wide front to be effective), became widely known. Not only did he take care of the exterior, but the interior also received significant enhancement. His replacement of the entrance-hall by a corridor

footnote 23 (*cont.*)
    dating from 1618. Its architect is unknown. H.J. Zantkuijl, *Bouwen in Amsterdam: het woonhuis in de stad* (Amsterdam, 1993), p. 242. On general classicist rules applied in building before, see Charles van den Heuvel, 'Stevins "Huysbou" en het onvoltooide Nederlandse architectuurtractaat', *Bulletin KNOB* 93 (1994), pp. 11, 14.
[24] Koen Ottenheym, 'Architectuur' in Jacobine Huisken, Koen Ottenheym and Gary Schwartz (eds.), *Jacob van Campen. Het klassieke ideaal in de Gouden Eeuw* (Amsterdam, 1995), pp. 158–60.
[25] John Summerson, *Architecture in Britain 1530–1830* (Harmondsworth, 1977), pp. 111, 120. The interchange between several Amsterdam and London architects was frequent: H.J. Louw, 'Anglo-Netherlandish Architectural Exchanges c.1600–c.1660', *Architectural History* 24 (1981), pp. 2–4, 15–16.
[26] This is Dutch classicism, the Dutch interpretation of antique and Palladian examples. The standard was furthered by the publication of *Architecture Moderna* (1631) by the painter/architect Salomon de Bray, which was widely used as a pattern book, not only in the Netherlands, but also in England and the German territories. The Coymans House stood therein as the ideal construction. Koen Ottenheym and Quentin Buvelot, 'Historiografie en mythevorming' in Huisken et al., *Jacob van Campen*, p. 13.
[27] He belonged to a famous family of painters, map-makers and architects, around whom a whole circuit of merchants, publishers, learned men and artists converged, e.g. Blaeu and Hondius. Koen Ottenheym, *Philips Vingboons (1607–1678), architect* (Zutphen, 1989), p. 16. On the crucial role of publishers, see chapter 12 by Paul Hoftijzer in this volume.

allowed for more spacious and lighter rooms inside.[28] Merchants hired Vingboons for the construction of their canal-houses. A fine example is the luxury city-palace for the burgomaster/merchant Joan Huydecoper, occupying the space of three standard lots, with a beautiful garden adorned with statues at the back. Inside, the spacious and lofty rooms allowed him to receive his guests in a grand fashion (see figure 6.3).[29]

Soon, the fame of the canal girdle spread. The concentric circles emphasized the centrality of the Dam Square. Remarkably, however, other Dutch cities failed to match Amsterdam's example of monumental canals. The Hague, housing the seat of the central government and also significantly enlarged, was the most appropriate candidate. There, the Prinsegracht was specifically modelled on one of Amsterdam's principal canals. In contrast to Amsterdam, however, far fewer residences were built than expected, and smaller dwellings appeared in between.[30] Similar plans in Utrecht failed. Apparently, there were enough opulent families willing to invest in such city-palaces only in Amsterdam.

So far, much in the creation of Amsterdam's monumentalism had been a private concern. During the 1630s however, the municipal authorities adopted a distinctive policy of displaying Amsterdam's power. This new attitude was propelled by political developments, the city competing with the rising power and dynastic ambitions of the *Stadhouder* Frederick Henry after his successes in the military campaigns. Serious conflicts arose with the government in The Hague concerning matters such as taxation and trade with Spain.[31] Despite Amsterdam's limited constitutional power, the economic upswing of the previous decades provided the basis for these audacious moves. Within the Republic, Amsterdam's credit became increasingly indispensable for all Dutch military and naval schemes.[32]

During the 1630s, several facilities and institutions were created or improved in Amsterdam: the Athenaeum Illustre (the would-be university, open to the public, inaugurated in 1632), the relocation of the public library (1632, with a renowned collection), the reconstruction of the public theatre (1637), the renovation of the anatomy theatre (1639, open

---

[28] The London architect Robert Hooke is known to have bought Vingboons' second book in 1674, just after it was published. Henry W. Robinson and Walter Adams (eds.), *The Diary of Robert Hooke* (London, 1935), p. 129; cf. Ottenheym, *Vingboons*, p. 8.

[29] Ottenheym, *Vingboons*, pp. 35–41. Huydecoper was a lover of architecture himself. He also subsidized a variety of painters and poets.

[30] H.E. van Gelder, *'s-Gravenhage in zeven eeuwen* (Amsterdam, 1937), p. 130. The other elite neighbourhoods of The Hague, around the Voorhout and the Fluwelen Burgwal, were interspersed with smaller houses too.

[31] Marjolein 't Hart, 'Staatsvorming, sociale relaties en oorlogsfinanciering in de Nederlandse republiek', *Tijdschrift voor Sociale Geschiedenis* 16 (1990), 80–1.

[32] 't Hart, *The Making of a Bourgeois State*, p. 177.

6.3 House of burgomaster Joan Huydecoper in Amsterdam (1638–1641), designed by Philips Vingboons; from Philips Vingboons, *Afbeelsels der voornaemste gebouwen uyt alle die Philips Vingboons geordineert heeft*, Amsterdam, 1648

to the public), and the laying out of the Botanical Garden in 1638.[33] Last but certainly not least, plans were drafted for new public buildings.

The burgomasters adapted the Palladian style for their schemes. One of the first institutions to be significantly upgraded was the girls' orphanage (1634), for which van Campen was commissioned. The enlargement included an inner court with a giant Ionic order. The evenly spaced pillars radiated a cool, abstract atmosphere. Van Campen also designed one of the city gates, the Heiligewegpoort, in a monumental classicist style (1636).[34]

The public theatre, partly a continuation of the Chambers of Rhetoric which had been united in 1632, obtained a new building in 1637, again by van Campen. The new structure promoted further professionalization and the theatre's repertoire was significantly extended in the following years. Drama especially flourished by comparison with other Dutch cities, and most of the Dutch plays which survive today were written by Amsterdam authors. Attempts in Rotterdam and Delft to establish public theatres faltered; only The Hague was adorned with a *schouwburg* from 1660.[35] In 1664, the Amsterdam theatre was extended with a deep stage, designed by the brothers Philips and Justus Vingboons, so as to allow for a proper presentation of Salomon's temple, hell, heaven, clouds, dragons, 'aeroplanes' or wagons for all sorts of gods, and other attractions.[36] By comparison, Antwerp's drama adhered for much longer to the semi-private tradition of the Chambers of Rhetoric. Yet while Amsterdam was outstanding in the Netherlands for its drama, London was far ahead of the Dutch (and actually of much of Europe) in this respect. London's first permanent public theatre dated from 1576 and its repertoire was impressive.[37]

In musical performances London also rose high above Amsterdam. In this respect, Antwerp clearly outstripped its Northern rival too. Musical

[33] See chapter 15 by Karel Davids in this volume.
[34] Zantkuijl, *Bouwen in Amsterdam*, pp. 267, 274.
[35] The Chambers of Rhetoric had been open to the public since 1610 and Samuel Coster's Academy had performed plays from 1617 to 1622. W.M.H. Hummelen, *Amsterdams toneel in het begin van de Gouden Eeuw* (The Hague, 1982), pp. 94–5; Mieke B. Smits-Veldt, *Het Nederlandse renaissance-toneel* (Utrecht, 1991), pp. 17, 22–3. The inauguration of 1638 was accompanied by Vondel's play *Gijsbrecht van Amstel*, which recalled the glorious past of Amsterdam's beginnings. The presentation was an enormous success (in fact, it is still performed on a regular basis).
[36] Ottenheym, *Vingboons*, p. 144. Louw, 'Anglo-Netherlandish architectural exchanges', p. 16, notes the similarity of van Campen's theatre to Inigo Jones' Theatre Cockpit-in-Court, Whitehall (1629–30).
[37] Roy Porter, *London. A Social History* (London, 1994), p. 177; Peter Burke, *Antwerp, a Metropolis in Comparative Perspective* (Antwerp, 1993), p. 39; see also chapter 11 by Werner Waterschoot in this volume. As for Dutch acting, British travellers regularly criticized the quality of performance: C.D. van Strien, *British Travellers in Holland during the Stuart Period* (Amsterdam, 1989), p. 108.

life in Amsterdam was restricted because the Calvinist church banned music during services, apart from chant. Despite the ban, lifted only in 1680, music could be heard in the church at regular times, the organists playing a variety of tunes to divert the people who were walking about. In fact, the organ was one of the city's proudest possessions. After a fire, the organ of the Nieuwe Kerk was rebuilt by van Campen and Quellien (see below). For the Oude Kerk, Amsterdam managed to hire the most famous composer of the Netherlands, Jan Pietersz. Sweelinck (1562–1621) as organist. During the intervals of drama performances, music was staged too. Further, every morning a company of musicians, paid by the city, performed music at the Dam. And although there were few public sites for the performance of art music, a flourishing domestic practice existed. Besides the regular music sessions of the *collegia musica* in the homes of wealthy merchants, music was to be heard at inns and taverns.[38]

Drama, poetry and music also found hospitality at the *Doelen*, the inns of the militia, which were frequented by magistrates and artists as well as by the militia captains. The Doelen were in use for the reception of official guests of the city too, at least up to the early 1650s. In the 1630s, the Kloveniersdoelen, the shooting-range of the arquebusiers, were significantly enlarged. As part of a general policy to improve the neighbourhood around this building, a rectangular structure was added, richly ornamented with columns and containing an immense hall measuring 9 by 18 metres.[39] The existence of this new building allowed a new series of enormous portraits of the militia captains to be painted. In fact, no other city in Holland had militia paintings which were so numerous and so large.[40] For lodging high-ranking foreign guests, a stately *Heerenlogement* was constructed in 1647.

In the meantime, the old Town Hall had grown too small for the many tasks of Amsterdam's government. The Gothic building, moreover, was regarded as unworthy of Amsterdam's new status as a leading economic centre. From 1639, several architects were asked to furnish designs for a

[38] The organists were paid by the church, the salary being augmented by the city, but the organs were often the property of the town, not the church. A.J. Gierveld, 'Het klavierinstrument in openbaar bezit in de eerste eeuw van de Republiek', *De Zeventiende Eeuw* 6 (1992), 79. Operas were seldom staged. D.J. Balfoort, *Het muziekleven in Nederland in de 17de en 18de eeuw* (The Hague, 1981), pp. 8–9, 21.
[39] P.T.E.E. Rosenberg, 'Doelengebouwen en doelenterreinen in de Hollandse steden' in M. Carasso-Kok and J. Levy van Halm, *Schutters in Holland. Kracht en zenuwen van de stad* (Zwolle, 1988), p. 69.
[40] C. Tümpel, 'De Amsterdamse schuttersstukken' in Carasso-Kok and Levy van Halm, *Schutters in Holland*, pp. 86–7, 93. Naturally, the militia pieces constituted a significant income for the local painters, stimulating Amsterdam painting in general. See also chapter 9 by Marten Jan Bok in this volume.

new Town Hall. Van Campen's submission won.[41] Its proportions were immense: in 1648, they were set at 280 by 200 feet, yet in practice the building became even larger. The final plan also involved a change of front. At first, the building had been oriented with the shorter side on the square, but a wide façade was regarded as more imposing.[42]

Not all burgomasters supported the plans for a new Town Hall. The religious-inspired opposition from the faction of Willem Backer, one of the more orthodox burgomasters, gained support in 1645 after a fire broke out in the Nieuwe Kerk, regarded by some as a 'token against Pompous Worldly Halls'. A compromise was reached: funds were to be provided for the Town Hall as well as for the reconstruction of the Nieuwe Kerk; the organ was to be reconstructed by the then famous duo of Van Campen and Quellien; the entrance of the church was to be directly from the Dam Square which involved a reorientation of the Town Hall; the church would obtain a steeple that would stretch far above the Town Hall (see figure 6.4); and the size of the Town Hall itself was to be restricted. Eventually, however, the Town Hall became larger and the steeple of the church was never completed. Lack of funds in the 1660s, due to the later town extensions, prevented the fulfilment of the Nieuwe Kerk project.[43]

Work on the pilings began in 1648. The Town Hall that emerged was to be the largest in Europe. The exterior and the interior of the building made an overwhelming impression, as many contemporary descriptions and prints attest. Built up in a strict mathematical order, the hall resembled the Renaissance palaces of Rome and Florence in both style and scale. According to the famous Amsterdam poet Joost van den Vondel, it was 'an undeniable token of majesty and power'.[44] The ornaments inside and outside stressed the superiority of Amsterdam over all other towns in Holland, and even over the whole world.[45]

[41] Vingboons' design provided severe competition for van Campen. Both Vingboons and van Campen had excellent contacts with the Amsterdam government. Van Campen's father had been an Amsterdam merchant. Around 1640, van Campen stayed with his friend P.C. Hooft, the poet and son of the famous burgomaster C.P. Hooft; Hooft's brothers-in-law were Pieter Hasselaer and Cornelis de Graeff, both the strongest advocates among the burgomasters for the new Town Hall. M.J. Bok, 'Familie, vrienden en opdrachtgevers' in Huisken et al., *Jacob van Campen*, pp. 28–31, 43–4.

[42] In Amsterdam feet (1 foot=28.3 cm). R. van Luttervelt, *Het Raadhuis aan de Dam* (Amsterdam, 1949), p. 21.

[43] J.F.L. de Balbian Verster, *Burgemeesters van Amsterdam in de 17e en 18e eeuw* (Zutphen, 1932), p. 46.

[44] Quoted by Fremantle, *The Baroque Town Hall*, p. 35. The term *paleis* was already applied by that time, although it was a real palace only at the beginning of the nineteenth century. Marijke Spies, 'De maetzang van Van Campen: de stem van de literatuur' in Huisken et al., *Jacob van Campen*, p. 235.

[45] Quentin Buvelot, 'Ontwerpen voor geschilderde decoratieprogramma's' in Huisken et al., *Jacob van Campen*, p. 142. In response, The Hague tried to copy the monumentalism

6.4 The Dam Square in Amsterdam *c.*1662 with the Weigh-house in the foreground, the new Town Hall at the back and the Nieuwe Kerk to the right. The projected steeple was never completed. Engraving after Jacob van der Ulft; from Olfert Dapper, *Historische beschrijving der stadt Amsterdam*, Amsterdam, 1663.

The correspondence to Antwerp's Town Hall, built in the 1560s, is striking. Although not as large as Amsterdam's hall, the wide front of Antwerp's hall with its classicist pilasters dominated the central square in a similar fashion. In all, it constituted a comparable imposing symbol of urban pride.[46] In contrast, London's magnificent medieval Guildhall, which was partly destroyed by the Great Fire, was reconstructed rather than totally rebuilt. Although finely decorated it was less overpowering than the halls in Antwerp and Amsterdam, being set well back from the chief public spaces of the city. In Amsterdam, the central location on the Dam Square was preferred above a more spacious situation in one of the extensions. In order to create a setting worthy of the new building, the Dam was to be reconstructed in a classicist *sistemazione*. From 1639 on, houses in the neigh-

---

footnote 45 (*cont.*)
    of Amsterdam's Town Hall for the Session Hall of the Estates of Holland. Van Gelder, *'s-Gravenhage*, p. 145.
[46] Holm Bevers, *Das Rathaus von Antwerpen (1561–1565). Architektur und Figurenprogramm* (Hildesheim, 1985), pp. 19, 36; see also chapter 5 by Piet Lombaerde in this volume.

bourhood of the old Town Hall were bought and pulled down. This operation involved considerable costs, rising to over 270,000 guilders annually in the 1640s.[47] Wide streets were allowed behind and next to the building, an operation that constituted a considerable achievement indeed.

The Town Hall itself housed the functions of the city government in a well-considered symmetrical and hierarchical system. Most important for the concept of public space were the Citizens' Hall and the *vierschaar*, the high court of justice where death sentences were pronounced. The latter, visible from the Dam Square, was lavishly decorated with marble sculptures, stressing the solemnity of the proceedings there. In the middle of the building, the immense Citizens' Hall (36 by 18 metres and about 30 metres in height) was flanked by two inner courts. It was perfectly located as a crossroads for the imposing corridors leading to the separate offices. Such a majestic hall, employed among others for the reception of foreign guests, had been the express wish of the city's magistrates. Its decorations, virtually all executed in marble, represented the universe, and included a depiction of the terrestrial hemispheres in coloured mosaic lines on the floor. Being open to the public, the hall became an important meeting point. Officials, merchants looking for the Bank of Exchange, and other visitors all strolled across it.[48]

Throughout the building, a wealth of decoration ornamented the simplicity of the structural parts. References to the world of Antiquity and the Old Testament abounded. The most famous artists were hired for the work. The sculptures were created by Artus Quellien, the Antwerp artist (1609–1688), based upon rough outlines by van Campen. Antwerp had remained the outstanding centre for religious and decorative sculpture, and so the influence of Petrus Paulus Rubens, the family of the sculptor Colyns de Nole and François Duquesnoy echoed through Quellien's work.[49] Large paintings were added by famous Amsterdam artists: Rembrandt, Govert Flinck and Ferdinand Bol, among others. Their work stressed Amsterdam's ruling and legal authority, and a dominant theme was the virtue of the Roman magistrates, to whom the Amsterdam burgomasters loved to be compared.[50] There were Roman allusions also in the

---

[47] Figures from Gemeentearchief Amsterdam, Archief Thesaurieren Ordinaris 5039, Memorialen. See also J.C. Breen, *Uit Amsterdam's verleden* (Amsterdam, 1934), pp. 78–82 for the details of this operation.

[48] Fremantle, *The Baroque Town Hall*, p. 42; Luttervelt, *Het Raadhuis*, p. 33.

[49] Eymert-Jan Goossens, 'De rol van de beeldhouwkunst' in Huisken et al., *Jacob van Campen*, p. 203. Quellien exerted a decisive impact upon sculpture in Amsterdam in general: Rombout Verhulst and Bartholomeus Eggers, for example, worked in his studio. Ottenheym, 'Architectuur', p. 196. See also chapter 5 by Piet Lombaerde in this volume.

[50] Albert Blankert, *Kunst als regeringszaak in Amsterdam in de 17e eeuw* (Amsterdam 1975); Marloes Huiskamp, 'Wijs als Salomo, onbaatzuchtig als Elisa. Het Oude Testament in 17de-eeuwse openbare gebouwen', *Spiegel Historiael* 27 (1992), p. 99.

official city descriptions of Amsterdam, dating from 1611 by Pontanus and from 1663 by Olphert Dapper.[51] The paintings also showed the revolt of the Batavians, who according to Tacitus were the original inhabitants of the Netherlands, signifying the revolt of the Dutch against Spain. This theme was advanced in particular by burgomaster Cornelis de Graeff.[52] Other burgomasters, too, showed a keen interest in the execution of the decorations. Many of them were well educated in classics, sciences, architecture and art.[53]

Poems also contributed to the glory of the Town Hall. They celebrated the intended schemes for the building, its inauguration or simply the coming of a new year for this splendid town. Poets also venerated the mathematical harmony of the Town Hall and the classical impact of Vitruvius upon it. In the building itself, many paintings were accompanied by verses explaining them. 'Architecture and Sculpture now [are] coupled to [the] brush [of painting]', stressed Thomas Asselijn, the poet and playwright in 1654.[54] The inauguration of the Town Hall in 1655 was grand, with festive dinners and extensive processions, even though the building was still far from complete.[55]

After the Town Hall was built, it became obvious that Amsterdam needed yet another major extension, and areas were assigned for the new shipyards of the admiralty and private companies. By the early 1660s, the city council had settled on the most appropriate system of fortifications, the completion of the semi-circular line (see figure 6.5). With these plans, the city gained so much territory that no further extensions were necessary until the second half of the nineteenth century. The administration of the new extension was superior to that of 1613. Building-lines were set, industries were allocated to certain areas and landowners were systematically dispossessed according to rules and prices set by the city government so as to prevent profiteering in land.[56] The general lay-out of

---

[51] H. van de Waal, *Drie eeuwen vaderlandsche geschied-uitbeelding, vol. 1* (The Hague, 1952), p. 216. The parallel with Rome was typical of the seventeenth century and could also be found in London. Several decades before, Amsterdam's leaders had been proud to compare the city with Venice. B. Bakker, 'Amsterdam en Venetië. Twee steden verbeeld' in Margriet de Roever (ed.), *Amsterdam: Venetië van het Noorden* (Amsterdam, 1991), pp. 15, 19; E.O.G. Haitsma Mulier, 'De eerste Hollandse stadsbeschrijvingen uit de zeventiende eeuw', *De Zeventiende Eeuw* 9 (1993), pp. 104–5.

[52] Van de Waal, *Drie eeuwen*, pp. 219–23.

[53] See also Peter Burke, *Venice and Amsterdam. A Study of Seventeenth Century Elites* (London, 1974), p. 98.

[54] Quoted by Fremantle, *The Baroque Town Hall*, p. 62. See also Marijke Spies, 'Minerva's commentaar: gedichten rond het Amsterdamse stadhuis', *De Zeventiende Eeuw* 9 (1993), pp. 15–33.

[55] Even the roof had not been finished. In 1708, the last vault was painted. H.J. Koenen, *Voorlezingen over de geschiedenis der finantien van Amsterdam* (Amsterdam, 1855), p. 24.

[56] Taverne, *In 't land*, p. 173.

6.5 Plan for the extension of Amsterdam in 1663; from Jan Wagenaar, *Amsterdam, in zyne opkomst, aanvas, geschiedenissen, voorregten, koophandel, gebouwen, kerkenstaat, schoolen, schutterye, gilden en regee- ringe*, Amsterdam, 1760

Amsterdam was by Cornelis Danckaertsz. de Jonge (who had cooperated regularly with Vingboons), in association with the city architect Daniël Stalpaert and the engineer Jan Heimansz Coeck. Famous fortification-builders were hired. The canal girdle was continued in the fashion of 1613, with a similar hierarchy.[57] A totally new neighbourhood, the *Plantage*, was also planned, to be developed in the eighteenth century with fair avenues and gardens.

The plans allowed for new enormous (semi-)public buildings to be constructed. The city architect (also stockbroker) Daniël Stalpaert (1615?-1676), formerly the overseer of van Campen's town hall, became famous for his huge edifices in a Dutch Palladian style. His storehouse for the Admiralty of Amsterdam was a vast, imposing, block of 210 by 225 feet, with a regular and harmonious façade. In size, the building was superseded by Stalpaert's storehouse for the Amsterdam Chamber of the Dutch East India Company, which became the largest construction of the whole Republic. Stalpaert also extended the office for the Amsterdam Admiralty and erected some enormous almshouses with an austere appearance. By that time, the old Bourse of De Keyser was in need of upgrading: Stalpaert converted it into a regular symmetrical structure of 124 by 250 feet, with giant Ionic orders.[58]

Such large constructions had their precursors in Antwerp. Apart from Antwerp's Town Hall, which must have been impressive in the setting of the sixteenth century, the Antwerp trade centre of the 1560s for Hanse merchants was enormous, in dimensions comparable to Stalpaert's constructions. In London, however, it was not until several generations after the Great Fire that new forms of large-scale public buildings gave a new monumental aspect to the city.[59]

Adding to the monumentalism of Amsterdam's public buildings were the private constructions for the elite. Most famous was the double house designed by Justus Vingboons for the wealthy arms-dealers Trip. It recalled one of Palladio's *palazzi*. Smaller structures added to the monumentalist image too, as they were increasingly built in rows. At first, these designs were initiated by the municipal offices for poor relief, but private schemes followed. With uniform heights for windows and roofs, sometimes with the same roof cornice for several houses, the new streets and canals became truly impressive. An outstanding example was constituted

---

[57] L. Jansen, 'De stadsuitbreiding van 1663', *Ons Amsterdam* 15 (1963), p. 380.

[58] Breen, *Uit Amsterdam's verleden*, p. 67; Zantkuijl, *Bouwen in Amsterdam*, pp. 404, 410, 422.

[59] As for monumentalism in London's financial district, realized in a cumulative process in the eighteenth and nineteenth centuries; see Keene, 'The financial district', pp. 280, 284, 289.

by the newly built area around the Amstel of 1660–84.[60] By comparison, London also applied stringent regulations in the reconstruction of the City after the Great Fire. With standard designs for housing, some parts of new-built London recalled the sober splendour of Amsterdam.[61]

Late seventeenth-century Amsterdam presented a striking image of modernity and amenity. Mercantile interests were prominent: hundreds of tall ships filled the harbour and the city's trade and bustle remained impressive. Burgomasters and magistrates, some of whom were eminent scientists, promoted scientific, artistic and other improvements. Since the beginning of the century, foreign visitors had praised the number, management and cleanliness of the city's welfare institutions. Street life was notably civilized. Every fifteen minutes various tunes were played by several carillons. According to John Evelyn, 'the harmony and the time . . . were the most exact and agreeable'.[62] The clarity of their sound was outstanding, owing to the foundry for pure bells of François and Pierre Hemony. Originally from Lorraine, they had moved via Zutphen to Amsterdam in 1655, making the city famous for an advanced method of bell-casting.[63] During the night, after 1669 the streets and canals were well lit by an unequalled system of street-lighting planned by the painter and engineer Jan van der Heyden (1637–1712). His 2,500 lanterns could be lit within 15 minutes. The lanterns allowed for a welcome extension of the public space for the hours after dusk. And, from the 1670s onwards, an improved drainage system, advanced by burgomaster Hudde, greatly reduced the smell of the canals during the summer.[64]

The costs of the second large extension, however, came to exceed all previous operations. Public works regularly constituted the largest single item in Amsterdam's overall expenses. The new fortifications alone must have amounted to over 21 million guilders. The new Town Hall had been a costly operation as well: in the end, it totalled almost 8 million guilders. Amsterdam's economic progress and population growth had long permitted such excessive spending. Besides, more than Antwerp or London, the city was also in a position to levy and allocate funds without interference by a central government. But, with the contraction of the economy in the last quarter of the seventeenth century, to which costly wars with England and France were added, the ceiling was reached. As figure 6.1 demonstrates, during the 1650s up to the end of the 1670s, there was a

[60] R. Meischke, 'Het Amsterdamse stadsbeeld en het nieuwe stadhuis', *Maandblad Amstelodamum* 45 (1958), pp. 205–7; I.H. van Eeghen, 'De geschiedenis van het eiland Vlooienburg', *Maandblad Amstelodamum* 40 (1953), p. 19.

[61] Reddaway, *The Rebuilding of London*, pp. 130, 298.

[62] William Bray (ed.), *The Diary of John Evelyn, from 1641 to 1705–6* (London, 1879), p. 29.

[63] Balfoort, *Het muziekleven*, p. 50.

[64] Joh.C. Breen, 'Jan van der Heyden', *Jaarboek Amstelodamum* 11 (1913), p. 44.

huge surge in expenses, which came to exceed by far any increase in the number of inhabitants. A thorough restructuring of the finances was undertaken in 1662, introducing a new system with double-entry book-keeping in order to exert better control over the annual expenses. A general reform followed in the later 1670s. In the 1680s, the number of public works contracted, followed by an overall stagnation in building activity during the eighteenth century.[65]

Despite the significant achievements in planning and architecture of the seventeenth century, the external public space was hampered by the absence of large thoroughfares, avenues and squares. As in Antwerp, no plazas were designed for ceremonial purposes, and statues and fountains were not yet part of the plans.[66] The new squares of the extension of 1663 were assigned a strictly economic function as markets. Almost all were irregular in shape, often as left-overs after the house lots had been measured along the canals.[67] The central square of Amsterdam, the Dam, wrestled throughout its history with one severe restriction: it was too small. No beautiful optical vistas were possible. Only the cupola on the roof of the Town Hall was a prominent landmark to be pinpointed by a visitor arriving from any direction.[68] In Antwerp, a particular vista of the Town Hall was possible from the Kaasrui. Moreover, after the fire of 1576, similar façades for the Market Square were ordained by the city council, resulting in a monumental effect.[69] In London after the Great Fire, Christopher Wren's proposals entailed wide streets and large open spaces. John Evelyn and Robert Hooke followed up with schemes for squares and vistas. In the end, because of the pressures of time and finance, London's medieval street-plan surfaced again, although many minor practical improvements and some significant new additions were made.[70]

Yet, overall, Amsterdam had grown more monumental since the 1630s. Several visitors praised the solemnity of the structures: 'The buildings are stately and so uniform without, that a whole street seems but one contin-

[65] Koenen, *Voorlezingen*, pp. 23–7. As for the double-entry system, Amsterdam was the most advanced of all towns in the whole Dutch Republic. W.F.H. Oldewelt, 'De boekhouding van Amsterdam', *Jaarboek Amstelodamum* 63 (1971), p. 18. On the building booms, see Ad Knotter, 'Bouwgolven in Amsterdam in de 17e eeuw' in P.M.M. Klep et al. (eds.), *Wonen in het verleden* (Amsterdam, 1987).

[66] Fabri, 'Het Vlaamse stadsbeeld', p. 77.

[67] Van der Hoeven and Louwe, *Amsterdam als stedelijk bouwwerk*, p. 72. See also Peter Burke, 'Investment and culture in three seventeenth century cities: Rome, Amsterdam, Paris', *Journal of European Economic History* 7 (1978), p. 336.

[68] Fremantle, *The Baroque Town Hall*, p. 37.

[69] Lombaerde, 'Overzicht', pp. 47–8. For Amsterdam's Westermarkt, however, standard designs for the houses had been ordered too: Bakker, 'De stadsuitleg', p. 91.

[70] Porter, *London*, pp. 88–9; Reddaway, *The Rebuilding of London*, pp. 111, 177; Keene, 'The Financial District', p. 280.

ued house,' wrote Robert Bargrave,[71] and an anonymous visitor to Amsterdam reported:

The best buildings are on the Keizers or Emperors Gracht and on the Herengracht; several of these are so stately that they may compare with some palaces . . .; the canals are planted on each side with limes, the water is broad and straight for a great way together, the buildings on each side are very noble and regular, besides the pleasure of seeing so many sorts of boats and vessels as are commonly here, so very delightful.[72]

The overall increase in scale had been a conscious policy, and constituted in this regard a significant achievement.[73] With the major extensions of 1663, the city was functionally more segregated, more spacious, cleaner, and a better place to live in compared with the earlier seventeenth century.

In hindsight, Antwerp's influence upon Amsterdam building had been strong up to the first decades in the seventeenth century. Yet from the 1630s, Amsterdam definitively went on its own specific monumentalist route, inspired by Roman classicist ideals and spurred on by political rivalries with the central state. No urban government in the Netherlands undertook so many initiatives in architecture and urban planning, even in comparison with Antwerp in the sixteenth century. Antwerp's government had also created the space necessary for urban development, but much had remained in the hands of private entrepreneurs.[74] Extensive migration and economic advantages strengthened Amsterdam's civic pride, which was expressed not only in the monumental buildings, but also in the impressive number of scientific institutions, the frequent processions by the militia, the enormous size and number of the militia paintings, and the outstanding position of the public theatre, to mention just a few of the most striking features. Some of these developments had been instigated by (semi-)private enterprises. Yet, without doubt, one of the most notable achievements of the seventeenth-century burgomasters was to endow Amsterdam with the physical form that expressed its powers.

London differed from Antwerp and Amsterdam because it was the capital of a dynasty which had adopted a self-consciously imperial role within Britain. The drive to improve the appearance of London came from the Stuart monarchs rather than from the city, whereas in Amsterdam the civic authorities took the initiative. The Stuart project was interrupted by the Civil War, but similar ideas, now powerfully informed by the Parisian projects of the French monarchy, were in the air

[71] Quoted by van Strien, *British Travellers*, p. 88.   [72] Quoted in Ibid., p. 89n.
[73] Meischke, 'Het Amsterdams stadsbeeld', p. 206; Henk Zantkuijl, 'Bouwen in de Hollandse stad' in Taverne and Visser, *Stedebouw*, p. 71.
[74] Fabri, 'Het Vlaamse stadsbeeld', p. 76.

when proposals were made for rebuilding the city after the Great Fire of 1666. Despite the prevailing influence of Dutch classicism in the vocabulary of English architects and builders,[75] Amsterdam's monumentalism was present only in part of the plans.

The architectural panache of Amsterdam had openly expressed the bourgeois and republican roots of its culture. The major architectural impact of London's rebuilding, in the form of the innovative and dominant cathedral and the many parish churches, stood in sharp contrast to the civic architecture of Amsterdam: its message was of an order derived from the king and backed up by the authority of the Anglican church.

[75] Summerson, *Architecture*, pp. 190, 206; Kuyper, *Dutch Classicist Architecture*, pp. 116–22.

7   Architecture and urban space in London

Judi Loach

For the purpose of examining London's achievement within the fields of architecture and urban space it seems sensible to redefine the timespan covered as 1620–1715. In order to appreciate the significance of architecture and planning from the Restoration onwards, one needs to understand the extent to which the Civil War and Commonwealth determined subsequent developments by bringing about so absolute a rupture with previous practice. Without such a contextualization there is a tendency to credit the radical changes which dominate the late seventeenth century wholly to the accident of the Great Fire, rather than to the revolution in thought instigated by those few intellectuals who dominated state policymaking, including urban reconstruction. One must also recognize that the change from Stuart to Whig government wrought such drastic effects in the domains of design for individual buildings and whole pieces of townscape that an entirely different narrative takes over in the 1720s, if not from 1715.

To what extent can this period then be considered one of architectural achievement? Certainly it has left us St Paul's Cathedral, and around it three dozen or so parish churches also by Wren. Furthermore, the Customs House and the Monument (both again by Wren) and virtually all the livery halls were built in the post-Fire reconstruction of the capital so that, even if visually they are overpowered by giant office blocks today, they remain a powerful presence; indeed, the vast majority of the City's extant public monuments were realized during this period.

Moreover, if one trespasses beyond the strict boundaries of the City, to consider London in its wider sense, the prime monuments to be found in the City of Westminster – notably Inigo Jones' Banqueting House in Whitehall and his Covent Garden Piazza (focusing on St Paul's Church) – bear eloquent witness to the high level of artistic achievement already attained prior to the Civil War. Looking slightly further afield, to the new suburbs arising around both cities in the later seventeenth century, we can see the parish churches designed by Wren's student and amanuensis, Hawksmoor, which must be counted amongst the most original and spatially exciting pieces of architecture ever realized in Britain. Moreover, the transformation of the lesser building stock – residential and commercial – from medieval timber-frames to more uniform brick façades, would have greatly increased the homogeneity of the city's appearance and so drastically modified one's impression of it.

But why should we consider this period to be one of architectural achievement – or rather (to make the issue clearer), one of architectural innovation? Certainly the civic monuments and general urban improvements both reflect a higher level of ambition, but can such products alone justify this accolade? Is it not rather a matter of developments in devising and producing built forms which are at stake? In this spirit I shall outline the developments experienced in London's architecture and urban spaces under five headings: the urge to plan; London's self-awareness of its status as a capital (and consequently its attempts to create an appropriate self-image); the introduction of effective controls over the construction process; the creation of new typologies for buildings (and urban spaces); and radical change within the design process itself.

In the seventeenth century the greatest change in orientation occurred in town planning, as London experienced the first conscious attempts systematically to impose physical order on the city. They began very early in the century, with the arrival of the Stuart dynasty, but were cut off abruptly by the Civil War; they were, however, taken up again under the Restoration. On the one hand, due to the arrival of a royal family more aware of, and more interested in, developments on the continent, they represented the introduction of truly Renaissance, classical ways of designing cities, which would be felt as much in architecture as in planning.[1] On the other hand, they represented a reaction against the frightening, seemingly uncontrollable, growth of the City. Those in authority implicitly believed in the ability of built form to determine society and its economy alike. They anticipated that by physically imposing order upon the City the national economy would prosper, and that by introducing material symbols of the monarchy into the suburbs (the overt intention of the Fifty New Churches Act of 1711) the citizenry would be turned back from dissent.[2]

[1] Graham Parry, *The golden age Restor'd: The Cult of the Stuart Court, 1602–42* (Manchester, 1981).
[2] In 1711 Jonathan Swift had claimed that there were 'at least three hundred thousand inhabitants in this town . . . (who for lack of churches) . . . either stay at home, or retire to the Conventicles' (*Examiner*, 24 May 1711, no. 42). See also H.Colvin, 'Introduction' in E.G.W. Bill, *The Queen Anne Churches* (London, 1979).

The nature of this new, Renaissance planning in London was but limited and fragmentary. The scheme proposed by Inigo Jones implicitly focused upon the ceremonial route from Whitehall to St Paul's, the respective seats of the monarch's secular and ecclesiastical power, its monumental structures – the complete sequence comprising Whitehall Palace with its Banqueting House, the Queen's Chapel at St James', Somerset House, Covent Garden (designed as the culmination of a vista from the Strand) Temple Bar and St Paul's Cathedral – each eloquent of the source of that power. More significantly, perhaps, they also served as fragments of a continuous façade along the ceremonial route, or as landmarks closing vistas from it.[3]

Likewise Christopher Wren's plan for the City of London (alone) prioritized this route along Fleet Street and up Ludgate Hill to St Paul's Cathedral, exploiting the monuments at Temple Bar and on the crown of the hill to clarify such a reading. Moreover, his other proposed thoroughfares served to link royal institutions within the one city of the realm independent of monarchical government. From St Paul's they led either to a new centre for royal institutions, clustering Post Office, Excise Office and Mint (together with insurance offices and goldsmiths) around the Royal Exchange, or to the Tower. *Rondpoints* facilitated the interconnection of these thoroughfares with secondary highways, so as to link principal royal institutions with other major edifices, notably the Customs House and London Bridge but also, albeit to a lesser degree, with the City gates.[4]

Inigo Jones' *piazza* at Covent Garden offered, through its tangible realization of a fragment, a vision of an entire ideal city: built in effect on an effectively 'green fields' site, it avoided any need for reconciliation with the extant medieval fabric: its planning could thus follow a strictly orthogonal geometry. Its introduction of open space into the urban fabric contrasted starkly with the dense medieval city all around. Its promotion of uniform façades, in a simplified classicism, gave visual expression to a priority of street – the civic realm – over that of individual dwelling, thus giving physical form to an alien, Renaissance, concept and thereby accentuating by visual means its distance from the medieval norms being observed all around it. Although it must be admitted that other post-Reformation developments, notably the nearby Inns of Court, had already incorporated comparable open spaces in the late 1550s and 1560s, the combination of all these various features of Renaissance town planning lacked any precedent in Britain. Similarly, although the

[3] Gillian Scampton, 'Idea and Image: the Concrete Embodiment of Stuart Ideology through the Work of Inigo Jones', Diploma in Architecture dissertation, University of Cambridge (1983).
[4] Viktor Furst, *The Architecture of Sir Christopher Wren* (London, 1956).

Renaissance style of architecture employed, both here and in the house
Jones designed for Lord Maltravers at Lothbury,[5] found echoes in other residential developments nearby realized before the Civil War,[6] the model as a
whole was adopted only after the arrival of the Hanoverians on the throne
(and in particular from the 1730s onwards), when it became the dominant
model for the development of the great estates across London and beyond.[7]

   This raises questions as to the real degree of success enjoyed by main-
stream (that is, international) classicism in Britain during the period
under consideration here. It should be remembered that Jones worked
virtually exclusively for the court, and that this represented an extremely
restricted circle within London as a whole. The bulk of buildings being
erected in the metropolis (and throughout the country) might incorporate classicizing motifs, along with others drawn from the continent, but
their designers remained immune to a classical system of design, in the
Palladian sense, as pioneered by Jones. The predominant mode was
therefore one which John Summerson has labelled 'Artisan Mannerism',
because it was 'essentially that of the best London craftsmen – joiners,
carpenters, masons and bricklayers'. Summerson identified its key features as: the suppression of roofs or the adoption of hipped roofs with
overriding eaves; Dutch (or 'Holborn') gables; the exploitation of cor-
nices, thus stressing the horizontal at the expense of the vertical; the use of
large wooden window frames, thus doing away with vertical mullions, in
brick or stone; cartouche-bearing pilasters; architraves decorated with
'exaggerated' lugs; and (often highly ornamented) broken pediments.[8]

   Although this mode was thus mannerist, insofar as it made original and
playful use of the extant vocabulary of architectural elements, it owed
little to engravings and other publications of continental origin. Instead it
was rather due to artisans' first-hand experience of continental, and (as
can rapidly be deduced from the above repertoire of preferred features) in

[5] John Harris and Gordon Higgott, *Inigo Jones, Complete Architectural Drawings* (London, 1989), nos. 84–5.
[6] Notably on William Newton's land, i.e. fourteen houses in Great Queen Street (1637) and thirty-two in Lincolns Inn Fields (1638–41) (John Summerson, *Architecture in Britain, 1550–1850*, The Pelican History of Art (Harmondsworth, 1953, 6th revised/2nd integrated edn), pp. 94–5).
[7] Summerson, *Architecture in Britain*, ch. 23: 'The House and the Street in the Eighteenth Century', pp. 227ff; John Summerson, *Georgian London* (London, 1945; 3d edn, London, 1978). Although there would be several somewhat classicizing terraces and even squares erected after the Restoration (Bloomsbury Square and St James's Square, 1661, Soho Square and Red Lion Square, 1666, and then Old Bond Street, Downing Street, Essex Street, Buckingham Street, Villiers Street and Great Ormond Street), none would, for instance, follow Jones' adoption of the Italian *piano nobile*, preferring to retain all floors at equal height. Such radical changes in house design would be accepted in London only from the advent of the Hanoverians, notably with Hanover Square (1717).
[8] Summerson, *Architecture in Britain*, ch. 10: 'Artisan Mannerism, 1615–75' (pp. 89–98).

particular Netherlandish, practice. The single most determining factor leading London artisans to turn in this direction for inspiration was no doubt the contemporary rise of brick as the major building material for the British capital. Whilst the lack of funds available to the court for anything other than military expenditure may also be held partially responsible for the comparative failure of full-blown classicism to take root in Britain, the independent development of a specifically native architecture in the post-Restoration period is also pertinent.

The Great Fire of 1666 offered opportunities for further pursuing such modern visions. That this was appreciated at the time is witnessed both by the considerable number of (unsolicited) proposals laid before the king[9] and by the nature of the preoccupations they reveal, being as much pragmatic responses to the urgent need to modernize the City's infrastructure in order to ensure its continuing functioning (principally for commercial purposes) as implementations of continental theories for Renaissance town design. Wren justified his strategies of widening streets and modifying their courses so as to approximate as nearly as possible to a grid precisely on the functional grounds of 'remedying' the 'deformity and inconvenience of the Old Town', an objective which was equally responsible for his proposals for a quayside all the way along the Thames (from Blackfriars to the Tower) and the enlargement of the principal crossroads into more efficient *rondpoints*.

Yet Wren's intentions were not merely rational, in the scientific, functionalist sense (displaying as they do considerable concern for monumentalizing institutions primarily those of the state). His prioritization of the ceremonial route was equalled by his desire to render all the parish churches (in effect symbols of state and monarchy) 'conspicuous and insular' and his idea of bringing together the halls of the twelve main City companies by arranging them around a single, regular square, with the Guildhall at its centre.

Although such a plan, on functional and symbolic levels alike, lacked British precedents, continental models were available of which Wren was certainly well aware. During his extended stay in France, only shortly before the Fire, he availed himself of the opportunity to visit recently completed gardens which, as examples of the new French classical approach to landscape design, demonstrated the application of a comprehensive geometry to encompass an entire terrain, and the principle of hierarchizing routes through the use of *rondpoints* (accentuated by statues or fountains) for interconnecting the major axes.[10]

---

[9] Their authors comprised John Evelyn, Sir William Petty, Richard Newcourt, Robert Hooke, Peter Mills, Valentine Knight and Christopher Wren.
[10] Summerson, *Architecture in Britain*, pp. 115–16.

In Paris he cannot have failed to notice innovations which made it contrast so sharply with the relentlessly chaotic medieval fabric of pre-Fire London. For, if the Bourbons Henri IV and Louis XIV paralleled the Stuarts in prioritizing a ceremonial route through their capital (in this case focusing on the Tuileries and Louvre palaces, and leading to the king's country seat of Vincennes), they also went far beyond this single aim.

The virtual razing of much of Paris prior to Henri IV's ascent to the throne required him to devise and implement a comprehensive plan for his capital, consisting as much of public works (in the sense of civil engineering) as of monumental architecture. As in Restoration London, priority had to be given to overall infrastructure (due to its neglect throughout the Civil War) rather than to individual monuments. Hence the construction of the Pont Neuf and the laying out of the rue Dauphine, Place Dauphine and associated quays, the construction of the Place Royale as Paris' first regular square (a traffic-free promenade bounded by aristocratic housing), and the project for a Place de France as a monumental entrance to the city went hand in hand with the opening up of nearly seventy new roads and attempts to pave all the streets and to resolve the problems of water provision and rubbish disposal throughout the city.[11] As Blunt astutely noticed, these models provided by early seventeenth-century Parisian developments brought together, for the first time, the monumentality inherent in the civic spaces created by Renaissance Italy with the less ostentatious grouping of smallish houses, executed in relatively inexpensive materials, typical of Flemish cities. Such models, uniting as they did princely magnificence with bourgeois pride, were, of course, particularly appropriate for seventeenth-century London.[12]

At the very moment of Wren's visit to Paris, Louis XIV's far more grandiose ambitions for the capital were just beginning to be realized. Once again, although Wren showed particular interest in the state monument then under construction, visiting the building-site of the Louvre virtually every day, he cannot have failed to notice the results of the drawing up of the town's first ever accurate survey (by Gomboust, in 1652)[13] and of measures then recently enacted for the lighting and paving of streets, sewage disposal and the banishment of noxious industries. His awareness of projects as carefully guarded as Bernini's for the

[11] Pierre Couperie, *Paris au fil du temps* (Paris, 1968; London, 1970), section Xa; Anthony Blunt, *Art and Architecture in France, 1500–1700*, The Pelican History of Art (Harmondsworth, 1953), pp. 113–17; Hilary Ballon, *The Paris of Henri IV: Architecture and Urbanism* (Cambridge, Mass., 1991), chs. 2, 3 and 5.
[12] Blunt, *Art and Architecture*, pp. 113–17.
[13] It would seem likely that Gomboust's survey at least partly inspired John Ogilby and William Morgan's production of *A Large & Accurate Map of the City of London* in 1676.

east façade of the Louvre makes it unlikely that he was not cognizent with such ideas already under discussion as the widening and alignment of all major thoroughfares, the founding of a state institution to take care of retired soldiers, the provision of drinking water throughout the city, and the project for developing the district on its northern boundary around two monumental city gates.[14] All in all, regardless of the large number of impressive state or quasi-state monuments then under construction or recently completed (notably the Collège des Quatre Nations, begun in 1663, and the Palais Mazarin, of 1645), not to mention a positive flurry of church building,[15] the measures being taken during this early period of Louis XIV's reign were intended as much to render the city more functional (by improving circulation) as to beautify or dignify its appearance.

Despite the widely held assumption, which these various proposals presented to the British monarch in the wake of the Great Fire all well demonstrate, that the overall planning of the capital was a royal prerogative, the reconstruction of the City would actually depend largely upon private and corporate finance, whose interests therefore impinged heavily upon the overall result. For private property ownership enforced certain constraints upon royal ambitions for the restoration of the City, precisely because of the needs for professions and trades to maintain their established patterns of concentration within specific districts and to maintain networks, including routes to ensure easy access between wharf, warehouse and market. Thus the relative powers of Crown and Merchant were demonstrated physically, the Crown's control citywide becoming restricted primarily to the imposition of legislative codes for construction.

Nevertheless, the principles behind Wren's highly symbolic plan for London were fulfilled, regardless of the refusal to accept the details of his – or indeed any – project. For the most evident changes to the City plan would be its overall hierarchization of streets, each of which would be widened and straightened, and the attempt to construct a quayside all the way along the Thames frontage. The ceremonial route culminating in the vista of St Paul's, and several of Wren's other thoroughfares linking major institutions (all housed in monumental edifices), would also be realized. Although the Anglican state suffered after the Civil War and Interregnum from a lack of fiscal capacity, it benefited from its more clearly defined literary and iconographic rhetoric through mythological allusions and historical references.

[14] Couperie, *Paris au fil*, section XIa.
[15] 1627–: St Paul-St Louis; 1629–: Notre-Dame des Victoires; 1630–: St Jacques-du-Haut-Pas; 1632–4: Visitation Ste Marie; 1645–78: St Sulpice; 1646–78: Val de Grâce; 1653–60: St Roch; 1656: St Nicolas Chardonnet; 1664: St Louis-en-l'Ile.

Wren's achievement is best appreciated by comparing late seventeenth-century London with contemporary Antwerp or Amsterdam. Although in all three the presence of the Church was signalled throughout by multitudinous spires punctuating the skyline, only in London did a new cathedral become the predominant monument, to the cost of the secular Guildhall or City Hall. Admittedly London's Guildhall was rebuilt before St Paul's, as indeed were most of the Livery Halls, for pragmatic, commercial reasons. Yet, given the widely publicized completion of Amsterdam's Town Hall around the time of the Great Fire,[16] one might have expected greater aesthetic pretensions to be displayed in London's new Guildhall. Whilst the merchant community's severe losses in the Fire no doubt engendered financial constraints, such a wholly pragmatic explanation is questionable in the light of contemporary ambitions for the Royal Exchange, even if these were never fulfilled. The competition between rival livery companies served to diminish the visible presence of the merchant community in relation to that of the Crown still further?

The urge to plan in turn illustrates a second innovation in the architecture and urban space of London in the seventeenth century, namely an awareness of the international significance of capital status and a concomitant desire to express this through built form. These were widely shared concerns, as evident in official sermons delivered to Parliament as it plans for the physical reconstruction of the City.[17] First, London was seen as the primary symbol, and embodiment, of the nation; hence its destruction by fire was perceived as punishment for the lack of godliness among all subjects. Second, Stuart London presented itself as a divinely sanctioned imperial capital, paralleling itself with Jerusalem, Rome and Constantinople, rather than with comparable commercial centres closer to hand, notably Antwerp and Amsterdam.[18] Like them, however, its material prosperity was seen to depend on the moral conduct of its citizens, rather than on any quality of its physical design. Spiritual and material reconstruction must advance hand in hand in order that the phoenix city (another widespread concept) 'would rise greater than before'.[19] This no doubt helped to legitimize

---

[16] Although the structure was completed, and dedicated, in 1655, work on the decorative schemes continued into the mid-1660s.

[17] For example, William Stillingfleet, *A Sermon Preached before the Honourable House of Commons at St. Margarets Westminster Octob. 10. Being the Fast-day Appointed for the Late Dreadfull Fire in the City of London* (London, 1666).

[18] Stillingfleet, *Sermon*; Parry, *Golden Age*; Scampton, 'Idea and Image'.

[19] Evelyn and Pepys were amongst those voicing this idea; see also the anonymous doggerel translation of Seneca's 91st Stoic letter, published in London in the wake of the Fire: *The Fourscore and Eleventh Epistle of Lucius Annaeus Seneca . . . written upon the sudden burning of Lions in France, translated out of the original into English Verse* (London, 1666).

the Crown's emphasis – visual as much as financial – on cathedral and parish churches.

A concomitant recognition, and fear, of foreign rivalry pre-dated, but was reinforced by, the experience of continental exile enforced on many courtiers by the Civil War. It had first appeared in the early Stuart period, with continental style princely entries for truly Renaissance architecture for all civic monuments, and the probable use of Henri IV's Place Royale in Paris, and/or the Piazza dell'Arme in Leghorn, as models for the Covent Garden Piazza. In post-Fire plans, such an awareness seems particularly acute, especially with regard to the treatment of waterways, which in all the detailed projects were given more serious consideration than had hitherto been the case in London. Wren's own proposals for the Thames quayside were at once utilitarian (improving both traffic circulation and access to water, in case of fire) and aesthetic, probably inspired by his observations of the French treatment of the Seine. His treatment of the Customs House, and notably of its river façade, seemingly designed to beautify the approach to the City by boat, is pertinent in this context. Furthermore, his project for the canalization of the Fleet River has been interpreted as reflecting Dutch townscape, with its relatively straight canals, crossed by high bridges and lined with pretty uniform brick houses.[20]

The specific emphasis on London's role as capital, and moreover as *imperial* capital (of Britannia), was clearly enunciated from James I's first entry into London onwards.[21] This theme was strongly recapitulated from the Restoration, with the support of royal propaganda such as Dugdale's history of St Paul's Cathedral (which aimed to validate Anglican claims to venerability equal to that of the Church of Rome, through his spurious account of England's conversion to Christianity through St Paul's personal mission to London!).[22] Certain overall tendencies and individual features indicate an awareness of how other European cities claiming imperial capital status had used town planning and architecture to provide the necessary tangible symbols for such status.

Since the Stuart monarchy promoted London's image as an ecclesiastical capital, and, as such, as an equal and alternative to Rome, it specifically evoked many of those features of urban design first comprehensively employed by Sixtus V in his reconstruction of Rome as the world capital of Christianity. Sixtus had not imposed an abstract, resolutely orthogonal plan upon the terrain without regard for its existing

[20] T.F. Reddaway, *The Rebuilding of London after the Fire* (London, 1940), pp. 200–43.
[21] Parry, *Golden Age*.
[22] Sir William Dugdale, *The History of St. Pauls Cathedral in London* (London, 1658).

street layout and monumental buildings. Instead he had driven wide streets through the medieval fabric so as to connect the long-established pilgrimage churches into a single circuit, and this infrastructure also defined the basis for the future development of unbuilt areas towards the city's edges. Such city planning was conceived from the point of view of a person moving along these streets through the city, and therefore paid especial attention to such a person's visual perception of the city: the exploitation of gradients to enhance the churches situated at their climax; the clearing of *piazze* in front of existing monuments in order to augment their dignity; the placing of new, or transporting of ancient, monuments – obelisks, columns or fountains – focus attenion on such monuments.[23]

Sixtus' programme thus combined functional objectives – such as improving circulation, encouraging future development and providing drinking water – with aesthetic ones. Nevertheless the relative finance and publicity devoted to the various aspects of this programme suggest that for this pope the most important elements were those that served most clearly to express the sacred, Christian nature of his reconstruction of an imperial capital (for example, the transportation of the obelisks across the city and their crowning with crosses, or the replacement of the statues of Roman emperors on the columns of Marcus Anthony and Trajan by those of the apostles Peter and Paul).[24]

This latter stratagem was first clearly evoked in Wren's (and Hooke's) second design for the Monument, crowned by a statue of Charles II (the Restorer and thus second founder of the Church of England) dressed as a Roman emperor, with a bas relief around the base in antique Roman style. It was evoked again at the close of the Stuart dynasty in the scheme for a column to be erected in the Strand, crowned by a statue of Queen Anne. Furthermore, the handling of the approach to St Paul's, including the laying out of a *piazza* in front of the west façade with, eventually, the erection of a statue of Anne at its focus, suggests a familiarity with the intentions of Sixtus and subsequent popes, as does the overall street layout and the attention paid by it to the symbolic role of city gates.[25]

[23] Sylvie Pressouyre, *Rome au fil du temps* (Paris, 1973).

[24] Domenico Fontana, *Della trasportazione dell'obelisco vaticano et delle fabriche di Nostre Signore Papa Sisto V* (Rome, 1590); B. Dibner, *Moving the Obelisks* (Cambridge, Mass., 1970).

[25] The erection of an equestrian statue of Charles II (albeit a statue of a Polish king whose head had been replaced by that of the British monarch!) by the goldsmith Robert Vyners in the Stocks Market was admittedly a privately funded venture. Yet Wren's subsequent design of a façade for the new St Stephen's Walbrook, so as to better set it off, would suggest that the Crown was ready to incorporate such independent initiatives into its own, broader strategy for reordering the city fabric, wherever possible.

Sixtus' use of urban design (rather than of 'architecture' in a narrow sense) to proclaim dogma obviously offered an appropriate model for the Stuarts and Bourbons alike. Both saw themselves as operating within the Catholic tradition but exercising a certain independence from the papacy and thereby, they believed, returning to a purer form of that tradition. It is therefore not surprising if British and French designs bore considerable resemblance to each other; it was not due merely to Wren and his peers being aware of their closest rival and its parallel ambitions to promote Paris as an imperial capital.

Furthermore, such papal ambitions for modernizing Rome – by straightening and enlarging streets and piazzas, and regularizing their boundaries, so as simultaneously to ameliorate traffic flow and dignify the city – had continued after Sixtus' death and currently, under Alexander VII (1655–67) were perhaps surpassing all previous ones. The contemporaneous creation of the Piazza S. Pietro (through the late 1650s and 1660s) was but one evident manifestation,[26] which seems to have pushed these rival 'empires' to fix their eyes on Rome as their prime exemplar to ape and outdo; hence, for instance, Louis XIV's idea – again at this very moment – of using the papal architect, Bernini, to design his own Louvre.

Yet, unlike Rome, Amsterdam, Antwerp and London each derived their supremacy from their roles as commercial centres. Their continued success therefore depended upon assuring satisfactory living and working conditions for a broad middle class of tradespeople and minor merchants, artisans and craftspeople. Under such circumstances these three cities could not afford such a discrepancy as Rome maintained between the world's noblest palaces and ecclesiastical buildings (flaunted to foreign dignitaries) and the slum conditions of most of the urban fabric – infrastructure and housing alike – behind them.[27]

Once more, the state impetus underlying London's reconstruction contrasts sharply with the urban development of either Antwerp or Amsterdam. After a republican Interregnum, Charles II had pragmatic political reasons (equivalent to Henri IV's earlier in the century) for modernizing his capital city; by attracting his most powerful subjects to spend more time there, he could control them more closely.

Nevertheless, the innovation within the field of architecture and urban space which may also have most affected achievement in other fields was the state's attempt to control the construction process itself, through the introduction, in the wake of the Great Fire, of legislation codifying such fundamental norms as the layout of buildings and the proscription of certain materials, together with legal and administrative bodies and

---

[26] Richard Krautheimer, *The Rome of Alexander VII 1655–67* (Princeton, 1985).
[27] *Ibid.*, pp. 126 and 131.

measures to ensure its enactment.[28] Certainly such legislative measures had been invoked elsewhere previously, but they had enjoyed comparatively little success. As early as 1547 Pope Gregory XIII had issued a bull decreeing the straightening of streets, the systematic elimination of alleyways (and indeed all spaces between neighbouring houses) and the facing of streets with walls to hide ruins or unbuilt sites.[29] In 1607, Henri IV had passed similarly ineffective legislation for aligning houses along street fronts, which forbade jettying out over streets and construction in timber, and attempted to enforce the paving of streets and the disposal of rubbish.[30]

Whilst the post-Fire legislation has been fairly criticized as simply acting upon past experience, rather than making any effort to foresee future needs, such conservative pragmatism seems to have been a more effective strategy, especially given the context of mass destruction and the pressing commercial need for rapid reconstruction.[31] This explains the choice of measures taken: the widening and straightening of streets, the removal or contraction of conduits within them; paving and drainage reforms; the proscription of jettying, and the consequent regularization of street frontages; the introduction of standard designs for housing (defined according to the importance of the street); the imposition of construction standards, governing building height, number of floors, thickness of walls, cellar depth and party walls; and the proscription of timber for use in external or loadbearing walls.[32]

Such regulations were, however, quite revolutionary within Britain, and had far-reaching effects. First, at a city scale 'eminent and notorious streets' were widened sufficiently to prevent any future fire crossing them and all streets were widened sufficiently to allow 'convenient passage' (many, if not most, alleys and minor lanes being suppressed in the process). The clear intention to extend the quayside (and with it the wharfage) along the entire riverfront of the Thames and to clean and canalize the Fleet (again increasing the available wharfage) would have further improved circulation, and thus concretely aided trade to and within the City.[33] The legislation also, albeit less successfully, included the first serious attempt to survey the City.[34]

[28] Although it was probably building on the practices established by the London Viewers, it went much further (and indeed operated separately from them): ed. J.S. Loengard, *London Viewers and their Certificates, 1509–1558* (London, 1989).
[29] Pressouyre, *Rome au fil.*
[30] Couperie, *Paris au fil*, section Xa.; Ballon, *Paris of Henri IV*, p. 7.
[31] Reddaway, *Rebuilding of London*, p. 79.   [32] *Ibid.*, pp. 79–82.
[33] See the Royal Proclamation of 13 September 1666 (Reddaway, *Rebuilding of London*, p. 49).   [34] Reddaway, *Rebuilding of London*, p. 289.

Second, at the scale of individual buildings, the legislation was equally radical, and probably even more influential in the long term, in that it eventually became the model followed (both in terms of regulations and in terms of the mechanisms set up to ensure their observation) throughout the country. Taking the house as the individual unit from which the City was constituted, the 1667 Act prescribed its scale, minimum standards for its construction (defined in terms of space and daylighting), uniform frontages (prohibiting jettying) and building materials. Most significantly, such standardization of design enabled much speedier reconstruction after the Fire than would otherwise have been possible.[35] Parliament was sufficiently foresighted to ensure the observation of this legislation through the simultaneous introduction of Surveyors to oversee its implementation (another measure which would eventually be adopted by boroughs throughout the land) and of appropriate administrative reforms, notably the handing over of authority for drains and sewers and for street levelling, paving and cleaning (including the levying of taxes required for these purposes) to a single body of Commissioners, who could operate more effectively than had their predecessors appointed by individual wards or parishes.[36]

Although some observers regretted the missing of a rare opportunity to build a truly Renaissance capital city in Britain,[37] the reconstruction achieved was far more than a mere re-creation of the previous settlement. Although its appearance was due to utterly pragmatic legislation, totally devoid of any aesthetic, let alone stylistic, considerations, an improved sewerage system, wider streets (now cleared of market stalls and paved), more open intersections, and more uniform (predominantly brick) façades not only made it more habitable but also made it appear much more modern, and thus 'beautiful' according to contemporary criteria.[38] In the longer term, the same legislation probably prevented the recurrence of any fire on such a scale, as well as (at least until the nineteenth century) any epidemic equivalent to the Plague which had preceded the Great Fire.[39]

A fourth major achievement (this time a more purely architectural one) concerned building typology. Although this was apparent across the country, Britain's particular politico-religious situation – where the summit of secular and ecclesiastical power was personified by a single figure, the monarch – concentrated the evidence for this within the capital. As in town planning, awareness of continental developments

---

[35] *Ibid.*, p. 129.   [36] *Ibid.*, pp. 56 and 286.
[37] Notably John Gwynne and Wren's own grandson, whom Reddaway takes firmly to task for misrepresentation (*Ibid.*, pp. 32–3).   [38] *Ibid.*, pp. 190–3 and 289–90.
[39] *Ibid.*, p. 299.

led to their emulation and often to attempts to supersede them. The institutions established for retired soldiers and sailors at Chelsea (built from 1681) and Greenwich (begun in 1694), respectively, would exemplify this tendency: Chelsea was probably inspired by the Invalides in Paris (1670), and possibly also by Kilmainham Hospital, Dublin (1680).[40]

Again it was the Crown's and the Anglican Church's recognition of foreign innovations and, equally, of foreign observation of Britain which spurred a greater concern with the image of the nation, as presented by its monuments. It is therefore not surprising to find that buildings displaying greatest innovation were precisely those perceived by the authorities as most clearly embodying the authority of the Anglican state. Most notably, the new model developed by Wren for the parish church represented a dramatic rupture with a European-wide tradition, continuous from the Middle Ages, of the cruciform plan (with its clear division between clergy in the choir and laity in the nave), in favour of a more unitary space. Admittedly, seventeenth-century churches in Amsterdam departed just as radically from the traditional Roman Catholic model, but here any similarity ends. For whereas the Dutch Calvinists, concerned with preaching the Word rather than participating in the Mass, devised compact, non-directional plans, the Anglicans continued to celebrate the Holy Communion regularly and thus maintained a strong sense of orientation towards the altar. Any resemblance between Wren's plans and those of his Dutch counterparts is merely accidental, due to the site constraints enforced upon him.

Restoration Anglicans, like their Gallican contemporaries, sought legitimacy by identifying themselves with a Church pre-dating Roman hegemony, and thus supposedly purer than their medieval antecedents. Both therefore turned to the 'Primitive' Church, evoking Byzantine models (albeit much limited by their deficiencies in knowledge and experience of these models!). Close investigation shows that Wren's centralized yet clearly orientated city churches were inspired by Byzantine *martyria*, rather than by Dutch hall churches, as has often been erroneously claimed, while his preferred model for the parish church, embodied in St James's Piccadilly, adopted a basilica form, which became explicit in the work of his pupil, amanuensis and successor, Nicholas Hawksmoor.[41] The latter's design for a 'basilica after the Primitive Christians' (which he offered as the prototype for all the parish churches to be erected as a result of the eighteenth-century Fifty One New Churches Act) explains the

[40] Summerson, *Architecture in Britain*, pp. 138 and 143–4.
[41] Kerry Downes, *Hawkesmoor* (London, 1959).

incorporation of various novel features, including a large entrance hall (evoking a narthex), clear glazing, galleries over the side aisles with corner stairtowers, an Eastern apse, etc. This 'primitivist' orientation explains the preoccupation of Wren and his Gallic contemporaries alike with the dome, an entirely novel feature in both British and French ecclesiastical architecture.

As in the field of building typology, so in that of the processes of architectural design and construction Britain's politico-religious situation led to innovations which set it apart from mainland Europe. In 1660, Britain was more independent of its immediate past, in this area, than were its European counterparts, owing to the rupture wrought by the Civil War, but equally by the subsequent return to monarchial rule.

Although a certain degree of continuity persisted in the building crafts, and therefore in vernacular building, the same could not be said of Architecture, and therefore of monuments. Moreover, even at the level of craft, much change occurred during the seventeenth century, owing not least to the arrival in England of significant numbers of immigrant craftspeople, and to the experience brought back by exiles returning from the continent. Historians have already noted the importation of building styles and methods, particularly from the Low Countries, probably because of their visible presence today in the form of such easily identifiable features as 'Dutch gables'.

Such historiography, however, directs attention towards the product, while neglecting the underlying design process. This exemplifies a problem inherent in all historical research into architecture, in that the tangible products are much easier to grasp than the mental processes responsible for their production. Yet in this case it is worth making the effort to uncover design, since it is here that the contrasts both between pre- and post-Restoration Stuart society and with continental practice are most acute.

For in design methodology the rupture wrought at the Restoration was almost total. After a long Interregnum devoid of funding or political ambition for monumental architecture, continuity with the past had been effectively broken, since all those responsible for prestige construction under the previous regime had now either died or fallen into political disgrace. Consequently, during the post-Restoration period, and despite the quantity of urgent building work apparent even before the disaster of the Great Fire (a backlog caused by two decades virtually devoid of state patronage, plus the degradations directly resulting from the Civil War), commissions fell overwhelmingly to a single individual from outside the architectural or construction milieu – Christopher

Wren. Moreover, this Oxford Professor of Astronomy was to hold the post of Surveyor of the Kings Works for nearly half a century, longer than any other in the entire history of the Office of Works.[42]

What Wren lacked in any sense of obligation to the (by now accepted) authority of codified classicism, or in experience of building construction, he made up for by applying his training as an experimental scientist to the design process. Freed from the conventions of the classical tradition, he pursued a more strictly functionalist approach to solving design problems, with a resultant originality that yielded improvements in, for instance, acoustic performance. He showed no fear of experimenting with unorthodox geometries (witness his city churches). His academic interest, and prowess, in mathematics enabled him to exploit calculation in order to experiment with structures, and thus achieve wider spans or exploit unusual structural solutions, often thereby expanding the spatial repertoire (domes, saucer domes, etc., in his city churches). His practice as a modern experimental scientist seems to have left him a preference for the model over the drawing in his development of designs, which further encouraged more plastic and spatial exploration, but probably at the expense of refinement of detail. His obsession, since childhood, with inventing machines, led to an interest in devising machines to improve the potential scale of buildings and the rate of construction. All in all he personified innovation.

Of course he was no lone genius, but rather the prime member of the modern scientific community (and, more precisely, of that court elite, the Royal Society) to be operating in the field of architecture. As such, his work should be considered as the fruit of a preceding period of incubation, namely the 1650s; whilst no money was being spent on the fabric of London's buildings and monuments, the evident backlog of work in this domain inspired many like minds (including Evelyn and Hooke as well as Wren) to reflect on future plans.

Yet this spirit of innovation and disregard for orthodoxy, far from dying with Wren, flourished and developed after his demise, becoming in the early eighteenth century what has too often been (mis)labelled as 'the English baroque'. This school of original and pungently witty mannerism was spearheaded by two rivals, as different as one could imagine, and yet equally expressing this quintessentially English and early modern approach to architectural design. One was Nicholas Hawksmoor, Wren's apprentice and eventual amanuensis, who developed his master's ideas, infusing them with a more profound understanding of building materials and a wider architectural culture. The other was Sir John Vanbrugh,

[42] H.M. Colvin, 'The Surveyorship of Sir Christopher Wren' in H.M. Colvin (ed.), *The History of the King's Works*, vol. V (London., 1976), pp. 19–38.

soldier and playwright, thus like Wren an outsider to the practice of designing and executing buildings.

Within the context I have outlined above, any modifications of 'style', of superficial decoration, seem relatively insignificant. Furthermore, the pattern here hardly differed from that already established a century earlier, if not before, and was in no way specific to London but rather was nationwide in occurrence. Decorative techniques, features and motifs diffused from the top down, from the court to the (often nouveau riche) merchant classes. Moreover, given the imposition of building codes in London, the domain available for individual display was somewhat curtailed. Decoration, however, is not so much a matter of architecture (of spatial design) as of craftsmanship. The availability of high-quality craftsmanship in England during this period – notably in wood carving and plaster decoration – may well further explain the propensity for private dwellings to have care and expense lavished on richly decorated interiors rather than on spatial innovation or on external decoration in this period.

Throughout the period, London benefited from the exceptional concentration of a flourishing trading economy and a monarchy within a single city and from a parallel concentration of population, and thus labour (especially skilled labour), as the City's commercial and political supremacy attracted large numbers both from the provinces and from abroad. This in turn enabled the development of financial and intellectual institutions, and of specialized communities of diverse trades or crafts. These peculiar circumstances ensured that, in terms of architecture and urban space, London maintained its priority over cities in the provinces and even achieved a certain advance upon cities of equivalent status abroad.

These achievements reflected several inherent tensions. The first attempts by the state to exercise planning controls were counter-balanced by its necessary reliance upon the private sector to finance the majority of new construction; private land ownership thus limited the scope for the imposition of order from above. Consequently the Crown's projection of its desired self-image, through the construction of an architecturally symbolic capital, was restricted to the erection of isolated monuments and fragments within a larger sea of privately commissioned buildings, which inevitably compromised any overall planning desired by the Crown.[43] Yet despite the relatively constrained sphere of operation open to the Crown, it was in the public sphere that the majority of innovations in design method and constructional techniques took place.

[43] This perhaps became most acute in the case of the Thames quayside (see Reddaway, *Rebuilding of London*, p. 225).

London was, by this date, an exceptional city within the kingdom. Nevertheless, it is important that these achievements are perceived not only in terms of understanding the phenomenon of London itself but equally as indications of what happened later elsewhere. That so much was achieved in this city at this time might have been due primarily to the particular concentration of financial and governmental power it enjoyed, but it was probably also sustained, at the end of the seventeenth century, by the financial revolution whereby, as a result of fiscal policy, money was disproportionately drawn into the capital from the provinces.

From the Renaissance, Britain had trailed far behind continental Europe in architecture and town planning. Indeed, several of the most salient innovations in London's architecture and planning noted above represent aspects of Britain's extremely late espousal of Renaissance ideas and practices. Yet this period also – and, in the context of an enquiry into 'achievement', perhaps more significantly – marked Britain's positive moves towards autonomy from continental models and practices and its development of entirely original ones in their place. More precisely, whilst the planning of urban spaces drew heavily on classicizing models offered by rival 'imperial' capitals, and despite the emergence across Europe of national identities leading to a parallel use of symbolic architecture to articulate underlying national ambitions, the somewhat fortuitous achievements in London in design processes and construction methods alike put Britain ahead of its continental rivals. In other words, the great achievements in this domain seem to be due to an unplanned rupture in the succession of architectural designers, coincident with the rise, and royal patronage, of modern experimental science.

Although the Great Fire certainly opened up opportunities and concentrated minds on the devising of a workable plan for the reconstruction of London and on its execution, rebuilding also reflected the influence of the Restoration that had so recently preceded it. For, without that prior cultural revolution, which made the British court more aware of its standing relative to continental rivals and of the potential propaganda usage of the capital's layout and architecture, the reconstruction was likely to have been less ambitious and yet, in consequence, more thoroughly pragmatic.

If we now find this period of British architecture of particular interest, it is probably partly owing to the sheer quantity of its artefacts – many of them monumental – that remain, not least in the City of London. It is hard not to notice, for instance, London's principal cathedral or the three dozen odd Wren parish churches which still remain in whole or part. Perhaps it is also, albeit less consciously, due to the originality, almost eccentricity (in comparison with their European counterparts), of these buildings. Yet, as has already been suggested, the most significant innovations, and achievements, within the fields of architecture and urban space in London during this period were not so much a matter of the built environment produced as of the processes through which it was conceived and realized. Moreover, the greatest achievement in the long term was perhaps not even the change wrought in the way in which individual architects designed, but rather the inception of a system of legislative and administrative controls which at once encompassed the development and execution of such designs, thus affecting all those involved in the construction process. It was not simply that the degree of standardization which this implied enabled the speedy reconstruction essential for preserving the continuation of the capital's economy, but that, in embracing such a modern approach (albeit almost inadvertently and for purely pragmatic reasons), the physical infrastructure required by a modern trading capital was put in place. More fundamentally, a system was set up that would promote its continued development.

Part 4

Fine and decorative arts

8   The fine and decorative arts in Antwerp's golden age

Hans Vlieghe

The artistic situation in sixteenth-century Antwerp was characterized by the rapid growth of the number of artists and artisans and by the geographical diversity of their origins.[1] According to Guicciardini, there were 300 artists among Antwerp's population of 100,000 by the year 1560, a figure that represented more than twice the number of bakers resident in the city. This striking development became apparent from the late fifteenth century onwards and was increasingly stimulated by the growing presence of a wealthy class of international merchants who were willing to spend conspicuously on luxury goods of various kinds.

In painting, the overall view of sixteenth-century Antwerp is a rather confusing one, which is typical for a period of intense growth and transition, moulded by so many new and often contradictory influences.[2] Nevertheless two phases can clearly be distinguished, with the middle of the century as a watershed between them. Before *c.*1500 Antwerp painting can best be defined as a transitional process. New external influences, of the Renaissance, became grafted upon a traditional pattern, but a successful amalgamation was not really achieved. The virtually unceasing growth in the number of painters forced them quite naturally into mutual competition, which in its turn gave birth to the typical Antwerp phenomenon of artistic specialization. These specialized areas met very specific needs.

---

[1] See Lodovico Guicciardini, *Description de tout le Pais-Bas* (Antwerp, 1567), p. 168.

[2] The most detailed recent general account of sixteenth-century painting in Antwerp is found in the relevant chapters in G. von der Osten and H. Vey, *Painting and Sculpture in Germany and the Netherlands: 1500–1600*, The Pelican History of Art (Harmondsworth, 1969); see also G.T. Faggin, *La pittura ad Anversa nel Cinquecento* (Raccolta Pisana di Saggi e Studi 24 (Florence, 1968). The relevant source material on which all later studies are based is to be found in Carel van Mander, *Het Schilder-Boeck* (Haarlem, 1604); P. Rombouts and T. van Lerius, *De Liggeren en andere historische archieven der Antwerpsche Sint-Lucasgilde*, 2 vols. (Antwerp, 1872); F.J. van den Branden, *Geschiedenis der Antwerpsche schilderschool*, 3 vols. (Antwerp, 1883). An excellent critical *status quaestionis* is C. van de Velde, 'De schilderkunst' in *Antwerpen in de XVIde eeuw* (Antwerp, 1975), pp. 419–45.

Thus, history painting in this first phase of the 'Antwerp Renaissance' remained almost exclusively devoted to religious imagery. It manifested itself in altarpieces but much more so in small-scale scenes of a more intimate character which functioned as precious interior decoration in the houses of the middle and upper-middle classes, as well as meeting their personal needs for devotion. From the beginning of the sixteenth century onwards it is also clear that the more important history painters deliberately began to adopt Renaissance forms and to mix them with style features and motifs of a more traditional Gothic origin.

Alongside the painters of traditional devotional imagery, some painters began to specialize in the field of portraiture, while others helped to give birth to landscape and so-called 'genre' painting. Portraiture must be seen in the first place as the expression of the self-assurance of the wealthy burgher class.[3] Landscape painting may also be regarded within the context of a growing interest in various kinds of natural phenomena, also manifested in map-making and the publication of herbaria. Thus, a very interesting and striking comparison has been drawn between the topographical style and the characteristic bird's eye view of sixteenth-century Antwerp landscape painting, as defined by such artists as Joachim Patinir and Pieter Brueghel the Elder, and similar features apparent in contemporary map-making.[4] At the same time, moralizing and satirizing company-pieces could be interpreted as representations – either *in bono* or *in malo* – of the merchant class's ethical standards.[5] In Antwerp this particular category of painting was initiated by Quinten Matsys. His scenes representing and satirizing situations which were considered examples of 'deviant' social behaviour and/or human folly inaugurated the specific evolution of one of the most genuine aspects of Antwerp painting, which would also become the starting-point for seventeenth-century Dutch genre painting.

Some painters, however, were successful in several specializations. Thus, the more outstanding history painters were frequently sought

[3] Flemish seventeenth-century portrait painting has been interpreted in a very penetrating study by Katlijne van der Stighelen, 'Burgers en hun portretten. Een dubbelzinnige liefdesrelatie' in *Stad in Vlaanderen. Cultuur en maatschappij 1477–1787*, exhibition catalogue (Brussels, 1991), pp. 141–56. No doubt her conclusions can likewise be applied to the sixteenth–century situation.

[4] See W. Gibson, *Bruegel*, The World of Art Library, (London, 1977), pp. 25–6, and, in greater detail, W. Gibson, *'Mirror of the Earth'. The World Landscape in Sixteenth-Century Flemish Painting* (Princeton, N.J., 1989), pp. 48–59.

[5] See e.g. the general introductions to genre painting and its functioning by P. Vandenbroeck, 'Van "hoge" normen en "laag" volk. Over de zin van de genreschildering' in *Van Bruegel tot Rubens. De Antwerpse schilderschool 1550–1650*, exhibition catalogue (Antwerp, 1992–3) (Ghent and Antwerp), 1992, pp. 29–36, and K. Renger, 'Flemish Genre Painting: Low Life–High Life–Daily Life' in P. Sutton (ed.), *The Age of Rubens*, exhibition catalogue (Boston and Ghent, 1993), pp. 171–81.

after as portraitists, often in response to commissions from outside the city. One may suppose that this aspect of their work was better rewarded than the many extant products of average portraitists.[6] Another typical feature which becomes apparent very early in Antwerp specialized painting is the phenomenon of collaboration. One of the earliest known examples is the collaboration between the landscapist Patinir and the figure painter Matsys, whereby the latter painted religious imagery in order to fill in the former's landscapes.[7] Specialization and collaboration would remain one of the most typical characteristics of Antwerp painting until late in the seventeenth century.[8] Subdivisions within the main genres proliferated, such as architectural painting, seascapes, still-life painting, flower pieces and kitchen scenes. A very striking example of a new topic which became increasingly popular and marketable in early sixteenth-century Antwerp painting is *grillen* (burlesque scenes), clearly derived from the work of Hieronymus Bosch but entirely out of its original visionary context.[9] This tendency towards further proliferation and subdivision would continue throughout the seventeenth century, thus proving that painters were constantly in search of new niches for selling their products.[10]

Indeed, to a very great extent paintings produced in Antwerp from the later fifteenth century onwards found their way onto the open market. They

[6] Judging from the innumerable anonymous portraits appearing in sixteenth- and seventeenth-century inventories, to a very important extent portrait painting must have been left to inferior artists in the 'bread-and-butter' category. Probably only the wealthiest citizens wanted some well-known history painter to draw their likeness, expecting this to give their portrait specific added value by enriching it with a well-balanced composition or enlivening it with a vivid expression. And this is what distinguishes portraits by such outstanding painters as Matsys, van Cleve or Floris from the work of the mere routine specialists. The fact that average portraiture was not esteemed very highly may also be seen in Carel van Mander's *Schilder-Boeck*, fol. 281r, where it is considered a minor branch of the arts (see also H. Miedema, *Karel van Mander. Den grondt der edel vry schilder-const uitgegeven en van vertaling en commentaar voorzien*, Utrecht, 1973, 2, p. 346), not really challenging the inventiveness of the artist.
[7] See J. Koch, *Joachim Patinir* (Princeton, N.J., 1968), especially pp. 49–55.
[8] See K. van der Stighelen, 'Produktiviteit en samenwerking in het Antwerpse kunstenaarsmilieu, 1620–1640', *Driemaandelijks Tijdschrift Gemeentekrediet* 44, 172 (1990), pp. 5–15; for a typical case study, see K. van der Stighelen, 'De (atelier-) bedrijvigheid van Andries Snellinck (1583–1653) en Co', *Jaarboek Koninklijk Museum voor Schone Kunsten Antwerpen* (1989), pp. 303–42.
[9] This phenomenon was studied at great length by G. Unverfehrt, *Hieronymus Bosch. Die Rezeption seiner Kunst im frühen 16. Jahrhundert* (Berlin, 1980); see also, in a more general context, W. Gibson, *Hieronymus Bosch*, The World of Art Library (London, 1973), pp. 163, 167. It should also be mentioned here that Pieter Bruegel the Elder's early activity as a copyist of Bosch motifs on behalf of Hieronymus Cock's print publishing house has to be understood in the same light (see e.g. Gibson, *Bruegel*, pp. 44–64).
[10] For the essence and mechanisms of artistic specialization in Antwerp, see the very enlightening article by Arnout Balis, 'De nieuwe genres en het burgerlijk mecenaat' in *Stad in Vlaanderen*, pp. 237–54.

176   *Hans Vlieghe*

were sold at the weekly Friday markets, but also at the more prominent Onze-Lieve-Vrouwepand. Apart from being presented there, paintings were also shipped as far as Spain and Scandinavia.[11] They were produced by individual masters but workshops must have been set up quite early for serial production, often with a repetitive character. The numerous small-scale religious scenes, especially *Adorations of the Magi* and *Passion* scenes, painted by the so-called 'Antwerp mannerists' from the first decades of the sixteenth century onwards, are among the first known examples.[12]

This, however, is not to say that commissions were unimportant. There is an obvious correlation with the fact that the growth of Antwerp's population stimulated the construction and enlargement of churches and other buildings with a more or less official character, which had to be decorated. The interior decoration of churches was by far the most important of these artistic commissions, but it was largely financed by the members of the wealthy bourgeoisie. They not only had luxurious epitaphs commemorating and glorifying themselves, but also paid for the many altarpieces that were needed. The same sponsors, however, were acting in a collaborative effort, as representatives of the main guilds. Apparently, some of the most outstanding works were the result of corporate sponsorship. The guilds, which incorporated some of the wealthiest among the many Antwerp professionally skilled craftsmen, acted as outstanding patrons of the arts by ordering altarpieces from the most prominent Antwerp painters.[13]

As we have seen, the style of these early sixteenth-century paintings, especially of the history paintings, makes a rather uneven impression, showing the typical features of a '*Mischstil*'. New forms originating in Italian Renaissance schemes were grafted onto an iconographical and typological system rooted in late-medieval imagery. A good example is offered here by the altarpieces of Quinten Matsys, where traditional fifteenth-century iconographical schemes were 'remoulded' in a typical Italian High Renaissance style clearly derived from Leonardo da Vinci.

[11] For the origins of Antwerp's art trade and selling for the open market, see D. Ewing, 'Marketing Art in Antwerp, 1460–1560: Our Lady's Pand', *The Art Bulletin* 72 (1990), pp. 558–84. See also the recent study by F. Vermeylen, 'Exporting Art across the Globe. The Antwerp Art Market in the Sixteenth Century', *Nederlands Kunsthistorisch Jaarboek* 50 (1999), pp. 13–29.

[12] For the specific paintings produced by the 'Antwerp mannerists' and their function, see van de Velde, 'Schilderkunst', p. 425.

[13] Unfortunately, as a result of iconoclastic actions in 1566 and 1581 we have only a fragmented idea of the original number of altarpieces adorning Antwerp's main churches during the earlier decades of the sixteenth century. Anyway, immediately after the re-Catholicization of Antwerp in 1585 this tradition was resumed: thus for years to follow commissions for paintings to adorn the various guild chapels in the Cathedral became the most important in the city (see in this respect, D. Freedberg, *Iconoclasm and Painting in the Revolt of the Netherlands 1566–1609* (New York and London, 1988), pp. 195–243).

Matsys was also influenced by the latter's '*sfumato*'. Joos van Cleve's work offers a rather different approach. His picturesque detail makes an undeniably late-Gothic flamboyant impression. Specific details, however, such as the stance of certain of his figures, have an obvious Italian Renaissance look.[14] The often rather bizarre and ambivalent character of this style may, to some extent at least, be explained by the fact that Renaissance forms and motifs resulted only partially from direct experience of the works of Italian masters and their antique prototypes. Initially, in an important number of cases, Antwerp-based painters must have become acquainted with the Renaissance through copies and engravings. Nevertheless, there was also personal contact with original works which were on view in the Netherlands, such as the famous Raphael cartoons in Brussels.[15] And, last but not least, an incessant need was felt to travel to Italy to study both Italian Renaissance and antique art *in situ*.[16]

Still, even in this 'mixed' and 'impure' form, the early stage of Renaissance adaptation in Antwerp painting undoubtedly betrays a growing interest in the new style. The cosmopolitan character of the class of wealthy merchants and entrepreneurs, their experience of travel and, not least, a growing familiarity with humanist teaching and learning must have quickly led them to appreciate the innovative Italianate and 'all antica' features and motifs we call 'Renaissance'.

It was only after the mid-sixteenth century that a purer form of Renaissance painting emerged in Antwerp as a result of improved knowledge of its concepts. This change is strongly linked to the activity of Frans Floris de Vriendt who, after a long stay in Rome, settled in Antwerp permanently in 1547.[17] His contemporary Lodovico Guicciardini had

[14] Characteristic examples of Matsys' style are the *St. Anne* altarpiece (ordered in 1507; Brussels, Musées Royaux des Beaux-Arts de Belgique) and the *Entombment* altarpiece (ordered in 1508; Antwerp, Koninklijk Museum voor Schone Kunsten); see L. Silver, *The Paintings of Quinten Massys with Catalogue Raisonné* (Oxford, 1984), pp. 201–5, cat. 10–11. A striking example from the œuvre of Joos van Cleve is his *Death of the Holy Virgin*, dated 1515 (Cologne, Wallraf-Richartz-Museum); see e.g. M.J. Friedländer, *Early Netherlandish Painting* (9a, Leiden and Brussels, 1972), p. 19, no. 16, pl. 32–3.
[15] For these famous and very influential cartoons, see especially J. Shearman, *Raphael's Cartoons in the Collection of Her Majesty the Queen and the Tapestries for the Sixtine Chapel* (London, 1972).
[16] See e.g. the essay by Nicole Dacos, 'Om te zien en te leren' in *Fiamminghi a Roma*, exhibition catalogue (Brussels and Ghent, 1995), pp. 14–31. The growing importance of the Italian journey may be reflected in the foundation in 1572 of the Antwerp Confraternity of 'Romanists', which grouped all those who had travelled to Rome, either as pilgrims or for business purposes. The latter group included a growing number of artists and artisans. See, in this connection, E. Dilis, *La Confrérie des Romanistes* (Antwerp, 1923).
[17] The historical importance of Frans Floris was first made clear by Carl van de Velde, in his monograph *Frans Floris (1519/20–1670). Leven en Werken*, Verhandelingen van de Koninklijke Academie voor Wetenschappen, Letteren en Schone Kunsten van België, 30 (Brussels, 1975), 2 vols.; see also Z. Zaremba Filipczak, *Picturing Art in Antwerp 1550–1700* (Princeton, N.J., 1987), pp. 11–44.

already praised him for his 'inventions'. Indeed, he made clear the distinction between the responsibility of the creative 'inventor' and the subordinate task of the 'executor' in his characteristic way of signing his works 'Frans Floris Invenit et Fecit'. He was acting as a true entrepreneur, supervising a number of skilled assistants who all had to work according to their master's directions and wishes. He also indicated his conviction that a painter's activity was an intellectual one and could best be defined as the work of the *'pictor doctus'*. Floris demonstrated this conspicuously by painting an allegory of the arts on the façade of his house in Antwerp, which by clearly being devoted to the promotion of painting as an *ars liberalis* must have impressed the onlooker as Italian art theory made visual.[18] Apart from Floris' activity, the legitimation of painting as a liberal art manifested itself in other instances. Thus, Dominicus Lampsonius began what he intended to be a true Vasarian history of Flemish painting. For several reasons his enterprise eventually became limited in 1572 to a series of artist's portraits with short Latin inscriptions.[19] Further, in 1594, the Theatrum Pacis, one of the stages erected on the occasion of the State Entry of Archduke Ernest of Austria, showed *Pictura* and *Sculptura* as the equals of the seven *artes liberales* and in their company.[20] Also after 1550, the *Liggeren,* or members' list, of the Antwerp St Luke's guild increasingly distinguished between the profession of *schilder* (painter) and that of the ordinary *huisschilder* (house painter), *doeckschilder* (painter of cheap work on canvas), or even *cladschilder* (dauber).[21]

Stylistic changes were most obviously manifested in a new monumentality that definitely broke with the *Mischstil*. The principles of the Italian

[18] Apart from the literature mentioned in the preceding note, see also C. van de Velde, 'The Painted Decoration of Floris's House', in G. Cavalli-Björkman (ed.), *Netherlandish Mannerism. Papers given at a Symposium in Nationalmuseum, Stockholm, September 21–22, 1984* (Stockholm, 1985), pp. 127–34.
[19] D. Lampsonius, *Pictorum aliquot celebrium Germaniae Inferioris Effigies* (Antwerp, 1572); see also J. Puraye (ed.), *Dominique Lampson. Les effigies des peintres les plus célèbres des Pays-Bas* (Bruges, 1956), and J. Becker, 'Zur niederländischen Kunstliteratur des 16. Jahrhunderts: Dominicus Lampsonius', *Nederlands Kunsthistorisch Jaarboek* 24 (1973), pp. 45–61.
[20] See J. Bochius, *Descriptio Publicae Gratulationis Spectaculorum et Ludium in Adventu Sereniss. Principis Ernesti* (Antwerp, 1595), p. 84; further to this subject, see A. Doutrepont, 'Martin de Vos et l'entrée triomphale d'Ernest d'Autriche à Anvers', *Bulletin de l'Institut historique belge de Rome* 18 (1937), pp. 137 ff. and Filipczak, *Picturing Art*, p. 17.
[21] This evolution, however, took time: see Filipczak, *Picturing Art*, pp. 20–1. In the course of the seventeenth century the distinction between the two categories was further defined, as has been shown by Lydia De Pauw-De Veen, *De begrippen 'schilder', 'schilderij' en 'schilderen' in de zeventiende eeuw*, Verhandelingen van de Koninklijke Academie voor Wetenschappen, Letteren en Schone Kunsten van België. Klasse der Schone Kunsten, 22 (Brussels, 1969), pp. 16–37.

High Renaissance were deliberately imitated in a purer form. Indeed, Floris inaugurated in Antwerp a concept of painting clearly inspired by the classicizing monumentality of the so-called *maniera grande*.[22] He was a very versatile painter. His œuvre comprises religious altarpieces, scenes from the Old Testament and portraits, but also numerous representations inspired by classical antiquity. The importance of the last category is especially revealing. It makes clear that the taste of the wealthy Antwerp buyers of these works must have become permeated, by degrees, by a more learned and humanist vein. For these works were largely destined for private commissions. In an important sense these monumental Antwerp paintings illustrating secular subject matter inspired by the ancients were an entirely new genre. It is striking that, from now on, collectors such as the famous Nicolaas Jonghelinck became more interested in themes derived from classical mythology and other learned subject matter.[23]

Style, as a qualitative aspect, can henceforth be considered a surplus value. Although the notion of a work of art bought for its intrinsic aesthetic value was especially common from the seventeenth century onwards, its origins may be found much earlier. Proof of this may be seen in the circumstance that, from the later sixteenth century onwards, collections of paintings were being built up in Antwerp which also became valued for their artistic or stylistic quality and for their rarity. A good example is the paintings of Joachim Beuckelaer, whose work in the years following his death fetched twelve times the initial price.[24]

We also see how a specialized art trade now began to organize itself. The growing importance of this trade was already evident in the opening in 1540 of the 'Schilderspand' in the then newly erected Exchange Hall. This was set up as a permanent gallery where painters had the opportunity to sell their works.[25] Art dealers in Antwerp also had to register as members of the St Luke's guild. To judge from the latter's lists, art dealers began to distinguish themselves as members of a specific professional group especially from about the middle of the sixteenth century onwards.[26] More and more, these dealers also began to act as middlemen

[22] The importance of Frans Floris as the herald in Antwerp of a typical High Renaissance monumentality is clearly demonstrated in van de Velde, *Frans Floris*.

[23] See van de Velde, 'Schilderkunst', p. 433.

[24] According to van Mander, *Schilder-Boeck*, fol. 238r: 'want de dinghen die hy binnen zijn leven veel maeckte / en voor cleenen loon / zijn nae zijn doot en tegenwoordigh in soo groot achten gheworden / dat se somtijts wel twaelfmael meer / als sy ingecocht waren / ghelden en geern betaelt worden'.   [25] See Filipczak, *Picturing Art*, p. 21.

[26] See Rombouts and van Lerius, *Liggeren*, vol. I, pp. 186 (Bartholomeus de Mompere, 1583), 220 (Gheert Gysbrechtssen, 1560), 229 (Merten de Backere, 1564), 240 (Cornelis Darthois, 1570), 246 (Lambertus Boxstaen, 1572), 250 (Adriaen Huybrechts, 1573), 262 (Goyvaert van Bredael, 1577), 272 (Gillis Sadeler, 1580), 279 (Hans Liefrinck, 1581).

between potential clients (including foreign dealers) and specific artists, some of whom were working in their personal service. A good example is offered here by the activity of the painter Jacob de Backer, who painted on behalf of the Antwerp dealer Antonie van Palermo between *c.*1575 and 1585.[27] The prominent role of art dealers further fostered the typical Antwerp specialization and division of labour: thus dealers could also act as middlemen in another way, for example by ordering landscape specialists to paint scenery details before passing the paintings to the workshops of other specialists who were expected to add human figures.[28]

The growing importance of artistic quality may finally become clear from the fact that the income of a painter such as Floris was seven times that of a stonemason.[29] Nevertheless, until the seventeenth century, the Italianate *pictor doctus* type, such as Frans Floris who was esteemed for the originality of his invention, was the exception rather than the rule. The financial position of artists must largely have remained determined by their artisanal skill and must also have been strongly tied to the purely 'physical' and quantitative aspects of the work of art, such as size, materials and number of figures. It has been shown that in the critical and dramatic years of 1584–85, the large majority of Antwerp painters belonged to the lower economic and social strata of the city's population: more than 80 per cent could be considered poor. Although this situation may be explained by the desperate state of the Antwerp economy, which was then at its most serious, it is nevertheless striking from tax records that the Antwerp painters as a group had much more limited financial means and spending power than merchants of all types and condition.[30]

The innovations of Frans Floris, especially his use of sophisticated subject matter of a profane and learned character, largely remained without any serious sequel after the painter's death in 1570. To an important extent, this had to do with the general economic collapse which set in shortly after the iconoclastic outburst of 1566, and which became manifest in the decline of spending power and the emigration of many merchants, entrepreneurs and craftspeople. Indeed, apart from their religious

[27] See C. van de Velde, 'Aspekte der Historienmalerei in Antwerpen in der zweiten Hälfte des 16. Jahrhunderts' in E. Mai and H. Vlieghe (eds.), *Von Bruegel bis Rubens. Das goldene Jahrhundert der flämischen Malerei* (Cologne, 1992), pp. 74–5.
[28] This practice is well documented for the seventeenth century (see especially the studies by K. van der Stighelen, mentioned in note 8); it seems likely to me that it was also current in the preceding century.
[29] See van Mander, *Schilder-Boeck*, fol. 240v, and Filipczak, *Picturing Art*, p. 42.
[30] See J. van Roey, 'De Antwerpse schilders in 1584–1585. Poging tot sociaal-religieus onderzoek', *Jaarboek Koninklijk Museum voor Schone Kunsten Antwerpen* (1966), pp. 107–31.

convictions, artists from Antwerp and other Flemish towns began to seek safer places to settle many years before the closing of the Scheldt and the re-establishment of Spanish and Roman Catholic power in 1585. It was doubtless for economic reasons that many sought their fortune in Fontainebleau, Paris, Venice, Rome and elsewhere from the 1570s onwards. After 1585, they settled more systematically in Dutch towns and the Palatinate. That the Antwerp art market began to suffer from a serious crisis soon after the beginning of the rebellion is also clear from the fact that the prices that paintings could fetch were falling dramatically.[31]

Even in the two decades after 1585, monumental secular history painting devoted to subject matter inspired by Greek mythology or Roman history remained exceptional and it is also characteristic that the sensual mannerist style, which during the late sixteenth century had become the main vehicle in western Europe for depicting profane subject matter (so-called *poesie*), did not play a role of any importance in Antwerp after the death of Floris, whose later works had been among the more important sources for the dissemination of that style in Northern art.[32] Apart from the fact that the power to purchase these expensive and sophisticated pictures was dwindling, a serious cultural obstacle must also have made it difficult to find buyers for these kind of works in Antwerp until the beginning of the seventeenth century. There was enormous pressure on Antwerp history painters of the post-Floris generation to direct all their resources to church decoration according to the principles laid down by the Council of Trent.[33] Further, the church authorities were very critical of all forms of nudity in art and in mythological pictures belonging to the private sphere.[34]

Only from about the beginning of the Twelve Year Truce, c.1609, did monumental secular history painting of this kind again become fashionable in Antwerp, alongside a new baroque monumentality in religious painting, strongly furthered by the activity of Rubens who had settled in Antwerp in 1608. This revival coincided with a general revival of the arts in Antwerp, especially of painting.[35] As a matter of fact, artistic expression

---

[31] See L. Smolderen, 'Tableaux de Jérôme Bosch, de Pierre Bruegel l'Ancien et de Frans Floris dispersés en vente publique à la Monnaie d'Anvers en 1572', *Revue belge d'archéologie et d'histoire de l'art* 64 (1995), pp. 33–41.

[32] See van de Velde, 'Aspekte der Historienmalerei', p. 76.

[33] See especially Freedberg, *Iconoclasm and Painting*, and D. Freedberg, 'Kunst und Gegenreformation in den südlichen Niederlanden, 1560–1660' in Mai and Vlieghe, *Von Bruegel bis Rubens*, pp. 55–70.

[34] Johannes Molanus' theological recommendations about imagery are especially to be mentioned here: see Freedberg, *Iconoclasm and Painting*, pp. 149–51.

[35] See H. Vlieghe, *Flemish Art and Architecture, 1585–1700*, The Pelican History of Art (New Haven and London, 1998), especially chs. 1–4.

in early modern Antwerp found its momentum in a period when the real peak of the city's 'golden age' had long passed. Nevertheless, the stupendous artistic achievement realized up to the middle of the seventeenth century by Rubens and the plethora of highly gifted artists following in his wake would not have been possible without the partial renaissance of Antwerp's economic and financial importance, which has been described very aptly by Roland Baetens as the 'Indian summer' of the city's prosperity.[36] If not a new golden age, it may nevertheless be considered at least a 'silver age'.

The stylistic mutations which were so typical of Antwerp painting were also apparent in Antwerp print-making and were, to some extent, even stimulated by that medium. A remarkable trend was that, from about the middle of the century onwards, print production became more and more concentrated in the hands of a few great entrepreneurs, whereas during the earlier decades of the century the engravers themselves were responsible for the sale of their products. To some extent this phenomenon ran parallel to that of the contemporary new workshop practice of the painter–inventor, who had skilful assistants working under his guidance.[37] The most important and influential among these print publishers was Hieronymus Cock, who showed himself to be innovative in another way. He was the first of the Antwerp print publishers to build up a very systematic and specific stock of engravings of copies of compositions by Italian but also Flemish painters. This is in striking contrast with the much more utilitarian output of the earlier publishers. This production must have met a growing need from the painters, for it is striking that, in Antwerp, this phenomenon occurred at the very moment when, in the œuvre of painters such as a Frans Floris, a more systematic orientation to the trend-setting masterworks of the Italian High Renaissance was becoming more and more important.

In the development of sculpture and the decorative arts during the sixteenth century, Antwerp's high-quality products also attained international recognition. Although their role and importance have been studied

---

[36] See R. Baetens, *De nazomer van Antwerpens welvaart. De diaspora en het handelshuis De Groote tijdens de eerste helft der 17de eeuw*, 2 vols. (Brussels, 1976); R. Baetens, 'Antwerpens Goldenes Jahrhundert–Konstanten und Wandel des wirtschaftlichen Lebens' in Mai and Vlieghe, *Von Bruegel bis Rubens*, pp. 27–38.

[37] See especially L. De Pauw-De Veen, 'De graveerkunst' in *Antwerpen in de XVIde eeuw*, pp. 447–83; T. Riggs, *Hieronymus Cock (1510–1570). Printmaker and Publisher in Antwerp at the Sign of the Four Winds* (New York and London, 1977); T. Riggs and L. Silver (eds.), *Graven Images. The Rise of Professional Printmakers in Antwerp and Haarlem, 1540–1640*, exhibition catalogue (Evanston, Ill., 1993); D. Landau and P. Parshall, *The Renaissance Print* (New Haven and London, 1994); J. van der Stock, *Printing Images in Antwerp. The Introduction to Printmaking in a City: Fifteenth Century to 1585* (Rotterdam, 1998).

in less depth than contemporary painting, some parallel conclusions can be drawn here.[38]

It was from about 1550 onwards that sculpture became a strongly centralized and well-organized business. The main protagonist was Cornelis Floris, Frans' brother. A further parallel with the role of Frans Floris is that Cornelis also introduced *maniera grande* forms imported from Italy.[39] The earlier decades of the sixteenth century witnessed the waning of the production of wooden retables carved in a late Gothic style or, more often, in the *Mischstil*, like that of early sixteenth-century painting. To an important extent this strongly standardized production was destined for export all over Europe.[40] Towards the end of the century, sculpture also became firmly established as an *ars liberalis* by breaking its traditional ties with the stonemasons' guild.[41]

In the various categories of the decorative arts a superior level of perfection was achieved in order to meet the growing demand for a luxurious life-style in Antwerp and elsewhere. To an important extent this was made possible by the immigration of skilled craftspeople from various European countries. Italy was the cradle of Antwerp's glassblowers[42] and majolica workers.[43] Leather workers came from

[38] See the general survey by A.K.L. Thijs, 'De Antwerpse luxenijverheid: winstbejag en kunstzin' in J. van der Stock (ed.), *Antwerpen. Verhaal van een metropool*, exhibition catalogue (Antwerp, 1993), pp. 105–13.

[39] The now somewhat out-of-date standard monograph by R. Hedicke, *Cornelis Floris und die Florisdekoration*, 2 vols. (Berlin, 1913), has recently been superseded by A. Huysmans, J. van Damme, C. van de Velde, and C. van Mulders, *Cornelis Floris 1514–1575. Beeldhouwer, architect ontwerper* (Brussels, 1996); see also the separate study on his activity as a tomb sculptor by A. Huysmans, 'De grafmonumenten van Cornelis Floris', *Revue belge d'archéologie et d'histoire de l'art* 56 (1987), pp. 91–122.

[40] On the main aspects of Antwerp sculpture from the earlier decades of the sixteenth century, see H.J. de Smedt, 'De beeldhouwkunst te Antwerpen, 1470–1530' in *Aspekten van de laatgotiek in Brabant*, exhibition catalogue (Louvain, 1971), pp. 272–83; F. Smekens, 'De beeldhouwkunst (1500–1550)' in *Antwerpen in de XVIde eeuw*, pp. 391–405; R. Szmydki, *Retables anversois en Pologne. Contribution à l'étude des rapports artistiques entre les anciens Pays-Bas Méridionaux et la région de Gdansk au début du XVIe siècle*, Verhandelingen van de Koninklijke Academie voor Wetenschappen, Letteren en Schone Kunsten van Belgie, 40 (Brussels, 1986); L. Jacobs, 'The Marketing and Standardization of South Netherlandish Carved Altarpieces: Limits on the Role of the Patron', *The Art Bulletin* 71 (1989), pp. 208–29.

[41] See C. Duvivier, 'Contestation entre la confrérie des maçons et des sculpteurs d'Anvers', *Revue d'histoire et d'archéologie* 3 (1862), pp. 91 ff1; M. Carsteels, *De beeldhouwers de Nole te Kamerijk, te Utrecht en te Antwerpen*, Verhandelingen van de Koninklijke Academie voor Wetenschappen, Letteren en Schone Kunsten van Belgie, Klasse der Schone Kunsten, 16 (Brussels, 1961), pp. 300–3; Filipczak, *Picturing Art*, pp. 16–17.

[42] See S. El Dekmak-Denissen, 'Glas te Antwerpen in de 16de en 17de eeuw', *Antwerpse vereniging voor Bodem- en grotonderzoek, Bulletin* (1988), pp. 15–34; S.El Dekmak-Demissen, 'De glasmanufacturen in Antwerpen' in L. Engen (ed.), *Het glas in België van de oorsprong tot heden* (Antwerp, 1989), pp. 121–33.

[43] See C. Dumortier, 'Les faïenciers italiens à Anvers au XVIe siècle. Aspects historiques', *Faenza. Bollettino del Museo Internazionale delle Ceramiche di Faenza* 73 (1987),

Spain[44] and the textile industry benefited from French immigrants.[45] This remarkable development would not have been possible without the crucial role of Antwerp as a market for raw materials, which highly skilled craftspeople could transform *in situ* into expensive luxury goods. This is confirmed in a letter written in 1574 by Christopher Plantin, who mentions that these favourable conditions had actually prompted him to set up his business in Antwerp around the middle of the century.[46] The refining of the raw material into attractive and highly valued luxury goods followed a process of stylization according to fashionable Renaissance ornamentation. From the middle of the sixteenth century onwards in particular, this ornamentation became 'normative' thanks to its dissemination by means of series of ornament and pattern prints, starting with those of Cornelis Bos and, especially, Cornelis Floris de Vriendt.[47]

It goes without saying that the wide circulation and dissemination of the very diverse products of Antwerp's decorative arts industry in the sixteenth century were largely made possible by the same well-organized trade system that enabled the enormous output of Antwerp painting to become internationally renowned. But the Antwerp art trade also marketed the artistic production of other towns in the Netherlands. Thus Brussels tapestries, the most famous and outstanding in Europe, were largely traded through Antwerp dealers.[48]

It is natural to make comparisons with the situation in Amsterdam, whose 'golden age' succeeded that of Antwerp, largely at Antwerp's expense. In both cities, artistic predominance became apparent in the increasing numbers of resident artists. Many of them were refugees from the Southern Netherlands who brought their specialist skills with them, and, as far as painting is concerned, the specializations typical of Antwerp. These became very characteristic of seventeenth-century paint-

footnote 43 (*cont.*)

pp. 161–72; C. Dumortier, 'Les ateliers de majolique à Anvers (1508–1585)', *Antwerpse vereniging voor Bodem- en grotonderzoek, Bulletin* (1988), pp. 23–38; C. Dumortier, 'Les majoliques anversoises "à la façon de Venise", de la première moitié du XVIe siècle', *Revue belge d'archéologie et d'histoire de l'Art* 59 (1990), pp. 55–74.

[44] See e.g. J.A. Goris, *Etude sur les colonies marchandes méridionales (Portugais, Espagnols, Italiens) à Anvers de 1488 à 1567. Contribution à l'histoire des débuts du capitalisme moderne* (Louvain, 1925), p. 432.

[45] See A. K. L. Thijs, *Van 'werkwinkel' tot fabriek. De textielnijverheid te Antwerpen (einde 15de–begin 19de eeuw)* (Brussels, 1987).

[46] See e.g. A. K. L. Thijs, 'Antwerpse luxenijverheid', p. 108.

[47] On these ornament prints, see R. Hedicke, *Cornelis Floris*; S. Schéle, *Cornelis Bos. A Study of the Origins of the Netherland Grotesque* (Stockholm, 1965); and Huysmans, van Damme, van de Velde and van Mulders, *Cornelis Floris*.

[48] On the Antwerp tapestry trade, see J. Denucé, *Antwerpsche tapijtkunst en handel*, Bronnen voor de geschiedenis van de Vlaamsche kunst, IV (Antwerp, 1936).

ing in Amsterdam too, as this was, in an even more striking way than Antwerp painting, especially destined for the open market. On the other hand, just as in Antwerp, the flowering of the arts in seventeenth-century Amsterdam, in their various forms and expressions, reflected the higher standard of living of the middle and upper-middle classes, and perfectly met the need for conspicuous display.

Comparison with Augustan London offers a rather different view. Art in late seventeenth and early eighteenth-century England flourished under an explicit princely and aristocratic patronage. The Restoration initiated a strong taste for luxurious high baroque interior decoration of palaces and churches which, furthermore, was fully in keeping with the monumental style of these buildings. Portraiture too played a very important role in mirroring the immense love of display of the court, the aristocracy and the parvenus. In order to meet these demands, important Italian history painters were stimulated to go to Britain to decorate palaces and large houses in London as well as great mansions in the countryside. Dutch, Flemish and German painters stayed in England too in order to meet the demands for portraiture, and landscape and genre painting. Gradually, however, and under their influence, genuine English artists began to emerge.

9   The rise of Amsterdam as a cultural centre: the market for paintings, 1580–1680

Marten Jan Bok

During the Middle Ages the northern parts of the Low Countries were a cultural outpost compared with the rich cities of Flanders and Brabant.[1] Between 1580 and 1660, however, the young Dutch Republic witnessed an extraordinary growth in the production of relatively small paintings, made for a middle-class public. The achievement of the Dutch painters of this 'golden age' seems to be twofold. On the one hand, the great Dutch masters succeeded in producing paintings of a quality which rivalled that of the great Italian masters. Rembrandt's work, to name but the most famous example, deeply influenced the art of painting for centuries to come. On the other hand, all Dutch painters achieved an unprecedented level of productivity, producing more than 5 million paintings during the seventeenth century.[2] Both phenomena are reflected in museum collections, as well as in catalogues of auctions of old master paintings, down to the present day.[3]

Though less conspicuous, the quality and output of other decorative arts, such as printmaking, silverware, sculpting, woodcarving, tapestry-

---

[1] The first version of this paper, presented at the 1994 Achievement Conference in Amsterdam, was later, after slight revision, published in Dutch in my dissertation: 'Vraag en aanbod op de Nederlandse kunstmarkt, 1580–1700 [Supply and Demand in the Dutch Art Market, 1580–1700]' (dissertation, Utrecht, 1994), pp. 97–130. An English translation of this dissertation is forthcoming. The original paper was later reworked for the 1995 Achievement Conference held in Antwerp. I wish to express my gratitude to Eddy de Jongh, Joy Kearney, Ad Knotter, Jan Lucassen, Neil de Marchi, J. Michael Montias, David Ormrod, Maarten Prak, Jan de Vries, Bert van der Wal, Diane Webb and Jan Luiten van Zanden for their help and advice.

[2] A.M. van der Woude, 'The Volume and Value of Paintings in Holland at the Time of the Dutch Republic' in D. Freedberg and J. de Vries (eds.), *Art in History. History in Art. Studies in Seventeenth-Century Dutch Culture* (Santa Monica, 1991), pp. 285–9; J.M. Montias, 'Estimates of the Number of Dutch Master-painters, Their Earnings and Their Output in 1650', *De werkelijkheid achter vernis: zeventiende-eeuwse schilderkunst, Liedschrift* 6, 3 (1990), pp. 59–74.

[3] For estimates of the number of Dutch paintings from this period in museum collections, see for example W. Brulez, *Cultuur en getal. Aspecten van de relatie economie–maatschappij–cultuur in Europa tussen 1400 en 1800*, Cahiers Sociale Geschiedenis, vol. 6 (Amsterdam, 1986), pp. 54–9; J. de Vries, 'Art History' in: Freedberg and de Vries, *Art in History. History in Art*, pp. 249–84; and van der Woude, 'Volume and Value'.

weaving and gilt-leather making, also rose to levels unprecedented in the Northern Netherlands.[4] In this development, Amsterdam, the biggest city and the commercial capital, played the leading role.[5] Amsterdam, however, did not serve as the Republic's metropolis, as Paris did for France or London for England. From the sixteenth century onwards the western part of what was to become the United Provinces had turned into a tightly woven network of cities, of which Amsterdam was only *primus inter pares*.[6] For the sake of clarity I will therefore concentrate my argument on Amsterdam, but readers should try to keep in mind that Frans Hals worked in Haarlem, Johannes Vermeer in Delft and the great silversmith Adam van Vianen in Utrecht.

The question why Amsterdam emerged as an important art centre after 1580 has been addressed by many scholars. Usually two important explanations are proposed: first, the enormous increase in wealth accruing to Amsterdam when it replaced Antwerp as the commercial pivot of the western world; and, secondly, the influx of painters and other skilled craftspeople from the Southern Netherlands after the fall of Antwerp to the Spaniards (1585). The former explains a large part of the rising demand for luxury goods, while the latter is generally seen as the catalyst for a greater supply of these goods.

Those who leave their homes to start a new life elsewhere tend to be more enterprising and ambitious than their neighbours at home.[7] Peter Earle has noticed for London that its immigrants were usually the more talented and better-educated youngsters from the English countryside. In

[4] In the case of woodcarving and sculpting, however, one might argue that new demand from the shipbuilding industry and for the decoration of houses and public buildings, may not have made up for the decline in demand from the Catholic Church caused by the Reformation.

[5] The Dutch printmaking trade rapidly expanded from the end of the sixteenth century. By the middle of the next century it had concentrated in Amsterdam, where a few very large publishers catered to the European market; see N. Orenstein, 'Noordnederlandse landschapsprenten en hun uitgevers in de Gouden Eeuw' in B. Bakker and H. Leeflang (eds.), *Nederland naar 't leven: landschapsprenten uit de Gouden Eeuw*, exhibition catalogue (Amsterdam, Rembrandthuis, 1993), pp. 33–41. In 1664 about 300 silversmiths were registered with the Amsterdam guild, making up almost half of the registered silversmiths in the province of Holland; J.H. Leopold, 'Zilver, zilversmeden en zilvermerken' in A.L. den Blaauwen (ed.), *Nederlands zilver, 1580–1830 / Dutch Silver, 1580–1830*, exhibition catalogue (Amsterdam, Rijksmuseum, 1979–80), pp. xxix–l, p. xxxiii. On the importance of Amsterdam in the international book trade, see chapter 12 by Paul Hoftijzer in this volume.

[6] In the twentieth century the preservation of this network even became the backbone of Dutch urban planning policies, until in the last decade it was swept away by the Thatcherite revolution. The open space between Dutch cities is now rapidly being filled in, thus finally creating a multi-million metropolis in the west of the country.

[7] The economic effects of this immigration are discussed in chapter 3 by Clé Lesger in this volume.

a way this rule seems to have been even more true for the immigrants who settled in Amsterdam from the Southern Netherlands. Many of those who came to Amsterdam were wealthy merchants and highly skilled craftspeople who took their families and their capital with them when they left their home towns. The immigration of scholars and scientists – as discussed in chapter 15 by Karel Davids in this volume – made the Republic a leading centre of science in Europe.

Culturally, these often self-confident immigrants deeply influenced their indigenous fellow citizens.[8] The Hollanders had for a long time been regarded as a simple and modest folk, not only by their more refined and cultured neighbours in Brabant and Flanders, but also by themselves. The older generation observed with regret that, soon after the Southerners started moving in, their sons and daughters began to 'ape' not only Southern trading practices, but also their dress, speech, manners, food and love of luxury in general. And, as more and more merchants from all over Europe started to frequent Amsterdam, the city became as cosmopolitan as Antwerp had been a generation earlier. Dutch trade with the Levant, the Americas and East Asia brought in luxury goods formerly unseen on the Dutch markets. As early as 1603, a year after the founding of the East India Company, the Haarlem merchant Jan Govertsz van der Aar had himself been portrayed as a shell collector by his friend Hendrick Goltzius. He is proudly holding up a *turbo marmoratus*, a species living in the seas of Indonesia and Australia (figure 9.1).[9] The new interest in luxury and the wonders of the world, which sparked a culture of collecting, also benefited painting and the decorative arts.[10] Here, too, immigrant artists and craftspeople from the Southern Netherlands played a leading role.

The main contribution of these migrant Flemish artists to Dutch painting may be regarded as the introduction of new genres. Although the Northern Netherlands already had a strong local tradition in history and portrait painting, other genres, such as still life, landscape, architecture, battle scenes and genre and animal painting, had hardly been developed. The work of Flemish genre painters such as David Vinckboons and

8 This subject is treated by J. Briels, *De Zuid-Nederlandse immigratie 1572–1630* (Bussum, 1978), pp. 45–66.
9 On this painting, see W.T. Kloek, et al. (eds.), *Dawn of the golden age. Northern Netherlandish Art, 1580–1620*, exhibition catalogue (Amsterdam, Rijksmuseum, 1993–4), pp. 584–5, cat. no. 256.
10 On collecting, see E. Bergvelt and R. Kistemaker (eds.), *De wereld binnen handbereik. Nederlandse kunst- en rariteitenverzamelingen, 1585–1735*, 2 vols., exhibition catalogue (Amsterdam, Amsterdams Historisch Museum, 1992); and M.J. Bok, 'Art-Lovers and Their Paintings. Van Mander's *Schilder-boeck* as a Source for the History of the Art Market in the Northern Netherlands' in Kloek, et al., *Dawn of the Golden Age*, pp. 136–66.

9.1 *Portrait of Jan Govertsz van der Aer* by Hendrick Goltzius

Adriaen van de Venne, still-life painters such as Ambrosius Bosschaert, or landscape painters such as Gillis van Coninxloo and Roelant Saverij had a lasting influence on Dutch art.[11] On the one hand they carried on Flemish traditions; on the other hand they paved the way for further development, leading in the first decades of the seventeenth century to the creation of the typical 'Dutch style' in many genres.

The introduction of new genres and the development of new painterly techniques could take place only in constant interaction with the ever-changing taste of the consumer. Yet it is very difficult to define the exact role of the consumer in this process. Around 1630, Constantijn Huygens, then secretary to the *Stadhouder*, wrote in the memoirs of his youth that the popularity of the art of painting had increased considerably during his lifetime.[12] Unfortunately Huygens fails to inform us why this change in public taste took place. All we know so far is that we can observe this development in the ever-growing number of paintings in Dutch households, as reflected in probate inventories. We can even see this fashion 'trickle down' from the most wealthy to the not so wealthy – a phenomenon which was later repeated in London from the 1690s onwards.[13] And yet, while searching for an explanation for Dutch achievement in the arts, the role of the consumer is the most difficult aspect to treat. Why did tens, even hundreds, of thousands of Dutchmen start to buy paintings, when they could have spent their money on other things? One might suggest many possible explanations for the observed shift in the demand curve, ranging from religious and political to more general cultural forces, but I think that we are partly dealing with a *faux problème*. They did, in fact, spend their money on other luxury goods too, such as jewellery. The crucial matter is that they had money to spend.

In the rest of this chapter, I will argue that the unique quality of the rise of the Dutch school of painting is the fact that, for about half a century, a larger proportion of the population than ever before could afford to buy paintings, so that Holland witnessed a virtual mass market for works of art. This made a large proportion of the production and marketing of paintings subject to the basic economic laws we all know so well. The emergence of numerous new genres (fish, still life, church interiors and game pieces, to name but a few odd ones), the specialization of artists in these genres and the development of less labour-intensive painting techniques led to new products and, although they may well have changed

---

[11] For an overview, see J.G.C.A. Briels, *Vlaamse schilders in de Noordelijke Nederlanden in het begin van de Gouden Eeuw, 1585–1630* (Antwerp, 1987). See also W.T. Kloek, 'Northern Netherlandish Art 1580–1620' in Kloek, et al., *Dawn of the Golden Age,* pp. 15–111, at pp. 55–60.

[12] C. Huygens (C.L. Heesakkers, transl. and ed.), *Mijn jeugd* (Amsterdam, 1987), pp. 70–1.

[13] Bok, 'Art-Lovers'. For London, see chapter 4 by Peter Earle in this volume.

consumers' tastes, they were first of all meant to cut costs and achieve economies of scale. Rising demand and increased productivity gave the Dutch art market an impressive dynamism. In this the art market of the Dutch 'golden age' differed fundamentally from the art market of the previous period, which, with the possible exception of Antwerp in the sixteenth century, had always been dominated by patrons and wealthy amateurs.

Before we turn to the development of general purchasing power, we need to pay attention to the growth in the number of painters active in Amsterdam and to the recruitment of apprentices. Thanks to the fact that from 1578 onwards most bridegrooms who had the banns for their first marriage published in Amsterdam registered their profession, we have fairly accurate data concerning the history of the Amsterdam labour market during the seventeenth century.[14] These data are of great importance for research into the art crafts, since, to a certain degree, they replace the lost membership rolls of the Amsterdam Guild of St Luke.[15]

It turns out that a total of 1,004 painters married in Amsterdam in the period 1585–1700.[16] Most of these were artist painters, the house painters and daubers making up only a minority. However, owing to the fact that not everyone married and that already-married painters settled in Amsterdam from elsewhere, these numbers reveal only general trends.[17] We observe a spectacular growth in absolute numbers, from one to two grooms a year before the turn of the century, to twelve to fourteen in the years between 1640 and 1670. The general trend will not surprise any specialist of the economic history of the Dutch Republic, because it shows a strong correlation with the development of the economy as a whole. The war of 1672–3, which caused such ravages in the art market

[14] S. Hart, 'Geschrift en getal. Onderzoek naar de samenstelling van de bevolking van Amsterdam in de 17e en 18e eeuw, op grond van gegevens over migratie, huwelijk, beroep en alfabetisme' in S. Hart, *Geschrift en getal. Een keuze uit de demografisch-, economisch- en sociaal-historische studiën op grond van Amsterdamse en Zaanse archivalia, 1600–1800*, Hollandse Studiën, vol. 9 (Dordrecht, 1976), p. 128.

[15] For the surviving documents concerning the guild, see D.O. Obreen, 'Het Sint-Lucas-Gild te Amsterdam' in D.O. Obreen (ed.), *Archief voor Nederlandsche kunstgeschiedenis 3* (1880–1881), pp. 89–196; W.F.H. Oldewelt, 'Het St. Lucasgilde' in W.F.H. Oldewelt, *Amsterdamse archiefvondsten* (Amsterdam, 1942), pp. 84–91; I.H. van Eeghen, 'Het Amsterdamse Sint Lucasgilde in de 17de Eeuw', *Jaarboek Amstelodamum* 61 (1969), pp. 65–102.

[16] Based on calculations by Simon Hart (Amsterdam, Gemeentearchief, collectie Hart, 725). The crafts included in the count are: painter (*schilder* [899]), fine artist (*fijnschilder* [31] and *kunstschilder* [14]), house-painter (*huisschilder* [15]), dauber (*kladschilder* [39]), painter's apprentice (*schildersknecht* [3]), 'room painter' (*kamerschilder* [1]) and portrait painter (*contrefeiter* [1] and *portretschilder* [1]).

[17] For a discussion of this source and for a more detailed analysis, see Bok, 'Supply and Demand', pp. 99–104.

and led to the bankruptcy of Johannes Vermeer of Delft, resulted in a 20 per cent drop in the number of painters marrying in Amsterdam after 1675. The number stabilized at the level of the period between 1615 and 1640.

Naturally these data tell us more about the assessment young painters made of their prospects than about the future course of their careers. Anyone establishing themselves as an artist at the beginning of the century profited from a booming market throughout their lifetime, whereas young artists who were trained in the years after 1650 could hardly make a living after 1673. In 1676, the Utrecht painter Adrianus van Ysselsteyn, for example, complained that he could not support himself with his painting 'since the economic climate has been so bad that for the past several years it has not been possible to earn a living as a painter'.[18] Many artists had to look for other sources of income, causing the number of active masters, as well as the recruitment of youngsters, to drop.

Comparison between the number of painters and that of all Amsterdam bridegrooms reveals that the years between 1611 and 1625 were the most favourable period, when one in every hundred young men declared himself to be a painter.[19] The years between 1641 and 1655 were likewise favourable, and in absolute numbers the level was actually substantially higher than in the first period of growth.

Amsterdam had a lively 'art scene', which must have greatly contributed to the interchange of ideas. Until 1619 the Amsterdam painters gathered in the inn 'de Drye Coningshoofden' in the Heintje Hoeksteeg, not far from the Oude Kerk.[20] In 1619 the Amsterdam Painters' Guild was granted a guild room in the former St Anthonispoort. From then onwards, many painters settled in the St Anthonisbreedstraat.[21] By the time Rembrandt van Rijn bought his house (now called het Rembrandthuis), the St Anthonisbreedstraat had become the centre of artistic life and art trade in the city. The St Anthonisbreedstraat retained this position until the 1650s, when many artists, including Rembrandt,

---

[18] '. . . vermits de conjunctuijre van tijden soo slecht geloopen sijn dat mette schilderconste in eenige jaren herwaerts niet te verdienen is geweest', quoted by M.G. Roethlisberger and M.J. Bok, *Abraham Bloemaert and His Sons. Paintings and Prints*, Aetas Aurea, vol. 8 (Doornspijk, 1993), p. 603.

[19] Bok, 'Supply and Demand', p. 102, graph 4.2.

[20] S.A.C. Dudok van Heel and J.H. Giskes, 'Noord-Nederlandse pre-rembrandtisten en Zuid-Nederlandse muziekinstrumentmakers', *Jaarboek Amstelodamum* 77 (1984), pp. 13–37, at p. 21.

[21] S.A.C. Dudok van Heel, 'Rembrandt van Rijn (1606–1669): Een veranderend schildersportret' in C. Brown, J. Kelch and P. van Thiel (eds.), *Rembrandt: de meester en zijn werkplaats. Schilderijen*, exhibition catalogue (Amsterdam, Rijksmuseum, 1991–2), pp. 50–67, at pp. 56–9.

moved to the neighbourhood around the Westerkerk. The large number of documents in which Amsterdam artists acted together bears witness to the close contacts that existed in this painters' 'milieu'.

The observed growth in the number of new master painters reflects the increase in the number of youngsters who were apprenticed, their success in completing their training, and their expectation of sustaining a family with their acquired skills. This increase would have been impossible without a wide recruitment base, which resulted from several favourable circumstances. First, artists would have taught their own children to draw, in order to determine whether it was worth training them to continue the workshop. Secondly, artists saw many boys who received basic training in draughtsmanship as part of their apprenticeship in other crafts (goldsmithing, carpentry, etc.).[22] Thirdly, we know from various sources that the children of the more well-to-do received drawing lessons as part of their education. The best-known example of this category is Constantijn Huygens, who as a boy was taught to draw and paint, and later was a prolific writer and composer.[23] Finally there were the schoolchildren who showed their masters more interest in drawing than in learning to read and write. In this respect the fact that a large majority of Dutch children went to school was of great importance.[24] We may add that schooling, be it with or without a few years in Latin school, was necessary for a successful career as an artist, because the painting of history pieces was impossible without at least some knowledge of the Bible and of classical mythology.[25]

Still, contemporaries were well aware of the fact that selection was not perfect. In 1604, Karel van Mander wrote:

> And thus it happens, alas, that sometimes
> natural painters go behind ploughs
> while peasants take up brushes.[26]

It is essential to our argument that society apparently showed a positive attitude towards the arts, since without such an attitude the artistic basis would never have become so wide, and the summit would never have reached such a height. I have already referred to Huygens' remarks on the increasing popularity of paintings during his lifetime. It had indeed

[22] Bok, 'Supply and Demand', pp. 178–88.   [23] Huygens, *Mijn jeugd*, pp. 70–1.
[24] See M. Spufford, 'Literacy, Trade and Religion in the Commercial Centres of Europe' in K. Davids and J. Lucassen (eds.), *A Miracle Mirrored: the Dutch Republic in European Perspective* (Cambridge, 1995), pp. 229–83, at pp. 263 and 270.
[25] I do not know any example of a Dutch painter of the seventeenth century who was illiterate.
[26] 'En so comet (eylaes) datter somwijlen / Natuerlijcke Schilders gaen achter ploeghen, / En Bouweren haer aen Pinceelen voeghen'; K. van Mander, *Het schilder-boeck* (Haarlem, 1604), fol. 1v.

increased to such an extent that even a large number of children from the higher ranks of society became artists.[27] That parents thought highly of a career as a painter becomes clear from the words of the Amersfoort bailiff Jan Haverman, who, in 1654, wrote that he intended to raise his children 'if possible (since they descend – without wanting to boast – from a good stock and family) in honesty, according to their quality, as he in fact is doing, sending one to study, having another paint, [etc.]'.[28]

Art historians have frequently noted that one of the most astonishing aspects of Dutch seventeenth-century painting is not just the sheer number of artists of more than national importance, but the generally high quality of the work of many artists of a lesser reputation.[29] Thorough training undoubtedly played a major role in this.

The training of an artist was expensive and parents would not have sent their sons as apprentices to painters unless they had a chance of success.[30] We should not think, though, that all Amsterdam painters had received their training in that city. Although Amsterdam had had its own local school of painting since the sixteenth century, it did not have many artists with a large workshop capable of employing many apprentices before 1630. Thus, for a long time, the artists' community grew mainly through immigration of masters who had been trained elsewhere. Briels estimates that at least 225 fully trained painters settled in the Northern Netherlands from the South, most of them in the years between 1580 and 1595.[31] A large proportion of this group settled in Amsterdam. But Amsterdam also attracted artists from other Northern Netherlandish cities, such as Haarlem, where Hendrick Goltzius trained extremely skilled engravers, or Utrecht, where Abraham Bloemaert and Gerard van Honthorst were influential art pedagogues.[32] It is assumed that Bloemaert, throughout his long career, trained between 70 and 100

[27] Bok, 'Supply and Demand', p. 187.

[28] '... gaerne (als sonder beroem gesprooten uijt een goede stamme en familie) eerelijk nae gelegentheijt soude opvoeden, gelijk hij ... oock doende is, laetende d'eene studeren, d'andere schilderen, [etc.].' Taken from a request to be allowed to sell goods from his children's maternal heritage (Utrecht, Rijksarchief, Hof van Utrecht, 252–48, stukken van de raadsheer G. van Dael, J25, 19 December 1654; kindly communicated by drs. E.A.J. van der Wal).

[29] G.J. Hoogewerff, *De geschiedenis van de St. Lucasgilden in Nederland* (Amsterdam, 1947), pp. 92, 223–4.

[30] On the investment required to train a boy as a painter, see J.M. Montias, *Artists and Artisans in Delft. A Socio-Economic Study of the Seventeenth Century* (Princeton, N.J., 1982), pp. 117–19, 153, 325; Bok, 'Supply and Demand', p. 187; and R. de Jager, 'Meester, leerjongen, leertijd. Een analyse van zeventiende-eeuwse Noord-Nederlandse leerlingcontracten van kunstschilders, goud- en zilversmeden', *Oud Holland* 104 (1990), pp. 69–111.   [31] Briels, *Vlaamse schilders*, p. 13.

[32] For a survey of painters settling in Amsterdam, see B. Haak, *Hollandse schilders in de Gouden Eeuw* (s.l., 1984), p. 352.

pupils, many of whom would later be active in Amsterdam.[33] In the middle of the 1620s Honthorst is said to have had no fewer than 25 pupils active in his workshop.[34]

After 1630 the workshops of Hendrick Uylenburgh ('la famosa accademia di Eeulenborg') and Rembrandt played an important role in the training of artists in Amsterdam.[35] We know that the talents of young artists apprenticed to masters such as Rembrandt were developed to the fullest, even to the extent that the quality of the work of some of them dropped considerably after they left Rembrandt's workshop and had to continue on their own. Next to that, artists in cities such as Haarlem and Utrecht, in some periods, provided apprentices and master painters with advanced training in drawing after the nude, more or less based on the example of the Florentine and Roman academies.[36] And, finally, hundreds of young artists continued their training in Italy, where they studied the works of the famous Italian masters, drew from examples from antiquity and gathered experience in the workshops of local masters.[37] Thanks to these *Wandergesellen* there was a continual exchange of artistic ideas and innovations between Italy and the Low Countries.

In 1678 the painter and art theoretician Samuel van Hoogstraeten wrote in his *Inleyding tot de hooge schoole der schilderkonst* (Introduction to the academy of painting):

Thus . . . a painter may not be able to enjoy completely the considerable pleasure he takes in art, unless he be relieved of the distressing anxieties of earning a living. Nor can the spirit give vent to the strong passions peculiar to art, so long as it is chained by domestic cares to warding off poverty.[38]

[33] Roethlisberger and Bok, *Abraham Bloemaert*, p. 574.

[34] J. von Sandrart (A.R. Peltzer, ed.), *Joachim von Sandrarts Academie der Bau-, Bild- und Mahlerey-Künste von 1675* (Munich, 1925), p. 173.

[35] On them see P. Huys Janssen, 'Rembrandt's Academy' in P. Huys Janssen and W. Sumowski (eds.), *The Hoogsteder Exhibition of Rembrandt's Academy* exhibition catalogue, ('s-Gravenhage, Kunsthandel Hoogsteder en Hoogsteder, 1992), pp. 20–35; J. Bruyn, 'Rembrandts werkplaats: functie en productie' in Brown, Kelch and van Thiel, *Rembrandt*, pp. 68–89; and S.A.C. Dudok van Heel, 'Het "Schilderhuis" van Govert Flinck en de kunsthandel van Uylenburgh aan de Lauriergracht te Amsterdam', *Jaarboek Amstelodamum* 74 (1982), pp. 70–90.

[36] On academies, see H. Miedema, 'Kunstschilder, gilde en academie. Over het probleem van de emancipatie van de kunstschilders in de Noordelijke Nederlanden van de 16de en 17de eeuw', *Oud Holland* 101 (1987), pp. 1–30; Bok, 'Supply and Demand', pp. 178–84; and Huys Janssen, 'Rembrandt's Academy'.

[37] A far from complete list of Dutch painters active in Rome in the seventeenth century has been compiled by G.J. Hoogewerff, *De Bentvueghels* ('s-Gravenhage, 1952), pp. 131–47. It comprises almost 300 names.

[38] 'Zoo en kan . . . een Schilder het behoorlijk vergenoegen in de konst . . . niet volkomen genieten, ten zy hy van het bitter zorgenpak des brootkommers ontlaeden zy. Noch de geest en kan met die hooge driften, die de konst eygen zijn, niet voort, zoo lang de huiszorg haer in d'engten van nootdruft geboeyt houdt'; S. van Hoogstraeten, *Inleyding tot de hooge schoole der schilderkonst, etc.* (Rotterdam, 1678, reprinted Utrecht, 1969), p. 351.

These words illustrate my proposition that talent and artistic skills could be deployed completely only in a society that enables artists to earn a living with their craft. Therefore, the art market deserves attention in our attempts to explain the rise of Amsterdam as an art centre.

Traditionally, a great demand for paintings has been regarded as being at the basis of the great expansion of the art market, first in the Southern Netherlands, and later in the Dutch Republic.[39] The French *homme de lettres* Samuel Sorbière, who spent the 1640s in Holland, even spoke of an 'excessive interest in paintings'.[40] And the same was observed by the English traveller John Evelyn.[41] Though certainly not every seventeenth-century Dutch household could afford to own paintings, nevertheless the ownership of paintings in the Northern Netherlands must have been much wider than elsewhere in Europe.

In my opinion the growth in demand for paintings can be explained by, on the one hand, the strong increase in per capita purchasing power in the Republic from about 1580 and, on the other hand, the relative drop in prices for paintings caused by the growing productivity of painters, as well as the introduction of new marketing techniques by the art trade. These mutually enforcing mechanisms set off a previously unseen dynamism in the art market. Add to that hundreds of large militia pieces – such as Rembrandt's *Nightwatch* – and equally large numbers of group portraits of the governors of public institutions, generating hundreds of thousands of guilders worth of commissions for artists, and we realize how attractive it may have been to become a successful painter.[42] How did this market work?

In his *Schilder-boeck* Karel van Mander has left us a snapshot of the Dutch art market in the years around 1600. The dozens of owners of paintings mentioned by van Mander belonged to a select group of wealthy merchants and patricians. They created a demand for costly paintings in cities such as Amsterdam, Haarlem and Leiden, only shortly after Antwerp had fallen to the Spaniards.[43] Contrary to one's expectations, this group did not consist exclusively of Southerners, but also

[39] H. Floerke, *Studien zur Niederländischen Kunst- und Kulturgeschichte: Die Formen des Kunsthandels, das Atelier und die Sammler in den Niederlanden von 15–18 Jahrhundert* (Munich, 1905; reprinted Soest, 1972), pp. 1–2, 6.

[40] 'L'excessive curiosité pour les peintures'; quoted in W. Martin, *Het leven en de werken van Gerrit Dou beschouwd met het schildersleven van zijn tijd* (Leiden, 1901), pp. 95–6.

[41] John Evelyn's observation, quoted by Floerke and many others, that every Dutch farmer invested his surplus capital in paintings because there were no other investment opportunities, has been sent to the realm of myth by J.M. Montias, 'Socio-economic Aspects of Netherlandish Art from the Fifteenth to the Seventeenth Century: A Survey', *The Art Bulletin* 72 (1990), pp. 358–73, at pp. 361–2.

[42] On the production of militia pieces, see M. Carasso-Kok and J. Levy-van Halm, *Schutters in Holland: kracht en zenuwen van de stad*, exhibition catalogue (Haarlem, Frans Halsmuseum, 1988).   [43] Bok, 'Art-Lovers'.

included indigenous Hollanders such as Jan Govertsz. van der Aar (figure 9.1 above). What these amateurs held in common, apart from their interest in the arts, was their great wealth, often newly accumulated in the trade with Russia, the Baltic or the West and East Indies. Van Mander was aware that 'art loves the company of wealth' – one of the classic observations of the art market – but was amazed that painting flourished in his time, because the Republic was still entangled in a destructive war.[44] Again and again he praises the small group of amateurs who had the money to buy expensive works by old masters, but also repeatedly patronized contemporary artists. They bought paintings by mannerist artists such as Cornelis van Haarlem, Cornelis Ketel and Abraham Bloemaert. In his last will the amateur Jacques Razet even founded an endowment for talented youngsters, including girls, who wanted to become artists.[45]

The dictum formulated by van Mander is still valid, as was recently put forward by the American economist William N. Goetzmann in his research on the development of the prices of paintings at auction over the past three centuries.[46] His analysis used sophisticated statistical techniques and came to the conclusion that there is a strong correlation between the prices paid for rare works of art and those of stocks and shares. In Goetzmann's words: 'demand for paintings increased when investor wealth grew'.[47] When he summarizes his findings in terms of 'a basic connection between art and money', we hear an echo of van Mander's words of almost four centuries earlier.[48]

Neither van Mander nor Goetzmann, however, manages to answer the question of why there was such a dramatic increase in the number of artists active in the Dutch Republic. Conspicuous consumption may have played a role at the beginning, though. At the top of the market, quality and rarity determine the price, governing as they do the desirability of works of art. They enhance the status of the owner, who is often willing to pay more than a 'reasonable' price to acquire that status. In London, such conspicuous consumption by the country gentry and the aristocracy within the metropolis seems to have been, the main source of growth of the urban economy for a long time.[49]

Neil de Marchi and Hans van Miegroet have argued that art theorists and *liefhebbers* (amateurs) 'thought in terms of artistic worth and prices as

[44] 'dat den const geern is by den rijckdom'; van Mander, *Het schilder-boeck*, fol. 219v, 299v.
[45] Bok, 'Art-Lovers', p. 143.
[46] W.N. Goetzmann, 'Accounting for Taste: Art and the Financial Markets over Three Centuries', *American Economic Review* 83 (December 1993), pp. 1370–6.
[47] Goetzmann used a 'repeat-sales regression'. This statistical technique is also used to analyse trends in prices in the real estate market.
[48] Goetzmann, 'Accounting for Taste', pp. 1370, 1375.
[49] As argued in this volume by both Ormrod (chapter 10) and Earle (chapter 4).

separate categories, not easily reconcilable'.[50] But they also demonstrated that seventeenth-century art dealers, to whom status was less important than profit, did take market mechanisms into account. The dealers may have been most innovative precisely in the sector of the art market concerned with less than 'top works', the buyers of which were more concerned with decorating their homes than with acquiring status.

The domination of the art market by wealthy art lovers is an age-old phenomenon and therefore insufficient explanation for the rapid growth in the number of active artists which took place in Amsterdam and other Dutch cities. It would therefore be worthwhile at this point to consider the role played by the growth in purchasing power, which enabled many burghers in the Dutch Republic, hitherto unable to do so, to spend part of their income on durable consumer goods (including works of art) rather than upon more basic needs of life.

The question of the development of per capita purchasing power and standard of living confronts historians with many pitfalls. For a long time they had to rely on indices based on the development of the daily wages of building craftsmen and of the prices of consumables such as bread grains. Jan de Vries has questioned the validity of such real wage calculations.[51] He noted that they fail to take into account that, at times of high prices for bread, consumers could substitute other foodstuffs for bread, or that they could improve the household's income by employing the labour of women and children.[52]

Elsewhere de Vries has argued that the purchasing power of wages, which had dropped severely in the Low Countries since 1500, started to rise from about 1570.[53] This rise continued for most of the seventeenth century, as a result of 'productivity-raising investments in agriculture, industry, and commerce'.[54] That productivity rose seems to be confirmed by estimates by Jan Luiten van Zanden, who calculated that 'per capita output rose by an average of at least 0.3 per cent per year between 1580 and 1650'.[55] However, he was less optimistic about the effect on the purchasing power of those who depended on wages: 'the resulting growth in

---

[50] N. de Marchi and H.J. van Miegroet, 'Art, Value, and Market Practices in the Netherlands in the Seventeenth Century', *The Art Bulletin* 76, no. 3 (September 1994), pp. 451–64, at p. 463.

[51] J. de Vries, 'Between Purchasing Power and the World of Goods: Understanding the Household Economy in Early Modern Europe' in J. Brewer and R. Porter (eds.), *Consumption and the World of Goods* (London, 1993), pp. 85–132.   [52] Ibid., p. 97.

[53] J. de Vries, 'The Labour Market' in K. Davids and L. Noordegraaf (eds.), *The Dutch Economy in the Golden Age*, Nederlansch Economisch–Historisch Archief (Amsterdam, 1993), pp. 55–79, at pp. 61, 68, 75.   [54] Ibid, p. 69.

[55] J.L. van Zanden, 'Economic Growth in the Golden Age: the Development of the Economy of Holland, 1500–1650' in Davids and Noordegraaf, *The Dutch Economy in the Golden Age*, pp. 5–26, at p. 17.

income per capita did not benefit labour.'[56] Here he is in conflict with the opinions of de Vries and van der Woude, who believe that the purchasing power of wages did increase considerably during the course of the seventeenth century, even beyond 1672.[57] This may be of lesser interest to our argument, as in Amsterdam a large proportion of the population consisted of self-employed merchants and craftspeople. It is not inconceivable that their purchasing power would grow at times when wage earners were unable to keep pace with inflation. This would fit van Zanden's observation that economic growth in the province of Holland led primarily to 'a significant increase in per capita income from capital', which continued down to the end of the eighteenth century.[58]

It is plausible that the boundary between those households that could afford to own works of art and those that could not to a large extent mirrored the boundary between the self-employed 'middling sort', whose wealth increased considerably, and those who lived by wages and did not share proportionately in the newly won wealth.[59] It is not easy to establish the proportion of the first group in the entire population, but we may assume that it grew considerably.[60] Amsterdam doubtless profited more from this process than did the other towns in Holland. By the beginning of the sixteenth century, per capita wealth in Amsterdam was already substantially higher than in most other towns and cities, and this disparity must have grown even stronger, at least for the middle and upper strata of population, as the city acquired a more prominent position.[61]

We now come to the question of to what extent increased purchasing power gave rise to a growing demand for luxury goods. We can deduce from Montias' research on Amsterdam that the market for paintings would indeed profit from growing wealth. He found a wealth elasticity of 1.42 for paintings in Amsterdam inventories from the period 1600–1669.[62] This means that, when the total value of movables in an average inventory increased by 1 per cent, the total value of works of art would increase by 1.42 per cent. The fact that elasticity is larger than unity shows that growing wealth must indeed have led to greater expenditure on paintings. The same seems to have happened in Delft,

[56] Ibid., pp. 17–18.
[57] J. de Vries and A. van der Woude, *Nederland 1500–1815: de eerste ronde van moderne economische groei* (Amsterdam, 1995), p. 721.
[58] Van Zanden, 'Economic Growth', pp. 18 and 23.
[59] For contemporary observations concerning the growth in wealth, see Bok, 'Art-Lovers', p. 150.   [60] For a more detailed argument, see Bok, 'Supply and Demand', pp. 112–14.
[61] Van Zanden, 'Economic Growth', p. 21.
[62] J.M. Montias, 'Quantitative Methods in the Analysis of 17th Century Dutch Inventories' in V.A. Ginsburgh and P.-M. Menger (eds.), *Economics of the Arts* (Amsterdam, 1996), pp. 1–26, at p. 8.

where Montias' calculations also demonstrate that the local art market consisted of several groups of consumers, each with its own pattern of demand.[63] Wealth elasticity for paintings turned out to be greater in the inventories of above-median value than in those of below-median value.[64]

I have argued that in Amsterdam, and in Holland as a whole, growing purchasing power benefited the art market, provided that prices of works of art remained stable. It is no more than an assumption, however, that price levels remained the same. Prices of primary produce showed a constant rise between 1550 and 1650.[65] One might expect this to have caused upward pressure on the price of handicraft goods, including of course the price of paintings. This seems not to have been the case, however. A considerable decline in the price of clothing and other durable consumer goods took place in Europe in the seventeenth and eighteenth centuries.[66] De Vries explains this by pointing out that price fluctuations for these goods was determined to no small degree by greater productivity, as well as by higher quality and increased durability.[67]

Little reliable information is available on the prices paid for paintings in the Republic. The widely varying value of the goods recorded in inventories, as well as the enormous range in quality of the paintings themselves, necessitates using very large samples indeed in order to obtain statistically significant comparisons over a longer period of time. Montias' Amsterdam sample was large enough to show a doubling of the number of paintings held per household, but did not produce hard data for the development of the price level for paintings.[68] However, we can say more about the development of productivity and the marketing of paintings.

Since 1580, technological innovations have contributed to a considerable growth in productivity in many sectors of the Dutch economy.[69] This must have happened in the arts sector as well. Montias has shown that painters used different methods to improve their incomes, of which 'process innovation', leading to higher productivity, was the first.[70] This

---

[63] He found a wealth elasticity of 1.23 for Delft in the period 1610–79 (Montias, *Artists and Artisans*, pp. 263–8). These Delft calculations were not, however, based on a random sample, as were those from Amsterdam.   [64] Montias, *Artists and Artisans*, pp. 265–8.

[65] De Vries and van der Woude, *Nederland 1500–1815*, p. 718. See also H. Nusteling, *Welvaart en werkgelegenheid in Amsterdam 1540–1860. Een relaas over demografie, economie en sociale politiek van een wereldstad* (Amsterdam, 1985), pp. 126, 260–1.

[66] De Vries, 'Purchasing Power' pp. 103–4.   [67] Ibid.

[68] J.M. Montias, '"Perspectiven" in zeventiende-eeuwse boedelbeschrijvingen' in J. Giltaij and G. Jansen (eds), *Perspectiven: Saenredam en de architectuurschilders van de 17e eeuw* exhibition catalogue (Rotterdam, Museum Boymans-van Beuningen, 1991), 19–9, at p. 27.

[69] K. Davids, 'Technological Change and the Economic Expansion of the Dutch Republic' in Davids and Noordegraaf, *The Dutch Economy in the Golden Age*, pp. 79–104, at p. 97.

[70] On this subject, see J.M. Montias, 'The Influence of Economic Factors on Style', *De Zeventiende Eeuw* 6 (1990), pp. 49–57; and J.M. Montias, 'Cost and Value in Seventeenth-Century Dutch Art', *Art History* 10 (1987), pp. 455–66.

was achieved through the introduction of more painterly techniques, which allowed artists to produce works of art with less cost of labour, without these works being considered inferior by their clients. In this sense, Montias considers the quickly worked landscapes of Jan van Goyen, with their almost monochrome tone, to be a technological improvement compared with the elaborate and laborious landscapes painted by his predecessors Hendrick Avercamp and Roelant Saverij. The artist making 'modern' landscapes could supply them more cheaply, without having to be content with lower profits. This led to competition from other artists wanting to profit from the technological edge, which resulted – as tradition has it – in artists such as Jan van Goyen, Jan Porcellis and Frans van Knibbergen painting 'a fairly large canvas' per day.[71]

The second method was 'product innovation': by adopting a unique personal style of painting, or by specializing in a genre not produced by anyone else, a painter could try to fill a 'niche' in the market. Another advantage of specialization was that the artists could work more quickly because of growing routine, or through standardization of part of the production process. All these new production methods led to growing competition, lower prices and a greater variety of products, all of which benefited the customer.[72]

Yet guild regulations restricting the import of paintings by out-of-town masters were aimed at limiting such competition. In cities such as Delft and Haarlem these restrictions in fact led to inventories listing more works by local masters than one would expect to find under unrestricted market conditions.[73] In small towns such restrictions may have frustrated artistic innovation, but in the bigger towns this policy seems to have fostered the development of local schools with their own artistic character and their own dynamism. Thus, providing that the number of painters active in a city was large enough (Montias speaks of a 'critical mass') competition at the local level induced the process of innovation and rising productivity outlined above. It took place simultaneously in several cities, resulting in the extraordinary variety of local styles in Dutch painting of the seventeenth century.

[71] A 'tamelyk grooten doek', according to Samuel van Hoogstraeten, as quoted by A. Houbraken, *De groote schouburgh der Nederlantsche konstschilders en schilderessen*, 3 vols. (The Hague 1718–21; reprint Amsterdam, 1976), vol. 1, pp. 166–8. In a booming market there is, in principle, unlimited space for growth in productivity. In practice, however, public taste sets a limit to this. One might argue that Hercules Seghers' failed attempt to introduce 'mechanical' painting is an indication of such a limit to contemporary taste. Without this, the simplification of style would not have had to stop with van Goyen, and in theory Dutch art could have arrived at minimal art in the seventeenth century.

[72] Montias, 'The Influence of Economic Factors on Style', pp. 54–5.

[73] J.M. Montias, 'Art Dealers in the Seventeenth-century Netherlands', *Simiolus* 18 (1988), pp. 244–56, at pp. 247–9.

Amsterdam was an exception to the rule that we usually find a disproportionately large percentage of works by local masters in probate inventories.[74] Although the city magistrates, urged by the guild of St Luke,
repeatedly introduced protective restrictions for the local art market, in
reality there was hardly any effective protection.[75] Contemporaries were
well aware of this, as becomes clear from a discussion within the Haarlem
guild of St Luke, in which it was noted that the local art trade could not be
compared with that in Amsterdam, 'for that is a mercantile city, and
should be excluded from the present discussion, since [trade] is pursued
there with different intentions'.[76] In this respect the Amsterdam luxury
industry resembled that of Antwerp, which was free for the same
reasons.[77] Both cities acted as a magnet for talented artists – the best-
known Amsterdam example being Rembrandt – wishing to profit from
the large local market and the manifold international trade links.
Thijs has argued that this was the main reason for the fact that the
sixteenth-century Antwerp school of painting did not develop a local
style.[78] To a certain extent Amsterdam struggled with the same problem a
century later. One dominating style never emerged. Rather, a wide variety
of styles existed, and there were certain specialities: the so-called pre-
Rembrandtists, the Rembrandt school and the typical Amsterdam city-
scapes produced from the 1650s onwards.[79]

The shift from patronage to the market system, which could be
observed in Antwerp in the sixteenth century, took place in the Republic
during the next century, when the Reformation put an end to the role of
the churches as patrons. Burke has pointed out 'the immediate gains in
creative freedom in the market system, in which one creates first and sells
afterwards'.[80] Yet, for most painters, this creative freedom was an ideal
rather than a reality.[81] In practice most of them had to follow the wishes of
a patron; this immediately becomes evident when we realize that portraits

[74] Ibid., p. 249.
[75] N. de Marchi, 'Matching Instruments and Goals: Traders' Practices in an Emerging Art
Market' (paper, Durham, Duke University, 1992), pp. 4–6, 10–12.
[76] '. . . also dat een Koopstadt is can die in deesen niet gerekent worden, ende wert sulcks
daer om andere insigten gedaen'; H. Miedema, *De archiefbescheiden van het St. Lucasgilde
te Haarlem*, 2 vols. (Alphen aan den Rijn, 1980), vol. 1, p. 249 (translation quoted from
Bok, 'Art-Lovers', p. 150.
[77] A.K.L. Thijs, 'De Antwerpse luxenijverheid: winstbejag en kunstzin' in J. van der Stock
(ed.), *Antwerpen, verhaal van een metropool 16de-17de eeuw*, exhibition catalogue Antwerp,
Hessenhuis, 1993), pp. 105–13, at p. 110.   [78] Ibid., p. 107.
[79] On the city scapes, see B. Bakker, 'Amsterdam en Venetië. Twee steden verbeeld' in M. de
Roever (ed.), *Amsterdam: Venetië van het Noorden* (Amsterdam, 1991), pp. 19–20.
[80] P. Burke, 'Cities, Cultures and Achievements: Some Preliminary Reflections' (unpublished paper, the Achievement Project, July 1993), p. 14.
[81] M.J. Bok and G. Schwartz, 'Schildezen in opdracht in Holland in de 17e eeuw', *Holland.
Regionaal-historisch tydschrift* 23 (1991), pp. 183–95.

make up about one-fifth of all paintings in inventories of the seventeenth century.[82] Art dealers often had dozens of paintings in stock by masters whose work is not known under the name of the artist today.[83] Thus the Amsterdam painter and art dealer Anthony Claesz. in 1625 sold 'one hundred paintings, all made by Master Franciscus and his assistant'.[84] The art dealer Cornelis Doeck in 1664 had forty-two paintings in stock by Leendert de Laeff, and his colleague Hendrick Meyeringh in 1687 had sixty-six paintings by the totally unknown painter Slort.[85] Such artists worked, as Houbraken put it, 'in slavery', while van Gool spoke of 'painting on the galley'.[86] They were employed by art dealers who operated at the lower end of the market, where quantity counted instead of quality. We have to distinguish these art dealers from their colleagues at the top of the market, who specialized in bringing together supply and demand for costly old master paintings and for works by the most prominent painters from the Low Countries and Italy. The dealers in this last group, whom Montias called 'high-class dealers', were already active in Amsterdam in the last decades of the sixteenth century.[87] They operated on an international scale and often traded in jewellery and other rarities as well as in paintings. The Haarlem artist who, in 1642, characterized the Amsterdam art market as that of a 'mercantile city' had the activities of these dealers in mind.

'Lower-class dealers', who were mainly interested in a rapid turnover of less expensive paintings, will have played a larger role in the increase in the number of paintings in Amsterdam households than their chic fellow dealers. They tried to maintain a continuous supply of paintings, through the import of cheap paintings – often copies – from the Southern Netherlands, or by contracting painters to make so-called 'work-by-the-dozen'.[88] They also introduced new marketing techniques, such as lotteries of paintings, raffles, street sales and auctions, all of

---

[82] Ibid., p. 192. In Dordrecht inventories from the period 1620–1719, 23.7 per cent of the paintings were portraits; J. Loughman, 'Een stad en haar kunstconsumptie: openbare en privé-verzamelingen in Dordrecht, 1620–1719' in P. Marijnissen, et al. (eds.), *De Zichtbaere Werelt. Schilderkunst uit de Gouden Eeuw in Hollands oudste stad*, exhibition catalogue (Dordrecht, Dordrechts Museum, 1992), pp. 34–64, at p. 46.

[83] For literature on the Amsterdam art trade, see Montias, 'Art Dealers', and de Marchi, 'Matching Instruments and Goals'.

[84] 'Ende noch hondert stucken schilderyen alle by Mr. Franciscus en synen knecht gemaeckt, 600.-'; A. Bredius, *Künstler-Inventare: Urkunden zur Geschichte der Holländischen Kunst des XVIten, XVIIten und XVIIIten Jahrhunderts*, 8 vols., Quellenstudien zur holländischen Kunstgeschichte ('s-Gravenhage, 1915–22), vol. 5, p. 1781.

[85] Montias, 'Art Dealers', pp. 255–6.

[86] Houbraken, *De groote schouburgh*, vol. 1, p. 322. J. van Gool, *De Nieuwe Schouburg der Nederlantsche kunstschilders en schilderessen, etc.*, 2 vols. ('s-Gravenhage, 1750–1), vol. 2, p. 472.   [87] Montias, 'Art Dealers', p. 252; Bok, 'Art-Lovers', pp. 148–51.

[88] Montias, 'Art Dealers', p. 246.

which aimed at attracting interest from new customers.[89] They tried to avoid guild restrictions as far as possible. De Marchi described the attitudes of these dealers as follows: 'The traders who imported and sold low quality works in volume, outside the purview of the St. Luke's Guild, held to a belief in the market-place rather than to some higher aesthetic art. In this, they were typical of merchants in general.'[90] The demand for dealers' services must have increased especially in the 1630s and 1640s, in Montias' view under the influence of a growing 'degree of the artists' specialization and on the variegation of consumers' tastes'.[91] The activities of the art dealers greatly contributed to the emergence of a mass market for paintings.

As we have seen, after the 1660s the number of painters marrying in Amsterdam declined considerably. De Vries' estimation of the trend in the number of Dutch painters, based on attributions in probate inventories and museum collections, shows a similar decline.[92] For a third indicator of decline we can turn to the occurrence of work by living masters in inventories. The percentage of paintings attributed to contemporary masters in a sample of Amsterdam inventories assembled by Michael Montias dropped below 50 per cent after the 1650s, and tumbled to less than 20 per cent after the 1670s.[93] Montias concluded: 'Since Amsterdam was such an important outlet for paintings, the shrinking of the Amsterdam market must have had a calamitous effect on the livelihood and prospects of Dutch artists.'[94] The observed decline was so dramatic that he even doubted the validity of his own data.[95]

Jan de Vries put into words what Montias could not yet face: 'The collapse after 1660 was much more abrupt than had been the surprising emergence of Dutch art early in the century.'[96] He compared the decline to 'the sudden pulling of a curtain.' What caused this decline? I see two important factors: failing demand and structural overproduction. According to contemporaries, failing demand was mainly caused by the consequences of war and changes in fashion.[97] Already in 1604 van

[89] De Marchi, 'Matching Instruments and Goals'. On lotteries, see R. Kosse, '"Een raere loterye." Het verloten van schilderijen in de zeventiende eeuw', MA thesis (Rijksuniversiteit Utrecht, 1992). See also N. de Marchi, 'The Role of "Dutch" Auctions, and Lotteries, in Shaping the Art Market(s) of 17th century Holland' *Journal of Economic Behavior and Organization* 28 (October 1995), pp. 203–21.
[90] De Marchi, 'Matching Instruments and Goals', p. 21.
[91] Montias, 'Art Dealers', p. 245.   [92] De Vries, 'Art History', p. 273.
[93] J.M. Montias, 'Works of Art in Seventeenth-Century Amsterdam: An Analysis of Subjects and Attributions' in Freedberg and de Vries, *Art in History. History in Art*, pp. 331–72, at p. 363.   [94] Ibid., p. 348.   [95] Ibid., p. 343.
[96] De Vries, 'Art History', p. 267.
[97] Houbraken, *De groote schouburgh*, vol. 2, pp. 130–6. For an excellent description of Johan van Gool's opinions, see Lyckle de Vries, *Diamante gedenkzuilen en leerzaeme voorbeelden: een bespreking van Johan van Gool's 'Nieuwe Schouburg'* (Groningen, 1990), pp. 87–101.

Mander had stated that Mars was a 'despoiler of art' and that the art of painting 'loved peace and prosperity'.[98] How few artists could avoid the consequences became clear when Rembrandt, Amsterdam's most famous painter, went bankrupt shortly after the First Anglo-Dutch War (1652–3).[99] The Third Anglo-Dutch War (1672–4) brought down Gerrit Uylenburgh, Amsterdam's foremost art dealer of his time.[100] Financial difficulties forced him to auction a large portion of his stock on 23 February 1673. The poet Joannis Antonides wrote an advertising poem for the occasion, echoing Karel van Mander's words of a lifetime earlier:

In Amsterdam, the art of Italian and Dutchman defies the raised banner of War, and gains sympathy from all connoisseurs. While Uylenburgh sells his paintings at a profit, in spite of all this war's furious raging which threaten us all with fire and sword, with gratitude from the gentlemen, who wish to adorn their rooms with these riches, gathered over a long time. Thus, however hit by the miseries of war, Pictura will lift her head.[101]

In spite of Antonides' poetic incitement to the amateurs, the auction did not generate enough money.[102] Shortly afterward Uylenburgh had to declare bankruptcy, which he explicitly blamed on 'these distressed times and the miserable state of the dear fatherland'.[103]

It is obvious that wars strongly influence the art market. In times of war everyone, including the rich amateur, has other things on their mind than the *beaux arts*. One sits on one's money until conditions improve. This causes a total failure of demand and acute loss in income for artists. This same mechanism takes place in times of generally felt economic decline. In short, the arts are a marginal economic activity subject to a high elasticity of demand.

We should not confuse elasticity of demand with wealth elasticity as discussed above. The wealth elasticity Montias found for Delft was based on probate inventories. These sources, however, are the written residue of

---

[98] Van Mander, *Het schilder-boeck*, fol. 299v.

[99] Dudok van Heel, 'Rembrandt van Rijn', pp. 60–1.

[100] Dudok van Heel, 'Het "Schilderhuis" van Govert Flinck'; Dudok van Heel, 'Rembrandt van Rijn', pp. 60–1.

[101] 'In Amsterdam trotseert de kunst / Van Italjaan en Nederlander / Den opgeregten Oorlogsstander, / En wint by alle kenners gunst. / Daar Uilenburg zyn schilderyen, / In spyt van alle razernyen, / Hoe elk ons dreigt te vier en zwaard, / Met winst vertiert, bedankt van Heeren, / Dien 't lust hun Zalen te stoffeeren / Met zulk een rykdom, lang vergaart. / Dies hoe de krygselenden treffen, / De Schilderkonst mag 't hoofd verheffen', quoted from Houbraken, *De groote schouburgh*, vol. 2, pp. 296–7.

[102] About a dozen of these paintings had recently been refused by Friedrich Wilhelm, the Grand Elector of Brandenburg. This may have made collectors even more wary.

[103] '. . . dese bekommerlijcke tijden en miserabele constitutie van het lieve Vaderlandt'; quoted from Dudok van Heel, 'Rembrandt van Rijn', p. 61.

purchasing decisions from the past and tell us little about consumer behaviour in the short run. This made Jan de Vries question whether, in general, there existed a strong relationship between growing wealth and a flourishing art market.[104]

In the short run, however, the pessimistic scenario may really have happened. The events of 1672 caused a crash on the Amsterdam stock market, from which it recovered only twelve years later. At the beginning of the 1680s the English consul in Amsterdam wrote that the city 'decayes in its riches and trade'.[105] Outside Holland, things were no different and probably even worse. In 1680, the Utrecht nobleman Adam van Lockhorst van Schonauwen wrote to Godard Adriaan van Reede van Amerongen: 'wealth is only fiction nowadays, since real estate goods do no longer have a price.'[106] Two years later, Gaspar Schade wrote to van Reede: 'besides, we are not as rich and liquid as we used to be before the year 1672, and in many of the poor provinces everything is going from bad to worse.'[107]

Owing to the high elasticity of demand for luxury commodities such as paintings, the decline in income of the richest inevitably caused a deep

---

[104] De Vries put forward the following argument: 'If the wealth elasticities estimated by Montias bear any resemblance to the income elasticities prevailing in seventeenth-century Dutch society, it becomes evident that the fall of income alone can explain only a minor part of the large decline in the number of painters and production of paintings . . . At the low end of the market, demand would have fallen no more than proportionately with income, yet it is precisely the cheap, mass-produced paintings that appear to have been hit hardest. At the high end of the market, demand would indeed have fallen more than proportionately with income, but an elasticity of 1.23 could account for the decline of demand only if upper- and middle-incomes plummeted, and even the most confirmed pessimists about the late seventeenth-century Dutch economy stop far short of such a claim' (de Vries, 'Art History', pp. 270–1).

[105] Quoted from J.I. Israel, 'The Amsterdam Stock Exchange and the English Revolution of 1688', *Tijdschrift voor geschiedenis* 103 (1990), pp. 412–40, at p. 421. The number of house sales under execution in Amsterdam doubled from 870 in the period 1664–73, to 1,760 in the following decade (Amsterdam, Gemeentearchief, Oud rechterlijk archief, 5061/2163–2176; kindly communicated by Ad Knotter). Apparently many families experienced serious financial difficulties (A. Knotter, 'Bouwgolven in Amsterdam in de 17e eeuw' in P.M.M. Klep et al. (eds.), *Wonen in het verleden, 17e–20e eeuw. Economie, politiek, volkshuisvesting, cultuur en bibliografie*, NEHA series, vol. 3 (Amsterdam, 1987), pp. 25–37, at p. 27). A temporary decline in the growth of the number of painters marrying in Amsterdam after 1625 coincided with another rise in the number of house sales under execution (Bok, 'Supply and Demand', p. 100).

[106] '. . . den rijckdom is nu maer imaginair, de vaste goederen hebben nu gheen prijs meer'. Quoted from M. van der Bijl, 'Utrechts weerstand tegen de oorlogspolitiek tijdens de Spaanse Successieoorlog. De rol van de heer van Welland van 1672 tot 1708' in H.L.P. Leeuwenberg and L. van Tongerloo (eds.), *Van standen tot staten. 600 Jaar Staten van Utrecht 1375–1975*, Stichtse Historische Reeks, vol. 1. (Utrecht, 1975), pp. 135–99, at p. 181, note 24.

[107] '. . . daerbij sijn wij soo rijck en geldigh niet als wel waren voort jaer 1672 ende in vele arme provintien loopt alles van slecht tot arger'; quoted from van der Bijl, 'Utrechts weerstand', p. 181, note 24.

crisis in the market for the more expensive paintings. Uylenburgh fell victim to this. But the demand for cheaper paintings must have collapsed too. No matter whether the price level for paintings dropped to such an extent that the percentage of the population able to afford to buy paintings remained stable, it is certain that living masters could no longer produce profitably at the current price level. Secondhand paintings drove new paintings out of the market completely.

The dramatic events of 1672 might almost make us forget that, as becomes clear from the falling number of new masters after about 1660, stagnation must have set in earlier than that. This did not elude contemporaries. Arnold Houbraken (1660–1719), who grew up in the period in which the crisis broke, explicitly points to the year 1660 as the watershed: '[in the Netherlands the arts] never [flourished] more beautifully than in the years between 1560 and 1660.'[108] This decline may be explained by a problem inherent in the Dutch art market of the seventeenth century: the durability of paintings.

The proportion of paintings by contemporary masters in Amsterdam probate inventories shows a constant decline from the 1630s, even at the time when the number of artists active in the city increased most rapidly. Apparently the durability of paintings was so high that there was insufficient demand for replacement.[109] As long as the total demand for paintings grew more vigorously than the supply of secondhand paintings, the market had room for new paintings. But the decline in market share for new paintings made artists more vulnerable to downward trends in the economy. When demand stagnated, painters saw their income fall rapidly because they had no instruments to influence either supply or the price level. There are two reasons for this. First, the supply of secondhand paintings was mainly determined by the number of paintings left by deceased individuals. The total volume of this supply was hardly influenced by short-term market changes. Secondly, the supply of paintings coming from individuals who had run into financial difficulties, whether leading to bankruptcy sales or not, increased. In a contracting economy these two factors together led to falling prices for paintings and consequently to erosion of the profitability of artistic activity. Because added value in works of art consists mainly of labour, artists had no other response to falling demand than to stop producing. De Vries has estimated that over some twenty years the number of painters active in the

[108] '[de kunsten bloeiden in de Nederlanden] nooit schooner als in den tusschentyd, van 't jaar 1560, tot 1660'; Houbraken, *De groote schouburgh*, vol. 2, p. 130.
[109] For the relationship between the durability of consumer goods and their price, and the influence thereof on demand and on the quantities of such goods in probate inventories, see de Vries, 'Purchasing power', pp. 102–4.

Republic dropped to about a quarter of the number reached at its summit, in the middle of the century.[110]

The process of marginalization which I described led to a final collapse of the art market only in the years after 1672, because demand did not bounce back to its previous level.[111] The mass market for paintings had vanished. Only the top of the market recovered to a certain extent. As van Zanden has demonstrated, per capita wealth in the Republic continued to grow until the end of the eighteenth century, but disparity in distribution grew also.[112] This explains the ongoing production of the costly cabinet pieces in the labour consuming style of the 'high finish' (*fijnschilderkunst*), which only the wealthiest amateurs could afford to collect.

The important achievements of Amsterdam and the Dutch Republic in the cultural field would not have been possible without the astonishing success of its economy. The growth in purchasing power of more and more layers of Dutch society in its golden age caused ever-increasing demand for luxury goods such as paintings.[113] To the economic historian the emergence of a mass market for paintings is no less an achievement than Rembrandt's *Nightwatch* is to the art historian. However, cultural achievement is not a simple function of economic growth and the production of works of art. We all know that this function should include many parameters which, unfortunately, are hard to quantify, such as changes in fashion, cultural policies or the religious or secular use of works of art. In this field much remains to be done.

In the first half of the seventeenth century many obviously considered painting to be an attractive profession. The time-consuming nature of the craft of painting, as well as the long and costly period of training, meant the supply of paintings could adapt only slowly to growing demand.[114] Given the expanding market of the time, this must have resulted in respectable profits for many painters. On the other hand, the great durability of paintings caused the market share of works by living masters to drop continuously. This increased the risk that economic decline, for example in times of war, would lead to failing demand. In this sense the

[110] De Vries, 'Art History', pp. 264 and 273.
[111] Production figures as calculated by van der Woude will have to be revised considerably. He estimated production to have been at an all-time high in the period 1680–99 (van der Woude, 'The Volume and Value of Paintings', p. 315). In reality production must have been dramatically lower than before. The same goes for the period 1660–79.
[112] Van Zanden, 'Economic Growth', p. 23.
[113] As a consequence, we might, as a hypothesis, add a second rule to Goetzmann's assumption that the price level at the top of the art market is indicative of the total wealth of the richest layers of society: the total number of active masters is indicative of the purchasing power of the middle classes and shows a broadly distributed wealth.
[114] As discussed, the possibilities for introducing innovations to raise productivity were limited by consumer taste.

art market proves to be a sensitive indicator of consumer confidence. After 1672 the purchasing power of large sections of society dropped to such an extent that the mass market for paintings disappeared.[115] It had lasted for only about half a century. Only the top of the art market still offered a decent income to painters, and then only to the most talented among them, who once again became more dependent on patronage.[116] In this respect the Dutch market for painting returned to 'normal'. As elsewhere in Europe, artists would have to look for patrons rather than for a niche in a mass market. In addition, after the middle of the 1670s, large numbers Dutch artists left their country to find employment elsewhere in Europe. Many of them settled in London.

[115] Another striking example of this phenomenon in the economic history of the Dutch Republic is the *trekvaart* (barge) system, which was the first public transportation system in the world 'that depended on the generation of mass demand for its success'; J. de Vries, *Barges and Capitalism. Passenger Transportation in the Dutch Economy, 1632–1839* (Utrecht, 1981), p. 183. The decline in per capita purchasing power made its services too expensive for many strata of society after 1670 (ibid., pp. 269–73). Here too this led to the collapse of the dynamics of the system.

[116] Lyckle de Vries, *Diamante gedenkzuilen*, p. 93.

10 Cultural production and import substitution: the fine and decorative arts in London, 1660–1730

David Ormrod

In contrast with the sphere of natural philosophy, the development of the visual arts in England experienced a major discontinuity during the 1640s and 1650s. No doubt Horace Walpole overstated the case when he remarked that 'the arts were, in a manner, expelled with the royal family in Britain'.[1] Nevertheless, the Civil Wars and the commonwealth period saw the departure of large numbers of immigrant artists and craftspeople, the disappearance of royal patronage and, with it, the key role of the Whitehall group and the conditions under which Inigo Jones launched a host of projects. The loss of momentum during the 1640s, symbolized in the sale of the royal picture collection, was not merely a royalist illusion.[2] From May 1644, the systematic destruction of religious art and church interiors increased under the supervision of the Parliamentary regional committees for the demolition of monuments. Stained glass, pictures, statuary, tombs, altars, screens and tapestries were lost on an enormous scale in areas occupied by Parliamentary forces, especially in London and East Anglia.[3]

It is difficult to estimate accurately the destructive impact of the Reformation and Civil War on the country's religious art. For contemporaries, a sense of loss must have been experienced in both real and psychological terms. Church building virtually ceased between 1534 and Wren's rebuilding of the City churches, with the exception of the 1630s, which saw the significant repair and remodelling of many London churches. In general, a protracted process of secularization affected most branches of the decorative and fine arts.[4] Within this vacuum, English

---

[1] H. Walpole, *Anecdotes of Painting in England*, ed. R. N. Wornum with additions by Rev. J. Dalloway, n.d. [1828 London], vol. II p. 76.

[2] Sales to the public began in October 1649. See A. MacGregor, 'The King's Goods and the Commonwealth Sale. Materials and Context', and F. Haskell, 'Charles I's Collection of Pictures', both in A. MacGregor (ed.), *The Late King's Goods* (London and Oxford, 1989), pp. 13–32 and 203–31.

[3] R. Strong, *Lost Treasures of Britain. Five Centuries of Creation and Destruction* (London, 1990), pp. 91–102.

[4] B. Denvir, *From the Middle Ages to the Stuarts. Art, Design and Society before 1689* (London, 1988), p. 19.

portraiture was virtually reinvented as a national art form in the seventeenth and eighteenth centuries, on foundations provided by continental practitioners. The return of royalist and other exiles and travellers after 1660 reopened the arts to European influences, especially those of France, and the influx of foreign artists and craftspeople increased. Horace Walpole commented wryly that 'the restoration of royalty brought back the arts, not taste'.[5]

The years 1660–85 formed a period of major dislocation in London's economic and social life. As provincial population growth slowed down, London continued to expand, and one of the social consequences of sustained inward migration was the westward expansion of London to accommodate the richer sections of metropolitan society. But an unpredictable series of events was to intensify and accelerate the changes already under way: the Great Plague and the Great Fire of 1665–6, and the Huguenot diaspora after 1685. The rebuilding process, of course, provided a major stimulus to the decorative arts, but was carried through in the face of major difficulties arising from disruption of business, loss of rents and property, and overcrowding.[6]

During the late 1660s and early 1670s, the nation's economy was in the grip of a serious trade and payments crisis, coinciding roughly with the Anglo-Dutch wars, at a time when the rural sector was weakened by the underconsumption of agricultural and other home-produced goods as the nation's population declined.[7] By 1678, the revival of trade was beginning to peter out and, as the political and economic situation deteriorated, a campaign against French luxury imports developed during the later 1670s. Unsurprisingly, the political economy of taste emerged as a major issue. Much has been written about the alternation of French and Dutch influences on English taste during these decades, or, to put it another way, the manner in which the components of the 'English baroque' were assembled. More important than the *form* in which hybridized versions of baroque taste were received, however, is the fact that England became heavily *dependent upon cultural imports*, whether French or Dutch adaptations of classical forms or European adaptations of

---

[5] Walpole, *Anecdotes*, pp. 76–7.
[6] N. Brett-James, *The Growth of Stuart London* (London, 1935), chapters 13–16; T.F. Reddaway, *The Rebuilding of London after the Great Fire* (London, 1940), pp. 256, 270–1. The value of furnishings and goods lost in the fire was almost as great as that of the buildings themselves, estimated by Strype at £3.65 million, compared with £4 million for the value of houses destroyed (Reddaway).
[7] W. R. Scott, *The Constitution and Finance of English, Scottish and Irish Joint-Stock Companies to 1720* (Cambridge, 1912), vol. I, pp. 284–92; a run on the banks caused widespread panic in 1667, and payments out of the Exchequer were stopped in 1671, followed by several banking failures in 1672. The trade depression continued until 1674.

oriental designs. This dependence lasted until the early decades of the eighteenth century, and involved humdrum imports of raw materials and artefacts by London merchants and retailers, alongside the transfer of skills and the absorption of stylistic influences from abroad which normally concern art historians.[8]

The post-Restoration decades also saw certain structural changes in the economy of the arts, but these should not be exaggerated. There was a *relative* decline in court patronage and a growing self-confidence amongst aristocratic patrons. This no doubt represented a major shift in the sources of social and political authority, especially after the Williamite revolution and the retreating claims of divine monarchy. As time went on, aristocratic taste was adapted to the more modest aspirations of the gentry and middling sorts, and a 'culture of politeness' spread across broad ranks of eighteenth-century British society. Its sources lay in the courts of Renaissance Italy, but in late seventeenth-century England it developed as a critique of the court and the godly: 'politeness' was defined against the forces which had produced the Civil Wars.[9] The spread of polite taste coincided with an improvement in standards of domestic comfort for the London middle class, reflected in household inventories. Post-Restoration interiors became much brighter, with the increased use of mirrors, sash windows, candlestands, high ceilings and plastered walls, set off with lighter furnishing fabrics, including silks and cottons. By the 1690s, pictures, prints and chinaware proliferated in many houses of the 'middling sort'.[10]

New consumption patterns provided an important driving force behind the refinement of the fine and decorative arts, and one in which market forces played an increasing role. The market for paintings, however, was slow to take off.[11] In the late seventeenth century, pictures were still acquired through commission if not abroad: the remnants of the Arundel collection, for example, were disposed of in Amsterdam in 1684. It was in the late 1680s and early 1690s that the 'massive boom' in

[8] Imports of art products and raw materials into London from France, Germany, Holland and Italy included pictures, prints and frames; pencils for painters, painters' colours, yellow ochre, turpentine, linseed oil, and gilded wax (Public Record Office [PRO] Customs 3/14, 1711).

[9] John Styles, 'The Culture of Politeness', seminar paper given at the Institute of Historical Research, London, 4 February 1994.

[10] P. Earle, *The Making of the English Middle Class: Business, Society and Family Life in London, 1660–1730* (London, 1989), pp. 290–301; and see chapter 4 in this volume.

[11] Lodewijk Huygens' visit to Somerset House in 1652 to view the disposal of pictures and other works of art formerly owned by Charles I suggests a rather low level of activity rather than a flourishing art market. See A.G.H. Bachrach and R.G. Collmer, *Lodewijk Huygens. The English Journal, 1651–1652* (Sir Thomas Browne Institute, Leiden, 1982), p. 61.

London art sales got under way, with over 400 auctions in the space of five years.[12] But it is likely that these early sales depended on imported pictures, and before about 1714 the fine arts were sustained by patronage as much as anonymous production for the market, especially that of the court. Here, we can see a crucial difference between London and Amsterdam. As Marten Jan Bok argues in chapter 9 of this volume, the rise of the Amsterdam art market between 1580 and 1660 is most readily explained by the rapid growth of domestic purchasing power, creating a 'veritable mass market' for home-produced works of art. In London, however, the art market was virtually invented from scratch during the half-century after the Restoration and depended, according to Pears, on the 'discovery of painting', the development of taste, the growth of foreign travel and the linking of taste with social authority. Defoe dated the English enthusiasm for pictures from the accession of William and Mary, when 'the love of fine paintings so universally spread itself amongst the nobility and persons of figure all over the kingdom, that it is incredible what collections have been made by English gentlemen since that time'.[13] The development of a public sphere for the visual arts, involving exhibitions, the sale of non-commissioned work and public discussion of artistic issues, occupied the period 1700–70, culminating in the foundation of the Royal Academy.[14]

Against this background, in what sense can we say that the fine and decorative arts emerged in late seventeenth-century London as a distinct cultural sphere and an autonomous economic sector, given the limited extent of market development and the complexities of the moral debate? In practical terms, it is probably most realistic to think in terms of a series of separate domains, defined by distinct skills and work practices, which became more closely integrated as the period progressed (see table 10.1). More than any other period, the 1690s have been seen as the critical decade during which an international style emerged in the decorative arts of the metropolis, described by some in terms of 'the triumph of the Baroque'.[15] More elaborate and integrated designs called for greater specialization, with at least two results. In the first place, some domains, such as those of the painter, the decorative artist and the goldsmith, generated large

---

[12] I. Pears, *The Discovery of Painting. The Growth of Interest in the Arts in England, 1680–1768* (New Haven and London, 1988), pp. 52 and 58.

[13] D. Defoe, *A Tour through the Whole Island of Great Britain* [1724], ed. D. C. Browning, (London, 1974), vol. I, p. 178.

[14] D. Solkin, *Painting for Money. The Visual Arts and the Public Sphere in Eighteenth Century England* (New Haven and London, 1993), pp. 2–3, 247.

[15] J. Hook, *The Baroque Age in England* (London, 1976), pp. 7–14; G. Jackson-Stops, 'Courtiers and Craftsmen. The William and Mary Style', *Country Life*, 13 October 1988, pp. 200–9.

Table 10.1 *The fine and decorative arts in 1700: a simple taxonomy*

Artists' work	1	Easel painting and drawing
	2	Drawing and engraving
	3	Decorative painting
	4	Stage design
Sculpture	1	Statuary and stonemasons' work
	2	Woodcarving
	3	Plaster and stucco work
Architecture	1	Architects
	2	Masons
	3	Carpenters, carvers and gilders
	4	Ironwork, gatesmiths
	5	Landscape gardening
Goldsmiths' work	1	Goldsmiths
	2	Jewellers
	3	Watchmaking
	4	Objects of vertu
	5	Coins and medals
	6	Banking and finance
Ceramics		
Glass		
Furniture & furnishing	1	Cabinet-making
	2	Upholstery
	3	Interior design
	4	Textile trades

clusters of moderately innovative individuals, populated by foreign practitioners, in which specialist skills and genres easily flourished. Amongst the large cluster of immigrant artists, the high quality of the van de Veldes' work was exceptional and established their unique position as the source for the English school of marine painting. Secondly, smaller and more specialized domains emerged, such as decorative woodcarving and ironwork, where exceptionally gifted individuals dominated the field, as the careers of Grinling Gibbons and Jean Tijou demonstrate.

Clearly, individual achievement within the fine and decorative arts depended on existing levels of excellence and technique within each domain, and within each of the crafts on which it depended (table 10.1). It would be a mistake, in other words, to give priority to individual creativity at the expense of the larger dimensions of collective achievement.

The work of the Huguenot goldsmiths of the 1680s and 1690s, a prime example of a cluster of several dozen individuals, involved the import of techniques required for mounting cast silver, in place of embossed work, together with new forms of design.[16] Overall, high levels of technical excellence were reached. For British goldsmiths, these were undoubtedly innovative practices, in an area which had been dominated by immigrant French, German and Dutch since Elizabeth's reign.[17] The fashioning of tableware and the provision of equipment to facilitate the increasingly popular rituals of tea- and coffee-drinking represented an important contribution to polite culture and domestic sociability. In terms of business organization too, such as increased division of labour within craft processes, subcontracting and retailing methods, London goldsmiths were in the forefront.[18] But, in general, silverware became less important as a store of wealth and fashionable taste could be satisfied with less weight and more elaborate designs.

In the field of painting, drawing and engraving, the late seventeenth century was notable for a major cluster of achievement, compared with the limited progress of earlier periods (shown in figures 10.1 and 10.2). The reign of Charles II, especially, was marked by the presence of equally large numbers of British and immigrant artists working in London. Amongst the immigrant group, Dutch painters far outnumbered the Flemish, an unusual situation explained by the crisis of the early 1670s in Holland.[19] The obsession with portraiture which characterized the period, in the hands of Lely and Kneller, has to a large extent obscured the importance of the minor Dutch masters working in London, especially the landscape painters. Although less distinguished than the earlier Anglo-Dutch painters, their work reached a wider public and provided a much more influential series of models for the future course of British painting.[20] The proliferation of genres which emerged marked a fertile stage of innovatory practice, including landscape, still life, marine painting, cityscapes, sporting and game pictures, 'house portraits' and the trompe l'oeil, in addition to portraiture. Historical and religious painting,

[16] T. Murdoch (ed.), *The Quiet Conquest. The Huguenots, 1685–1985* (London, 1985), p. 229.

[17] R. D. Gwynn, *Huguenot Heritage. The History and Contribution of the Huguenots in Britain* (London, 1985), pp. 72–4.

[18] D. Mitchell, 'Innovation and the Transfer of Skill in the Goldsmiths' Trade in Restoration London' in D. Mitchell (ed.), *Goldsmiths, Silversmiths and Bankers: Innovation and the Transfer of Skill, 1550 to 1750* (London, 1995), pp. 5–22.

[19] At least twenty-two Dutch artists were working in London during the reign of Charles II, compared with seven from the Southern Netherlands. Those from the Northern provinces were Bol, Hoogstraeten, Hondius, Buckshorn, Borselaar, Boon, Paling, Danckerts, Verelst, Roestraten, Loten, Coloni, Jan Griffier I, Edema, Caspar Netscher, Pen, Sunman, Waggenar, the van de Veldes, Vorsterman and Wissing; those from the Southern provinces were van Lemput, Vanzoon, van Lemens, Gaspars, van der Heyden, Huysmans and Stoop.

[20] O. Millar, 'Painting', in *The Orange and the Rose. Holland and Britain in the Age of Observation, 1600–1750*, catalogue of an exhibition arranged by the V&A, London, 1964, pp. 22–5; O. Millar, *The Tudor, Stuart, and Early Georgian Pictures in the Collection of Her Majesty the Queen* (London 1968), pp. 20–32; C. White, *The Dutch Pictures in the Collection of Her Majesty the Queen* (Cambridge, 1982), pp. xxxix-l.

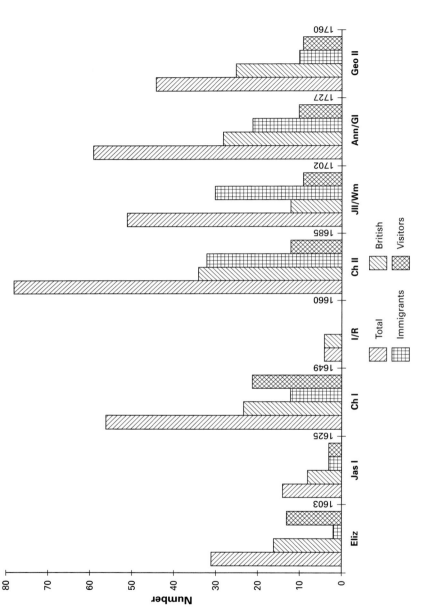

10.1 Numbers of British, immigrant and visiting artists working in England, 1558–1760 (Sources: H. Walpole, *Anecdotes of Painting* (see note 1), vols. I–III; M. Bryan, *Biographical and Critical Dictionary of Painters and Engravers*, London 1816; E. Waterhouse, *Dictionary of Sixteenth and Seventeenth Century British Painters*, Woodbridge, 1988; I. Scouloudi, *Returns of Strangers in the Metropolis, 1593, 1627, 1635, 1639. A Study of an Active Minority*, London, 1985 (Quarto Series of the Huguenot Society of London, vol. LVII))

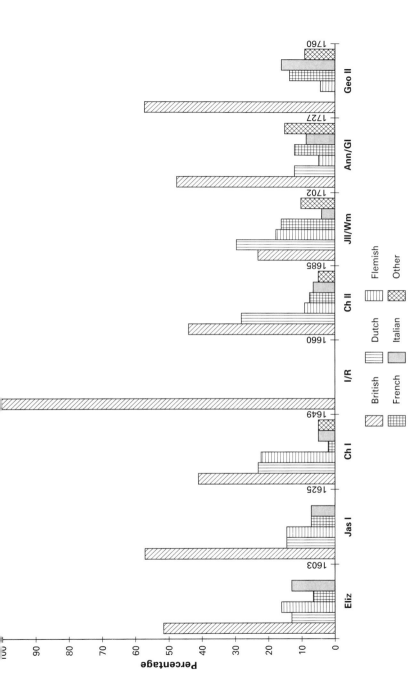

10.2 Proportions of British and foreign artists working in England, 1558–1750 (Sources: H. Walpole, *Anecdotes of Painting* (see note 1), vols. I–III; M. Bryan, *Biographical and Critical Dictionary of Painters and Engravers*, London 1816; E. Waterhouse, *Dictionary of Sixteenth and Seventeenth Century British Painters*, Woodbridge, 1988; I. Scouloudi, *Returns of Strangers in the Metropolis, 1593, 1627, 1635, 1639. A Study of an Active Minority*, London, 1985 (Quarto Series of the Huguenot Society of London, vol. LVII))

on the other hand, were not part of the repertoire of this cohort. Horace Walpole was doubtless justified in writing, in 1762, that 'Britain had rarely given birth to a genius in painting', yet the sector as a whole showed notable incremental improvement and infrastructure deepening, of a kind that laid the basis for a future golden age.[21]

Especially important was the development of better training facilities for artists through the establishment of the drawing academies in 1712 and 1718, under the direction of Kneller and Cheron, respectively.[22] Hitherto, apprentices had relied on drawing books, principally those of Henry Peacham (1606) and William Sanderson (1658) and numerous imported Dutch and Flemish authors, and they copied engravings and existing pictures and drawings in the hands of patrons, artists and collectors.[23] Van Dyck, in particular, was much copied. Drawing from life and from nature was previously rare in the training of young artists; indeed it was frowned upon. It is significant that the most innovative practices in the 1660s and 1670s were those of the immigrant topographical and landscape painters, drawing masters and engravers from the Netherlands, including Danckerts, Siberechts, Vorsterman, the Wycks, the Griffiers, and the Knyffs.[24] The work of this group was very much in the Dutch cartographic tradition, and the ability to record visual information, knowledge of perspective and basic draughtsmanship should be recognized as key skills which were essential to achievement across wide areas of the fine and decorative arts. Drawing ability was essential to the engraver, to the silversmith's chasing-work, to the carver and even for the modification of imported French designs, such as those of Le Pautre.[25]

From the middle of the seventeenth century, the output of prints and illustrated books increased enormously. The engraver, to a much greater degree than the painter, brought the possibility of an interest in the visual arts to a wide public. John Evelyn's pioneering work on engraving, *Sculptura*, appeared in 1662, in which he publicized the new process of mezzotint, introduced to England by Prince Rupert, with help from Wren. Evelyn recommended the collection of prints to those unable to afford original works of art, and unsurprisingly, in a book dedicated to

[21] Walpole, *Anecdotes*, I, ix.
[22] Discussed in I. Bignamini, 'Art Institutions in London, 1689–1768: A Study of Clubs and Academies', *The Walpole Society* 44 (1988), 1991.
[23] The enormous range of Dutch and Flemish pattern books is listed by J. Bolten, *Method and Practice. Dutch and Flemish Drawing Books, 1600–1750* (Landau, Pfalz, 1985); M. Whinney and O. Millar, *English Art 1624–1714* (Oxford, 1957) pp. 12–13.
[24] L. Stainton and C. White, *Drawing in England from Hilliard to Hogarth* (London, 1987), pp. 13–27.
[25] Whinney and Millar, *English Art*, chapter XI; Stainton and White, *Drawing in England*, pp. 29–42; Thornton, *Seventeenth Century Interior Decoration in England, France and Holland* (New Haven and London, 1978), pp. 66–7.

Robert Boyle, hoped that 'such as are addicted to the more noble mathematical sciences, may draw, and engrave their schemes with delight and
assurance'.[26] The best mezzotinters in Europe were attracted to London
during the second half of the seventeenth century, when the art became
known as engraving 'in the English manner'.[27]

The case of sculpture and carving may be contrasted with that of easel
painting, drawing and engraving. Here, a small field was dominated by a
single genius, Grinling Gibbons, who raised the status of the craft of
woodcarving to a position of enhanced importance within the broad
range of the decorative arts as a whole. Gibbons' exceptional abilities
were fostered by the time he spent in the Quellin workshops in Antwerp
and Amsterdam during the late 1650s and early 1660s. Sources for his
later work included Hubertus Quellin's two volumes on the statuary and
carvings at the new Amsterdam Town Hall, as well as the work of several
Dutch still-life painters, especially Justus van Huysman the Elder and
Seghers.[28] Artus Quellin I (1609–1668) had spent nine years in Rome
working for Francois Duquesnoy, who in turn had worked with Bernini.
His brother, Artus Quellin II, also went to Italy and spent two years in
Amsterdam. It was Arnold Quellin, son of Artus II, who arrived in
England in 1678 and later married Frances Siberechts, daughter of the
immigrant Flemish painter Jan Siberechts. In the early 1680s, Arnold
entered into partnership with Gibbons, though it is likely that they had
worked together from an earlier date. In ways such as these, personal contacts and family connections provided the basis for the careers of a high
proportion of painters and sculptors in the period before professionalization was established. In the case of Grinling Gibbons, it is possible to link
his work directly with the practice of high baroque decoration and its
Dutch variants.[29]

Organizationally, and to some extent stylistically, the domain of sculpture can be divided between those who were trained and worked in the
traditional artisanal mode and those who did not. Thomas Burman,
Edward Pierce, Joshua Marshall, Abraham Storey and Thomas Green
were members of the masons' company and worked with building
contractors. John Bushnell, Gabriel Cibber and Francis Bird, however,
worked outside the company and described themselves as statuaries; all
three had travelled extensively and worked in a classical baroque manner,
drawing inspiration from the work of Bernini and his followers.[30] This

[26] Whinney and Millar, *English Art*, pp. 11–12.
[27] A. M. Hind, *A History of Engraving and Etching, from the fifteenth Century to the Year 1914* (London, 1923), pp. 258 and 272.
[28] This paragraph is based on G. Beard, *The Work of Grinling Gibbons* (London, 1989).
[29] Beard, *Grinling Gibbons*, pp. 10, 51–3.

distinction was replicated in other domains. For example in the 1620s, a major rift had opened up between native painters working within the artisanal structure of the Painter-Stainers Company, and the increasingly successful immigrant artists from the Low Countries associated with the court.

In the field of furniture-making and upholstery, the post-Restoration period saw a high rate of innovation and diversification of production. Again, we see the familiar dominance of foreign craftspeople, and a growing tension between native workmen trained in the traditional way as carpenters and joiners, subject to restrictive practice, and Dutch and Huguenot cabinet-makers operating outside the control of the companies. For instance, the most fashionable chairs of the late seventeenth century involved the integration of four sets of craft skills, controlled by four separate companies, the Joiners, Turners, Carvers and Upholsterers.[31] It was principally the Dutch, admittedly drawing much from French examples and techniques, who transformed the backward state of the craft in England from the 1660s onwards. Gerreit Jensen and Cornelis Golle were the most outstanding representatives, the former acting as cabinet-maker to four successive monarchs. Their success was such that, by 1700, Dutch craftspeople at the Hague had to submit an 'English cabinet' as their masterpiece.[32] In the intervening period, they instigated a series of changes connected with the growing taste for more portable, smaller items of furniture, frequently veneered, in place of heavy oak pieces. Exotic veneers, marquetry work and inlays of king-wood, ebony and amboyna were used, as well as walnut (most of it imported). It was during the 1720s and 1730s that the use of mahogany greatly increased.[33]

The reorganization of domestic space, to meet an increasing desire for privacy, developed rapidly in seventeenth-century England, especially in London.[34] In great houses, the apartment evolved as a series of linked rooms which became increasingly private as one moved through them,

---

[30] Whinney and Millar, *English Art*, p. 237; Hook, *Baroque Age*, p. 124.

[31] P. Kirkham, 'The London Furniture Trade, 1700–1870', *Furniture History*, 24 (1988), pp. 11–12; G. Beard, *English Furniture* (London, 1985), pp. 15–19.

[32] T. H. Lunsingh Scheurleer, 'The Decorative Arts', in *The Orange and the Rose*, pp. 27–8. For a comparison with Dutch and Flemish pieces within a single collection, see P. Thornton, 'Furniture from the Netherlands at Ham House', *Nederlands Kunsthistorisch Jaarboek* 31 (1980), pp. 239–43.

[33] Whinney and Millar, *English Art*, pp. 225–9; Edwards, *The Shorter Dictionary of English Furniture* (London, 1964), p. 342.

[34] F. E. Brown, 'Continuity and Change in the Urban House: Developments in Domestic Space Organization in Seventeenth Century London', *Comparative Studies in Society and History* 28 (1986), p. 587, argues that specialization and differentiation of room functions probably began earlier in London than in other parts of the country.

culminating in one or more comfortably furnished closets.[35] It was in these small spaces that innovations in decoration and furnishing were often first tried out, such as upholstery, the display of ceramics, the setting of mirror glass into panelling and the use of oriental laquer. Such ideas could be readily adapted to modestly proportioned London houses in the later seventeenth century, as greater emphasis was placed on the front parlour as a space for withdrawal or interaction with visitors, when space was at a premium.[36] The demand for portable and more compact furniture was increasing, and this was facilitated by the replacement of oak by lighter woods. The taste for greater intimacy and for diary-keeping and collecting was accommodated in a diverse range of chests, bookcases, bureaux, writing tables and cabinets with fitted drawers, symbolizing secrecy, possessiveness and total privacy.[37] There was thus a multiplication of specialized types of furniture. Evelyn noted in 1669 that the fashion developed of dining in small parties at separate tables.[38] If British painters in the late seventeenth century prioritized the head at the expense of the body, furniture makers did the opposite, by providing much more comfortable upholstered seating and more elaborate bedding.[39] By 1700, London had become the centre of a flourishing furniture industry, with expanding export markets, and by the 1720s, as Defoe noted, it was possible to distinguish town from country-made pieces.[40] But in the early eighteenth century, as Pat Kirkham shows, leading London furniture makers still combined the roles of craftsman, manager and designer.[41]

In the 1690s, after more than a century of manufacture in England, the quality of home-produced 'delftware' (tin-glazed earthenware) was still rather indifferent compared with Dutch and Flemish products. The role of Antwerp was critical in the transfer of the art of tin-glazing

[35] P. Thornton, *Authentic Decor. The Domestic Interior, 1620–1920* (London, 1984), p. 18.
[36] Brown, 'Domestic Space Organization', pp. 577, 583–4; A.F. Kelsall, 'The London House Plan in the Later 17th Century', *Post-Medieval Archaeology*, 8 (1974), pp. 80–91. Thornton, *Seventeenth-Century Interior Decoration*, pp. 296–303. For a well-documented example of the arrangement and decoration of the baroque enfilade in a great London house, see G. Jackson-Stops, 'Daniel Marot and the 1st Duke of Montagu', *Nederlands Kunsthistorisch Jaarboek*, 31 (1980), pp. 244–60.
[37] G. Willis, *Craftsmen and Cabinet-makers of Classic English Furniture* (Edinburgh, 1974), pp. 21–2; R. Edwards, *English Furniture*, p. 13.
[38] Edwards, *Shorter Dictionary*, p. 12.
[39] Thornton, *Seventeenth-Century Interior Decoration*, chapters IV–VIII.
[40] Kirkham, 'The London Furniture Trade', p. 3; Defoe, *A Tour*. The early eighteenth-century Customs ledgers list furniture exports from London (*ad valorem*) in the following categories: cabinets (£9–26 each), escritoires (£5–12 each), chairs, cane chairs, chests of drawers (£10 each), clock cases (£2–3 each), looking glasses, upholstery ware; the most important markets were Holland, Germany, Spain, Portugal and the West Indies (PRO Customs 3/14, 1711).   [41] Kirkham, 'The London Furniture Trade', p. 82.

from Urbino in Italy to northern Europe, largely through the agency of one family, the Savini (anglicized to Andries).[42] It was Jasper Andries and his son, together with Jacob Jansen, who set up the first London pottery in Aldgate, in 1571. All the known potters employed there, totalling thirteen, were Flemish. During the first half of the seventeenth century, three further potteries were established in London, all in Southwark. That at Pickleherring was operated from 1618 by Christiaen Wilhelm, also a maker of smalt and vinegar and a member of the Dutch Church. By 1700, nine delftware factories were functioning in London, including those of the Rotterdam immigrant potter John de Wilde, founded at Vauxhall in 1683, and of Jan van Hamme, who established the Copthall pottery, also in Lambeth. The latter arrived from Delft in 1676 accompanied by his family and sixteen servants and workmen.

By the 1630s, it seems that distinctively English forms of delftware were emerging from the London potteries, differentiated from the earlier Flemish majolica. Barrel-shaped mugs, straight-sided posset pots, wine bottles and dishes decorated with English inscriptions were produced, and the interchange of English and Dutch potters led to a general diversification of designs.[43] For much of the seventeenth century however, the Dutch potteries maintained a clear lead over their London rivals, not least because of the excellence of Dutch decoration and artistry. Engravings provided a common fund of design motifs, particularly the prints of van Dalen, Crispin van den Passe, Goltzius and de Vos.[44] The paintings of Hobbema, van Berchem and van Goyen had a direct influence on the potters of Delft after the mid-century.[45] Since the 1460s, however, the import of foreign painted wares into England had been prohibited and reaffirmed at various times: by proclamation in 1676 and in further statutes of 1689 and 1694.[46] Illegal imports continued to flow into London, but the prohibition probably stimulated English and immigrant potters to achieve higher standards.

The case of ceramics clearly illustrates both the routes and the mechanisms by which innovations in manufacturing and design were transmitted from southern to northern Europe, and the continuing dependence on imported and immigrant skills. When the craze for collecting oriental porcelain and delftware reached the dizzy heights of

---

[42] Most of the information in this section is drawn from Frank Britton, *London Delftware* (London, 1986), pp. 8–23. The process of transmission from Italy to Holland and England, via Antwerp, can be reconstructed as follows: Middelburg 1564, Norwich 1567, Haarlem 1568, Aldgate 1571, Delft 1584, Amsterdam 1584, Rotterdam 1600, Harlingen 1600, Southwark 1615, Leeuwarden 1616, and Utrecht 1616 (ibid., p. 22).
[43] F.H. Garner and M. Archer, *English Delftware* (London, 1948), p. 6.
[44] Ibid., pp. 11–12.   [45] Ibid., p. 16.   [46] 3 Edw. IV c.4; 2 W. & M. c.4; 6 & 7 WIII. c.7.

'Chinamania' after the accession of William and Mary, the more discerning purchasers preferred illegally imported Dutch wares which, according to Defoe, they piled 'upon the tops of cabinets, scrutores, and every chymney-piece, to the tops of the ceilings'.[47] It is doubtful that many of them would have had the opportunity to see the magnificent collections assembled at Hampton Court, Dyrham or Chatsworth, but the evidence of surviving examples suggests a connection between the 'fatal excesses' of the 1690s and the growth of a more sophisticated metropolitan taste.[48]

It is possible, then, to observe individual achievement and innovation in different domains, and there is a sense in which each exhibits its own history and peculiar characteristics. In several fields, high standards of workmanship and technique were the norm. But more significant than the level of achievement within each separate domain was the totality of achievement within the sector as a whole. As classical models were better understood and as experimentation proceeded, it seems that a threshold was crossed, in terms of both design and workshop practice. A small number of individuals succeeded in bringing together several activities which were only loosely integrated hitherto, so as to create entirely new possibilities and forms of creative expression. The pioneer, of course, lies outside our period: Inigo Jones. But the Huguenot architect and *ornemaniste* Daniel Marot combined an equally impressive range of skills, including those of artist, engraver, architect, landscape gardener and producer of designs for furniture, silver and ceramics. Furthermore, he was able to draw on the accumulated skills of a generation of Dutch, Huguenot, Italian and other immigrant craftspeople in a way that Jones was not.

Marot worked as an engraver at the court of Louis XIV before leaving for Holland, where he became 'dessinateur-en-chef' to William III. From the palace of Het Loo, he moved to Hampton Court in 1694 and for a period of at least four years produced designs for interior decorations and garden plans. He was the first architect in Holland (and England) to coordinate and design all the decorative elements in a room.[49] In several respects, he represents a new kind of figure who was able to orchestrate all the possibilities inherent in what J.U. Nef described as the new 'economy of delight' of seventeenth-century France, which emphasized luxury and quality at the expense of abundance. It would be easy to exaggerate Marot's contribution to the decorative arts in England, and he was

---

[47] Defoe, *A Tour*, I p. 166.
[48] The production of chargers, for example, seems to have waned in the London potteries during the first quarter of the eighteenth century (Garner and Archer, *English Delftware*, p. 11).   [49] Murdoch, *The Quiet Conquest*, p. 183.

certainly the 'representative of a more generally diffused, French-inspired, court culture'.[50] But his engravings, issued in sets of six during the 1690s, undoubtedly secured for him an extremely wide influence. The collected Amsterdam edition of 1700 became a much-used pattern book for craftspeople throughout Holland, Britain and the colonies, as the most comprehensive outline available of the international baroque interior.[51]

The idea of contriving a unified furnishing scheme – a full *ameublement* of hangings, upholstery, movable furniture and a *garniture* of vases and clocks – arrived in England from France in the early seventeenth century. Ham House is one of the most complete surviving examples. The practice spread beyond fashionable court circles after the Restoration, and by 1700 English architects were accustomed to thinking about how a room should be furnished in advance of building.[52] The overall conception depended upon the act of visualization, and it has been suggested that the immigrant Anglo-Dutch school of painting provided the British public with a new range of possibilities.[53] On balance however, French influences were more powerful, especially in promoting the new ideals of personal luxury and domestic grandeur and in 'investing private space with public meaning'.[54] In practical terms, the production of architectural drawings – first established by Inigo Jones, followed by John Webb and William Talman – was the essential preliminary. The publication of pattern books for fireplaces, panelling and architectural details began earlier, and multiplied after the Great Fire. The fire, indeed, gave an enormous impetus towards standardization in building and furnishing. The emergence of interior design thus depended upon the coordination of at least four sets of skill: those of the architect, the artist and decorative painter, the furnishing trades and the building trades, including carpenters and plasterers.

The period saw a high rate of improvement and innovation in cabinet-making, upholstery, the use of mirrors and pier-glasses and the arrangement of pictures. New possibilities arising from the use of large raised and fielded panels in place of the small flat panels characteristic of Tudor and Jacobean wainscoting allowed for a much more interesting and symbolic hanging of pictures and the incorporation of decorative painting into the

[50] Saumarez-Smith, 'Decorative Arts', in R. P. Maccubbin and M. Hamilton-Phillips, *The Age of William II and Mary II. Power, Politics and Patronage 1688–1702* (London, 1989) p. 299.   [51] Jackson-Stops, 'Courtiers and Craftsmen', p. 203.

[52] Thornton, *Seventeenth-Century Interior Decoration* (New Haven and London, 1978), chapter 2; C. Saumarez-Smith, *Eighteenth Century Decoration. Design and the Domestic Interior in England* (London, 1993), p. 39.

[53] Saumarez-Smith, *Eighteenth Century Decoration*, p. 31.

[54] The phrase is Saumarez-Smith's; ibid., p. 19.

domestic interior.[55] It was during the 1690s, in particular, that London merchants first began to install chimney glasses and to place pier-glasses between windows.[56] The period saw the increased use and display of ceramics, glass-fronted cases, cabinets of curiosities, and the furnishing of print rooms and libraries. Out of all these elements, there emerged a new conception of the interior as a total design. Baroque art, as an art of the 'total environment', was the first manifestation of this, but the Palladian revolution made similar demands. The architectural interior and its furnishings provided a new context within which the fine and decorative arts became more closely integrated, in which private space became an arena for the expression of taste and public meaning.[57] It is more easily understood as the outcome of several clusters of achievement, rather than the work of specific individuals.

The harmonious integration of these various elements and skills, which was arguably the main achievement of the period, came into being via three channels, at a time when the arts were still dominated by patronage rather than the market. First, the role of the architect was crucial in bringing together and controlling elite teams of craftspeople, for major projects such as St Paul's, Windsor, Hampton Court, Montagu House, or more modestly at Ham House, all of which are well-documented examples.[58] With the exception of William Winde, the entire succession of seventeenth- and early eighteenth-century architects were native-born, which differentiates this particular field from all others.[59] As Sacheverell Sitwell put it, the career of Wren was *the* opportunity for great craftspeople, but others such as Hugh May, Robert Hooke and William Talman coordinated, trained and organized large groups of leading craftspeople, with great success, including Tijou, Gibbons, Verrio, Laguerre and Cibber.[60] Several of these elite craftspeople themselves acted as master contractors: Gibbons, for example, employed up to fifty men in his own workshops and during the 1680s was executing very little work himself.[61]

Secondly, the important role of social networks must be emphasized, formed from marriage, kinship and common religious affiliations, all of which were especially common amongst painters and elite craftspeople,

[55] On the sixteenth-century introduction of small panels, see Willis, *Craftsmen and Cabinet-makers*, pp. 14–15; G. Beard, *The English House Interior* (London, 1990), p. 86.
[56] Saumarez-Smith, 'Decorative Arts', p. 293.
[57] Saumarez-Smith, *Eighteenth-Century Decoration*, pp. 19–21.
[58] See especially, P. K. Thornton and M. F. Tomlin, *The Furnishing and Decoration of Ham House* (London, 1980); G. Beard, *Craftsmen and Interior Decoration in England, 1660–1820* (London, 1981), pp. 115–65.   [59] Winde was born in Holland of English parents.
[60] S. Sitwell, *British Architects and Craftsmen* (London, 1945), p. 5.
[61] G. Beard, 'The Furniture Trades in the Seventeenth Century', paper given at the seminar in Preindustrial History, Institute of Historical Research, 10 March 1995.

especially immigrants. Networks became denser when sons and (more rarely) daughters followed their father's craft. These minor dynasties are too numerous to list, but include the Quellins, Marots, Golles, Cibbers and Riccis; amongst painters, there were the de Critz, van de Velde, Griffier, Vanzoon, Hoogstraeten and Hondius families, amongst many others.

A third transformative agency was the experience of workshop training, especially where English craftspeople succeeded in breaking free from local restrictions and travelling abroad.[62] The examples of painting, sculpture and carving, and ceramics indicate clearly how workshop training and social networks functioned to provide the routes and mechanisms by which skill and innovation were transmitted from southern to northern Europe. The role of Antwerp was critical. In spite of economic decline, Antwerp retained its identity as an economic *and* artistic metropolis during the first half of the seventeenth century, while, to the north, these functions were shared amongst the towns and cities of Holland.

This brief review has attempted to highlight a number of infrastructural improvements in the decorative and fine arts in London. The sector as a whole was characterized by the overwhelming predominance of foreign artists and craftspeople, particularly in the years following the Huguenot diaspora from 1685 to 1702. The example of immigrant and visiting painters working in London points to the reign of Charles II as something of a minor golden age when large numbers of (mainly Dutch) immigrant painters were working alongside equally large numbers of British artists. During the reigns of James II and William III, the proportion of foreign painters was much higher, within a smaller overall total. Overall, the most significant achievements arose from the efforts of a handful of individuals to draw together and coordinate the creative activity of immigrant craftspeople, particularly Wren and his circle, whose skills encompassed draughtsmanship, mathematics and architectural history and theory. The achievement was a collective one, however, in which the question of nationality took on an increasing significance amongst those who would nowadays be described as cultural theorists.[63] British architects continued to depend on the skills of foreign craftspeople and decorative teams, and the debt to immigrant artists was evident,

---

[62] Beard, *Craftsmen and Interior Decoration*, pp. 11–13.

[63] As early as 1658, William Sanderson had raised the question of nationality in relation to the production and consumption of pictures, long before the early eighteenth-century debates established by Pope, Steele, Shaftesbury, Richardson and others; see, for example, J. Murdoch, 'Painting: from Astraea to Augustus' in B. Ford (ed.), *The Cambridge Cultural History of Britain*, vol. 4, *Seventeenth Century Britain* (Cambridge, 1989), pp. 262–4.

less directly perhaps, in fostering the capacity to visualize and delineate the built environment.

By the early eighteenth century, when the art market was more firmly established than had been the case during the reign of Charles II, this developing network of cultural transactions was increasingly conditioned by the efforts of the Whig aristocracy to establish national control of a 'national culture'. In 1711, Pope had complained that, compared with France, Britain remained unconquered but uncivilized.[64] The Whig propagandists, especially Shaftesbury, responded with the suggestion that 'newly united Britain' should indeed reduce its dependence on imported French fashions and cultural products, and at the same time develop its own national culture, drawing inspiration directly from classical sources. Shaftesbury went on to propose the establishment of academies of painting, sculpture and architecture, in which the vigorous Palladianism of Inigo Jones would be revived, to replace the 'licentious' baroque designs of Wren and indeed of Counter-Reformation art in general. It was, in short, a Whig-inspired plea for a form of Protestant classicism, set out 'in terms of value of the discourse that we now describe as civic humanism.'[65]

If the close of the so-called Baroque Age was not as abrupt as some art historians suggest, however, it is equally true that opposition to French cultural dominance had grown steadily from the 1670s onwards. The remedy which gradually emerged is perhaps better known to economic historians than to art historians, since its rationale was commercial: import substitution. It has often been emphasized that London was both a centre of fashionable, conspicuous consumption and the country's most important manufacturing centre, particularly of high-quality luxury goods.[66] As Marcia Pointon puts it, London was seen as the place where 'the exotic was turned into art'. As a developing world entrepôt, replacing Amsterdam by 1730, London was the centre of a growing import trade in an increasingly diverse range of raw materials: hardwoods, dyestuffs for textiles and artists' pigments, and the industrial raw materials upon which artists and craftspeople depended, including potters, bookbinders and workers in stucco,

[64] A. Humphreys, 'The Arts in Eighteenth Century Britain' in B. Ford (ed.), *The Cambridge Cultural History of Britain*, vol. 5, *Eighteenth Century Britain* (Cambridge, 1991), p. 4.

[65] Following J. G. A. Pocock, John Barrell discusses these lines of thought, mainly in relation to painting, in terms of the discourse of civic humanism and the effort to establish a 'republic of taste' within the fine arts, J. Barrell, *The Political Theory of Painting from Reynolds to Hazlitt* (New Haven and London, 1986), pp. 1–27. See also Solkin, *Painting for Money*, chapter 1.

[66] F. J. Fisher, 'The Development of London as a Centre of Conspicuous Consumption in the Sixteenth and Seventeenth Centuries', *Transactions of the Royal Historical Society*, 4th. series, 30 (1948), pp. 37–50; reprinted in E. M. Carus-Wilson (ed.), *Essays in Economic History*, vol. II (London, 1962), pp. 197–207.

amongst others.[67] On the other hand, the flow of exotic imports of finished goods from Asia was growing rapidly – silks, japanned ware, porcelain and a host of minor curiosities – in addition to French luxury goods. Chinaware was an ideal complementary cargo to go with tea, and heavy porcelain chests provided the necessary ballast for the East India Company's ships.[68] The 1660s saw the acceleration of an import-led phase of commercial growth, occurring at a time when London's population was expanding much more rapidly than that of the rest of the country. Not until the mid-1740s did British trade again surge forward in such a dramatic way.[69]

As we have already noticed, however, import-led growth was producing serious balance of payments problems during the 1670s, and the increasing consumption of imported French luxury goods by the prosperous minority took on a particularly menacing aspect. The growing campaign against imports of French luxury goods reached a climax during the wars of the 1690s, when francophobia, economic nationalism and fiscal necessity combined to encourage a major protectionist drive. Tariffs were raised against a range of European imports such as paper, linen and silk, while various initiatives were undertaken to encourage home production.[70] The purpose of import substitution in the fine and decorative art trades was to ensure the continued flow of necessary raw materials and immigrant skills, while discriminating against or prohibiting the import of finished art products. We have already noted how steps were taken to reaffirm and strengthen the long-standing prohibition of imported painted earthen-

[67] M. Pointon, 'Diamonds Are a Girl's Best Friend', paper given at the V&A/RCA MA Seminar on the History of Design, 2 December 1993. In addition to imports of exotic woods, dyestuffs and raw silk entering the port of London, the Customs ledgers list numerous types of raw material for the luxury trades rarely noticed or quantified by historians, including Italian marble imports, German goldsmiths' tools, printers' ink and unbound books from Holland, painters' colours from Flanders, France and Holland, and upholstery wares from France (PRO Customs 3/1, 1697–8).

[68] K. N. Chaudhuri, *The Trading World of Asia and the English East India Company, 1660–1760* (Cambridge, 1978), pp 406–7; J. Villiers, 'Oriental Influences on English Taste', *History Today* 25 (1975), pp. 164–74. On the import of French luxuries and the adverse balance of trade since the 1660s, see D. C. Coleman, 'Politics and Economics in the Age of Anne: the Case of the Anglo-French Trade Treaty of 1713', in D.C. Coleman and A.H. John (eds.) *Trade, Government and Economy in Pre-Industrial England. Essays presented to F.J. Fisher* (London, 1976), pp. 188–90; M. Priestley, 'Anglo-French Trade and the "Unfavourable Balance" Controversy, 1660–85', *Economic History Review*, 2nd series, 4 (1951).

[69] P. Deane and W.A. Cole, *British Economic Growth, 1688–1959* (Cambridge, 1964), pp. 41–50.

[70] R. Davis, 'The Rise of Protection in England, 1689–1786', *Economic History Review*, 2nd series, 19 (1966); P. K. O'Brien, T. Griffiths and P. Hunt, 'Political Components of the Industrial Revolution: Parliament and the English Cotton Textile Industry', *Economic History Review*, 2nd series, 44 (1991); N. B. Harte, 'The Rise of Protection and the English Linen Trade, 1690–1790' in N. B. Harte and K. Ponting (eds.), *Textile History and Economic History* (Manchester, 1973).

ware (majolica or 'delftware') in 1689 and 1694. In the case of pictures, discriminatory tariffs were applied. In 1695, the first steps were taken to discourage the import of pictures by levying a 20 per cent *ad valorem* duty, 'whether for private use or sale'.[71] It has been wrongly assumed that imports of paintings were prohibited before this date; in fact the earlier prohibitions related only to imports by strangers (of 1483) and paintings and artefacts that could be described as 'popish images' of 'vain and superstitious things' (of 1570).[72] The 1695 duty was continued by a further statute of 1704, and strengthened in 1721 when it was replaced by a scale of specific duties related to the size of the painting.[73]

It is unlikely that protectionist measures such as these had more than a marginal impact on the art trade, although examination of the outport customs letter books and merchants' correspondence shows that importers took elaborate steps to avoid payment of the substantial increases of 1721. In September 1726, for example, the Commissioners of Customs in London felt it necessary to warn their officers in the outports that London merchants were increasingly importing 'several small pictures which to evade the dutys were placed in large frames, consisting of ten or twelve pictures in each', thus calling for stricter supervision.[74] At the same time, prints were imported from Holland, sewn together and bound up as books simply to avoid duty when in fact they were intended to be framed 'proper for furniture'.[75] In the early 1750s, a prominent Leeds merchant importing pictures from Holland informed his Amsterdam agent that these should be rolled up and 'introduced carefully as they are subject to a large duty'.[76]

[71] 6 & 7 Will. III, c. 7.
[72] Pears, *The Discovery of Painting*, pp. 53–4. It was the ambiguity of the earlier legislation in the changing climate of religious ideology, rather than outright prohibition, which lay at the root of the problem. The late fifteenth- and sixteenth-century legislation undoubtedly discouraged the import of religious and historical paintings. The relevant statutes are 1. Rich. III c.12, which related to imports by merchant strangers of painted cloths and painted images, and 13 Eliz. I c.2 .
[73] 3 & 4 Anne c.4, 8 Geo. I c.18, and 11 Geo. I c.7; H. Crouch, *A Complete View of the British Customs* (London, 1738), pp. 200–2; S. Forster, *A Digest of all the Laws Relating to the Customs, to Trade and Navigation* (Cambridge, 1727). Three categories of picture, distinguished by size, were established by the act of 1721. This was clarified in 1724, so that size was measured according to surface area. Pictures measuring 16 square feet and above paid a duty of £3; those of 4–16 square feet paid £2; and those under 4 square feet paid £1. These represented substantial duty increases, given that pictures were usually given low valuations by importing merchants before specific duties were introduced in 1721; valuations normally fell in the range of 10s–£2 during the later 1690s, producing duties of 2s–8s per picture.
[74] PRO Customs Letter Books, Customs 97/74B (Yarmouth, Board to Collector), 17 September 1726; 17 September,1726; Customs 64/63 (Exeter, Board to Collector), 27 September 1726.   [75] PRO Customs 64/55 (Exeter, Board to Collector), 3 June 1729.
[76] Gemeente Archief, Amsterdam, Archief Brants 1343, William Denison, Leeds, to Jan Isaac de Neufville, Amsterdam, 21 April 1753.

The legislation of 1695 and 1704 was clearly intended to encourage the re-export of European pictures from London, as two-thirds of the duties were drawn back on export. According to Defoe, these were the years when London's expanding art market took on a more speculative character: since the turn of the century, 'all Europe has been rumag'd . . . for pictures to bring over hither, where, for twenty years, they yielded the purchasers, such as collected them for sale, immense profit. But the rates are abated since that, and we begin to be glutted with the copies and frauds of the Dutch and Flemish painters, who have imposed grossly upon us.'[77] Although interpretation of the customs statistics in relation to the art trade is fraught with difficulty, particularly before 1721 when pictures were entered *ad valorem*, the customs ledgers suggest that London was already a net exporter of pictures by the late 1690s.[78] The early history of the London art market has hitherto been considered almost entirely in terms of European imports from Flanders, France, Holland and Italy, but these were more than balanced by an outflow of pictures to Germany, Portugal, Ireland, the plantations and colonial consumers. It seems, in fact, that the process of import substitution operated in ways which differed little in their essentials from those that applied to manufactured goods in general. It is arguable that the existing accumulation of imported skills was greater in the artistic field than was the case with manufactures such as paper and linen, the classic import-substitution industries of the late seventeenth century. The silk industry, on the other hand, was characterized by a slow build-up of immigrant skills, dating from the 1570s, as was the manufacture of ceramics.

The commercial background to the history of the decorative and fine arts deserves more attention than it has so far received. It is clear that the assumptions of late mercantilist thinking were consistent with the programme of Shaftesbury and his circle, in which Britain would emerge as 'the principal Seat of the Arts', and this serves to remind us of the underlying link between the arts and cultural politics in the Augustan age. The often-repeated notion that the visual arts somehow express the 'character of the age' is perhaps a less helpful observation than one which seeks to emphasise their capacity to function as symbols or emblematic representations of power, capital and status, and indeed, as mere commodities.

---

[77] Defoe, *A Tour*, I p. 178.
[78] PRO Customs 3/1 (Michaelmas 1697–8) shows that exports of pictures from London exceeded imports by 37 per cent.

Part 5

Books and publishing

11 Antwerp: books, publishing and cultural production before 1585

Werner Waterschoot

In the 1581 edition of his well-known *Descrittione de tutti i Paesi Bassi*, Lodovico Guicciardini praised the printing house of Christophe Plantin as unrivalled throughout Europe.[1] This contemporary eulogy has been supported by posterity. To late-twentieth-century eyes, the activity of the Officina Plantiniana marks one of Antwerp's most characteristic cultural achievements in the sixteenth century. Guicciardini mentioned no other printer besides Plantin. Nevertheless, Plantin was not the only printer in Antwerp at that time, nor was he the first. Antwerp had played a prominent part in Dutch typographical history since 1481. By the end of the fifteenth century, the greatest share of book production in the Southern Netherlands was contained within the city. With 432 titles produced before 1501, Antwerp surpassed the university town of Leuven (270 titles), while all other Southern towns together produced no more than 131 books. At that time, only the cities of Zwolle and Deventer (600 titles) in the North were more important in the same field. Both cities profited from the presence of famous schools, run by the Brethren of the Common Life, and, as a consequence, enjoyed an avid reading public.

The rise of Antwerp as a typographic centre, however, was due to different circumstances. Printing needed capital, first of all for establishing and equipping the shop, but, still more importantly, for financing forthcoming publications. The cost of paper was the heaviest burden on the printer's budget and had to be paid before production began. On the other hand, the profit made from selling copies came in only slowly. The necessary finance, then, was most easily supplied in a dynamic and growing city such as Antwerp. Its expanding hinterland and developing network of communications facilitated and accelerated the sale of the printer's output.

The career of Antwerp's earliest important printer is representative in this respect. Gerard Leeu had been active as a printer at Gouda in Holland, where he produced some 60 books between 1477 and 1484. He

[1] L. Guicciardini, *Descrittione di tutti i Paesi Bassi* (Antwerp, 1581), p. 162.

then went to Antwerp, where he was described as 'a man of grete wysedom in all maner of kunnying'.[2] In Antwerp he printed more than 150 books, apparently for a much wider, even international public. He issued liturgical texts and schoolbooks in Latin and devotional works and romances in Dutch, as well as in French and English. After Leeu's death, Dirk Martens, the earliest printer in the Southern Netherlands, left his native town (Aalst) for Antwerp, where he stayed between 1493 and 1498 and between 1505 and 1512 before practising in Leuven. In Antwerp, he printed both pious works and the *Epistola de insulis nuper inventis* ('Letter on the recently discovered isles') by Christopher Columbus.

As with Antwerp's foremost merchants and captains of finance, many of the printers were of foreign origin. Christophe Plantin and Maarten de Keyser (or Martin Lempereur) came from France, Gerard de Jode from Guelders, Arnold Mylius and Tielman Susato from the Rhineland. This was no barrier to setting up in the printing business, for access to the trade was by patent from central government and thus free from civic and guild control. Nevertheless, from 1558 onwards printers had to join the guild of St Luke to allow better control. As a result, the sector expanded continuously: between 1501 and 1510, forty-five people were active in the typographic trade; by the 1570s, this number was ten times greater. In contrast to Paris, where publishers without a printing house of their own dominated the trade, in Antwerp it was the printers who controlled all aspects of printing and distribution.[3]

As in other economic respects, Antwerp surpassed the rest of the Netherlands. Ghent and Brussels both had some ten printers, and Leuven had as many as forty-two, but their output was of only local significance, by comparison with that of Antwerp's outstanding masters from the first half of the sixteenth century onwards.

Between 1506 and 1546, Michael Hillen van Hoochstraten published more than 150 books, ranging from writings by the humanists Erasmus, Jacobus Latomus and Adrianus Barlandus to almanacs. He published the first book in the Netherlands directed against Luther, the *Articulorum doctrinae Lutheri* by Latomus, as well as the first edition of John Fisher's attack on Luther. Subcontracting his publications, he had some of them printed by his Antwerp colleagues Christoffel van Ruremund and Jan van Doesborch, at Delft by Cornelis Lettersnider and in Paris by Joannes Kaerbriand. He also worked for the English market, as did van Doesborch, who associated himself with Laurence Andrewe of Calais, a

[2] A. Rouzet, *Dictionnaire des imprimeurs, libraires et éditeurs des XVe et XVIe siècles dans les limites géographiques de la Belgique actuelle* (Nieuwkoop, 1975), p. 122.
[3] L. Voet, 'De typografische bedrijvigheid te Antwerpen in de 16de eeuw' in *Antwerpen in de XVIde eeuw* (Antwerp, 1975), p. 240.

printer and bookseller in London. Van Doesborch offered a variety of subjects to his English customers: schoolbooks, currency regulations, prognostications and travel stories.[4] Cornelius Grapheus worked also for Hillen van Hoochstraten. He published almost 300 books under his own name, or on contract for Antwerp publishers, for Reginaldus Oliverius at Ipswich, and for Jean Bourgeois at Arras. Grapheus issued ordinances, prognostications, the famous geographical work of Petrus Apianus, and books in Latin, Greek, Hebrew, Dutch, French and English. Yet more impressive was the career of Willem Vorsterman, who published about 400 books in the period 1504–43. Besides contract work for colleagues in Ghent (Gillis van de Walle), Amsterdam (Bartholomeus Jacobs), Ypres (Jaspar van den Steen), Konstanz (Johannes Haselberch) and other cities, he put work out to other Antwerp firms and to Jodocus Badius in Paris. Consequently, his was a polyglot output, comprising books in Dutch, French, English, Spanish and Danish. Vorsterman published chap-books, devotional works, Bibles, ordinances, almanacs and one music book. The preponderance of Antwerp printers made that city the natural place for the production of important, voluminous and illustrated books in the Netherlands.

The runaway success of the Antwerp printing houses manifested itself in three very specific features of their output: diversification, topicality and mass production. At the beginning of the sixteenth century, as every-where in Europe, religious literature represented a large segment of the book market: between 1500 and 1539, of 2,650 books printed in Antwerp, no fewer than 1,164 belonged to the pious sector, of which a third (371 titles) were traditional devotional works. The predominance of this late-medieval genre diminished as the Reformation progressed. In August 1520 Hillen van Hoochstraten issued a text by Luther. By the end of 1522 twelve Latin and ten Dutch Luther editions had left the Antwerp presses.[5] The activity of Luther's fellow-Augustines in their Antwerp convent, the presence of a powerful group of German merchants and not least the tolerance of the city magistrates aided this proliferation. Giving priority to the commercial interests of the city, the municipal government did not wish to upset the foreign residents. As late as 1567 Guicciardini stated that foreigners enjoyed more freedom in the Netherlands and in Antwerp in particular than anywhere else on earth.[6] In fact, of the 161 people executed for the sake of religion in Antwerp between 1525 and

---

[4] J. van der Stock (ed.), *Antwerp. Story of a Metropolis, 16th–17th Century* (Ghent, 1993), p. 220.

[5] D. Imhof, G. Tournoy and F. de Nave (eds.), *Antwerpen, dissident drukkerscentrum. De rol van de Antwerpse drukkers in de godsdienststrijd in Engeland (16de eeuw)* (Antwerp, 1994), p. 15.   [6] Guicciardini, *Descrittione di tutti i Paesi Bassi* (Antwerp, 1567), p. 116.

1566, only five were Lutherans. The others were Anabaptists or held related beliefs.

As a result, the most daring among the Antwerp printers played an important part in propagating the new doctrines. After Hillen van Hoochstraten and Vorsterman, the most active participants in this risky business between 1520 and 1545 were Adriaan van Berghen, Jacob van Liesvelt and Maarten de Keyser. Van Berghen started as the most important publisher of Dutch books on theology and moved in the direction of heterodoxy.[7] After 1522 he became the most assiduous printer of Protestant books in the Netherlands. Ultimately, the magistrates banished him from Antwerp in 1536, sentencing him to a pilgrimage to Nicosia. Instead of travelling to Cyprus, he left for the Northern Netherlands, where he sold Protestant books while wandering from town to town. In the meantime, his press in Antwerp remained active and in about 1536 produced nine tracts by the 'arch-heretic' David Joris. No wonder that the court in The Hague sentenced him to death on the scaffold on 2 October 1542.

Van Liesvelt was a second victim. From 1536 onwards he was continually accused of printing heretical works, and in 1545 was charged with producing a Protestant Bible. Despite the assistance of several lawyers, his defence was unsuccessful and he was beheaded in Antwerp on 28 November 1545.

De Keyser followed a more subtle path. Originally from Paris, he was especially active as a printer in Antwerp between 1525 and 1536. He is said to have left France on the advice of Jacques Lefèvre d'Etaples, whose translation of the Bible had been forbidden in France and who wanted to have it printed elsewhere. De Keyser managed to publish his work in the years 1528–32 without being harassed by the authorities. He then issued many tracts by German and English Protestant authors.[8]

Frans Fraet was known as a rhetorician and as a minor printer of predictions. On 3 January 1558, however, he was sentenced to death for circulating heretical works. That judgement was severe by comparison with those meted out to others in the book trade. Under the pseudonym Magnus Vanden Merberghe he was the most energetic Protestant publisher of his time, and it was only after his death that the town of Emden took over Antwerp's position as the leading centre of Dutch Protestant printing.

---

[7] P. Valkema Blouw, 'The Van Oldenborch and Vanden Merberghe Pseudonyms or Why Frans Fraet Had to Die', *Quaerendo* 22 (1992), p. 257.

[8] P. Valkema Blouw, 'Early Protestant Publications in Antwerp, 1526–30. The Pseudonyms Adam Anonymus in Bazel and Hans Luft in Marlborow', *Quaerendo* 26 (1996), p. 101.

From the beginning of Luther's publishing activity, the imperial government issued strict edicts intended to prevent the spread of heresy. Consequently, an Antwerp municipal ordinance of 14 February 1524 obliged printers to include the author's name, their own name and mark, and the year and the place of publication in all editions. The printers circumvented this measure by using false or fictitious imprints, by ante-dating their books or by hiding in anonymity. These procedures were effective, sometimes for centuries. The name Niclaes van Oldenborch became famous for many daring Protestant publications, yet the man never existed. The name was a pseudonym used between 1527 and 1559 by seven or eight publishers, including van Berghen, Mattheus Crom, Steven Mierdmans, Hans de Laet and, last but not least, Fraet. The dynamic business activities of these people knew no national or linguistic limits. Most of de Keyser's publications, for example, were in French or Latin, and so intended to be sold abroad.

Through Vorsterman's and van Doesborch's contacts with the English book market, English works on the religious controversies found their way to the continent via Antwerp. John Fisher, bishop of Rochester and champion of the Catholic orthodoxy in England, responded to early Protestant attacks with books printed by Vorsterman in November 1522 and by Hillen van Hoochstraten in January 1523. English Protestants had a much greater impact through the Antwerp market. In the autumn of 1528 William Tyndale arrived in Antwerp and stayed there for most of the rest of his life. His presence led to a flow of clandestine editions. Tyndale's translation of the Pentateuch bears the imprint 'Marlborow, Hans Luft'. In fact, it came out in 1530 from de Keyser's printing house. De Keyser had entrusted part of the work to Grapheus, probably because his own setting capacity was insufficient. An edition of the New Testament 'dylygently corrected and compared with the Greke'[9] was produced by de Keyser in November 1534. He also circulated two influential tracts by Tyndale, 'The Parable of the Wicked Mammon' and 'The Obedience of a Christen Man'. Simon Fish, the most influential early English Protestant after Tyndale, also gained an audience through the Antwerp printing world. In 1529, Grapheus issued two of Fish's works, including 'A Supplication for the Beggars', a short work against the Catholic clergy, which proved to be the most widely read *libellus* of the early English Reformation.

Smuggling this contraband into England was risky. The Antwerp printer Hans van Ruremund was arrested in London for the illegal importation of Tyndale's New Testament. His relative Christoffel van

---

[9] Imhof, Tournoy and de Nave, *Antwerpen*, p. 26.

Ruremund was imprisoned for the same reason in Westminster, where he died.

Later in the century, after the Anglican Settlement, Antwerp became a centre for recusant printing. Thus, the tradition of clandestine production for the English market was continued, but now for the use of English Catholics.

At one point Vorsterman even produced Protestant texts in Danish. However, that was not on his own responsibility, for the books, including a New Testament and works by Luther, were ordered by Canon Christiern Pedersen when staying in the Netherlands. Pedersen himself supplied some of the typefaces.

Clandestine publishing undoubtedly favoured the development of the Antwerp printing industry. A number of the people involved certainly acted from personal engagement. However, a considerable part of the Antwerp trade issued both Protestant and Catholic books simply for profit. Hillen van Hoochstraten produced the first Luther editions in Antwerp as well as Henry VIII's rebuttal of the German reformer. Gillis Coppens van Diest, who printed recusant authors such as John Rastell and Richard Shacklock, was in 1567 (correctly) under suspicion of having circulated a clandestine Protestant pamphlet. (His mark, by the way, read: 'A fructu dignoscitur' – 'By his fruit ye shall know him'.) Willem Silvius, the Royal Typographer, was suspected in 1568 of having participated in the iconoclasm of 1566.

Only when pressed by the central government did the Antwerp aldermen take action against the multitude of heretic printers, and then reluctantly and ineffectively. The Brussels authorities were aware of the situation and of the measures to be taken. In 1562 Margaret of Parma, the Regent of the Netherlands, instructed the margrave of Antwerp to track down the person responsible for a heretical book. She advised him to enquire carefully among the printers so as to identify the letter-type.[10] Of course, the Antwerp printers were struck blind on this matter. In a similar case in 1566, the Antwerp aldermen summoned Coppens van Diest, Grapheus and two of their colleagues to identify the printer of a clandestine admonition to the people of Brabant. Coppens, who had himself printed the text, declared that the type was in use everywhere. Grapheus said that he too used this type of letter, but that the text was in Dutch, whereas he preferred to print in Latin. The case came to nothing.[11]

As in all other European countries, texts concerning the religious controversy predominated. Nevertheless, the Antwerp presses produced a

[10] H. Vervliet, *Sixteenth-Century Printing Types of the Low Countries* (Amsterdam, 1968), p. 4.
[11] Rouzet, *Dictionnaire des imprimeurs*, pp. 45 and 80.

wide range of books.[12] Songbooks and chap-books for common entertainment were printed in great quantities, but few have been preserved. Sixteenth-century inventories do not record this type of book, which was of low monetary value. Schoolbooks and dictionaries were steady sellers. The presence of merchants with interests in many countries created a market for books presenting colloquial phrases in seven languages. Books on accountancy also appealed to the same public. Most manuals of surgery, midwifery and pharmacy were printed in the vernacular, for use by the practitioners in the crafts. Cartography in its most advanced form was represented by the maps and atlases of Gerard Mercator and Abraham Ortelius.[13] Works on mathematics, astronomy, physics, botany, zoology and technology found their way to scholars and scientists.[14] Nor did Antwerp printers and publishers neglect the foreign vernacular market, if it was sufficiently large. Between 1545 and 1570 Antwerp produced more Spanish works than did printers in Spain itself.[15] In this vast array of books for all sorts of customers, belles-lettres represented no more than a modest share of the whole. Printing was above all a matter of business and profit. Remuneration for an author was exceptional. In a letter of 17 November 1586 to his nephew Emmanuel van Meteren, the geographer Ortelius expressed his particular pleasure that his publisher Plantin had presented him with twenty-five copies of his latest book. He knew of other men who had paid Plantin to print books which hardly sold.[16]

Topicality was key to the printing industry of a commercial centre such as Antwerp. The presence of so many diverse nations and languages made Antwerp an obvious centre for the exchange of all kinds of information. The people of Antwerp were known for their linguistic proficiency. Guicciardini spoke highly of the Antwerp merchants and their wives, who mastered three or four languages, and sometimes five to seven.[17] News sheets, mostly about political subjects, were distributed in large numbers, usually by the lesser printers. In 1587, for example, Matheus de Rische published a 'True Report' of the death of Mary Stuart immediately after her execution. Prognostications too ensured a steady and guaranteed income for their publishers. Nor should the role of prints in the diffusion

[12] L. Voet, De gouden eeuw van Antwerpen. Bloei en uitstraling van de Metropool in de zestiende eeuw (Antwerp, 1973), p. 395.
[13] F. de Nave, D. Imhof and E. Otte (eds.), Gerard Mercator en de geografie in de Zuidelijke Nederlanden (Antwerp, 1994), p. 15.
[14] E. Cockx-Indestege and F. de Nave (eds.), Christoffel Plantijn en de exacte wetenschappen in zijn tijd (Brussels, 1989), p. 19.
[15] F. de Nave, 'A Printing Capital in its Ascendancy, Flowering and Decline' in van der Stock, Antwerp. Story of a Metropolis, p. 92.
[16] L. Voet, The Golden Compasses. A History and Evaluation of the Printing and Publishing Activities of the Officina Plantiniana at Antwerp, 2 vols. (Amsterdam, 1969–72), vol. II, pp. 284–5.   [17] Guicciardini, Descrittione (1581), p. 167.

of information be underestimated. The most notorious print dealer was Hieronymus Cock. As a publisher of woodcuts and engravings he covered wide areas. A quarter of his output consisted of religious images, after which came allegories, ornaments, landscapes, portraits, mythological subjects, townscapes, maps, ships and reproductions of works of art. At the end of the century, the Galle workshop took over Cock's position as a publisher and dealer in prints with an international reputation. Filips Galle, a native of Haarlem, was helped as head of the firm by his many relatives. Their output was more homogeneous and religious in character, in accordance with the spiritual climate of Counter-Reformation Antwerp.

Antwerp publishers revealed their awareness of the market by very quickly reprinting the books that sold best. The first edition of Sigismund von Herberstein's *Rerum Moscoviticarum commentarii* came out in Basel in 1555. A year later the book was published in Antwerp. Distance was no obstacle. Antonio Possevino's *Moscovia* appeared in Wilna (now Vilnius in Lithuania), but the work did not escape the attention of Plantin, who managed to bring out his edition only a year afterwards, in 1587.[18] In 1566 Plantin printed a Hebrew Bible, which was in part intended for the Jewish communities in North Africa. Three of Antwerp's foremost merchants, Johan Rademaker, Gaspar van Zurich and Gillis Hooftman, competed for the profitable contract to distribute this edition.[19]

The increasing scale of book production was in the size of the Antwerp printing houses, about a quarter of which were large businesses. In the second half of the century the firms of Martinus Nutius, who specialized in Spanish printing, Arnold II Birckman, Joannes Bellerus and Jan van Keerberghen were outstanding for their size. Over the sixteenth century as a whole, 194 masters associated with the printing industry were listed in the guild of St Luke (48 printers, 72 booksellers, 7 punch-cutters and type-founders, 62 engravers and 5 print dealers).

The most representative Antwerp typographer was, of course, Christophe Plantin.[20] Antwerp became a decisively influential typographic centre through his activity alone. He was born in about 1520 of humble stock in a village near Tours in France. Having been trained as a bookbinder at Caen, he emigrated to Antwerp in 1548/9 and initially worked there as a master craftsman in leather.

From the beginning, however, he must have had the ambition of becoming a printer. In 1550 he enrolled himself as a printer in the guild of St Luke. In his letter to Pope Gregory XIII of 9 October 1574 Plantin

18 Voet, *De gouden eeuw*, pp. 20–3.
19 L. Voet, *The Plantin Press (1555–1589). A Bibliography of the Works Printed and Published by Christopher Plantin at Antwerp and Leiden*, 6 vols. (Amsterdam, 1980–3), vol. I, p. 325.
20 Voet, *The Golden Compasses*, vol. I, p. 3.

explained his choice of Antwerp in terms of three reasons: the availability of materials, the abundance of craftspeople and easy access to the market.

With the help of the heretic Hendrik Niclaes, the founder of the Family of Love, he set up a printing workshop. In the first phase of his activity (1555–62) he printed 141 works. In 1562, the business stopped for a while. Plantin stayed in Paris when three of his journeymen were surprised printing a heretical work. For safety's sake the printer remained in Paris for a year and a half. In the meantime, all his goods had been sold under process of law. He then started anew in association with four (later five) companions. Three of them being staunch Calvinists, the company ended in 1567 when the duke of Alba arrived in the Netherlands. By then, the company had put 209 editions on the market.

In that same period Plantin did not neglect the profitable business of printing heretical texts, especially Bibles in translation. But he did not risk this traffic in Antwerp. So, in the greatest secrecy, some of his men were for that purpose sent to work at Kampen in 1562 and at Wesel in 1566.[21] It is no wonder that he later felt obliged to emphasize his Catholic orthodoxy to his Spanish patrons. One of these was Gabriel de Çayas, the secretary to Philip II, for whom Plantin had done some leather work. Through de Çayas, Plantin made a proposal to the sovereign for publishing a scholarly edition of the Bible. By interesting the king, Plantin avoided any possible persecution and obtained financial support to realize a vast enterprise. The Spanish scholar Arias Montanus came to oversee the work. In five years, between 1568 and 1573, the *Biblia Polyglotta* or *Biblia Regia* was finished. At the zenith of his activities in the 1570s, Plantin had at least sixteen presses working and had twenty compositors, thirty-two pressmen and three proofreaders in his service, in addition to the servants in his house and bookshop.

Before the Polyglot Bible was finished, Plantin conceived another great project. The Council of Trent had decided upon a revision of liturgical books, with the result that all previous editions were to be replaced. Through his patron Antoine Perrenot Cardinal de Granvelle, Plantin obtained from the authorities in Rome and their privileged printers the sole rights for the project in the Netherlands. This business was undermined, however, by the activities of some Liège and Cologne printers, who ignored the privileges and turned out breviaries and missals. Luckily, the Spanish market was more promising. The king, well disposed to the successful publisher of the *Biblia Regia*, granted him a virtual monopoly for the sale of breviaries and missals in Spain and its dominions overseas.

[21] P. Valkema Blouw, 'Geheime activiteiten van Plantin, 1555–1583', *De Gulden Passer* 73 (1995), p. 6, note 3.

Meanwhile Plantin had become Europe's leading printer of humanist, scientific and religious literature, paying great attention to new genres, for example emblems. In an emblem, the central element is an illustration with a motto above and a subscription below it, these three components interpreting and clarifying each other. Plantin was famous for his press-work, set in type designed by the best French and Dutch specialists. He deliberately preferred copperplate illustrations to woodcuts. As a result, copperplate illustration became predominant in the next century. The quality of his work was such that scholars from all over Europe offered him their writings for publication.

Immediately after the Spanish Fury (4–6 November 1576), during which Plantin was obliged to ransom his life and property several times, he left the city to borrow money from friends in Liège, Paris, Cologne and Frankfurt. He was able to resume his business, but expansion ceased. Under the regime of the States General, the work for the king of Spain came to an abrupt end. Plantin was still to print many impressive works – herbals by Carolus Clusius and Mathias Lobelius, Guicciardini's *Descrittione* and the atlases of Ortelius – but his personal initiative was restricted. Now many of his publications were printed 'to order' or were financed by publishers in Paris and Cologne.

In 1583 he set up a branch in the town of Leiden in Holland as printer to the newly established university. Plantin was organizing a reserve press should the Spaniards besiege Antwerp, which they did in 1584–5. Plantin avoided royal displeasure by observing strict neutrality in his Leiden publications. Thus he had no difficulty when he returned to Antwerp in 1585 immediately after its surrender to Alexander Farnese. In spite of the unfavourable times, Plantin managed to produce forty volumes a year. He was an exhausted man, however, and died on 1 July 1589. Between 1555 and 1589 he had produced some 2,450 books.

After Plantin's death, his son-in-law Jan I Moretus became manager of the Officina Plantiniana. In his time, the Spanish regime and the Old Church had stabilized. Like his predecessor, Moretus published important works such as the *Annales ecclesiastici* of Cesare Baronius, new editions of Rembert Dodoneus, Clusius and Lobelius, and learned works by Ortelius and Justus Lipsius. The former variety of Plantin's production was no longer maintained, however, and the true glory of the press in Jan Moretus's time was its liturgical and devotional output. These books were illustrated by the best craftspeople of the Antwerp school: the three Wierix brothers and the Galle family. They spread the fame of the Officina throughout the Catholic world. This increase in Catholic devotional publications was paralleled by the evolution of the Giolito firm in Venice, which under the influence of the Counter-Reformation restricted itself to religious books in Italian for a geographically limited market.[22]

Guicciardini was moved to praise many of Antwerp's cultural accomplishments in addition to Plantin's Officina. They included the arts of singing and dancing. 'All over the city', he said, 'one sees everywhere weddings, banquets and dancings. Everywhere, one hears cheerful singing and clincking'.[23] The Venetian ambassador Vincenzo Quirini characterised the music in Antwerp at the beginning of the century as 'perfect' and his colleague Bernardo Navagero considered the inhabitants of the Netherlands to be born musicians.[24] The most stable and most important musical focus in Antwerp was provided by the Church. Antwerp cathedral had twelve choristers, who lived in a private house, where they received instruction from their master. On high feast-days, hours and masses were sung in descant. The singing master was also a composer. At the beginning of the sixteenth century, the office was held by the famous Jacob Obrecht. Between 1512 and 1516 Benedictus de Opitiis was active as an organist to the chapel of Our Lady's Praise in the cathedral. He then entered the service of the English king, Henry VIII. The city itself had a company of fiddlers in its service. They presumably accompanied voices in both secular and ecclesiastical performances. The four parish churches and many monasteries also contributed to the musical culture of the city. Under the Calvinist regime (1578–85) the Huguenot psalter was not confined to religious services. Some composers found inspiration in it to write spiritual chansons for singing at home.

Antwerp had many composers, who were also active as singers, clergymen or schoolmasters or who were in private service. There was presumably a lively concert life, very little of which is known. Andries Pevernage, the singing master of the cathedral after 1585, is said to have organized weekly concerts at his home, where compositions by Italian, French and Dutch masters would be performed. Upper-class youths received musical instruction from private teachers. Some texts by the foremost Renaissance poet Jan van der Noot were set to music by four of the best composers: Hubert Waelrant, Andries Pevernage, Grégoire Treschault and Cornelis Verdonck, all living in Antwerp at that time.[25] When

---

[22] P. Burke, 'Antwerp, a Metropolis in Europe' in van der Stock, *Antwerp. Story of a Metropolis*, p. 55.   [23] Guicciardini, *Descrittione* (1581), p. 169.
[24] A.-M. van Passen, 'Antwerp under the Magnifying Glass. An Anthology' in van der Stock, *Antwerp. Story of a Metropolis*, p. 60.
[25] W. Waterschoot (ed.), *De 'Poeticsche Werken' van Jonker Jan van der Noot. Analytische bibliografie en tekstuitgave*, 3 vols. (Ghent, 1975), vol. II, p. 204; vol. III, p. 69; J.W. Bonda, *De meerstemmige Nederlandse liederen van de vijftiende en zestiende eeuw. The Polyphonic Songs in Dutch of the Fifteenth and Sixteenth Centuries* (Hilversum, 1996), p. 148.

enumerating the merits of the Antwerp city clerk Cornelius Grapheus, Guicciardini pointed out that this gentleman was also well versed in music. As late as the 1650s, the Dutch poet and diplomat Constantijn Huygens greatly appreciated the musical culture which he encountered in the Duarte house in Antwerp.

Antwerp was also a centre for the production of music books.[26] Tielman Susato, an immigrant from Cologne, was the first to gain an international reputation for music printing. Another important master, Jan de Laet, published advanced music such as motets. The indefatigable Plantin produced the finest choir books. From the 1570s onwards, the Bellerus and Phalesius families were leading houses for this musical production. The entire contemporary repertoire was made available by the Antwerp presses: vernacular songbooks and psalms, as well as polyphonic secular and ecclesiastical music. Works by all the famous European composers were offered by the Antwerp publishers, if sometimes after great delay. Nicholas Yonge's *Musica Transalpina*, published in 1588, was the first London edition of Italian madrigals in English and drew one third of its content from Antwerp music books.[27]

Another feature which characterized Antwerp as a centre of music was the production of musical instruments. Hans Ruckers from Mechelen, the well-known builder of harpsichords, managed a company of a size comparable to Plantin's Officina.[28] His products, like Plantin's, were sent all over Europe. Although Ruckers was the leading manufacturer of these instruments, he was not the only one. Another important business in this field was the building of organs. They were exported as far as Spain and Scandinavia. Gillis Brebos, as the leading organ-builder, not only worked for the cathedrals of Antwerp and Malines, but was invited by King Philip II to Spain to make organs in the Escurial. In Antwerp cathedral itself, no fewer than four organs were set up at this time.

Literature and the performing arts flourished in this prosperous and stimulating setting. Humanists were usually closely tied to royal patronage, and so other towns offered them more advantages: Brussels as a seat of the court, Malines as a juridical centre and Leuven as the leading place of learning. Hence the humanists residing in Antwerp were high-ranking civil servants who wrote in their spare time. Although in the sixteenth century the Netherlands produced a plethora of scholars and scientists, the most prominent of them did not live in Antwerp: not Andreas

[26] R. Dusoir and E. Otte (eds.), *Antwerpse muziekdrukken. Vocale en instrumentale polyfonie (16de–18de eeuw)* (Antwerp, 1996), p. 18.
[27] G. Persoons, 'Muziekleven' in *Antwerpen in de XVIde eeuw*, p. 505.
[28] G. O'Brien, 'The Cultural and Economic Importance of the Ruckers Family in Antwerp' in van der Stock, *Antwerp. Story of a Metropolis*, p. 351.

Vesalius, or Gerard Mercator, or Simon Stevin, or Rembertus Dodonaeus. They visited Antwerp, however, to meet their colleagues and to have their works printed. Thanks to the skills of the Antwerp publishers, there was a continuous flow of distinguished men of learning. Humanists such as Erasmus and Thomas More, religious reformers such as Tyndale and Philippe de Mornay, and philosophers such as Cornelius Agrippa von Nettesheim and John Dee passed through Antwerp. Many foreign writers who had their works printed in Antwerp stayed there for a while, including the Hungarian physician and author of emblems Joannes Sambucus. The Antwerp government welcomed the gift or dedication of important books to the city. Guicciardini, Lobelius and Dodonaeus received substantial sums of money for the dedication of their chief works to the city of Antwerp. Ortelius was rewarded with a cask of Rhine wine, while Lipsius was honoured with gilt plate in return for the offer of his *De constantia*. On the other hand, the building up of a public library took time, and was not realized until 1608. Then, by an agreement between the bishop and the magistrates, the library of the Antwerp chapter and the books in the Town Hall were united into one institution.

In the second half of the sixteenth century, Plantin's Officina became a centre of humanism. The process began with the Polyglot Bible, his greatest editorial enterprise, on which many scholars worked under the supervision of the Spanish theologian Arias Montanus. Plantin's printing of Latin literature, old and new, did the rest. Together with his friend, the geographer Abraham Ortelius, he served as a core around which men such as Justus Lipsius, Joris Hoefnagel and Gerard Mercator could organize their Antwerp editorial and financial affairs. After Plantin's death in 1589, Ortelius became the undisputed head of learned society in Antwerp. In particular, he acted as a benevolent intermediary between European scholars concerned with antiquity. In their letters these humanists touched on questions of scholarship, but they also discussed the exchange of seeds and bulbs. Gardening must have been a favourite topic for many of these people.

Although Antwerp's humanists enjoyed a solid reputation in the European republic of letters, they were not conspicuous in the streets. More popular tastes were served by the Dutch rhetoricians. Since the fifteenth century, chambers of rhetoric had been the chief focus for vernacular literary life in the Netherlands. They were meeting places for men who wrote poetry in mutual competition. The phenomenon spread rapidly in the most urbanized regions of the Netherlands, and chambers sought recognition from town authorities. By this means, their statutes were assured and they were enabled to act as guilds. They collaborated with town governments in organizing all kinds of festivities: processions, receptions of the sovereign and of foreign visitors, and other public celebrations. Naturally, the chambers competed in producing poetry and drama. Their dramatic productions took place in the open air, usually in the market-place with the whole population as spectators. The authorities willingly supported these ambitious entertainments, which enhanced the reputation of the town. As Protestantism spread, the chambers became important focuses for intellectual debate. A gathering of chambers in Ghent in 1539 alarmed the central authorities because Lutheran opinions were expressed.

The duchy of Brabant was home to a particular type of competition known as the 'Land's Jewel', held exclusively between a group of Brabant chambers. The winner of the first match was awarded a silver plate. That chamber was obliged to organize the next contest and to add another plate to the prize. The cycle ended after seven meetings, when the ulti-mate winner gained seven plates. Antwerp had three chambers of rheto-ric: the 'Gilliflowers', united with the guild of St Luke in 1480; the 'Marigold', founded in 1488; and the 'Olive branch', dating from 1510. The 'Gilliflowers' chamber was twice victorious in the 'Land's Jewel' and had to organize the next festival, which they did in 1496 and 1561, respectively. Nothing is known of the 1496 festival other than the list of prizes. Some scattered archival material was left from the meeting in 1561. A bulky volume printed in 1562, however, provides details of the organization of the festival of 1561, as well as the texts of most of the poems and plays.[29] The introductory pages describe the entry into Antwerp of the fourteen participating chambers as a magnificent spect-acle. There were 1,328 men on horseback as well as many actors on 23 antique chariots and 196 illuminated ones. Although such an entry was primarily a display of the wealth and splendour of the Brabant towns, as represented by their chambers, Antwerp was responsible for its organiza-tion and had summoned the whole duchy to participate in the contest.

The 'Gilliflowers' depended heavily on the Antwerp authorities for the organization of the festival, and those authorities in turn had to obtain the consent of the central government for such a comprehensive display. Collaboration between the city and the guild was assured by the presence of several aldermen on the committee of the chamber. Not surprisingly, one of the items in the program was a 'Eulogy of the honest merchant'. Administrative matters were settled by the governors of the visiting cham-bers, who assembled with the Antwerp civic authorities in the Town Hall. Minutes were taken by the city clerk Alexander Grapheus himself. The victor of the contest was designated by a jury consisting of prominent

---

[29] E. Cockx-Indestege and W. Waterschoot (eds.), *Uyt Ionsten Versaemt. Het Landjuweel van 1561 te Antwerpen. Inleiding D. Coigneau* (Brussels, 1994), p. 25; W. Waterschoot, '3 augustus 1561', in *Een theatergeschiedenis der Nederlanden* (Amsterdam, 1996), p. 120.

members of the participating chambers. Prizes were offered, not only for purely dramatic matters such as best actor, but also for the most impressive entry, the finest allegorical blazon, the most solemn presence in church and the most brilliant illumination of lodgings. The committee of judges took account of public opinion. For that purpose the jury, like the aristocracy, enjoyed the privilege of reserved places. Some minor prizes, however, were awarded by a committee on which only men of the 'Gilliflowers' and Antwerp aldermen participated.

The festivities lasted from the 3rd to the 26th of August. Trade was slow during that period, because all attention was concentrated on the stage for the performances set up in the market-place. Richard Clough, the agent of Thomas Gresham in Antwerp, reported the entry to his master: 'Thys was the strangyst matter that ever I sawe, or I thynke that ever I shall see – I wolde to God that some of owre gentyllmen and nobellmen of England has sene thys . . . and then it would make them to thynke that ther ar other as wee ar, and so provyde for the tyme to come; for they that can do thys, can do more.'[30]

Antwerp was crowded with visitors from all over the Netherlands. This great event marked the end of the 'Land's Jewel' competition, but its fame, consolidated by the 1562 publication, set standards for similar assemblies in the Northern Netherlands for the rest of the century.

Entries for new sovereigns were one occasion on which humanists, artists and rhetoricians joined forces to prepare a pageant of major political and cultural significance. These celebrations were high points in sixteenth-century urban life. Exceptionally, foreign nations too participated in the decoration of the streets and the homage to the prince. In 1520, when honouring the emperor Charles V, the city clerk Cornelius Grapheus and the clerk Petrus Aegidius composed Latin, Greek and Hebrew inscriptions for the triumphal arches and *tableaux vivants*. The project was executed by 250 painters and 300 carpenters. Other such occasions were the presentation of Prince Philip as the heir to the throne in 1549; the inauguration in 1582 of the Duke of Anjou by the provinces which had deserted the Spanish king; the welcoming of Archduke Ernest as a representative of Philip II in 1594; and the entry of Albert and Isabella as new sovereigns in 1599. Accounts of each of these celebrations were published with a view to emphasizing the city's loyalty and power, as demonstrated by the ingenuity and opulence of the festivities. The entry of Prince Philip in 1549 must have been the most grandiose spectacle of them all. Cornelius Grapheus, now in his old age, drew up the programme, while the artistic organization was entrusted to Pieter

---

[30] C. Kruyskamp (ed.), *Het Antwerpse landjuweel van 1561. Een keuze uit de vertoonde stukken* (Antwerp, 1962), p. xxi.

Coecke van Aelst, who was in charge of every well-known artist. The entire city was covered with triumphal arches and stages. More than 2,000 columns had to be painted. Since the old Town Hall was in disrepair, a temporary wooden palace was erected in the market-place.

The only comparable spectacle in Antwerp's history was that in honour of Cardinal-Infante Ferdinand in 1635.[31] The staging of that entry was entrusted to Peter Paul Rubens, who created a flamboyant apotheosis of the Habsburgs as a world power. The spectacle also revealed the progressive separation of ruler and subject. On that occasion the performances of the rhetoricians seemed old-fashioned when set beside Rubens' stylish and imposing triumphal arches. The gap between the elite and the mass of the people widened during the seventeenth century. Theatrical performances came to take place in playhouses, which became more and more exclusive. From the 1640s an entrance fee was charged that represented half a day's wage.[32]

What survived of Antwerp's cultural achievements after 1585, when the city surrendered to Farnese in the name of the Spanish king? Broadly speaking, they stood firm for a while. The most conspicuous break with the past was the attack on the chambers of rhetoric. The Duke of Alba had declared them to be hotbeds of heresy and for the rest of the century they were prohibited. The era of the 'Land's Jewel' was over. The next representative meeting of the chambers took place at Malines in 1620. However, musical life continued to flower in Antwerp during the seventeenth century. Book production went on too. In 1585 the Protestants were given four years to embrace Catholicism or leave the country. Consequently, from 1589 many printers and journeymen left Antwerp for the Northern Netherlands, where they instigated the rise of Holland's printing business. The Counter-Reformation stimulated a new flourishing of religious orders, convent schools and pious literature. Heterodox visitors, however, avoided the now rigidly Catholic city. Uniformity of mind prevailed over diversity of opinion. By 1600, devotional literature represented a substantial share of Antwerp book production, as it had done a century before. In 1601, the Officina Plantiniana began the remarkable series of emblem books by the Jesuit Joannes David, which initiated a glorious sequence of spiritual emblem literature lasting fifty years. After that, the Moretuses turned again primarily to the Spanish liturgical market. They still enjoyed an international reputation for splendidly produced liturgical works. International discourse between intellectuals, however, had now shifted to other sites.

---

[31] W. Waterschoot '17 april 1635' in *Een theatergeschiedenis der Nederlanden*, p. 186.
[32] H. Soly, 'Social Relations in Antwerp in the Sixteenth and Seventeenth Centuries' in van de Stock, *Antwerp. Story of a Metropolis*, pp. 42–3, 45.

12   Metropolis of print: the Amsterdam book trade in the seventeenth century

Paul Hoftijzer

Around 1600, printing and bookselling in the newly created Dutch Republic went through a period of rapid and unprecedented growth. This remarkable phenomenon has been called 'the Dutch miracle',[1] and rightly so, for whereas until the 1580s the book trade in the Northern Netherlands had been a fairly modest activity, within only a few decades it grew into a full-blown and flourishing enterprise. In towns all over the country, but particularly in the densely populated province of Holland, new printing establishments and bookshops were opened and the output of books and other printed matter multiplied. The books were on all subjects and in all formats and languages. In contrast to the sixteenth century, they were no longer intended only for the local or regional market, but increasingly meant for international distribution. Thus an industry came into being, which would eventually make the Dutch Republic – as one historian has put it – 'the intellectual entrepôt of Europe'.[2]

One city took pride of place in this development: Amsterdam. Nowhere else in Europe during the seventeenth century were so many books printed. Of a total estimated Dutch book production of well over 100,000 titles for this period, the great majority were produced in the Republic's unofficial capital.[3] Thousands of highly specialized and skilled people earned a living in the Amsterdam book trade: type-founders, paper merchants, typesetters, printers, correctors, booksellers,[4]

---

[1] H. de la Fontaine Verwey, 'Het Hollandse wonder' in P.F.J. Obbema et al., *Boeken in Nederland. Vijfhonderd jaar schrijven, drukken en uitgeven* (Amsterdam, 1979), pp. 46–64.

[2] G.C. Gibbs, 'The Role of the Dutch Republic as the Intellectual Entrepôt of Europe in the Seventeenth and Eighteenth Centuries', *Bijdragen en Mededelingen betreffende de Geschiedenis der Nederlanden* 86 (1971), pp. 323–49.

[3] The estimate is based on J.A. Gruys et al., 'Dutch National Bibliography 1540–1800; The STCN', *Quaerendo* 13 (1983), pp. 149–60. For a first attempt at a statistical analysis of Dutch seventeenth-century book production based on the *Short-Title Catalogue, Netherlands* (*STCN*, compiled by the Royal Library in The Hague) for the year 1650, see also J.A. Gruys and J. Bos, *T'Gvlde Iaer 1650 in de Short-Title Catalogue, Netherlands* (The Hague, 1995), esp. pp. 26–7.

[4] In the seventeenth-century Dutch book trade, the later separate functions of publisher and bookseller were still combined in one person.

bookbinders, hawkers, illustrators, woodcutters, engravers, and illuminators, as well as, of course, authors, translators, editors, and journalists.

This contribution aims to present a survey of the Amsterdam book trade during the seventeenth century, giving particular attention to the factors that contributed to its unparalleled success.[5] With a view to developing the broad comparison between the 'achievements' in various fields of three major European cities, which is the theme of this book, the question will also be addressed of why Antwerp and London were unable to follow Amsterdam's shining example in this field during the seventeenth century.

This overview uses a model first introduced in 1980 by the American historian Robert Darnton. In a conference paper entitled 'What Is the History of Books?' he argued that book history should be concerned with what he called the 'communications circuit', the life cycle of books from authors, via printers, publishers and booksellers to readers. Naturally, the circuit is not cut off from society at large: it should be seen, according to Darnton, 'in all its variations over space and time and in all its relations with other systems, economic, social, political, and cultural, in the surrounding environment'.[6] When speaking about the Amsterdam book trade, one should, therefore, first ask in which environment and under what conditions printers and booksellers in this city operated.

'The greatest city in all the Low Countries, and one of the richest and best traded empories of the whole world.' Thus the English naturalist John Ray described Amsterdam in his travel journal, first published in London in 1673.[7] The basis of this great prosperity, of course, was the city's thriving economy. As has been described in more detail elsewhere in this book, between the end of the sixteenth century, when it replaced Antwerp as the main trading city of the Low Countries, and about the 1660s,

---

[5] For another recent survey, see J.A. Bots and O.S. Lankhorst, 'Une librarie universelle. Amsterdam, ou la scène fructueuse d'une union entre l'écrit et la marchandise' in H. Méchoulan (ed.), *Amsterdam au XVIIe siècle. Marchands et philosophes: Les bénéfices de la tolérance* (Paris, 1993), pp. 124–37.

[6] R. Darnton, 'What Is the History of Books?' in K.E. Carpenter (ed.), *Books and Society in History. Papers of the Association of College and Research Libraries, Rare Books and Manuscripts Preconference, Boston (Mass.), 24–28 June, 1980* (New York/London, 1983), pp. 3–28. Also published in R. Darnton, *The Kiss of Lamourette. Reflections in Cultural History* (New York, 1990), pp. 107–35. For criticism on and an extension of Darnton's model, see T.R. Adams and N. Barker, 'A New Model for the Study of the Book' in N. Barker (ed.), *A Potencie of Life. Books in Society. The Clark Lectures 1986–1987* (London, 1993), pp. 5–44.

[7] Quoted from the second edition, John Ray, *Travels through the Low-Countries, Germany, Italy and France* (London, 1738), vol. I, p. 34.

Amsterdam's shipping, trade and industry expanded at breakneck speed, making it the commercial clearing house of Europe and, at the same time, its financial centre.

Printers and booksellers greatly benefited from the favourable economic and financial situation. As printing was a capital-intensive enterprise, the easy availability of capital at low rates of interest significantly lowered the production costs of books, which could then be distributed via an extensive international trade network. In many ways, the operation of the book trade was similar to that of other branches of trade and industry in Amsterdam's advanced market economy, that is as a commodity subject to supply and demand. Foreign books were imported, for instance, via the Frankfurt book fairs, both for sale at home and for re-export to other countries. Some Amsterdam printers produced books simply as bulk commodities, to be shipped to those places where they were most in demand: cheap English Bibles to Britain and its colonies, Hebrew and Yiddish texts to Poland, Catholic church books to Germany and the Southern Netherlands, pirate reprints of French bestsellers to France.

The same mechanism can be seen in related activities. The large quantities of paper which local merchants imported from France were only partly consumed by Amsterdam printers; the rest was sold to other countries.[8] Moreover, much of the printing type cast by Amsterdam typefounders found its way across the Republic's borders, especially to England, where Dutch type remained in general use well into the second half of the eighteenth century.[9]

Another economic advantage enjoyed by the Amsterdam book trade was the absence of strict external and internal regulation. The authorities rarely interfered with this branch of industry and the rules and regulations of the Amsterdam guild of printers and booksellers, which was not founded until 1662 (previous to that printers and booksellers belonged to the guild of St Luke), were fairly lenient. In practice, membership was not obligatory; women were allowed to succeed to the businesses of their deceased husbands or fathers; and even Catholics and Jews were admitted as members.[10]

---

[8] See I.H. van Eeghen, *De Amsterdamse boekhandel* (Amsterdam, 1978), vol. V, pp. 35–7. After the revocation of the Edict of Nantes by Louis XIV in 1685, when Dutch paper imports from France came to a standstill, paper mills established in the Veluwe region in Gelderland and along the river Zaan were quickly able to offset paper shortages.

[9] V. Barbour, *Capitalism in Amsterdam in the Seventeenth Century* (Baltimore, Md., 1950), pp. 64–5.

[10] See I.H. van Eeghen, *De gilden. Theorie en praktijk* (Bussum, 1965), pp. 100–30; L.P. Leuven, *De boekhandel te Amsterdam door katholieken gedreven tijdens de Republiek* (Amsterdam, 1951), pp. 11–15.

Last but not least, economic and maritime activities made
Amsterdam into an important communications centre. From all over
the world, information of all sorts was sent and brought to Amsterdam,
by merchants, couriers, diplomats, travellers, boatmen and others. On
arrival in the city it was published and distributed by printers and booksellers in the form of price currents, pamphlets, newspapers, travel
accounts, etc.[11]

In the wake of the flourishing economy, the Amsterdam population
underwent enormous growth. Between 1600 and 1660 the number of
inhabitants steadily increased from about 60,000 to some 200,000. Most
of these people were born outside Amsterdam, being immigrants from
other parts of the Dutch Republic or from abroad. In the decades around
1600 large numbers of immigrants arrived from the Southern
Netherlands; later, many also came from Germany, Britain, France and
eastern Europe. The predominant motive of these newcomers was to participate in Amsterdam's prosperity, but many came also for religious
freedom, and some for intellectual freedom. A decentralized political
structure, the absence of an established national Church and deep-rooted
notions of tolerance made the Dutch Republic, and Amsterdam in particular, a place of refuge for those who in their own country were prosecuted
for their beliefs and ideas, whether they were Flemish Protestants,
Sephardic and Ashkenazic Jews, Polish Socinians, English Nonconformists or French Huguenots.

The sympathy shown by the Amsterdam population and magistrates
to immigrants and refugees also encouraged foreign printers and booksellers to settle and work in the city. That particularly applied to the
many experienced printers and booksellers coming from the Southern
Netherlands at the end of the sixteenth century, and from France
during the final decades of the seventeenth. The most important
Amsterdam booksellers of the period around 1600 – Cornelis Claesz
(active 1582–1609), Jan Commelin (active 1582–1615) and the
engraver and map publisher Jodocus Hondius (active 1593–1612) – all
came from the South.[12] Amsterdam was also an important centre of
Hebrew printing. Most Jewish printers had come from the Iberian
peninsula, among them the prominent Hebrew teacher and rabbi

---

[11] See J.J. McCusker and C. Gravesteijn, *The Beginnings of Commercial and Financial
Journalism. The Commodity Price Currents, Exchange Rate Currents, and Money Currents of
Early Modern Europe* (Amsterdam, 1991), ch. I, 'Amsterdam Commercial and Financial
Newspapers'; F. Dahl, 'Amsterdam, Earliest Newspaper Centre of Western Europe', *Het
Boek* 25 (1938–9), pp. 160–97.

[12] J.G.C.A. Briels, *Zuidnederlandse boekverkopers en boekdrukkers in de Republiek 1570–1630*
(Nieuwkoop, 1974).

Menasseh Ben Israel, who set up a successful printing house in 1627.[13] The large number of French printers and booksellers residing in Amsterdam at the end of the seventeenth century were all Huguenots, who had fled from religious oppression under Louis XIV. The influx of many French printers and booksellers may well have reversed a decline in the Amsterdam book industry: whereas the numbers of booksellers in other Dutch cities fell after 1670, those in Amsterdam remained stable.[14]

Other nationalities were less well represented, but there were always a few German and English printers and booksellers in town, the latter mostly exiled Puritan Nonconformists, who looked upon the printing press as a powerful ally in the struggle against their enemies in England.[15] Other strangers came to Amsterdam simply to learn the trade, for example the famous Hungarian punch-cutter Miklos Kis, who, after having served an apprenticeship at the type foundry of Joan Blaeu in the 1680s, returned to his native country.[16] Another interesting figure is the Armenian printer Mattheus Avac, who was sent by his church to Amsterdam around 1658 to order type and print a Bible in the Armenian language.[17]

An additional result of the remarkable tolerance found in Amsterdam was freedom of printing. This is not to say that censorship did not exist, but the various decrees against illicit and seditious books were often ignored by both printers and authorities alike.[18] Sometimes patronage played a part in this, as in the case of the Amsterdam printer Willem Jansz

[13] R.G. Fuks-Mansfeld, 'The Hebrew Book Trade in Amsterdam in the Seventeenth Century' in C. Berkvens-Stevelinck et al. (eds.), Le Magasin de l'Univers. The Dutch Republic as the Centre of the European Book Trade. Papers Presented at the International Colloquium, Held at Wassenaar, 5–7 July 1990 (Leiden, 1992), pp. 155–68.

[14] See the graph in J. de Vries and A. van der Woude, Nederland 1500–1815. De eerste ronde van moderne economische groei (Amsterdam, 1995), p. 374.

[15] K. Sprunger, Trumpets from the Tower. English Puritan Printing in the Netherlands 1600–1640 (Leiden, 1994); P.G. Hoftijzer, Engelse boekverkopers bij de Beurs. De geschiedenis van de Amsterdamse boekhandels Bruyning en Swart (1637–1725) (Amsterdam/Maarssen, 1987).

[16] G. Haiman, Nicholas Kis. A Hungarian Punch-Cutter and Printer, 1650–1702 (Budapest, 1983).

[17] See P. von Zesen, Beschreibung der Stadt Amsterdam (Amsterdam, 1664), pp. 370–1: 'Ja die Perser selbsten haben, im vergangenen Jahre, eine Armenische Drükkerei, darinnen die heilige Schrift in Armenischer Sprache sol zu lichte kommen, alhier anrichten laszen'. See also D.W. Davies, 'The Geographic Extent of the Dutch Book Trade in the 17th Century', Het Boek, new series, 31 (1952–4), p. 19.

[18] Cf. H.A. Enno van Gelder, Getemperde vrijheid. Een verhandeling over de verhouding van kerk en staat in de Republiek der Verenigde Nederlanden en de vrijheid van meningsuiting inzake godsdienst, drukpers en onderwijs gedurende de zeventiende eeuw (Groningen, 1972), ch. 4, 'De drukpers'. See also S. Groenveld, 'The Mecca of Authors? States Assemblies and Censorship in the Seventeenth-century Dutch Republic' in A.C. Duke and C.A. Tamse (eds.), Too Mighty to be Free. Censorship and the Press in Britain and the Netherlands (Zupthen, 1987), pp. 63–86.

Blaeu, whose good connections among the city magistrates in the 1620s and 1630s protected him from complaints by the local Reformed church council about his printing Catholic and Socinian books. But the authorities also realized that in some cases action against an illicit publication would only draw more attention to it. At least, that was the impression of the English envoy Thomas Chudleigh, who in 1683 had complained to the States General in The Hague about the publication in Amsterdam of two pamphlets against the English government. According to the report he sent to London, the *griffier* (clerk) of the States General had answered that his action would 'onely serve to publish the thing & make people curious to gett the libells, but doe no good as to suppressing of them'.[19] Even if a printer or bookseller was caught, punishment normally was relatively mild: they might be fined, their printing equipment confiscated, or their shop closed for a while, but for seventeenth-century Amsterdam it is difficult to find examples of more severe punishment for printing or selling prohibited books.[20]

Apart from their cosmopolitan character, the inhabitants of Amsterdam were relatively well educated. Partly because of efforts by the Reformed and other Protestant churches to enable their believers to read the Bible, but perhaps even more as the result of commercial needs, by 1650 over half of the adult males and about one-third of the women in Amsterdam had had some form of elementary education, proportions that were higher than those in many other areas in Europe, and were rising.[21] In addition, many members of the higher strata of Amsterdam society had received some form of secondary education, for instance in the municipal Latin School, in the numerous privately run 'French' schools or, even better, at the Amsterdam Athenaeum Illustre or the University of Leiden. Schooling gave strong impulses to local cultural and intellectual life, which was further enhanced by various literary and scholarly societies and by public institutions such as the City Library, open, to quote one contemporary, 'to all enthu-

---

[19] Hoftijzer, *Engelse boekverkopers*, p. 143.

[20] Enno van Gelder, *Getemperde vrijheid*, p. 162, gives one rare example of an Amsterdam publisher who in 1651 was first put into the pillory, then flogged, and finally banned from the province of Holland for publishing a slanderous pamphlet against the local magistrates, as well as for committing theft.

[21] See S. Hart, 'Geschrift en getal. Onderzoek naar de samenstelling van de bevolking van Amsterdam in de 17de en 18de eeuw, op grond van gegevens over migratie, huwelijk, beroep en alfabetisme' in his *Geschrift en getal. Een keuze uit demografisch-, economisch- en sociaal-historische studiën op grond van Amsterdamse en Zaanse archivalia, 1600–1800* (Dordrecht, 1976), pp. 115–81. The preponderance of the commercial necessity of literacy over religious incentives is argued by Margaret Spufford, 'Literacy, Trade and Religion in the Commercial Centres of Europe' in K. Davids and J. Lucassen (eds.), *A Miracle Mirrored. The Dutch Republic in European Perspective* (Cambridge, 1995), pp. 229–83.

12.1 The Amsterdam City Library *c.*1620, when it was housed in an annexe of the New Church on the Dam. Device of the Amsterdam bookseller Lodewijck Spillebout; from B. Platina, *'t Leven der Roomsche Pausen*, Amsterdam, 1650; Amsterdam University Library

siasts who did not have the means to buy all sorts of books themselves' (figure 12.1).[22]

High levels of literacy and education and the lively cultural climate in Amsterdam boosted printing and bookselling. In studies of the seventeenth-century Amsterdam book trade much emphasis has always been put on its international outlook, but is has recently been argued that the Dutch, and indeed the Amsterdam book industry, cannot properly be understood without reference to the substantial national and local book market.[23] Not only was there a continuous supply of a great variety of copy from Dutch authors, who now began to be paid for their work (the emergence of the Dutch Grub Street writer dates from this period), but there was also an increasing demand for all sorts of printed matter, from expensive and serious books to cheap popular print: newspapers, pamphlets, almanacs, godly tracts, chap books, songbooks and illustrated broadsheets. The great popularity of these publications can be

[22] H. de la Fontaine Verwey, 'The City Library of Amsterdam in the Nieuwe Kerk 1578–1632', *Quaerendo* 14 (1984), pp. 163–206, at p. 165.
[23] B. van Selm, 'Johannes van Ravesteyn, "libraire européen" or Local Trader?' in Berkvens-Stevelinck et al., *Le Magasin de l'Univers*, pp. 251–63; B. van Selm, *Inzichten en vergezichten. Zes beschouwingen over het onderzoek naar de geschiedenis van de Nederlandse boekhandel* (Amsterdam, 1992), esp. ch. 5.

judged from the impressive numbers printed. For example, the dramatic account of the adventures of the East India skipper Willem IJsbrantsz Bontekoe, first published in 1646, had been reprinted at least seventy times by 1800.[24]

Economic prosperity, an open and permissive society, a literate and relatively well-educated population and a thriving cultural and intellectual climate all provided a fertile breeding ground for the Amsterdam book trade. Yet its great success can be only partially explained by these general circumstances. Printing and bookselling also involved the actions of individual human beings, people with professional skills, a talent for business and the genius to perceive what the public wants. Perhaps the favourable conditions in Amsterdam created an opportunity for such qualities to come to the fore. Whatever the case may be, the great renown of the seventeenth-century Amsterdam book trade was also the product of the skills and commitment of many individual printers and booksellers. Clustering together along 'Het Water' (the old inner port of the city), on the Dam Square next to the Town Hall and the Exchange (figure 12.2), or in the adjacent streets and alleys, they all tried to find their niche in the market.

One such printer and bookseller was Willem Jansz Blaeu. He began his career in 1599 when he opened a shop on Het Water. From his youth, Blaeu had a great interest in the mathematical sciences and initially he specialized in making navigational instruments, maps and globes, for which there was a great demand in this city of seafarers. Despite strong competition, he managed to expand his business into a printing and publishing house of the first rank, which his descendants kept up into the early eighteenth century. Blaeu's publishing list was extremely varied. Apart from books on mathematics, astronomy, geography and the art of navigation, including his own seaman's guide *Het licht der zee-vaert* (1608; translated into English in 1612 under the title *The Light of Navigation*), he published fine editions in small pocketbook format of the classical authors, works on calligraphy, emblem books, travel journals and the writings of leading Dutch scholars and literary writers such as Daniel Heinsius, Hugo Grotius, Joost van den Vondel and Pieter Cornelisz Hooft. His greatest fame, however, he achieved through the publication of his maps and atlases, in particular the two-volume *Theatrum orbis terrarum*, which appeared in four different language editions in 1634 and 1635. When Blaeu died, in 1638, he left his sons a new printing establishment, which accommodated nine printing presses,

---

[24] See G. Verhoeven and P.J. Verkruijsse (eds.), *Iovrnael ofte Gedenckwaerdige beschrijvinghe vande oost-Indische reyse van Willem Ysbrantsz. Bontekoe van Hoorn. Descriptieve bibliografie 1646–1996* (Zutphen, 1996).

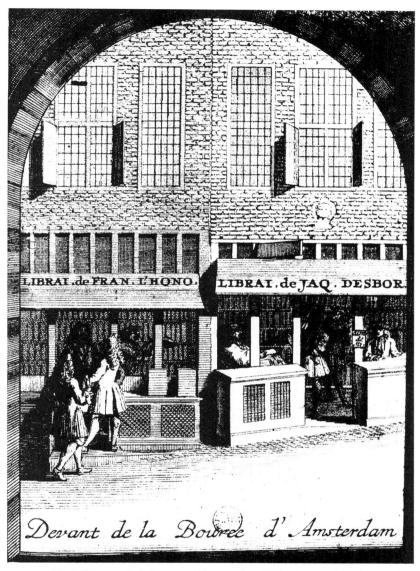

LIBRAI . de FRAN . L'HONO .

LIBRAI . de JAQ . DESBOR .

Devant de la Bourse d'Amsterdam

12.2 'Devant de la Bourse d'Amsterdam.' The shops of the Amsterdam Huguenot booksellers François l'Honoré and Jacques Desbordes seen from the arcade of the Amsterdam Exchange; frontispiece in J.P. Ricard, *Les loix et coutumes*, Amsterdam, 1715

named after the Muses, and six plate presses for producing maps and illustrations. According to the French traveller Claude Joly, who visited the new workshop in 1646, it was 'l'imprimerie la plus belle de toute l'Europe'.[25]

Willem Jansz Blaeu belongs to the first generation of great Amsterdam booksellers of the golden age. Louis and Daniel Elsevier, who came to Amsterdam from Leiden around the middle of the century, belong to the second. Louis Elsevier, who in contrast to his Leiden relatives held unorthodox beliefs and was interested in modern philosophy (that may have been one reason he left Leiden in 1637), was entrusted by René Descartes to print all his works and subsequently became the publisher of all major Dutch Cartesian scholars. He also published books by Pierre Gassendi, Thomas Hobbes and John Milton. Daniel Elsevier, Louis' nephew and associate between 1655 and 1664, continued along these lines. He also collaborated with his friend, the great scholar and diplomat Nicolaas Heinsius in the publication of a famous series of editions of classical authors. Moreover, he was one of the best general wholesale booksellers of his time, as can be seen from his 1674 stock catalogue, which in nearly 800 pages lists some 20,000 titles from all over Europe.[26]

Daniel Elsevier's death in 1680 marks the end of the second period of great Amsterdam booksellers. As representatives of the next generation one could mention such lesser-known figures as Daniel Elsevier's former assistant Hendrik Wetstein, or Johannes and Gillis Janssonius van Waesberge, whose activities extended as far as Danzig, where they had a branch store. Perhaps more characteristic of this period, however, are the many French printers and booksellers who worked in Amsterdam at the end of the century. The most prominent were the brothers Jean, Pierre and Marc Huguetan, from a great Lyons printing dynasty. What makes them important is not so much the quality of their publishing list as the sheer scope of their activities. With a partnership that may have been worth more than half a million guilders and with immense book stocks all over Europe and in the Levant, they truly can be seen as pre-modern book trade tycoons. Their unscrupulous way of doing business, however, was not much liked by their colleagues. One complained that the Huguetans had twelve to thirteen printing presses at their disposal, which

[25] H. de la Fontaine Verwey, 'Willem Jansz. Blaeu, "Mercator Sapiens"' in his *Uit de wereld van het boek*, vol. III, *In en om de 'Vergulde Sonnewyser'* (Amsterdam, 1979), pp. 9–34.

[26] *Catalogus librorum qui in bibliopolio Daniels Elsevirii venales extant* (Amsterdam, 1674). For extensive information on the Amsterdam Elseviers see A. Willems, *Les Elzevier. Histoire et annales typographiques* (Bruxelles, 1880) and D.W. Davies, *The World of the Elzeviers 1580–1712* (The Hague, 1960).

they kept in constant operation, 'without making any distinction whom they damage or where'.[27]

Much of the activity of the French booksellers was indeed in the printing and trading of pirated French books. But they also produced original publications, mostly written by Huguenot refugees who tried to scrape a living in the book trade. Among these publications were various newspapers and periodicals, which, because they were in French, found an audience throughout Europe. In particular, scholarly journals such as the renowned *Nouvelles de la République des Lettres* had a great impact. This critical journal, published by the Amsterdam bookseller Henry Desbordes and edited by Pierre Bayle and others from 1684 onwards, would serve as the model for numerous other French periodicals subsequently to be published in Amsterdam, Rotterdam and The Hague.[28]

Printers and booksellers such as the Blaeus, Elseviers, van Waesberges and Huguetans were the elite of the Amsterdam book trade. But many lesser-known entrepreneurs also left their mark. One of them was Broer Jansz, who as early as 1619 began the publication of a weekly Dutch newspaper, the *Tijdinghe uyt verscheyden quartieren* (News from various quarters), which also appeared in an English edition.[29] Another of his initiatives was the serial publication *Catalogus universalis* (1640–52), the first Dutch trade catalogue of newly published books.[30] An equally interesting figure is Gillis Joosten Saeghman, a nephew of Broer Jansz, who during his long career became the leading publisher of almanacs, of which he printed hundreds of thousands of copies in various forms.[31] There was the dissenter Jan Rieuwertsz, who remarkably combined his official

[27] '. . . zij hebben 12 of 13 perssen, en zouden die graag gaande houden, zonder ondescheid wie of waar zij iemand benaadeelen, gelijk wij zulks daaglijks zien en bespeuren'; letter by the Amsterdam paper merchant IJsbrand Vincent to Balthasar Moretus at Antwerp of 24 January 1695, cited in van Eeghen, *Amsterdamse boekhandel*, vol. III, p. 175. See also van Eeghen, 'Europese "libraires": de gebroeders Huguetan in Amsterdam (1686–1705)', *Documentatieblad Werkgroep 18e Eeuw* 53–4 (1982), pp. 1–9.

[28] See J.A. Bots, 'Le Réfuge et les *Nouvelles de la République des Lettres* de Pierre Bayle' in J.A. Bots and G.H.M. Posthumus Meyjes (eds.), *La Révocation de l'Édit de Nantes et les Provinces Unies* (Amsterdam/Maarssen, 1986), pp. 85–95. See also E.L. Eisenstein, *Grub Street Abroad. Aspects of the French Cosmopolitan Press from the Age of Louis XIV to the French Revolution* (Oxford, 1992).

[29] See Dahl, 'Amsterdam, Earliest Newspaper Centre', pp. 160–97; F. Dahl, 'Amsterdam, Cradle of English Newspapers', *The Library*, 5th series, 4 (1950), pp. 166–79.

[30] H.W. de Kooker (introd. and ed.), *The Catalogus Universalis. A Facsimile Edition of the Dutch Booktrade Catalogues Compiled and Published by Broer Jansz, Amsterdam 1640–1652. With an Introduction and Indexes* (Utrecht, 1986).

[31] J. Salman and G. Verhoeven, 'The Comptoir-Almanacs of Gilles Joosten Saeghman. Research into Seventeenth-Century Almanacs in the Dutch Republic', *Quaerendo*, 23 (1993), pp. 93–114.

position as town printer with publishing banned works by Spinoza and his followers, and whose shop was a meeting point for radical philosophers.[32] Of the numerous women engaged in the Amsterdam book trade, Susanna Veselaer should be mentioned. During the second half of the seventeenth century she expanded the business of her late husband, Jan Jacobsz Schipper, into one of the city's largest printing establishments. Together with the Jewish printer Joseph Athias she pirated large numbers of English Bibles and other profitable books of foreign publishers.[33] An astounded Oxford student, who visited her printing house in 1678, wrote in his travel diary:

> [T]here were 18 hard at work printing and 6 or 7 setting letters. They print here many English bibles of all sizes; upon the title-pages of which they sett: *London printed by R. Barker and the Assigns of John Bill &c.* And they were (whilst I lookt on), printeing a small English bible in octavo, which they sett printed by the aforesaid A.D. 1669. They showed me also severall books printed here with the title pages as if at Collen, Leipsick, Mentz, &c. whence it comes to pass that you may buy bookes cheaper at Amsterdam, in all languages, then at the places where they are first printed: for here the copy cost them noething.[34]

One often finds such mixed expressions of admiration and envy in comments by foreign authors on the flourishing state of the Amsterdam book trade – admiration for the industry and accomplishments of these printers and booksellers; envy of the fame and fruits it brought them, and not their own countrymen. Why then were printers and booksellers in other places unable to challenge Dutch supremacy? Let me, by way of comparison and conclusion, try to answer this question with a few general remarks about the book trade in Antwerp and London in the seventeenth century, paying particular attention to its international outlook.

The great flourishing of the Antwerp book trade in the sixteenth century was largely due to circumstances similar to those responsible for the miracle of Amsterdam in the seventeenth century.[35] But after the fall of Antwerp in 1585 a slow but gradual decline set in. The city's main economic artery, the Scheldt, was cut off by the Dutch, the Counter-Reformation, personified by the Jesuits, restricted the city's varied religious and cultural life, and a northward drain of capital, talent and

---

[32] See P. Visser, '"Blasphemous and Pernicious": The Role of Printers and Booksellers in the Spread of Dissident Religious and Philosophical Ideas in the Netherlands in the Second Half of the Seventeenth Century', *Quaerendo* 26 (1996), pp. 303–26.

[33] Van Eeghen, *Amsterdamse boekhandel*, vol. IV, pp. 96–117; van Eeghen, 'De befaamde drukkerij op de Herengracht over de Plantage, 1685–1755', *Jaarboek van het Genootschap Amstelodamum* 58 (1966), pp. 82–100.

[34] See P.G. Hoftijzer, 'A Study Tour into the Low Countries and the German States. William Nicolson's *Iter Hollandicum* and *Iter Germanicum*, 1678–1679', *Lias* 15 (1989), pp. 73–128, esp. p. 100.   [35] See Werner Waterschoot's contribution to this volume.

experience bled the city dry. Among the expatriates were, as we have seen, many printers and booksellers, some of whom had previously worked in the establishment of the great Christopher Plantin. Indeed, the reversal in the fortune of the Antwerp book trade can best be seen in the activities of the Plantin–Moretus firm. Although Plantin's descendants in Antwerp continued to be the largest printers of the city, producing an impressive number of still beautifully executed books, the enterprising, humanistically oriented spirit of the sixteenth century had gone. Instead of the great diversity of publications in all fields – theology, law, philology, literature, history, geography and science – produced during Plantin's day, theological and liturgical books now became the mainstay of the firm.[36] That was profitable business, to be sure, but it could not make Antwerp recover its former prominent position.

The serious lagging behind of the London book trade has a much longer history. Since the introduction of printing in London by William Caxton, the development of publishing and bookselling in the city had been slow. The peripheral location of the British Isles, the lack of knowledge of the English language on the Continent and poor typographical standards hindered its expansion beyond national boundaries. Moreover, tight control of the press by the government and the Anglican Church, combined with strict internal regulation by the all-powerful Stationers' Company, frustrated domestic growth. On top of that came the severe disruption of the trade caused by the Civil War and by the destruction of great stocks of books during the Great Fire of 1666.

Only at the end of the seventeenth century could a new mood be discerned. New publishing and distribution methods, developed to gull the official censors and the monopolists of the Stationers' Company, together with the lapse of the Printing Act in 1695, provided a better environment for the London book trade.[37] From an international point of view, however, booksellers in the English metropolis continued to lag behind, as can be illustrated by Anglo-Dutch book trade relations around 1700. During that period, when trade with France had come to a standstill because of the ongoing wars, the English booksellers became almost completely dependent on their Dutch colleagues for book imports. One of the participants in this trade was the London bookseller Samuel Smith, who was the main supplier to the Royal Society. Fortunately, part of his

[36] L. Voet, *The Golden Compasses. A History and Evaluation of the Printing and Publishing Activities of the Officina Plantiniana*, vol. I, *Christophe Plantin and the Moretuses: Their Lives and Their World* (Amsterdam, 1969).

[37] G. Mandelbrote, 'From the Warehouse to the Counting-House: Booksellers and Bookshops in Late 17th-Century London' in R. Myers and M. Harris (eds.), *A Genius for Letters. Booksellers and Bookselling from the sixteenth to the 20th Century* (Winchester, 1995), pp. 49–84.

business correspondence with a number of Dutch booksellers (including, in Amsterdam, Hendrik Wetstein and Johannes and Gillis Janssonius van Waesberge) is preserved at the Bodleian Library in Oxford, and provides a fascinating insight into the practices and vicissitudes of the international book trade.[38]

Smith's main problem was that he could not deal with his Dutch colleagues on equal terms. Normally, books would be exchanged on the basis that each partner sold as much to the other as he bought from him, thus avoiding costly financial transactions in the annual settling of accounts. But the books Smith had to offer were not very attractive to his correspondents, because they were mostly in English and besides were far too expensive. Anyone who bought these books ran the risk of being stuck with them, particularly when they were undercut by a pirated edition. So the trade balance between Samuel Smith and his Dutch colleagues was always to his disadvantage, and each year he had to transfer large sums of money to his correspondents, a highly unattractive position for a bookseller to be in.

This situation lasted well into the eighteenth century. For many decades Dutch booksellers supplied over a third of the bound (that is, second-hand) books imported to England from the Continent and more than half of the unbound (i.e. new) books. Exports of English books to the Dutch Republic were minimal.[39] In 1733 a frustrated London bookseller wrote:

Great estates have been gained in Holland by reprinting books written in France, with which, as well as with the classics, and other books of literature, the Dutch have for many years largely supplied England, Scotland, and Ireland, as well as Germany and the Northern parts of Europe.[40]

Eventually the hegemony of the printers and booksellers of Amsterdam came to an end. In the second half of the eighteenth century the roles were reversed. Booksellers in other countries (in France, Switzerland, Germany and, to a lesser extent, also England) finally caught up with them. The causes were many. In 1783, at a time when the Republic was in

[38] For a discussion of the Smith correspondence, see C. Blagden and N. Hodgson, *The Notebook of Thomas Bennet and Henry Clements (1686–1719), with Some Aspects of Book Trade Practice* (Oxford, 1956); P.G. Hoftijzer, 'Religious and Theological Books in the Anglo-Dutch Book Trade at the Time of the Glorious Revolution' in J. van den Berg and P.G. Hoftijzer (eds.), *Church and Society in Change. Papers of the Fourth Anglo-Dutch Church History Symposium, Exeter, 1988* (Leiden, 1991), pp. 167–78.

[39] G. Barber, 'Aspects of the Book Trade between England and the Low Countries in the Eighteenth Century', *Documentatieblad Werkgroep 18e Eeuw* 34–5 (1977), pp. 47–63.

[40] Quotation taken from a petition by the London bookseller Samuel Buckley to the English Parliament in 1733 for a ban on imports of possible piracies of his Thuanus edition; van Eeghen, *Amsterdamse boekhandel*, vol. V, p. 102.

both an economic and a political crisis, a Leiden bookseller observed, having summed up the assets of the Dutch book trade in the past:

Nothing is left of these advantages but licentiousness instead of *freedom*, all the rest is gone. Elsewhere they now have paper of the same quality but cheaper than ours; they print as well but cheaper than we and they have more beautiful type; and although we may have political hackwriters in abundance, we lack serious scholars.[41]

Other changes were more fundamental. The economic balance had turned against a country and a city that had dominated the European market for a disproportionally long time. Moreover, the book trade everywhere went through a period of profound change as a result of the gradual disappearance of Latin as the universal language of the Republic of Letters, the rise of the vernacular languages and the emergence of new markets and publics. Contrary to what most contemporary Dutch booksellers hoped, the crisis could not be redressed. The miracle had simply worn off.

[41] Translated quotation taken from Elie Luzac, *Hollands rijkdom*, 4 vols. (Leiden, 1783–4), vol. IV, p. 425.

13 Printing, publishing and reading in London, 1660–1720

Adrian Johns

Late seventeenth-century Londoners were steeped in the printed word. By its means, citizens learned how to act, what to know and even who to be. The history of print consequently underpins much that was distinctive about the period, from high science to low politics. This chapter provides the raw materials for an understanding of what is therefore an extremely important subject. It describes the making, circulation and consumption of printed materials in the Restoration metropolis.

In modern collections, those materials are systematically distinguished from other relics of past communication. The distinction, however justified in the present, is historically unfortunate. Print did not exist in isolation. It is significant that some of the most important texts of the time, even when they were in fact printed, appeared in the form of 'speeches' (Milton's *Areopagitica* being one example), 'letters' (such as Shaftesbury's major manifesto against popery and arbitrary government), 'discourses' (such as Locke's on government), or 'sermons' (including Sacheverell's fateful diatribe on 'the perils of false brethren'). Some, to be sure, did indeed originate in these other forms. But others did not. The persistence in print of rhetorical and stylistic idioms derived from manuscript or oral modes of communication testified to a continuing relation between all three forms of activity. In some cases, for example ballads, printed materials were expressly intended from the start as facilitators of oral performance. We shall see that much the same was true of learned printing too. In each case, then, these materials were never meant to stand alone as self-sufficient artifacts. It is therefore essential for the historian to attend to the practices of sociability, among which reading was one, pursued with their aid.[1]

---

[1] J. Milton, *Areopagitica; a Speech of Mr. John Milton For the Liberty of Unlicenc'd Printing, To the Parlament of England* (n.p., 1644); *A Letter from a Person of Quality to his Friend in the Country* (n.p., 1675); [J. Locke], *Two Treatises of Government* (A. Churchill, 1690); H. Sacheverell, *The Perils of False Brethren, both in Church, and State, set forth in a Sermon preach'd before the Right Honourable the Lord-Mayor* (H. Clements, 1709). For the general point, see D.F. McKenzie, 'Speech–Manuscript–Print', in D. Oliphant and R. Bradford (eds.), *New Directions in Textual Studies* (Austin, Tex. 1990), pp. 87–109, and R. Chartier, 'Leisure and Sociability: Reading Aloud in Early Modern Europe' in S. Zimmerman and R.F.E. Weissman (eds.), *Urban Life in the Renaissance* (Newark, Del., 1989), pp. 103–20.

Hand-written communication in particular remained a viable – and in many cases a preferable – alternative to print throughout the seventeenth century. Organized workshops dedicated to the production and circulation of manuscripts survived and indeed prospered. Poetry and news were their most consistently successful products, but Harold Love has also identified music and parliamentary compilations as principal beneficiaries. The Scriveners' Company, refounded in 1617, united a community of manuscript-writers and copiers among whose responsibilities were the accuracy and authenticity of documents. Less commercially, correspondence and the circulation of written texts were the dominant means of communication in many learned domains, including natural philosophy and mathematics. Well into the eighteenth century, both Swift and Sterne participated in 'scribal publication', and Richardson, himself a printer, dedicated long hours to letter-writing. The relation between these activities and the practices surrounding the manufacture, circulation and reception of printed materials was by no means a simple or consistent one. Certainly, it was not a matter of unambiguous inferiority, whether in terms of the credibility of the materials concerned or their cultural consequences. Sir Roger L'Estrange was given to remarking that manuscript newsletters were in certain circumstances more dangerous than printed ones. Nor is it necessarily to be supposed that their success was anomalous, let alone that they were doomed to extinction as print culture acceded to inevitable dominance. This was, after all, some two centuries after Caxton had first introduced the press to London, and that is too long a lag to be disregarded. In fact, it may far more plausibly be argued that manuscript and oral modes were not just alternatives to print, but complements to it. More radically, this chapter claims that the impact of print actually depended on their presence.[2]

Yet when visitors came to London it was the ubiquity of printing and publishing which they noticed. Such observers often expressed surprise at the size of the city's book trade. It seemed at once both impressively large and puzzlingly small. On the one hand, there were over 150 bookshops in the capital, not to mention countless temporary stalls, and their numbers were continuing to increase. Tramping through their 'particular Quarters', Samuel de Sorbière claimed to count 'twice as many' as he had seen in the rue Saint-Jacques, the corresponding precinct in Paris. Printing houses, too, flourished. There were at least fifty-three in 1661–2, some forty at the time of the Fire in 1666, and over sixty by 1705. Two decades later Samuel Negus could count a dozen more still. At the Restoration, a government inclined to view printed pamphlets as major fomenters of rebellion had set a statutory limit of twenty on the number of

---

[2] H. Love, *Scribal Publication in Seventeenth-Century England* (Oxford, 1993), pp. 3–137 (esp. pp. 74, 94–5), 297.

printing houses; this limit was always exceeded. On the other hand, however, individual premises, be they printing houses or bookshops, remained small in size, and were dedicated overwhelmingly to local markets. There was no London printing house comparable to that of a Plantin, a Blaeu or an Elzevier. Not even the royal printers themselves could match those great Continental establishments. And although individual booksellers – Samuel Smith being the best-known example – did deal with counterparts in Amsterdam and Hamburg, they experienced recurrent problems of credit in doing so. They found payment in kind by the exchange of books – the preferred *modus operandi* of the international book trade – difficult to sustain, largely because the titles London dealers had to offer were of little interest to a European readership which found English affairs provincial and the English tongue incomprehensible. So the London trade thrived, bursting the bonds of Stuart regulation, yet remained focused on the City and nation rather than reaching out to the world. The distinctive culture of print which emerged in the metropolis may plausibly be understood in terms of this seeming paradox of scale.[3]

Where would an early modern Londoner go to see books being made and sold? The question is worth asking. There was a distinct topography of print in the City, with booksellers concentrated around a small number of thoroughfares and precincts. The best known of these was the area around Amen Corner, St Paul's Churchyard and Ave Maria Lane. This was the zone which so impressed Sorbière. It had been the principal centre for the book trade since long before the invention of printing, and continued as such throughout the early modern period. Characterized by its established prosperity, it had become a popular rendezvous for people of quality. Even the Great Fire of 1666, which laid waste the entire area, proved no more than a temporary reverse. Some of the more prosperous citizens took the opportunity to decamp west into new and fashionable squares such as Covent Garden. But the booksellers stayed put, finding the area still 'well situated for learned and studious Mens access'. In fact, the catastrophe provided an opportunity for the more enterprising among them, in that it created a dire need for more books to replace those

---

[3] M. Treadwell, 'The English Book Trade' in R.P. Maccubbin and M. Hamilton-Phillips (eds.), *The Age of William III and Mary II: Power, Politics and Patronage 1688–1702* (Williamsburg, 1989), pp. 358–65, esp. p. 360; M. Plant, *The English Book Trade: An Economic History of the Making and Sale of Books,* 3rd edn. (London, 1974), p. 64; S. Sorbière, *A Voyage into England* (London, 1709), p. 16; J.S.T. Hetet, 'A Literary Underground in Restoration England' (unpublished PhD thesis, Cambridge University, 1987), pp. 104–5, 244, 257; Stationers' Company, Court Book D, fol. 82ʳ; K. Maslen and J. Lancaster (eds.), *The Bowyer Ledgers* (London, 1991), p. xxiii. The incoming correspondence of Samuel Smith is preserved in the Bodleian Library, Oxford, as Bodl. Ms. Rawl. Letters 114.

destroyed by the flames. Fortunes could be made in the book trade during the years of the rebuilding. Before long, recovery was an established fact. There were some thirty bookshops in St Paul's Churchyard itself by 1700, and the trade was fast expanding into adjoining Paternoster Row. Well into the nineteenth century it remained a flourishing centre.[4]

From this central location, the trade extended tentacles towards all four points of the compass. Moving east from St Paul's, a late seventeenth-century pedestrian would find perhaps twenty more booksellers along the major City concourse extending from Cheapside to Cornhill. Since 1668 the richest of all, Thomas Guy, had lived here, at the corner of Lombard Street. Or one could go west instead, walking along Fleet Street towards the Strand. There were around twenty-five booksellers' shops on this thoroughfare by the 1690s, including that of Jacob Tonson. In this direction one ultimately reached Westminster, where still more bookshops could be found. Alternatively, more venturesome individuals might want to descend southwards from the cathedral towards the Thames, to glimpse an unknown number of printing presses half-concealed in the labyrinthine alleys between Blackfriars and Barnards Castle. The biggest operation of all, the royal printing house, occupied a large but decrepit building on the westernmost periphery of this zone. It was a precinct of distinctly dubious character, overcrowded, noisy and full of uncharted crannies well suited to conventicles and cabals. But if, finally, one went north from St Paul's, one found relief in Little Britain. This was home to a cluster of second-hand book dealers, and one or two more substantial premises too. Brave or lusty individuals might then wish to turn east, and proceed past Bartholomew Close and Aldersgate Street – both home to more printing houses – towards Grub Street and Moorfields. These were London's most notorious bawdy-house districts. But men such as Robert Hooke frequented them for their bookstalls too, and they offered afford-able refuge to the swarming hacks pilloried in Pope's *Dunciad*.[5]

Fleet Street and Cornhill were major thoroughfares; so was London Bridge, the only span across the Thames, which likewise housed a few booksellers' premises. In common with other major European cities such as Paris and Amsterdam, bookshops in London clustered along such

[4] J. Stow (ed. J. Strype), *A Survey of the Cities of London and Westminster*, 2 vols. (London, 1720), vol. I, p. 195; R. Porter, *London: A Social History* (London, 1994), pp. 70–1, 95–116.

[5] M. Treadwell, 'London Printers and Printing Houses in 1705', *Publishing History* 7 (1980), pp. 5–44; Hetet, 'Literary Underground', p. 17; Treadwell, 'English Book Trade', pp. 360–1; P. Rogers, *Grub Street: Studies in a Subculture* (London, 1972), pp. 256–7; 'The Diary of Robert Hooke, Nov. 1688–Mar. 1690 and Dec. 1692–Aug. 1693' in R.T. Gunther (ed.), *Early Science in Oxford*, 15 vols. (Oxford, 1923–67), vol. X, pp. 69–265, esp. p. 223.

routes and in places which accorded ready markets. St Paul's Churchyard itself was one example. Elsewhere, the Royal Exchange and (for mariners) the Tower furnished others. Unlike other cities, however, bookshops did not congregate along the banks of the capital's river. This was largely because London lacked a promenade (as, for the most part, it still does); but also because importers were compelled to channel all their shipments through both the Customs House and Stationers' Hall, thus removing the advantage offered by a position close to the wharves. The result was a series of locations dense in book-trade associations. Paul's Churchyard in particular was an area in which virtually every building had a role to play in the manufacture and circulation of words. The Castle tavern in Paternoster Row became a key meeting-point for writers, booksellers and printers. Sales of 'copies' were held at another tavern nearby, called the Queen's Head. In the Churchyard itself, Child's coffee-house became the favoured haunt of physicians and Fellows of the Royal Society. The book trade's own church, St Faith's, was to be found in the crypt of the cathedral itself. And just to the west stood Stationers' Hall itself, home to the Company that oversaw the trade in its entirety.[6]

The proprietors of these premises followed a trade which was pervaded by representations of domesticity and kinship. Most printing houses and bookshops were dwellings too. The same building which contained the presses would often house the master printer and his or her family – and not uncommonly the apprentices and journeymen. As if this were not claustrophobic enough, they might also coexist with other trade premises. John Dunton, for example, rented 'half a Shop', a warehouse and 'a fashionable Chamber'. Booksellers and printers made creative use of these conjoined places, moving between them to forge alliances, negotiate agreements, preserve secrecy where necessary and foster mechanisms of circulation. For the printing house in particular, moreover, the juxtaposition of domestic and vocational spaces affected the character of the workplace, the practices believed appropriate within it and their material consequences in the form of printed books. The book trade was in this sense entirely representative of a society conceiving of itself as an aggregate of patriarchal households, held together by fragile attributions of credit. And, as the prime source of morality and authority in the early

[6] T. Belanger, 'Booksellers' Sales of Copyright: Aspects of the London Book Trade 1718–1768' (unpublished PhD thesis, Columbia University, 1970), pp. 49, 158–9; B. Lillywhite, *London Coffee Houses: A Reference Book of Coffee Houses of the Seventeenth, Eighteenth and Nineteenth Centuries* (London, 1963), pp. 151–2, 156–8. A definitive survey of part of the area around St Paul's for a slightly earlier period is presented in P.W.M. Blayney, *The Bookshops in Paul's Cross Churchyard* (London, 1990). For Paris, compare H.-J. Martin, *Le Livre Français sous l'Ancien Régime* (Paris, 1987), pp. 90–1, 103–4.

modern world, the patriarchal household was held to guarantee certain ethical standards too. These standards here became the foundation of a reliable and safe print culture. They underwrote authenticity, security and authorship in print. Absentee masters, like absentee fathers, were on the other hand held to foster lax conduct. In the book trade, such nefarious dereliction manifested itself in the form of three notorious evils threatening to the credit of print itself: inaccuracy, sedition and piracy.[7]

This juxtaposition of the domestic and the vocational was common throughout western Europe. However, for the most part London printing houses were smaller than Continental ones. They would contain two or at most three presses; a substantial proportion had only one. The number of workmen varied similarly. Not counting elusive and possibly transitory participants, such as proofreaders, 'devils' and 'flies', they ranged from just one in some of the smallest houses up to eighteen in the king's. It is admittedly the case that these numbers grew somewhat over the years. By the mid-1720s, when Benjamin Franklin worked there, John Watts' printing house was employing about fifty people. Nonetheless, London printing remained predominantly a small-scale craft enterprise throughout most of this period. This compactness no doubt exacerbated the familial connotations of printing work.[8]

The culture and practices of a printing house were revealed *in extenso* in Joseph Moxon's *Mechanick Exercises on the Whole Art of Printing*. Published in 1683–4, Moxon's work provided the only thorough account of a late seventeenth-century London printing house. Its author exercised the craft himself, and could therefore specify a wealth of practical detail which only a practitioner would know. Moreover, as the son of a separatist printer previously exiled to the Low Countries, Moxon was well placed to compare British and Dutch practices. He noted, for example, that English houses generally placed cases of type in a different chamber from presses, whereas in Holland (as contemporary images indeed show) they shared the same room. Moxon also advocated using type manufactured in Amsterdam – or, at a pinch, his own, which was modelled on Amsterdam

---

[7] J. Dunton, *The Life and Errors of John Dunton late Citizen of London; written by Himself in Solitude* (London, 1705), p. 70. For the realities of printing-house life, see D.F. McKenzie, 'Printers of the Mind: Some Notes on Bibliographical Theories and Printing-House Practices', *Studies in Bibliography* 22 (1969), pp. 1–76. For the moral implications of the patriarchal household, see S. Shapin, 'The House of Experiment in Seventeenth-Century England', *Isis* 79 (1988), pp. 373–404. The connection to print culture is made far more extensively in A. Johns, *The Nature of the Book: Knowledge and Print in the Making* (Chicago, 1998), ch. 2.

[8] E. Arber (ed.), *A Transcript of the Registers of the Company of Stationers of London; 1554–1640 A.D.* 5 vols. (Birmingham, 1875–94), vol. IV, p. 533; McKenzie, 'Printers of the Mind', pp. 54–7; B. Franklin (ed. J.A. Leo Lemay and P.M. Zall), *Autobiography* (New York, 1986), pp. 36–7.

designs. And he recommended a design for the press itself which was rarely used in London, and which he attributed to the Amsterdam printer, globe-maker and cartographer Willem Jansen Blaeu.[9]

Moxon's description was of a craft workshop centred on its master, who acted as the 'Soul' of the entire enterprise. The other participants were then governed by the master's natural authority as if they were 'members of the Body'. The most important distinction between these 'members' was that between compositor and pressman. The former arranged the type into formes, and the latter operated the press. Each task required no little skill. A compositor would be expected to set about 1,000 characters an hour – about an octavo page. Thus prepared, the formes were then printed by pressmen working in pairs with fast, physical and highly coordinated actions. Each press might be expected to make about 250 impressions an hour. Together, working for up to fourteen hours a day, their combined labours would translate into some 1,200–1,500 sheets of printed paper.

The strongly felt identity of the master printer had implications for the work carried out in the printing house. A compositor, for example, should actively seek out occasions to amend the manuscript delivered by an author lacking (as almost all did) the skills to compose adequately. 'His care may not suffer such Work to go out of his Hands as may bring . . . Scandal and prejudice upon the *Master Printer*'. Patriarchal authority thus cut both ways: it buttressed the reliability and credit of printed materials, yet demanded alterations to authors' words to secure its own endurance. Moxon insisted that such a worker must be a 'Scholler' to achieve this delicate balance, and a rather formidable one at that. Pressmen, too, needed 'a competency of the Inventers Genius' to operate their machines with the precise and choreographed virtuosity required of them. Foreign workers often possessed the necessary capabilities, it seemed, which was why the Dutch could produce correct editions with such facility. British workers all too often did not.[10]

Such a rapport clearly did not come about naturally. The workers of every house maintained their own rules and conventions, generally unwritten, observance of which unified them into so many quasi-familial communities. By a custom which in Moxon's era had already existed since 'time out of Mind', each such community was called its house's 'chapel'. Its oldest member would be known as the chapel's father, and any journeyman marrying or becoming a parent was expected to signal as much communally. To enter, newcomers and apprentices alike had to pay

---

⁹ J. Moxon (ed. H. Davis and H. Carter), *Mechanick Exercises on the Whole Art of Printing* *(1683–4)* 2nd edn. (London, 1962), pp. xix–xxi, 16–17, 22–3, 45–9.
¹⁰ Ibid., pp. 15–18, 191–311.

a fine called a '*Benvenue*', and apprentices had also to undergo an elaborate initiation; as late as 1800, an apprentice would still talk of 'burying his wife' – that is, of ending his apprenticeship – with a ribald bacchanal. Breach of chapel rules was then punishable by a penance called a 'Solace'. Offences included excessive inebriation, fighting, abuse and the inappropriate use of equipment. The chapel thus created and enforced a collective morality. It need not be opposed to the master's interests. So much so, in fact, that the master even sponsored some of its activities, such as the feast held every autumn to mark the beginning of working by candlelight.[11]

The conventional boundaries of a chapel coincided with the physical walls of its particular printing house. Yet journeymen seem to have encountered few problems in moving between different establishments. In fact, a wider unity embraced every participant in the London book trades. All of them, including booksellers, printers, journeymen, binders and hawkers were in theory assembled in the community of the Stationers' Company. This Company, chartered by Queen Mary in 1557, provided the central defining conventions of the craft. It oversaw quality – by means of regular searches carried out on its members' properties – and acted against threats to its members' livelihoods. A principal occasion for such activity was provided by its monthly courts held at Stationers' Hall, in which matters of 'propriety' (as it was termed) were resolved by means of negotiation and penalty. In particular, the Company maintained a 'register book', in which members would enter the titles of books they were to publish. Once entered, such a title denoted its enterer's right to the 'copy' concerned. In principle that right would last forever. Violations of a Stationer's copy, by comprinting or otherwise, were frequently denounced before the court, which would act to forestall such 'piracy'. In this way, the Stationers' Company founded a civility of the book trade which centred on the concept of copies.[12]

One of the principal differences between London's print culture and that obtaining in cities such as Amsterdam was that the Stationers' Company was charged with embracing all participants in the trade, without exception. Indeed, in the Restoration this ambition reached its peak, and deputies (especially the Stationer William Lathom) were hired to enforce inclusion of the countless stallholders and hawkers operating

---

[11] Ibid., pp. 323–31.
[12] For the Stationers' Company, see C. Blagden, *The Stationers' Company: A History 1403–1959* (London, 1960). The procedures of registration, 'copy' and 'propriety' are discussed at length in Johns, *The Nature of the Book*, ch. 3. For a treatment in terms of the origins of copyright, see M. Rose, *Authors and Owners: The Invention of Copyright* (Cambridge, Mass., 1993), pp. 9–30.

in the capital's streets without oversight. Similar corporate bodies certainly existed in other European cities, but the structure of the London Company was as distinctive as its inclusivity. In German guilds, for example, master printers, booksellers and journeymen were generally admitted with equal status, whereas in France and the Netherlands master printers alone participated. Moreover, in Amsterdam until late in the century mastership was conveyed by dispensation, not company convention. The difference was not so great as to be irreconcilable – indeed, much to James II's dismay, conspiratorial Whig Stationers such as Awnsham Churchill fitted remarkably easily into the homes and lives of Amsterdam booksellers – but it existed nonetheless. Journeymen and booksellers did sometimes try to form their own collectives in these countries, but the masters forbade them, with occasionally violent results. In London, the Stationers' Company at least aspired to be comprehensive – but so did the strict hierarchy it established. This hierarchy pervaded the culture of the book trade. So prevalent was it that Restoration journeymen could cite France, Holland, Italy and even Spain as countries in which their fellows received more favourable recognition.[13]

The ranking of the book trade took two forms. First, the Stationers' Company divided its members according to the customary City ranks of Freeman, Liveryman and Assistant. Most members never made it beyond the first of these, and to be an Assistant – that is, to enter the oligarchy which took virtually all the Company's decisions – was a privilege accorded only a very few. Secondly, however, the register system became the foundation of an occupational hierarchy. This occupational distinction may have been less explicit than the civic tripartite division, but it was probably more significant both economically and culturally. For perhaps a century, booksellers had been rising in prosperity and status compared with printers. In the Restoration, this ascendancy was resoundingly confirmed. It was increasingly evident even in the formal hierarchy of the Company. By 1663, journeymen complained, the booksellers had grown so powerful that 'there is hardly one Printer to ten others that have a share in the Government of the Company'. And even those printers who did reach the rank of Assistant 'either dare not stand for the Interest of Printing, for fear of losing a Work-Master; or will not, because they have an interest among them'. In the next century, William Strahan would

[13] Stationers' Company Archives, Suppl. Doc. I.A, Env. 10, I (for Lathom); *A Brief Discourse Concerning Printing and Printers* (London, 1663), p. 23. For Churchill, see R. Ashcraft, *Revolutionary Politics and Locke's* Two Treatises of Government (Princeton, N.J., 1986), pp. 462–3; the hospitable reception accorded such refugees continued a tradition extending back beyond Moxon's father to the Marian exiles. For a comparison with sixteenth-century Antwerp, see L. Voet, 'The Printers' Chapel in the Plantinian House', *The Library*, 5th series, 16 (1961), pp. 1–14.

recall the position his fellow printers had then occupied as one of 'slavery'. There were recurrent suggestions that the disgruntled printers might even secede to form their own company.

This occupational divide was now itself followed by a further rift. It was copy-owning booksellers in particular who now came to prominence, leaving in their wake those who merely retailed volumes to lay customers. The Restoration trade would be dominated by those whose 'chief Riches and Profit' lay in 'the Property of valuable Copies'. These men and women made their fortunes by exploiting the Stationers' propriety, and not directly by retail or manufacturing. Some abandoned the latter two activities altogether, and developed new strategies of wholesale publishing to optimize their gains. With capital – and sometimes a lot of it – secured in the perpetual rights established by the register system, a small number of such booksellers could wield disproportionate influence over the industry and its products.[14]

One result was that certain individuals and syndicates could afford to concentrate their energies on particular markets. Already in the Interregnum Livewell Chapman and Giles Calvert had been instrumental in the creation of a corpus of radical politics and philosophy. Now, John Martyn and James Allestrey pioneered the publishing of experimental natural philosophy; Moses Pitt projected a huge and, as it turned out, doomed project for a multi-volume *English Atlas*; John Streater and others attempted to monopolize law books; and literature attracted its own magnates. Humphrey Moseley's extensive holdings in pre-Civil War drama and poetry were snatched up on his death by Henry Herringman, who put this wealth and renown to use to sponsor new works for the next four decades. Dryden was a major beneficiary. Jacob Tonson then inherited Herringman's mantle in the early eighteenth century. Tonson would be instrumental not just in the maintenance of authorial figures such as Shakespeare and Milton, but in their very creation. It was in the century after 1660, not in the century before, that Shakespeare in particular attained his status as a national literary icon.[15]

However, not all the 'copies' underpinning the prosperity of these booksellers were creations of the Stationers' register. The Crown itself

---

[14] On the tripartite hierarchy, as well as the other rules of the Company, see ordinances of 1678 and 1682 reprinted in Arber, *Transcript*, pp. I, 3–19, 20–4. For complaints against the rise of the booksellers, see *Brief Discourse*, pp. 3–6 and 12, and *The London Printers Lamentation, or, the Press opprest, and overprest* ([London], 1660), p. 2. For the prospect of a separate company, see C. Blagden, 'The "Company" of Printers', *Studies in Bibliography* 13 (1960), pp. 3–17.

[15] J. Feather, *A History of British Publishing* (London, 1988), pp. 56–7; H.M. Geduld, *Prince of Publishers: a Study of the Work and Career of Jacob Tonson* (London, 1969); M. De Grazia, *Shakespeare Verbatim: The Reproduction of Authenticity and the 1790 Apparatus* (Oxford, 1991).

intervened in the book trade – as it did in many others – by means of patents, or privileges. These were formal manifestations of royal prerogative, deployed to vest specific powers in their holders. So, for example, capital-intensive publishing projects which might otherwise be too risky to pursue could be underwritten by a royal privilege granting their proposers exclusive rights for a given period. For example, a nine-volume collection of theological commentaries proposed by Cornelius Bee and others in the early Restoration cost about £1,000 for preparing and 'methodizing' the manuscripts, even before paper and printing for the six-year project had been accounted for. The existence of just one rival threatened Bee with utter ruin. Charles II granted him a fourteen-year patent forbidding others from printing 'any *part* or *parcell*' of the work.[16]

Such a privilege, unlike an entry in the register, was defensible at law. Some felt that the mechanism should be extended to replace the Stationers' own system of copies, since they argued that the latter was necessarily tainted by commercial interests. Richard Atkyns and John Streater advocated this policy with particular vehemence, while also proposing a separate Company of Printers. But it was never really endorsed, and privileges remained a supplement to the Stationers' culture rather than its replacement. In fact, the Company itself operated perhaps the most lucrative privilege of all. This was called the English Stock, and covered a number of rights. Most notably, the Stock held a monopoly in all almanacs. This gave it dominance over what was a huge and growing market – perhaps the single largest of them all. In the Restoration, the Stock oversaw the annual publication of perhaps 300,000 almanacs, rising to 500,000 by around 1700. This yielded some £1,000–1,500 in yearly profits. With its work being distributed to support the trade's most needy members, and with the Stockkeepers regularly diverting funds to finance the Company's search-and-seizure efforts, it would scarcely be an exaggeration to say that much of the Stationers' realm depended on this one enterprise.[17]

The Company's searches served a dual purpose. First and foremost, they bolstered the Stationers' regime against piracy and cognate offences. But they were also part of a state effort to regulate the book

---

[16] *The Case of Cornelius Bee and his Partners* ([London], n.d. [1668?]). For a brief general account of privileges, see J. Feather, *Publishing, Piracy and Politics: An Historical Study of Copyright in Britain* (London, 1994), pp. 10–14.

[17] R. Atkyns, *Original and Growth of Printing* (London, 1664); [R. Atkyns and/or J. Streater], *The Kings Grant of Privilege for Sole Printing Common-Law-Books, defended* (London, 1669); C. Blagden, 'The English Stock of the Stationers' Company', *The Library*, 5th series, 10 (1955), pp. 163–85; C. Blagden, 'The Distribution of Almanacks in the Second Half of the Seventeenth Century', *Studies in Bibliography* 11 (1958), pp. 107–16.

trade. From the start, the restored monarchy had felt itself entitled and obliged to mount such an effort, both to underpin the trade's success (by protecting favoured members from domestic and foreign competition) and to prevent the printing of seditious or libellous works. Charles II personally urged haste in constructing a regime of press regulation from almost the moment he arrived back in Britain in 1660, and by 1662 Parliament was ready to oblige. The so-called Press Act which then passed into law closely resembled an earlier measure of 1637, which had lapsed with the abolition of the Star Chamber at the onset of the Civil War. It provided for licensers who should peruse any work before permitting it to be published. These licensers were to be ecclesiastical officers or appointees of the Secretaries of State. In a separate commission, Sir Roger L'Estrange, a proven Cavalier – and himself an adept participant in political pamphlet wars – was appointed Surveyor of the Press. L'Estrange, with the support of assorted 'messengers of the press' and financed by a patent on the printing of news, accepted a broad mission to monitor the London book trade, support loyalist publications and suppress opposition tracts. For a quarter of a century he personified the restoration regime's effort to mould a print culture in its own image.[18]

What emerged from these measures was a pragmatic alliance between Company and Crown. L'Estrange's roving commission excepted, enforcement, in an age before regular police forces, remained the preserve of the Stationers themselves. In return, the Press Act enjoined entrance in the Stationers' register for all publications, thus sanctioning the Company's conventions of propriety in law. But it did not do so to provide a foundation for perpetual properties. The court's intent was to aid in the prosecution of opposition works. This it did in two ways: by using the protection against piracy offered by the register as an incentive to Stationers to have their books properly licensed (since entry required the approbation of a licenser); and by explicitly identifying a figure responsible for each published title, who could be prosecuted for it. The lack of a licence was not generally in itself sufficient grounds to go to the trouble of a prosecution. But it did provide the *potential* for pursuit, and this potential constituted a large part of the system's utility. Moreover, books which *did* carry a licence were held to display not just a permission but an active badge of distinction. A comparison was often drawn with the impresa stamped on a newly minted coin. Here, readers were

---

[18] 'An Act for preventing the Frequent Abuses in Printing Seditious Treasonable and Unlicensed Bookes and Pamphlets and for Regulating of Printing and Printing Presses', 14 Car. II, c.33; G. Kitchin, *Sir Roger L'Estrange: A Contribution to the History of the Press in the Seventeenth Century* (London, 1913).

supposed to infer, could be found safe and reliable knowledge. Whether or not readers actually made that inference is moot, but licensers, writers and Stationers all liked to suppose that they did.[19]

As a result, the history of the book trade in this period falls into three distinct phases, in which local practices and statutory regulation were inextricable. The first was that of explicit regulation, whether by the Press Act, which was renewed periodically, or, in times when the Act had fallen into abeyance, by the exercise of royal prerogative. This lasted beyond the advent of William III, until the Act lapsed for what proved to be the last time in 1695. The result was not the utopia of press freedom which we might suppose. On the contrary, with the register system now deprived of legal sanction, the Stationers feared that an anarchic dystopia of piracy would prevail. So for the next decade or so the booksellers themselves were vociferous in clamouring for a replacement. They also developed their own mechanisms for protection, adapting and expanding practices mooted in preceding years to safeguard particularly vulnerable fields such as legal publishing. By early in the next century a system of wholesaling syndicates called 'congers' had been established, protecting members' copies and sharing large-scale publishing projects. Members of a conger would collaborate to blacklist rivals accused of unsound practices, especially piracy. They also partially dissolved the identities of particular craftspeople and shopkeepers into the collective, giving rise in turn to fears that a given group might abuse its power and descend into nothing but a 'pyrate-Conger'. Finally, in 1710 Parliament passed an 'Act for the Encouragement of Learning', which endorsed a qualified notion of the Stationers' 'copy'. The Act recognized a right on behalf of the writer of a work for a limited period, with extensions if he or she were still alive at the end of that period. Some Stationers were already referring to this as one's 'copy' 'right', and by the mid-eighteenth century the two words would have been conflated to become 'copyright'.[20]

[19] In this sense, as Chartier has argued more generally, authorship was defined by a practical conjunction of two concerns, namely property and regulation: compare R. Chartier (trans. L.G. Cochrane), *The Order of Books: Readers, Authors, and Libraries in Europe between the Fourteenth and Eighteenth Centuries* (Cambridge, 1994), pp. 39–43, 61–88; and Chartier, *Forms and Meanings: Texts, Performances, and Audiences from Codex to Computer* (Philadelphia, Pa., 1995), pp. 36–7. For an example of the comparison with coinage, see *Arguments Relating to a Restraint upon the Press* (London, 1712), p. 16.

[20] For the making of the so-called 'Copyright Act' (8 Ann., c.21), see J. Feather, 'The Book Trade in Politics: The Making of the Copyright Act of 1710', *Publishing History* 8 (1980), pp. 19–44. There is an extensive literature on the subsequent forging of the proprietal author: see especially Rose, *Authors and Owners*; Feather, *Publishing, Piracy and Politics*; D. Saunders, *Authorship and Copyright* (London, 1992); and M. Woodmansee and P. Jaszi (eds.), *The Construction of Authorship: Textual Appropriation in Law and Literature* (Durham, NC, 1994).

It is tempting to speculate on what might have been had the Press Act and the interventions of royal prerogative survived into the eighteenth century. The appropriate comparison in such an event would not be with Amsterdam or other Dutch centres, since the limited and divided powers of local and state authorities in such cities severely qualified any attempts at regulation. In all probability, the London of James III would have seen a baroque system come into being similar to that developed in Bourbon Paris. There, as Robert Darnton, Roger Chartier and others have revealed, printers, booksellers, hawkers and readers learned to negotiate a complex realm of policing. In theory, books were either licensed or illicit. In practice, in both seventeenth-century England and eighteenth-century France, many occupied a hazy space between the two. An increasing proportion – perhaps the majority – were never explicitly licensed, yet very few were pursued for the omission. In France, they might, for example, be accorded a 'tacit permission', in which case the police would allow publishing to proceed without prejudice to future efforts at suppression. And the chief superintendant himself became a vital defender of such works as the *Encyclopédie*. L'Estrange's successors in London might well have learned to play a similar role. Indeed, in patchy testimony from the later seventeenth century we can perhaps discern the emergence of just such a flexible, oral and face-to-face culture. After experiencing problems with earlier texts, Henry More found that the best way to ensure safe passage past the licenser at Lambeth Palace was to go to London in person and have dinner with him. This emerging culture was abandoned in 1695, with nothing to replace it.[21]

In the meantime, however, the Stationers' Company, licensing and privileges had structured an entire culture of print. The material products of that realm culminated in some remarkable books, including John Milton's *Paradise Lost* and Isaac Newton's *Principia*. But these were rather exceptional achievements. A community composed of small-scale craft workshops in a city without sophisticated banking arrangements spent most of its time pursuing correspondingly small-scale enterprises in a more or less undignified scramble for survival. A master printer was more likely to survive by frequent commissions for pamphlets and ephemera,

---

[21] For Dutch regulatory efforts, see S. Groenveld, 'The Dutch Republic, an Island of Liberty of the Press in Seventeenth-Century Europe?' in H. Bots and F. Waquet (eds.), *Commercium Litterarum: Forms of Communication in the Republic of Letters 1600–1750* (Amsterdam, 1994), pp. 281–300. For the French regime, see R. Chartier (trans. L.G. Cochrane), *The Cultural Origins of the French Revolution* (Durham, NC, 1991), pp. 38–91; and R. Darnton, *The Forbidden Best-Sellers of Pre-Revolutionary France* (New York, 1995). For the role of the Directeur de la Librairie, Malesherbes, in protecting the *Encyclopédie*, see R. Darnton, *The Business of Enlightenment: A Publishing History of the* Encyclopédie, *1775–1800* (Cambridge, Mass., 1979), pp. 9–14.

which offered a constant flow of funds, than by infrequent large projects. The latter might involve long delays between payments and unpredictable lapses in work while cloistered academics, unused to the disciplines of the printer's chapel, feuded over mathematical calculations or pondered the dichotomies of translating ancient Chaldean. Both left the master dangerously exposed. Moreover, large projects necessitated venturing a substantial investment – and quite possibly one's entire livelihood – on a single work. This could be risky to the point of foolishness. For all these reasons, printing houses generally preferred to produce small, frequent pieces. Even those engaged in large projects would in practice retain the prerogative to set aside such prestigious work for the sake of small jobs. It has been realistically claimed, then, that the majority of printed material from the period was of this form. Virtually all of it disappeared shortly after its production, leaving a material archive which, for all its glories, does not represent accurately the printing industry as it really was.

As it was, the printing industry favoured the small scale and the short term. Learned publishing was accommodated in the interstices of this culture as best as possible. Scarcely any printing houses operated for the purpose of such work. John Fell's efforts at Oxford University Press succeeded only in the teeth of reluctant readers and an actively hostile Stationers' Company. Richard Bentley's at Cambridge also encountered difficulties, although Bentley took care to recruit Tonson as a London ally. But these two were the only operations in Britain whose *raison d'être* was learned publishing. By contrast, Addison estimated that 200–300 families lived by scribbling, and the printers themselves reckoned that two-thirds of their number depended on pamphlets for their survival. Quantitatively, and perhaps qualitatively too, the face of the London author was that of the professional hack.[22]

Contemporaries tried various approaches to accommodate the production of substantial or learned works to this unwelcoming realm. Authors could guarantee to purchase a certain number of copies themselves in order to underwrite publication, as did the Royal Society; or a lottery might be held, as John Ogilby enterprisingly ventured in order to support his edition of Virgil. But the most important strategy was that of subscription publishing. The technique seems to have been invented by London booksellers, and was relatively well established among them by the time the first Amsterdam equivalent was mooted in 1661 (for an

---

[22] D.F. McKenzie, *The Cambridge University Press 1696–1712: a Bibliographical Study*, 2 vols. (Cambridge, 1966), vol. I *passim*; D.J. McKitterick, *A History of Cambridge University Press*, 2 vols. to date (Cambridge, 1992–), pp. 319–62; [J. Addison], *The Thoughts of a Tory Author, Concerning the Press* (London, 1712), p. 30; D.F. McKenzie, 'The London Book Trade in the Later Seventeenth Century' (unpublished Sandars Lectures, Cambridge, 1976), p. 25. The world of the hack is described in Rogers, *Grub Street*.

obscure religious text in untranslated Hebrew, a work which the Dutch themselves would find it hard to sell – it at first generated precisely no subscribers even at a theologians' conference). In Restoration London, on the other hand, subscription was a relatively common means of publication. From Walton's polyglot Bible of 1657 through to Catesby's natural history in the 1730s, many substantial works were introduced on the basis of this mechanism.[23]

Subscription publishing involved issuing a prospectus of the intended work, which would include an invitation to would-be purchasers to pay up front. If all proceeded to plan, these investors would receive their books for a lower price than retail customers, in return for which their early payment would have provided sufficient capital to permit production. Both the economic viability of the project and the worth of the text to be produced had to be established in the proposals inviting such contributors. In this campaign, building up a list of notables prepared to venture money was itself very important. Subscription lists themselves became instruments for establishing the viability of the projects concerned, and not just in an economic sense. They buttressed both the commercial propriety of the publication and, not independently, its worth as a work of learning. Such lists were thus printed in careful order of rank and quality, and circulated in efforts both to attract more subscribers and to create a market for the work when it eventually appeared. They were not always successful, however. By 1700, if not before, subscription appeals were notorious for the frequency with which the books they advertised failed to appear.[24]

Another way to reduce the risk inherent in major publishing projects was to approach them collaboratively. Cooperations between publishing booksellers were known before the Civil War, but it was in the Restoration that such ventures became something close to routine. John Streater, a printer consistently troublesome to the Stationers' hierarchy, was a major pioneer of such efforts in his publishing of folio law books. The concept of the 'conger' evolved partly out of Streater's efforts. As well as dispersing the consequences of failure and defusing the threat of piracy, however,

[23] K.S. Van Eerde, *John Ogilby and the Taste of his Times* (Folkestone, 1976), pp. 85–6; R.W.F. Kroll, '*Mise-en-Page*, Biblical Criticism, and Inference during the Restoration', *Studies in Eighteenth-Century Culture* 16 (1986), pp. 3–40; H. McBurney, *Mark Catesby's Natural History of America: The Watercolors from the Royal Library, Windsor Castle* (Museum of Fine Arts, Houston, London, 1997), pp. 17–18; P.T. van Rooden and J.W. Wesselius, 'Two Early Cases of Publication by Subscription in Holland and Germany: Jacob Abendana's *Mikheal Yophi* (1661) and David Cohen de Lara's *Keter Kehunna* (1668)', *Quaerendo* 16 (1986), pp. 110–30. I am most grateful to Amy Meyers for telling me about Catesby's subscription publishing.

[24] F.J.G. Robinson and P.J. Wallis, *Book Subscription Lists: A Revised Guide* (Newcastle, 1975); J. Feather, *English Book Prospectuses: An Illustrated History* (Newton, Pa., 1984).

collaboration also had the benefit of reducing the prospects for retribution if a work were called in by L'Estrange. In this context, such strategies stabilized into the practice known as 'trade publishing'. This involved a proxy Stationer being paid to put his or her name on a title-page in place of that of the party actually responsible. It was one way to avoid the identification of a given title with the party actually funding its production. With such decoys in play, their 'syncopated or fictitious Names' made it hard to mount a successful prosecution. One Tory – himself discreetly anonymous – complained that those who used such mechanisms were tantamount to 'Highway-men in Masks'.[25]

London printers required not just small-scale publications, but regular ones. The events of the 1640s had established that there was a large potential market for just such manageable, periodical packets, especially when they dealt with current political events. Regulation notwithstanding, the book trade acted to foster and exploit that market from then on. L'Estrange's provision by means of a monopoly on news represented ironic recognition of its vitality. In fact, the very concept of 'news' was in a sense an invention of the Stationers. But so was that of false news. Printed newsbooks were notorious for their unreliability, and even more so for their prodigious claims to veracity. The more newsmen proclaimed truth, it seemed, the likelier it was that their publications were fraudulent, inauthentic, inaccurate or simply wrong. One of the running jokes of the later Interregnum and Restoration was this contrast between announced veracity and actual falsity, or, given a slightly different twist, between announced permanence and actual transience. The essence of news was supposed to be factual truth, and truth should be eternal; yet a periodical press required the rapid turnover of facts in order to survive. This paradox characterized not just news publishing, indeed, but the entire realm of the Stationers. Theirs was a world in which radically opposed representations of truth and falsity, and of permanence and transience, brutally collided. Print underpinned urban culture, that all could admit; but piracy and libels threatened its stability.[26]

The impact of print was thus instantiated in the most notorious site at which news was consumed: the coffee-house. Offering opportunities for

---

[25] *Arguments Relating to a Restraint upon the Press*, pp. 26–7. For congers, see N. Hodgson and C. Blagden, *The Notebook of Thomas Bennet and Henry Clements (1686–1719)* (Oxford, 1956). For trade publishers, see M. Treadwell, 'London Trade Publishers, 1675–1750', *The Library*, 6th series, 4 (1982), pp. 99–134.

[26] For the effects of periodicity, see C.J. Sommerville, *The News Revolution in England: Cultural Dynamics of Daily Information* (New York, 1996). Newspapers themselves are discussed in detail in J. Raymond, *The Invention of the Newspaper: English Newsbooks, 1641–1649* (New York, 1996); and J. Sutherland, *The Restoration Newspaper and Its Development* (Cambridge, 1986).

even the illiterate to comprehend the latest printed papers, and combining facilities for both rabble-rousing and caballing, the coffee-house epitomized the possibilities for disorder raised by the press. Ink and coffee flowed in concert during the Restoration years, and addiction to both could be satisfied in the same location. It is striking that several of the best-known coffee-houses either abutted or shared premises with bookshops. Only in the 1720s would the *de facto* alliance come under strain, when coffee-house owners and printers would fight for control of the newspaper press. In the meantime, it was the influence of printed materials as manifested in places such as these which made the combination of authority and licence a frightening one. The possibilities were only confirmed during such crises as that of 1679–83, when the Press Act lapsed and the London populace was inflamed as never before by pamphleteers and newsmongers.[27]

How best to counteract these threats? The alliance between licensing and propriety was one means. Later, a new sacrosanct principle would be found on which a similar conjunction of regulation and property could rest: that of authorship, as certified by copyright. But the point of application for both these strategies was the moment of production, and it was not so clear that this was the source of the problem. Newspapers and pamphlets would be of little consequence without the coffee-house cabals prepared to make so much of their contents. What if not just production, but use, could be transformed?

Concern therefore centred not just on printing and publishing, but on reading. L'Estrange himself wanted to license coffee-houses to ensure their propriety as sites for the consumption of texts. Others proposed new sites altogether. Circulating libraries – the first of them launched by the enterprising Francis Kirkman in the 1660s – prospered, and were destined for enormous success in the succeeding century. Societies for the reformation of manners assisted, one of them led by the Whig bookseller John Dunton. Such organizations filtered materials to be read in the home. Dunton created his own periodicals, the most successful of them being the *Athenian Mercury*, partly to further this end. Nonetheless, fears persisted. In the eighteenth century they focused more and more on the distinctive literary form to emerge out of the conjunction of credibility and transience characteristic of London publishing, namely the novel.

---

[27] There is now an extensive literature on coffee-houses. The main reference source is Lillywhite, *London Coffee Houses*. For print and coffee in the Restoration, see M. Knights, *Politics and Public Opinion in Crisis, 1678–81* (Cambridge, 1994); and T. Harris, *London Crowds in the Reign of Charles II: Propaganda and Politics from the Restoration until the Exclusion Crisis* (Cambridge, 1987). For the war between printers and coffee-house owners in the 1720s, see M. Harris, *London Newspapers in the Age of Walpole: A Study of the Origins of the Modern English Press* (London, 1987), pp. 30–1.

Kirkman had pioneered this idiom, too, by means of his engaging *English Rogue* series. Novels fascinated new audiences, especially (and, to some, notoriously) female ones. Critics were bewailing their moral effects on such readers well after the time of Richardson.[28]

A particularly striking proponent of the regulation of both publishing and reading together was the Royal Society. Chartered in 1662, the Society aimed to further experimental philosophy, and was responsible for some of the most important developments in natural knowledge. Among its more notable attainments was a set of protocols for conducting philosophical work through the production, circulation and discussion of written and printed words. Created in an urban environment in which such materials were readily discredited, and in which authorship was both fragile and contentious, the Society moved rapidly to establish conventions by which both problems might be remedied. It established a register system, like that of the Stationers' Company, by which theories and designs could be attributed to their proper creators. It obtained by royal patent a right to license its own printed books and the capacity to appoint privileged printers to produce them. And, less formally, it instituted conventions for the 'perusal' of incoming papers, their reading before the collected virtuosi and their circulation to the republic of letters. Such practices stimulated continuing discourses and experimental investigations. The Society's secretary, Henry Oldenburg, also created the first 'scientific' periodical, the *Philosophical Transactions*, as a vehicle for these developments. The *Transactions* was not only the distinctive creation of experimental civility, but the projection of that civility into the troubled culture of Restoration print. It survived harrowing troubles over its first few decades to become an icon of the Enlightenment.[29]

The Royal Society thus tied the reception of printed documents to those of written ones, and secured both to the maxims of civility which governed polite conversation. But, in doing so, it was merely making manifest something modern historians are all too apt to forget. At every stage – in the domestic printing house, upstairs behind the bookshop, in the street, before the quizzical licenser and in the coffee-house – the meaning of print was shaped by reading, writing, speech and gesture. The Society's

[28] Again, there is a substantial literature now on the practices, sites, regulation and effects of reading. See especially J. Raven, H. Small and N. Tadmor (eds.), *The Practice and Representation of Reading in England* (Cambridge, 1996); and A. Bermingham and J. Brewer (eds.), *The Consumption of Culture, 1600–1800: Image, Object, Text* (London, 1995), pp. 23–74.

[29] E.N. da C. Andrade, 'The Birth and Early Days of the *Philosophical Transactions*', *Notes and Records of the Royal Society* 20 (1965), pp. 9–22; C.A. Rivington, 'Early Printers to the Royal Society, 1663–1708', *Notes and Records of the Royal Society* 39 (1984), pp. 1–28. This story is told in detail in Johns, *The Nature of the Book*, ch. 7.

success lay in subjecting print culture to the rules of decorum governing these social practices. The extent of that success may be gauged by the accomplishment of Isaac Newton in attaining supremacy through the three editions of his *Principia*. By 1720, Newton was President of the Society, and unrivalled as the greatest philosophical author in Europe.[30] Beginning in 1660 and culminating in the 1720s, the process by which London's virtuosi had built the grounds for this feat spanned almost exactly the period of the present chapter. It demonstrated a truth both simple and, to modern historians, unfamiliar: that a reliable and creditable print culture was indeed an achievement – and a remarkable one.

[30] For the continuing strength of conversational civility and its central relevance to print, see A. Goldgar, *Impolite Learning: Conduct and Community in the Republic of Letters, 1680–1750* (New Haven, Conn., 1995). On the authorship of Newton, see especially R.C. Iliffe, ' "Is He like Other Men?" The Meaning of the *Principia Mathematica*, and the Author as Idol', in G. MacLean (ed.), *Culture and Society in the Stuart Restoration: Literature, Drama, History* (Cambridge, 1995), pp. 159–76.

Part 6

Scientific and useful knowledge

14   Science for sale: the metropolitan stimulus for scientific achievements in sixteenth-century Antwerp

Geert Vanpaemel

During the sixteenth century, the rich and populous provinces of the Spanish Netherlands harboured a considerable number of scholars and scientists. The University of Leuven, founded in 1425, was widely known for its promotion of the mathematical and astrological sciences. Among its justly famous students were the anatomist Andreas Vesalius, the botanist Rembert Dodoens and the cartographer Gerard Mercator, each of them holding a prominent place in the development of early modern science. Humanism also took root in the academic milieu, supported by the presence of Erasmus, who was responsible for the creation of the Collegium Trilingue in 1517. By the middle of the century, Leuven counted as one of the major intellectual centres in northern Europe.[1]

However, after 1550 the momentum of the Leuven development started to slow down. The remarkable generation of the early sixteenth century had died or had emigrated. The Leuven printing industry showed a continuous decline towards the end of the century, when only five printers remained.[2] Books on medicine, mathematics and science were then mostly published in Antwerp.[3] The decline of Leuven (and of Brussels) was paralleled by the rise of Antwerp as the scientific capital of the Spanish Netherlands.[4] Major figures of the late sixteenth century, such as the cartographer Abraham Ortelius, the pharmacist Peter van

---

[1] H. De Vocht, *History of the Foundation and the Rise of the Collegium Trilingue Lovaniense 1517–1550*, 4 vols. (Leuven, 1986). For science in particular, see G. Vanpaemel, 'Gerard Mercator and the Scientific Renaissance at the University of Leuven' in H.H. Blotevogel and R. Vermij (eds.), *Gerhard Mercator und die geistigen Strömungen des 16. und 17. Jahrhunderts*, Duisburger Mercator-Studien 3 (Duisburg, 1995), pp. 33–48.

[2] J. Dauwe, 'Het Leuvens boekbedrijf' in R. van Uytven (ed.), *Leuven, 'de beste stad van Brabant'. I. De geschiedenis van het stadsgewest Leuven tot omstreeks 1660* (Leuven 1980), pp. 263–71. In fact, decline had set in from the beginning of the century but, at least until 1550, the book industry remained an important supporting element of university life.

[3] Examples are the mathematical and cosmographical works of the Leuven professors Cornelius Valerius and Adrianus Romanus.

[4] During the first half of the century, science was also well represented in Brussels through the presence of Vesalius at the imperial court and the activity of printers such as Thomas van der Noot.

Coudenberghe and the mathematician Michiel Coignet, lived and worked in Antwerp and had no connection whatsoever with the university, while others, such as Dodoens and his fellow botanists Clusius and Lobelius, found a stimulating working environment among the Antwerp printers and artists. Undoubtedly, the wealthy city of Antwerp attracted scholars of all sorts, looking for patrons to support their work. Also, the deteriorating economic and political situation in the Spanish Netherlands caused many to look for a safer place in times of war and repression. But the concentration of scholars was not merely a temporary demographic result of economic factors. In the metropolis, a new kind of science emerged which differed in many respects from the academic traditions dominating the Leuven university. Antwerp science was aimed at a public of merchants, entrepreneurs, sailors and travellers, and was primarily based on practical, useful knowledge. It enlisted the cooperation of a large number of artists, printers and scholars, and it could be made to sell on the market. Of course, these aspects had not been completely absent from the humanist science at Leuven, but they now became dominant and characteristic features of the scientific endeavour, betraying the unique combination of cultural cross-fertilization and economic opportunities only to be found in a metropolis in its golden age.

The continuing scholarly interest among historians in Antwerp's golden age has over the years produced a large amount of literature attempting to capture the essence of this urban phenomenon. Significantly, the historiography of science has been strongly underrepresented. A recent book by a select team of experts on Antwerp's golden age has no chapter on science and, although some names are dropped in different chapters, science was apparently not recognized by the authors as a significant cultural sphere of metropolitan life.[5] To historians of science, this comes as something of a surprise, and is even a matter of outright embarrassment. The fact that from an overall perspective the scientific achievements appear hardly noticeable is, to say the least, somewhat disturbing.

It is perhaps too easily taken for granted by historians that in a large and wealthy metropolis science cannot but develop and flourish. This is, however, not necessarily the case and certainly it precludes all further investigation on the complex relationship between urban environment and scientific achievement. Here the comparative perspective offered by the almost contemporary development of science in Leuven can be revealing. The scientific renaissance of Leuven was predominantly based on the particular circumstances provided by the university environment. Antwerp had no institution for higher learning until the foundation of mathematical courses

---

[5] Jan van der Stock (ed.), *Antwerp: Story of a metropolis, 16th-17th century* (Ghent, 1993).

by the Jesuits in 1617. In general, theoretical or speculative science would not be valued very highly in a commercial environment. Conversely, the scientific achievements of Antwerp scholars in botany, engineering or instrument building were not easily integrated into the academic life at Leuven. Thus, the urban atmosphere of the metropolis must be taken into account to fully understand the specific scientific achievements in Antwerp.

The first problem at hand is to identify the scientific achievements of the sixteenth century linked with Antwerp. This is more difficult than it may seem. It will not suffice to list all the scholars working in the city at one time or another, or to make a census of all the books published. Antwerp was of course the most important centre of book production in the Spanish Netherlands, and scholars from the whole region and even from abroad had their works published there. For our purposes, however, it is not the mere numbers of publications that count, but rather the social and intellectual stimuli to a particular scientist to work in the Antwerp region. So it will not help to take as a starting point the fact that the majority of scientific books and pamphlets in the Southern Netherlands were indeed published by Antwerp printers.[6] Many of these books were written by scientists who were not resident in or even linked with Antwerp. On the other hand, the Antwerp scientific scene is not to be equated entirely with book production. We should not ignore the large number of anonymous schoolmasters, herbalists, surveyors, architects and instrument builders who certainly contributed to the peculiar circumstances in which the more renowned scientists worked. The availability of printing presses was certainly a positive inducement to go to Antwerp or to do a particular kind of work, but the production of books was primarily an economic achievement of the Antwerp printers, not of the Antwerp scientists. Indeed, as one author has put it: 'One cannot escape the feeling that the large production of scientific books in sixteenth-century Antwerp was due more to the initiative of printers and publishers than to the creative work of Antwerp scientists.'[7]

Another method might be to examine the biographies of the most important scientists, where they are available.[8] Science in the Spanish Netherlands during the sixteenth century did not lack great names. But, from the existing

---

[6] Much research on the intellectual life in Antwerp is being done in connection with the Museum Plantin-Moretus, which naturally pays much attention to the role of the Plantin house and, by extension, of the Antwerp printers; for example, E. Cockx-Indestege and F. de Nave (eds.), *Christoffel Plantijn en de exacte wetenschappen in zijn tijd* (Brussels, 1989).

[7] P. Boeynaems, 'De wetenschappen te Antwerpen in de 16de eeuw' in *Antwerpen in de XVIde eeuw* (Antwerp, 1975), pp. 349–60, at p. 354.

[8] Actually, not many biographies are available, and most of them are outdated. References can be found in A. Meskens, *Wiskunde tussen Renaissance en Barok. Aspecten van wiskunde-beoefening te Antwerpen 1550–1620*, Publicaties SBA/AMVC 41–43 (Antwerp, 1994).

biographies, it is often very hard to determine to what extent the urban environment of Antwerp had a particular influence on their work. Biographies of great scientists tend to concentrate on personal effort and individual genius, rather than on the relevance of the social circumstances upon which their achievements were based. The golden age of Antwerp was also too short to encompass the whole of a scientist's career. Fame brought invitations from rich patrons or foreign courts: all but three members of what we can consider the core group of Belgian scientists indeed migrated abroad.[9]

More might be learned from analysing a larger group of scientists, but then this might weaken our definition of 'achievement'. Large numbers are not necessarily a sign of outstanding intellectual activity. One might, for example, be tempted to consider the wealth of medical publications as an indication of stimulating scientific interactions among Antwerp physicians. But, in fact, once we leave out the books published in Antwerp by Leuven professors or the translations of renowned treatises on surgery and midwifery, we are left with only a few minor and unimportant pamphlets, written in the wake of epidemic diseases. One exception was David van Mauden, an Antwerp physician who had studied in Padua. Even then, his *Bedieninghe der anatomien* (1583), based on the work of Vesalius, was a quite elementary anatomical textbook for surgeons, written in the vernacular.[10] His colleague Jan Fyens (or Fienus) wrote a more learned treatise at about the same time on human gases, *De flatibus humanum corpus molestantibus* (1582), hardly a great scientific achievement, although the book was republished in Frankfurt (1592) and Amsterdam (1643), even into the eighteenth century.[11]

Another area where numbers do not equal quality was astrology. There was a continuing and even growing interest in astrology among Dutch scientists during the sixteenth century. It was well represented at the University of Leuven, where it influenced the revival of medico-mathematical studies in the first half of the century. But astrology was also a widely debated subject among the educated classes. This interest was supported by an endless series of books, pamphlets and almanacs based on astrological principles. Not surprisingly, there was a large market for such publications in Antwerp. Between 1555 until 1589, no fewer than 126 different Dutch almanacs were published.[12] Other books

[9] Ortelius, Coignet and van Coudenberghe.
[10] R. van Hee (ed.), *In de voetsporen van Yperman. Heelkunde in Vlaanderen door de eeuwen heen* (Brussels, 1990), p. 96; F. de Nave and M. de Schepper (eds.), *De Geneeskunde in de Zuidelijke Nederlanden (1475–1660)* (Antwerp, 1990), p. 139.
[11] De Nave and De Schepper, *De Geneeskunde in de Zuidelijke Nederlanden*, p. 115.
[12] R. Jansen-Sieben, 'Christoffel Plantijn en zijn Nederlandstalige drukken op het gebied van de *artes mechanicae*', in F. de Nave (ed.), *Exacte wetenschappen rondom Christoffel Plantijn (ca. 1520–1689)* (Antwerp, 1990), pp. 55–65.

discussed astrological conceptions in connection with medicine or theology, such as the Antwerp physician Cornelius Schylander's *Medicina Astrologica* (1577) or the humanist Cornelius de Schepper's *Assertiones Fidei adversus Astrologos* (1523). Some of these publications were well argued and of high quality, based on sound mathematical knowledge and actual astronomical research.[13] On the whole, however, the Antwerp astrologers did not generate a coherent research programme such as occurred in Leuven in the circle around Gemma Frisius.[14] Compared with the creative atmosphere of Leuven around 1550, the medical and astrological contributions by Antwerp scholars appear rather insignificant. Moreover, in view of the fact that many of the Antwerp physicians had studied at Leuven University and that interest in astrology had first peaked in Leuven, it may be correct to consider these sciences as a derived effect of the Leuven revival, rather than as a genuine Antwerp phenomenon. Probably before the end of the century, Antwerp mathematicians were turning away from astrology, although the lucrative business persisted.[15]

The examples of medicine and astrology show that neither a large group of educated scholars nor continuing market demand for 'scientific' publications could guarantee a high level of 'achievement'. This is not to say that these aspects were without any relevance in fostering an appropriate atmosphere. We will return to them as a part of the broader constellation of intellectual life. As independent fields of achievement, however, they cannot meet the high standard that we attribute to the scientific work of some of their contemporaries.

The strong dependence of the scientific activities in Antwerp on the prior scientific renaissance at Leuven is but one problem in defining the nature of the metropolitan achievement. Another is concerned with the overall migration patterns in the Netherlands, marked by religious repression and political rebellion during the sixteenth century. The migration of scholars (and many others) to the safer and more tolerant

[13] The history of astrology in the Spanish Netherlands has never been fully studied. An attempt is made in A. Brokken (ed.), *Sterren en Beelden. Astrologie in de eeuw van Mercator* (Sint-Niklaas, 1994), concentrating, however, on the pictorial and artistic aspects of astrological images. The main intellectual centre of astrology was not Antwerp but Leuven. See W. Shumaker and J.L. Heilbron, *John Dee on Astronomy* (Berkeley, Calif., 1978), pp. 55–9.

[14] On Gemma Frisius and his circle, see F. van Ortroy, *Bio-bibliographie de Gemma Frisius* (Brussels, 1920); E.H. Waterbolk, 'The "Reception" of Copernicus' Teachings by Gemma Frisius (1508–1555)' *Lias* 1 (1974), pp. 225–42. A. de Smet, 'Gemma Frisius', *Nationaal Biografisch Woordenboek* 6 (1974), col. 315–31; A. de Smet, 'Gérard Mercator (1512–1584) et les sciences occultes', *Scientiarum Historia* 16 (1990), pp. 5–10; Vanpaemel, 'The Scientific Renaissance'.

[15] Meskens, *Wiskunde tussen Renaissance en Barok*, pp. 190–2.

city of Antwerp does not necessarily reflect a positive attraction of the metropolis. The rise of Antwerp was paralleled by the political, social and intellectual decline of other cities.[16]

The turning point around the middle of the sixteenth century coincided with a more general reorientation of Antwerp humanism. Whereas early humanism in Antwerp was predominantly concerned with classical culture and philology, after 1550 it became increasingly linked with a pronounced interest in natural science.[17] At about the same time, Christoffel Plantin settled in Antwerp to found one of the major printing houses in Europe. His *officina* served as a meeting place for all sorts of scholars, and Plantin himself would often encourage scholars to publish their work or to cooperate on translations and new editions.

The heyday of Antwerp science undoubtedly should be placed between 1550 and 1585. The period falls neatly after Antwerp had already peaked as the leading economic centre in Europe.[18] It is convenient to draw a line in 1585, when Antwerp was sacked by Parma's Spanish troops and the Scheldt was closed, causing economic decline and massive emigration. Both dates are to be taken as approximate. Before 1550 the main contributions to science in the city were derived from scientific activities going on in Leuven or other places (Ghent, Brussels, Malines, etc.), and were not particularly outstanding. In putting the closing date at 1585, it should be borne in mind that not just Antwerp but the whole region entered a dark period of decline. Very little is known about the history of science in the Spanish Netherlands during the following decades, although at least by 1600 things had stabilized. In particular, during the first half of the seventeenth century the city again witnessed an increase in scientific activities, in which the Antwerp Jesuits and the Moretus printers played a prominent role. Yet this time the 'magic' of the metropolis had gone. Leuven had regained the intellectual leadership in the Southern Netherlands, and Antwerp was not even second best.

The scientific disciplines that can be considered to represent the

[16] Among the various factors affecting scientific work in other cities, we may point to the departure of the Spanish court (abdication of Charles V in 1555), the growing religious intolerance (which may have been less severe in a populous city), the threat of war (although Antwerp also suffered in 1576, 1579, 1583 and 1585) and the economic decline, which may have been less pronounced in Antwerp before the massive emigration movement started.

[17] M. Nauwelaerts, 'Humanisme en onderwijs', in *Antwerpen in de XVIde eeuw*, pp. 257–300; M. de Schepper, '*Sola una totus mundus est Antverpia*: humanisme en humanisten te Antwerpen (1470–1648)' in T.A.J.M. Janssen, P.G.M. de Kleijn and A.M. Musschoot (eds.), *Nederlands in culturele context* (Antwerp, 1995), pp. 181–202.

[18] F. Braudel, *Le temps du monde* (Paris, 1979). Yet, on a cultural level (in particular painting and printing), Antwerp may have peaked somewhat later. See P. Burke, *Antwerp, A Metropolis in Comparative Perspective* (Antwerp, 1993).

scientific achievements of Antwerp best can be grouped into two clusters: botany and mathematics. The first cluster also contains pharmacy and horticulture, while the second ranges from bookkeeping to fortification.[19] Both clusters fully qualify to be called areas of achievement. On the one hand, the Dutch botanists Dodoens, Clusius and Lobelius, who at least for some time worked in Antwerp, occupy a major place in the history of botany, both for their monumental and beautifully documented herbals and for their new approach in describing and cataloguing plants. The link with the metropolis is immediate and clear: during the sixteenth century Antwerp printers took the lead in the publication of botanical books. Between 1531 and 1562, they produced 18 of a total of 382 botanical publications in Europe, a feat that placed Antwerp in seventh place (after Strasbourg, Paris, Lyons, Basle, Venice and Frankfurt). After 1563, Antwerp even took the lead, with 37 editions out of a total of 278 before 1600.[20] The study of botany was connected to a strong interest in horticulture in the Antwerp region and to the presence of an international herb market. It is appropriate to consider botanical research in Antwerp as a major scientific achievement of the city.

The second cluster relates to the mathematical sciences. Here the problem is somewhat different. The mathematical 'movement' in the Southern Netherlands undoubtedly originated in Leuven, under the influence of Gemma Frisius and Gerard Mercator. Yet the mathematics that flowered in Antwerp may be considered as resulting from a different approach. Whereas Leuven mathematics was the outcome of a philosophical programme, centred on cosmography, astrology and the occult sciences, Antwerp mathematics had a more practical bent. A clear example may be offered by the difference between Mercator's maps on the one hand, produced in Leuven, destined for scholars (philosophers, theologians, etc.) and made according to Mercator's longstanding research on magnetism and, on the other hand, Ortelius' maps, which were commercial products, often reproduced from existing maps, to be sold to travellers and merchants, who would use them for practical ends. Nor is the cosmographical inspiration of Frisius and Mercator reflected in the navigation manuals of Everaert and Coignet, or the treatises on bookkeeping by Stevin or Raets, although admittedly in some cases the

---

[19] In our discussion of Antwerp science, we have deliberately left out technology. From the secondary literature, it appears that Antwerp did not produce any technological achievements in, say, dyeing, shipbuilding or smithing. The 'art' of military and civil construction may be classified under 'mathematics'.

[20] A. Louis, *Geschiedenis van de plantkunde* (Ghent/Leuven, 1977). A useful overview of recent work on botany in the Southern Netherlands (with further bibliographical references) is F. de Nave and D. Imhof (eds.), *De Botanica in de Zuidelijke Nederlanden (einde 15de eeuw–ca. 1650)* (Antwerp,1993).

difference may be rather slight (the most published books were indeed reprints of Frisius' practical manuals).[21]

During the period 1550–85, several outstanding 'mathematical' achievements ought to be considered. In 1570 Abraham Ortelius published his *Theatrum orbis terrarum*, the first book of maps which heralded a new age in cartography. The work was the result of impressive cooperation between merchants, cartographers, engravers, painters and printers. In subsequent years it was edited no fewer than twenty-five times, including translations into French, German, Dutch, Italian and Spanish. With Ortelius, Antwerp became a renowned centre for cartography, in particular because the maps of Mercator, who was befriended by Ortelius and maintained good relations with Antwerp, could also be easily obtained from Plantin.

Apart from Ortelius, mention should be made of Michiel Coignet, a mathematician who worked as a teacher, a wine-gauger and an instrument maker. Coignet is recognized as one of the inventors of the proportional compass.[22] At least one other instrument can be credited to him: the nautical hemisphere. While being a gifted instrument maker, he was also a keen mathematician. His book on navigation (1580) influenced several other authors, and his name occurs in the writings of Galileo and Kepler. As with Ortelius, Coignet represents only the culmination point of a wider group of mathematical practitioners, none of whom, however, reached a comparable level of achievement.

Fortification was a third area of mathematical achievement. Antwerp itself became the centre of fortification innovation through the construction of its citadel in 1567 by the Italian engineer Francesco Paciotto. People from all over Europe, among them the famous German engineer and mechanic Daniel Speckle, visited Antwerp to have a good look at the work under construction. Fortification was indeed a major activity in the Netherlands throughout the century; the Spanish War, which had such devastating effects on the country, stimulated the application of new techniques and inventive warfare. The Spanish army often enlisted the services of Italian engineers, who brought their skills and knowledge to the Netherlands. The innovative Italian system of fortification was soon taken over by Dutch engineers and considerably improved. Simon Stevin, one of the main architects of the Dutch fortification system, lived in Antwerp for some time, working as a bookkeeper but certainly also watching with great interest the work on the citadel.

[21] Antwerp mathematics is analysed by Meskens, *Wiskunde tussen Renaissance en Barok.*
[22] A. Meskens, 'Michiel Coignet's Contribution to the Development of the Sector', *Annals of Science* 54 (1997) pp. 143–60.

The question to ask now is how the urban environment of the commercial metropolis could and did contribute to the promotion of scientific research. In general, one can think of five possible inducements to scientific work. Scientists may have found opportunities in Antwerp for an education in science that they could not get elsewhere. This would have been important for those disciplines in which the universities did not provide any education or for people who could not attend a university for social or political reasons. A second inducement was the opportunity to earn a living. Although university teaching was still the main profession for scientists or 'natural philosophers' in the sixteenth century, a city such as Antwerp could provide many jobs for skilled scholars: teachers, architects, garden designers, pharmacists, bookkeepers, engineers and, of course, physicians. The variety of jobs and the number of potential customers or patrons may have induced scholars and skilled workers to look for a living in the metropolis. Thirdly, the city may have offered possibilities for doing scientific work that could not be found elsewhere. The availability of libraries or natural history collections, and also of information from seamen, merchants and travellers was certainly attractive to many scholars. Scholars may also have gone to Antwerp to have personal contact with colleagues and to cooperate in mutual research programmes. The urban concentration of people may thus have generated something like a scientific community, a coherent group of scholars comparable to the academic professorial community. Finally, a large city such as Antwerp may have held advantages in terms of freedom and tolerance, which to many intellectuals have always been very important, for obvious reasons.

Antwerp had no university, but offered many schools and teachers. There were no fewer than 150–200 'small' elementary schools.[23] Although the level of education was probably very low, this large number is evidence of a desire for education among the Antwerp population. Mostly, this education was directed towards commerce and, to a lesser extent, towards navigation. In addition, the many translations printed in Antwerp perhaps indicate a more than usual knowledge of modern languages.

At a more advanced level, there were Latin schools, concentrating on classical literature. The number of such schools in Antwerp rose from one to five by 1529. In 1575 the Jesuits opened a college which soon attracted 300 students from all classes of the population. The advance of education did not stop in 1585. Still more new colleges were to be founded at the beginning of the seventeenth century.

[23] H.L.V. de Groote, 'De zestiende-eeuwse Antwerpse schoolmeesters', *Bijdragen tot de geschiedenis* 50 (1967), pp. 179–318; 51 (1968), pp. 5–52.

Apart from general education, there were also plenty of opportunities to learn a profession as an apprentice in a guild or as the younger member in a family business. This applies in particular to printers, engravers, goldsmiths, teachers, merchants and bookkeepers, all professions closely linked to mathematics. It was not unusual for children to be sent to a parent in Antwerp to learn a trade. Among the more famous students were Simon Stevin, who learned the trade of bookkeeping in Antwerp, and the Dutch mathematician Ludolf van Ceulen.

The situation was somewhat different for botany: the great botanists were all educated at a university. Pharmacists, on the other hand, were part of the *De Meersse* guild, and learned their trade through apprenticeship. There is no indication that the level of pharmaceutical knowledge in Antwerp was more advanced than anywhere else, but the fact that most pharmaceutical books in the second half of the sixteenth century were published in Antwerp suggests a lively interest in botanical matters and medical recipes.[24] Finally, horticulture was part of the engineering profession, which had no proper place in the education system. But, precisely for this reason, young engineers may have been attracted to the metropolis in order to get some informal education with a renowned master.

A wealthy city such as Antwerp undoubtedly attracted people seeking to earn a living. Yet surprisingly few scientists actually moved to Antwerp for this reason. Ortelius and Coignet, whose trade was destined for an international market such as could be found in Antwerp, were born in the city and lived there all their lives. Dodoens, Clusius and Lobelius on the other hand did not live permanently in Antwerp and did not seek proper employment there. However, the Italian military engineer and mechanic Federigo Giambelli, having left the Spanish service, settled in Antwerp and married a local girl.

Evidently, the large number of schools implies that there was a great demand for teachers. Also, the city of Antwerp offered employment for such professions as wine-gaugers and fortification builders. Mathematicians of all trades could earn a living as teachers, bookkeepers, city officials or surveyors. The flourishing book trade also provided opportunities for correctors, engravers, translators or authors. Some of the city's better-known mathematicians did indeed come from abroad: Valentin Mennher (teacher and merchant), Pierre Savonne (teacher), John Weddington (accountant, merchant) and Hans Vredeman de Vries (painter, architect, surveyor).

---

[24] L.J. Vandewiele, *Geschiedenis van de Farmacie in België* (Beveren, 1981), pp. 134–51.

Antwerp may also have served as a labour market for specialized trades-people. The Dutch architect and engineer Willem de Raet, who arrived in Antwerp probably in 1558, was contacted there in 1573 by the merchant Willem de Vos, acting as an agent for the duke of Braunschweig, to enter the service of the duke. A few years later, de Raet was approached by an Italian merchant in Antwerp wanting him to go to Lucca.[25] Antwerp may thus have been an ideal place for engineers (or other trades) to find new employers all over Europe.

The same probably applies to horticulture, insofar as architects also served as garden designers. For example, Vredeman de Vries worked on the fortifications of the city while publishing a book on garden design.[26] Yet the famous Antwerp botanists may not have been very dependent upon the city to find employment. Dodoens was a city physician in Malines before he obtained a professorship in Vienna and later in Leiden. Clusius worked in several gardens in various places, but none of them in Antwerp (e.g. the gardens of Laurens in Bruges or de Brancion in Malines).[27] However, we should bear in mind that Clusius travelled extensively through Europe as a tutor to several rich young men. Although these contacts were not established in Antwerp, we can assume that in general the cosmopolitan culture of Antwerp made it a place where people could easily meet and make arrangements of this kind.

Finally, some of the Antwerp merchants are known to have been gener-ous patrons. In particular, we often encounter Gillis Hooftman, a rich merchant and shipowner who acted as a Maecenas to Ortelius and Coignet, making suggestions for research and supporting their publica-tions.[28] And, of course, Christophe Plantin was an enlightened patron who did much more than just print books. In particular, Plantin employed many people as translators, illustrators and correctors, as well as authors. Another example is the printer Jan van der Loe, who acquired the woodblocks of Fuchs' herbal in Frankfurt and asked Dodoens to

[25] O. de Smedt, 'Willem de Raet, Bouwmeester en Ingenieur (ca. 1537–1593). Een voorlo-pig bestek', *Bulletin de l'Institut Historique Belge de Rome* 36 (1964), pp. 33–68.

[26] H. Vredeman de Vries, *Hortorum viridariorumque elegantes & multiplices formae, ad archi-tectonicae artis normam affabre delineatae* (Antwerp, 1583).

[27] F.W.T. Hunger, *Charles de l'Escluse (Carolus Clusius). Nederlandsch kruidkundige 1526–1609*, 2 vols. ('s Gravenhage, 1927–43); J. Theunisz, *Carolus Clusius. Het merkwaar-dige leven van een pionier der wetenschap* (Amsterdam, 1939). Lobelius mentions some Antwerp owners of gardens, such as Philips Marnix of St Aldegonde, Jan van Hoboken and Madame de Brimeu, who obtained new varieties of tulips and other flowers.

[28] For Hooftman and Ortelius, see H. Wauwermans, 'Ortelius', *Biographie Nationale XVII* (Brussels, 1903), cols. 291–332; for Hooftman and Coignet, see Meskens, *Wiskunde tussen Renaissance en Barok*.

create a new edition. This started Dodoens on his career as one of the foremost authors of botanical works.

Apart from the financial support scientists could find in Antwerp, other particular circumstances may also have furthered scientific research. As a port, Antwerp was an important centre for information about geography and botany. When Paracelsus went to Antwerp in 1519, he was very impressed: in true Paracelsian manner, he stated that he had learned more from a visit to the Antwerp herb market than from all the universities of Europe.[29]

It was in Antwerp that the first private botanical garden was founded by the apothecary Peeter van Coudenberghe. His garden had some 600 plant species. Van Coudenberghe's enormous botanical knowledge enabled him to produce an edition of Valerius Cordes' *Dispensatorium* (1568) for Plantin with some 400 corrections. Many new plants and flowers (such as the tulip and the tobacco plant) were introduced in Antwerp at an early date, stimulating botanical and pharmaceutical research.[30]

It is not just the information obtained from travellers and sailors that may have been of interest to the scholar. The continuous stream of published books, manuals and, in particular, broadsheets (e.g. on astrology), which were perhaps more difficult to obtain outside the Antwerp region, should also be considered as a notable source of information. It would always be worthwhile for a scholar to make the round of the Antwerp bookshops. In addition to books, all kinds of art items, curiosities and antiquities were on sale, or could be looked at in the galleries of rich collectors (Ortelius was an antiquary who only by chance turned to geography). Coins and flowers, fossils and paintings, minerals and jewels, books and globes were all represented in the typical art gallery to demonstrate the profusion of nature's wonders.[31]

Another stimulus provided by the city was the possibility for scholars to travel in the service of a merchant. Ortelius made several journeys with a commercial purpose. The German merchant Johan Radermacher, who lived for many years in London as an agent for Hooftman, was a typical example of a *mercator sapiens*. He was well versed in the arts and sciences and was a source of reliable information for his correspondents at home.

It is not appropriate to apply the definition of a scientific community as

---

[29] Quoted in Vandewiele, *Geschiedenis*, p. 134.

[30] Aegidius Everaerts, *De herba panacea, quam alii tabacum . . . vocant* (Antwerp, 1587).

[31] Science was an integral part of the art collections of the bourgeoisie. U. Härting, 'Doctrina et pietas. Über frühe Galeriebilder', *Koninklijk Museum voor Schone Kunsten Antwerpen. Jaarboek 1993* (Antwerp, 1993), pp. 95–133.

it was developed for nineteenth-century science to the circumstances of the sixteenth century. Science as such was not yet a recognized profession and scholars were not devoted to a common research programme in which each one had a well-defined role. The closest resemblance to a scientific community in the sixteenth century would be a 'school' formed by a teacher and his students. Thus, we can describe the group around Gemma Frisius in Leuven as a scientific community.

The situation in Antwerp was different. There was in fact a well-defined group of scholars, mainly centred on Plantin and Hooftman, who knew each other well and cooperated on their mutual enterprises. A good example might be Clusius, who brought back from Salamanca a number of letters by the deceased humanist Cleynardus, which he handed over to Plantin for publication. He also passed on some ancient inscriptions that he had noted in Valencia to Martinus Smetius, an archaeologist. His map of Spain was printed in 1570 with the help of Ortelius. Similar links can be found with Ortelius and Coignet, or with artists such as Joris Hoefnagel.[32]

Such cooperation might indicate a scientific community, but the relations were personal rather than intellectual. The scientific achievements of the Antwerp group always carry the mark of a commercial enterprise, rather than of a common spiritual quest. Conflict and rivalry, as between Ortelius and de Jode or Heyns, were just as frequent as cooperation. It has indeed never been established that the scholarly group around Plantin shared anything more than material interests. It is still not clear whether the frequently mentioned 'House of Love', a secret religious movement to which Plantin, Ortelius and others belonged, can be regarded as the expression of a genuine ideological movement among Antwerp intellectuals.[33] In general, Antwerp printers are considered to have adopted a very pragmatic attitude towards religious conflicts, selling both Catholic and Protestant books as far as it was safe and possible.[34] Perhaps a more spiritually coherent group was formed later around Rubens and Lipsius,[35]

---

[32] Further observations about the circle around Ortelius, Hoefnagel and Radermacher can be found in Thoma da Costa Kaufmann, *The Mastery of Nature. Aspects of Art, Science, and Humanism in the Renaissance* (Princeton, N.J., 1993).

[33] R. Boumans, 'Was Abraham Ortelius katholiek of protestant?' *Handelingen der Zuidnederlandse Maatschappij voor Taal- en Letterkunde en Geschiedenis* 6 (1952), pp. 109–27.

[34] G. Marnef, 'Repressie en censuur in het Antwerps boekenbedrijf, 1567–1576', *De Zeventiende Eeuw* 8 (1992), pp. 221–31.

[35] M. Morford, *Stoics and Neostoics. Rubens and the Circle of Lipsius* (Princeton, N.J., 1991). Rubens was also involved with the Antwerp Jesuits, cooperating with Franciscus d'Aguilon on his *Opticorum Libri Sex* (Antwerp, 1613). See A. Ziggelaar, *Franciscus de Aguilon (1567–1617). Scientist and Architect*, Bibliotheca Instituti Historici S.I., 44 (Rome, 1983).

but not even in this case can we speak of a scientific community, delegating roles and tasks to its various members.

Many of the scientists active in Antwerp's golden age were either first- or second-generation immigrants who presumably moved for economic reasons. During the second half of the century, however, more and more immigrants arrived in Antwerp as refugees from the military violence in their home regions. Clusius was one of them; Plantin's botanical engraver Peter van der Borght another. Guicciardini, in his well-known description of the Netherlands, noted the massive influx of people, especially from the Southern provinces, to Antwerp, a wealthy but, even more importantly, a well-fortified city.

Immigrants were able to settle quite easily in Antwerp, as a result of (or causing?) a large measure of (religious) tolerance. Around 1550 the situation was described in alarmed terms by Rogier de Tassis, the deacon of the collegiate chapter of Our Lady.[36] There is no indication, however, that on the whole repression was less severe in Antwerp than in other cities. The Antwerp magistrates may have been only somewhat more tolerant towards the sources of the city's wealth – in particular to merchants and foreigners, but also to printers and booksellers.[37] It is not clear how safety and tolerance can account for the scientific achievements in a more than self-evident way. As we indicated above, the religious tolerance of the city did not inspire Antwerp printers and their allied scholars to any especially motivated or enlightened sort of scientific achievement. On the other hand, it offers a plausible explanation for the 'suction effect' of Antwerp, drawing people from the neighbouring countryside. As other places were being evacuated, Antwerp remained (at least until 1585) the only safe haven for intellectual adventures of any sort.

Reflections of this kind presuppose, however, a special link between scientific investigations and intellectual freedom, two phenomena which do not necessarily have to be interdependent. The political rulers, and in general the settled establishment, were in fact among the main employers of scientists. We have no reason to assume that scientists needed any special form of intellectual freedom that they could not get in other cities (provided a certain measure of peace and security). On the contrary, the science produced in Antwerp was far removed from any subversive religious or political meaning. It was both pragmatic and saleable, not educative or reforming.[38] Although the spirit of tolerance and freedom may

---

[36] P. Valvekens, *De Inquisitie in de Nederlanden der zestiende eeuw* (Brussels/Amsterdam, 1949), pp. 260–3.   [37] Marnef, 'Repressie en censuur'.
[38] This should be compared with the astrological and occult scientific movement in Leuven, where the attainment of personal enlightenment and the good Christian life were the foremost aims of scientific endeavour.

have had direct social implications by allowing a mixture of quite diverse people to engage in urban life, its influence upon the science produced was actually negative: by addressing the larger audience of the metropolis, Antwerp science lost the idiosyncratic characteristics it might have retained in a smaller circle of devoted scholars.

From the foregoing remarks, it emerges that Antwerp provided some interesting inducements to scientific research that attracted scientists and scholars. Yet, on the whole, this attraction had a limited effect on the formation of a specific scientific environment within the metropolis. First of all it should be stressed that the scientists appeared to be quite mobile. They did not settle for long in one place, in contrast to, for example, the university professors of Leuven. The more practical science that was typical of Antwerp offered many opportunities for work in different places. This was certainly the case for the more famous botanists who were invited to foreign courts and universities. But other less distinguished professionals travelled too: Simon Stevin came to Antwerp from Bruges at an early point in his career, but travelled on to other mid- and northern European countries, finally settling in the Dutch Republic. If Antwerp was a good place to visit, it was not necessarily the final goal of the journey. Still, it acted as a go-between for information and contacts on a wider scale.

The conclusion is further supported by the fact that none of the great Antwerp scientists, all of them descendants of immigrant families, moved to Antwerp because of their scientific ambitions. The Antwerp scientific achievements were rather 'native'. Foreigners such as the Neapolitan astronomer Ottavio Pisani, who lived in Antwerp at the close of the century, were exceptional figures in the scientific life of the city. The presence of foreign merchants was not reflected in pronounced activity by foreign scientists, apart perhaps for the Italian engineers working on the citadel.

The Antwerp scientific community may have been too diverse to be properly delineated as such, but we can still take into account the wider support for science that stimulated the rise of commercial scientific production. In describing the historical role of science in society, Joseph Ben-David has made use of a distinction between scientific experts and the scientistic movement at large.[39] The scientific experts are the active workers in a field of science, who have expert knowledge that is not accessible to people outside the scientific community. But the success and viability of any scientific community depend on the support it

---

[39] J. Ben-David, *The Scientist's Role in Society. A Comparative Study* (Chicago, 1971), p. 78. Ben-David uses this distinction only in his analysis of eighteenth- and nineteenth-century science, but it can easily be applied to earlier periods.

receives from other, more powerful, groups in society. These groups are not usually scientists themselves, but they can be described as having a scientistic attitude. The scientistic movement is characterized by the adoption of a scientific style or ethos in tackling human and social problems. Ben-David's distinction can be extended to apply to the Antwerp situation. Science and education were held in high regard in the metropolis. Military engineering and fortification became important aspects of the city administration, and merchant patrons promoted research in navigation, cartography and botany. The expert scientists were not themselves a separate social group, but they found support from the elite circles of the city, with whom they shared entrepreneurial and aesthetic values.

The existence of a scientistic movement in the metropolis was, however, not a sufficient condition for great scientific achievements. Although economic wealth and an international network of information and contacts created the right opportunities for expert scientists to pursue their research work and to occupy leading positions in the scientific world, these opportunities were not equally well suited for all kinds of science. Indeed, none of the greatest scientists of the Spanish Netherlands (Vesalius, Mercator and Dodoens) lived in Antwerp. Stevin, Clusius and Lobelius remained there only for a short period of time; they were able to transport their business just as easily to other places. The scientism of Antwerp not only served as an attraction pole for scientists, it also selected the kind of science it would and could support. The greatest achievements were made in botany and geography, two fields that relied on large amounts of information, and that were of immediate use to the scientistic circles promoting them. Significantly, medicine, astrology and natural philosophy were much less well represented in terms of expert scientists.

The golden age of Antwerp coincided with the rise of a new scientific ethos, which brought to the fore the practical skills and knowledge of engineers and mechanics and stressed the empirical study of nature, in contrast to the scholastic methods of earlier times or the intellectual or humanist discourse of philosophers. This new ethos was not well received at traditional universities, and needed another environment in which it could flourish. A metropolis was the ideal setting. The open and varied opportunities it offered provided a breeding ground for those professionals who did not have any interest in a university milieu. In this way, the Antwerp metropolis foreshadowed the atmosphere to be found in London in the eighteenth century, though with some important differences. The Antwerp scientists had to rely on the support of social elites, and their practical science did not develop into a 'philosophy' that shaped their political and social views. Perhaps in this respect the Antwerp phenomenon was nearer to the Dutch example, where science was supported by the town rulers and had a very practical bent. But, in the Dutch Republic, a truly metropolitan scale was lacking, although Amsterdam did take over some of the economic functions of Antwerp. In this respect, Antwerp was perhaps an exception even in its own time. The general development of the Netherlands in the sixteenth century was based on a dense network of cities that vied for intellectual superiority. The sudden rise of Antwerp as a metropolis was at least partly caused by the historical coincidence of civil war, forcing people to migrate. Without the particular circumstances caused by war and rebellion, the economic prosperity and the urban atmosphere of Antwerp might have acted differently on the development of new scientific activities. Science would probably not have been concentrated to any great extent in one place, but would have been scattered over the numerous cities of the Netherlands, all within of one day's journey of Antwerp. The wider network of rival and fairly independent cities, rather than the urban network of the metropolis, would have been the landscape of sixteenth-century science.

The concentration of scientists and scholars in Antwerp in the second half of the sixteenth century was an exceptional and short-lived development, and should therefore not be confused with the metropolitan model of London or Paris. During the seventeenth century, the urban network again became dominant in intellectual life in the Spanish Netherlands, Leuven in certain respects being the main intellectual centre, but with equally interesting work going on in other cities, in particular Antwerp, Ghent and Brussels. The Antwerp Jesuits offer an example: in 1617 they started their mathematical courses in Antwerp at the behest of the city officials, but during subsequent decades they transferred their institution several times between Leuven and Antwerp. They also maintained important colleges in other Flemish towns, such as the one in Ghent where the mathematician Gregorius a Sancto Vincento worked on the development of the calculus. The Leuven professors still went to Antwerp for the publication of their books, while several mathematicians were employed at the court of the Archdukes in Brussels for astronomical and technical duties.

The science of the Jesuits also reveals how much the commercial atmosphere of the city had faded, and indeed become unimportant, as a stimulus for scientific work. The Jesuits' real aim was not to provide practical learning, although because of the monopoly of Leuven University they were obliged to concentrate on this part of the 'market'. On every possible occasion they strove to take a stand on matters of general philosophy and theology. They opposed the Jansenism of Leuven University and the adoption of Cartesianism by the Faculty of Arts and they publicly commented on Copernican astronomy and on the condemnation of Galileo. In short, they tried to imitate in every respect the workings of a true university. In their achievements, however great, nothing remains of the urban atmosphere that had caused the rise of a commercial science in the Antwerp metropolis during the late sixteenth century.

15 Amsterdam as a centre of learning in the Dutch golden age, c.1580–1700

Karel Davids

In a survey of the growth of the scientific community in the western world between 1450 and 1900 Robert Gascoigne drew attention to a 'unique' pattern in the Netherlands from the late sixteenth to the late seventeenth century. He saw a 'broad-based peak' in the number of distinguished scientists in Holland which coincided with the very period of 'political, economic, and cultural eminence when this small country ranked as one of the leaders of Europe'.[1] Although the absolute numbers involved were smaller than those in France, Britain, Germany or Italy, the singularity of the Dutch case lay precisely in the fact that the number of 'achievers' in the domain of science was markedly larger among generations born after c.1580 than in the period that went before.

Scholars from the Dutch Republic in this period made outstanding contributions both to what Thomas Kuhn has called 'the classical physical sciences' and to a broad group of fields that can be described as 'the life sciences'.[2] In the former tradition, their achievements ranged from improvements in methods of reckoning (by Simon Stevin, Ezechiël de Decker and Adriaen Vlacq) and innovations in mechanics, hydrostatics and optics (by Stevin, Willebrord Snellius and Christiaan Huygens, for example) to pioneering advances in Cartesian geometry by a small band of scholars gathered around the Leiden professor of mathematics Frans van Schooten jr. (including Huygens, Johan de Witt, Hendrick van Heuraet, Johannes Hudde and Joachim Nieustadt) and the development of overarching theories, notably by Huygens and Isaac Beeckman, that contributed to the rise of the mechanical world view.[3] In the life sciences,

---

[1] Robert Gascoigne, 'The Historical Demography of the Scientific Community, 1450–1900', *Social Studies of Science* 22 (1992), pp. 559 and 561.

[2] T.S. Kuhn, 'Mathematical versus Experimental Traditions in the Development of the Physical Sciences', *Journal of Interdisciplinary History* 7 (1976), pp. 1–31; Geert Vanpaemel, *Een standbeeld voor Stevin. Wetenschap en cultuur in de Nederlanden* (Nijmegen, 1995).

[3] D.J. Struik, *Het land van Stevin en Huygens*, 2nd edn (Amsterdam, 1966); K. van Berkel, *In het voetspoor van Stevin. Geschiedenis van de natuurwetenschap in Nederland 1580–1940* (Amsterdam, 1985); J.A van Maanen, *Facets of Seventeenth-Century Mathematics in the Netherlands* (Utrecht, 1987), pp. 19–30, 37; E.J. Dijksterhuis, *Simon Stevin* (The Hague,

scholars from the Netherlands excelled in continuous, extensive, detailed enquiries in the fields of medicine and natural history. What they were aiming at, in Harold Cook's words, was first and foremost 'getting the details straight'. This style of research was carried to a high degree of perfection by Jan Swammerdam, Reinier de Graaf, Frederik Ruysch, Antoni van Leeuwenhoek and Nicolaas Hartsoeker.[4] In the course of the golden age, a gradual shift of emphasis in scientific activities in the Netherlands can be detected from enquiries and explorations in physics and mathematics to investigations in the life sciences. While the achievements of the Dutch in the former sphere mostly date from the period 1580–1670, the role of the Dutch in the latter field became more prominent only from the 1630s onwards and reached its zenith between the 1660s and 1730s.

Describing the geographical context of this community I have up to now used terms such as 'Holland', 'the Netherlands' or 'the Dutch Republic' rather than 'Amsterdam'. In the world of scholarship, Amsterdam during the time of the Republic never reached the dominant position it attained in other fields of culture and in economic life. The peak in scientific achievements in the Netherlands between the late sixteenth and late seventeenth centuries was also broad based in the sense that these activities took place in a plurality of centres instead of being concentrated in a single metropolis. Amsterdam was just one centre among many, albeit one of the most important. These centres of scientific activity were almost exclusively located in cities. Scientific scholarship in the Dutch Republic was by and large an urban affair.

This contribution aims to analyse more closely the relation between the cluster of achievements in science in the Dutch Republic between *c.*1580 and 1700 and their urban context, with a focus on Amsterdam. It seeks to answer the questions how and to what extent the urban environment in the Dutch Republic, and more specifically in Amsterdam, during the golden age facilitated achievements in science and in what respects the relationship between science and the urban environment in Amsterdam resembled or differed from the one prevailing in Antwerp and London.

footnote 3 (*cont.*)
1943); J.A. van Maanen, 'Korrespondenten von G.W.Leibniz. 6. Joachim Nieustadt', *Studia Leibnitiana* 15 (1983), pp. 115–19; J. MacLean, 'De nagelaten papieren van Johannes Hudde', *Scientiarum Historia* 13 (1971), pp. 144–9, K.Haas, 'Die mathematischen Arbeiten von Johann Hudde (1628–1704), Bürgermeister von Amsterdam', *Centaurus*, 4 (1956), pp. 235–84; A.J.E.M. Smeur (ed.), *Ezechiël de Decker. Tweede Deel van de Nieuwe Telkonst 1627* (Nieuwkoop, 1964); H.J.M. Bos et al. (eds.), *Studies on Christiaan Huygens* (Lisse, 1980); C.D. Andriesse, *Titan kan niet slapen. Een biografie van Christiaan Huygens* (Antwerp, 1993).
[4] Harold J. Cook, 'The New Philosophy in the Low Countries' in Roy Porter and Mikulás Teich (eds.), *The Scientific Revolution in National Context* (Cambridge, 1992), pp. 115–16, 131–4, 141–2.

Long before the outbreak of the Revolt that gave birth to the Republic of the United Provinces, the North Netherlands already knew a quite elevated level of urbanization. Although the percentage of the population living in cities in the northern part of the Habsburg Netherlands nowhere reached the levels attained in Flanders or Brabant, the concentration of people in cities by the first quarter of the sixteenth century was higher than in any other region in Europe at the time, northern Italy excepted. The average level in the Northern provinces around 1525 has been estimated at 27 per cent and in Holland at 44 per cent. This urbanization took the form of a proliferation of small or medium-sized cities rather than the concentration of the population in a few large centres – in the early sixteenth century, there were thirty-eight towns with 2,500 inhabitants or more – and, even if variations in size grew larger during the phase of rapid growth between 1580 and 1675, multipolarity remained an essential feature of the Dutch urban landscape. By the last quarter of the seventeenth century, the total number of towns in the United Provinces with 2,500 or more inhabitants had grown to sixty-one, twenty-three of which were situated in the province of Holland.[5]

City descriptions (or *stadsbeschrijvingen*) published in the Dutch Republic from the early seventeenth century onwards, which contained detailed overviews of the history, topography, form of government and principal economic activities of particular cities,[6] reveal that many of these towns from the late Middle Ages onwards boasted of quite a number of people whom contemporaries considered to be eminent achievers in the field of scholarship. A city description almost invariably included a section devoted to the illustrious men who had been born within its walls, which grew longer in the course of time. Next to artists, office-holders and war heroes, this muster-roll normally also contained a list of *geleerde mannen*, or 'learned men' (and, occasionally, learned women). Going through these lists, the modern reader is first of all struck by the realization that the most of them are hardly known to posterity at all (and, with few exceptions, did not make it into Gascoigne's data base either) and, secondly, by the observation that these worthies more often than not at some point in their life left their home town in the Northern Netherlands and pursued their training or career in Flanders, Brabant,

[5] Jan de Vries and Ad van der Woude, *Nederland 1500–1815. De eerste ronde van moderne economische groei* (Amsterdam, 1995), pp. 35, 82–95; W. Prevenier and W.P. Blockmans, *De Bourgondische Nederlanden* (Antwerp, 1983), pp. 30–4, 391.
[6] E.O.G. Haitsma Mulier, 'De eerste Hollandse stadsbeschrijvingen uit de zeventiende eeuw', *De zeventiende eeuw* 9 (1993), pp. 102–5.

Italy, France or southern Germany.[7] The North did not lack potential talent in the world of scholarship, even before the onset of the Revolt. City descriptions of Amsterdam list theologians, physicians and philologists such as Kornelis Krook, Sybrant Okko and Martinus Koster.[8] But scores of gifted men sooner or later drifted to the South, if only because none of the cities in the Northern provinces of the Habsburg Netherlands yet housed an institute of higher learning. Paris, Padua or Leuven still exerted a powerful attraction to men of talent from Holland, Utrecht or Friesland. Desiderius Erasmus from Rotterdam and Gemma Frisius from Dokkum are but the best-known minds of this brain-drain from the North. The total outflow of learned men was many times larger.

But this pattern was completely reversed during the Dutch Republic. First of all, in the last decades of the sixteenth century the Northern Netherlands received a large quota of immigrants from Flanders and Brabant, including such gifted scholars as the botanist Carolus Clusius, the astronomer Rev. Philips van Lansbergen, the cosmographer Rev. Petrus Plancius and the mathematician Simon Stevin, along with some twenty mathematical practitioners from Antwerp.[9]

[7] I have consulted the city descriptions by Samuel Ampzing, *Beschrijvinge ende lof der stad Haerlem in Holland* (Haarlem, 1628), Mathijs Balen, *Beschrijving der stad Dordrecht* (Dordrecht, 1677), Henricus van Berkum, *Beschrijving der stadt Schoonhoven* (Gouda, 1762), Dirck van Bleyswijck, *Beschrijvinge der stadt Delft* (Delft, 1667), Valentyn Jan Blondeel, *Beschrijving der stad Utrecht* (Utrecht, 1757), Reinier Boitet, *Beschrijving der stadt Delft* (Delft, 1729), C. Booth, *Beschrijvinge der stadt Utrecht* (Utrecht, 1685), Gerard Brandt, *Historie der vermaerde zee- en koopstadt Enkhuizen* (Enkhuizen, 1666), Casparus Commelin, *Beschrijving van Amsterdam*, 2 vols., 2 edn (Amsterdam, 1693, 1726), Olfert Dapper, *Historische beschrijving der stadt Amsterdam* (Amsterdam, 1663), Tobias van Domselaer, *Beschrijvinge van Amsterdam*, 2 vols. (Amsterdam, 1665), M. Fokkens, *Beschrijvinge der wijdt-vermaarde koop-stadt Amstelredam* (n.p., 1662), Abraham Kemp, *Leven der doorluchtige heeren van Arkel ende jaar-beschrijving der stad Gorinchem* (Gorinchem, 1656), Simon van Leeuwen, *Korte beschrijving van het Lugdunum Batavorum van Leiden* (Leiden, 1672), Frans van Mieris, *Beschrijving der stad Leiden*, 3 vols. (Leiden, 1762–84), I.I. Orlers, *Beschrijvinge der stadt Leyden*, 2nd edn (Leiden, 1641), Johannes Isacius Pontanus, *Rerum et urbis Amstelodamensium historia* (Amsterdam, 1611) and *Historische beschrijving der seer wijt beroemde coop-stadt Amsterdam* (Amsterdam, 1614), Theodorus Schrevelius, *Harlemias ofte, om beter te seggen. de eerste stichtinge der stad Haarlem* (Haarlem, 1648), Geraard van Spaan, *Beschrijving der stad Rotterdam en eenige aanleggende dorpen*, 2nd edn (Rotterdam, 1713), Dirk Velius, *Chronyk van Hoorn*, 3rd edn (Hoorn, 1648), Jan Wagenaar, *Amsterdam in zijne opkomst, aanwas, geschiedenissen*, 13 vols. (Amsterdam, 1760–68), Ignatius Walvis, *Beschrijving der stad Gouda* (Gouda, 1714), Cornelis van der Woude, *Kronycke van Alcmaer met syn dorpen* (Alkmaar, 1645), Filip von Zesen, *Beschreibung der Stadt Amsterdam* (Amsterdam, 1664), Cornelis van Zomeren, *Beschrijvinge der stadt Gorinchem* (Gorinchem, 1755).
[8] See, for example, van Domselaer, *Beschrijvinge*, pp. 94–5; Commelin, *Beschrijving*, pp. 860–6; J. van der Zande, 'Amsterdamse stadsgeschiedschrijving vóór Wagenaar', *Holland* 17 (1985), pp. 218–30.
[9] Struik, *Het land van Stevin*, pp. 40–1; A. Meskens, *Wiskunde tussen Renaissance en Barok. Aspecten van wiskunde-beoefening te Antwerpen 1550–1620* (Antwerp, 1994), p. 85.

Secondly, informal clusters of scientific activity emerged in various towns in the North. Alkmaar between 1570 and 1610, for example, was the residence of such distinguished scholars as Adriaen Anthonisz., Adriaen Metius, Jacob Metius, Cornelis Drebbel, Willem Jansz. Blaeu and Cornelis Pietersz. Schagen.[10] Enkhuizen in the period 1580–1600 numbered among its citizens learned men such as Bernardus Paludanus, François Maelson, Lucas Jansz. Waghenaer and Jan Huyghen van Linschoten.[11] Thirdly, after the Revolt, cities in the Northern Netherlands saw the creation of a dense grid of public institutional facilities which to Dutchmen and foreigners alike provided an environment at least as favourable for the cultivation of scholarship as institutions in other parts of Europe had already offered for a long time. An overview can be found on the maps in figures 15.1, 15.2 and 15.3 and in Table 15.1.

These newly created facilities in cities in the Northern Netherlands were of various types. Besides universities established in Leiden, Franeker, Groningen, Utrecht and Harderwijk, the Dutch Republic saw the foundation of a large number of 'illustrious schools', i.e. institutes of higher learning which were largely similar to universities except for the possession of the *ius promovendi*. Nineteen cities, including the university towns and Amsterdam, boasted of the creation of a permanent *theatrum anatomicum* for the public dissection of bodies. A city which housed an anatomical theatre commonly also provided for a public lectureship in anatomy and/or surgery; in addition, several theatres were endowed with cabinets of *naturalia*.[12] Botanical gardens were a normal facility in university towns. But they could be found in a few other places as well. Amsterdam acquired a *hortus medicus* in the 1640s and saw it greatly expanded after 1682. A *hortus* in The Hague was laid out in the 1750s. And with the creation of a garden went, in both cases, the foundation of a municipal chair in botany.[13]

[10] H.A.M. Snelders, 'Alkmaarse natuurwetenschappers in de 16e en 17e eeuw' in *Van Spaans beleg tot Bataafse tijd. Alkmaars stedelijk leven in de 17e en 18e eeuw* (Zutphen, 1980), pp. 101–22.

[11] René Willemsen, *Enkhuizen in de tijd van de Republiek* (Hilversum, 1988), pp. 161–2; Brandt, *Historie*, pp. 21–30; E. Bos-Rietdijk, 'Het werk van Lucas Jansz. Waghenaer' in *Lucas Jansz. Waghenaer van Enchuysen. De maritieme cartografie in de Nederlanden in de zestiende en het begin van de zeventiende eeuw* (Enkhuizen, 1984), pp. 21–46.

[12] Jan C.C. Rupp, 'Matters of Life and Death: The Social and Cultural Conditions of the Rise of Anatomical Theatres, with Special Reference to Seventeenth Century Holland', *History of Science* 28 (1990), pp. 272, 277–8.

[13] W.H. van Seters, 'De voorgeschiedenis der stichting van de eerste Amsterdamse hortus botanicus', *Jaarboek van het Genootschap Amstelodamum* 46 (1954), pp. 42–4; D.O. Wijnands, *The Botany of the Commelins* (Rotterdam, 1983), pp. 3–4; L.J. Endtz, *De Hageprofessoren. Geschiedenis van een chirurgische school* (Amstelveen, 1972), pp. 97 and 99.

15.1 Institutional facilities for science in cities of the Dutch Republic,
*c.*1600

The combination of institutions differed by city, as the maps show.
Amsterdam, Leiden, Utrecht and Franeker possessed a broader mixture of
facilities than Deventer, Delft, Dordrecht or Rotterdam. These institutions
also varied in size and importance. The number of chairs and the number
of students at the University of Leiden were greater than at any other university in the United Provinces. The range of subjects taught at universities
was wider than that covered at illustrious schools. Anatomical theatres in
Amsterdam or Leiden, which could accommodate up to 400 people, were

15.2 Institutional facilities for science in cities of the Dutch Republic, *c*.1650

much bigger than those in small or medium-sized cities such as Franeker or Groningen; besides, they were more regularly in use.[14] As for botanical gardens, no town in the Republic could compete with the collections of Amsterdam or Leiden in sheer size, variety and rarity of items.

By the second quarter of the seventeenth century it was rare indeed to find a Dutchman pursuing a scholarly career abroad. Christiaan

[14] J.A.M. Slenders, *Het theatrum anatomicum in de Noordelijke Nederlanden 1555–1800* (Nijmegen, 1989), pp. 66–8.

15.3 Institutional facilities for science in cities of the Dutch Republic, *c*.1700

Huygens, who accepted a pension from the king of France, was the exception rather than the rule. The number of Dutch graduates at universities in the United Provinces consistently surpassed the number of taking a degree at a foreign university.[15] The Dutch Republic moreover quickly turned into a pole of attraction for students and scholars from other parts of Europe. The universities that were founded after 1575 saw their enrolment swelled by a considerable number of foreign students. Their share

[15] W.T.M. Frijhoff, *La société néerlandaise et ses gradués, 1575–1814* (Amsterdam, 1981), p. 383.

of the total number of graduates rose from around 25 per cent up to 1675
to 28 per cent in the last quarter of the seventeenth century to nearly 33
per cent in the period 1700–25.[16] The bulk of this inflow of foreign students came from the Holy Roman Empire; the coastal area from East
Frisia to East Prussia, the Calvinist territories in inland Germany and the
whole region adjacent to the Republic supplied the largest number. The
British Isles were mostly a distant second.[17]

Professors at universities and illustrious schools were often recruited
from abroad as well. The majority of professors appointed to the chairs of
divinity, philosophy and philology in Leiden during the first fifty years following its foundation in 1575 were not born in Holland or Zeeland, but
originated from France, Germany or the Southern Netherlands.[18] The
greatest catch of all was of course the classicist Joseph Scaliger, who
exchanged Saumur for Leiden in 1593. At the University of Franeker,
established in 1585, foreign-born professors in the period 1600–1750 constituted 25–40 per cent of the total staff. At the University of Groningen,
founded in 1614, the share of foreign professors before the middle of the
eighteenth century always amounted to more than 50 per cent.[19] The
University of Utrecht, founded in 1636, included twelve foreigners among
the fifty-two professors appointed in the period up to 1700.[20] Among the
twenty-two professors appointed at the illustrious school in Amsterdam
(known as the Athenaeum Illustre) between its foundation in 1632 and the
end of the seventeenth century, nine had immigrated from Germany,
France, England or the Southern Netherlands; among the thirteen
Dutchmen, four had been born in the city itself.[21]

The growth of cities in the Northern Netherlands as centres of science
in their own right and as poles of attraction for foreign scholars was the
result of a combination of changes in the wider context of Dutch society
which gathered speed in the last decades of the sixteenth century. Owing
to the expansion of commerce and ocean shipping, the growth of the military establishment, the increase in land reclamation and the introduction

[16] Ibid., p. 379.   [17] Ibid., pp. 98–103, 380.
[18] J.J. Woltjer, 'Introduction' in T.H. Lunsingh Scheurleer and G.H.M. Posthumus Meyjes
(eds.), *Leiden University in the Seventeenth Century. An Exchange of Learning* (Leiden,
1975), pp. 14–16; J.J. Woltjer, 'Foreign Professors' in Lunsingh Scheurleer and
Posthumus Meyjes, *Leiden University*, pp. 461–5.
[19] F.R.H. Smit, 'Over honderdzevenenzeventig Franeker professoren' in G.T. Jensma,
F.R.H. Smit and F. Westra (eds.), *Universiteit te Franeker 1585–1811* (Leeuwarden,
1985), pp. 101–18; W.B.S. Boeles, 'Levensschetsen der Groninger hoogleeraren' in
W.J.A. Jonckbloet, *Gedenkboek der hoogeschool te Groningen* (Groningen, 1864), pp. 1–74.
[20] G.W. Kernkamp, *De Utrechtsche academie 1636–1815*, 2 vols. (Utrecht, 1936), vol. I, p.
124.
[21] *Gedenkboek van het Athenaeum en de Universiteit van Amsterdam 1632–1932* (Amsterdam,
1932), pp. 34–41, and the biographies of professors on pp. 539–715.

of numerous projects for town extension, demand for experts in the mathematical arts considerably increased. All these activities involved the employment of a large group of people with arithmetical and/or geometrical skills, such as bookkeepers, gaugers, navigators, gunners, engineers or surveyors. Engineers, for instance, were employed during the war against Spain to design and build fortifications that would protect Dutch cities against enemy forces (or to assist in capturing fortified places held by the Spanish army). Surveyors were involved in projects for impoldering, draining and town extension. They drew up plans for the profiles and traces of dikes, designed engineering constructions, mapped out new roads and waterways, drafted overall plans for the extension of cities and made detailed schemes for the parcelling out of plots.[22] In the last phase of its extension drive, during the mid-1660s, the city of Amsterdam had no fewer than fourteen surveyors on the pay-roll of its department of public works.[23] The total number of newly admitted surveyors in the United Provinces saw a continual rise up to about 1670.

As in Antwerp before and in London later on,[24] the most usual way in which this growing class of bookkeepers, gaugers, navigators, gunners, engineers or surveyors acquired their mathematical skills was by taking courses with private mathematical practitioners. Between about 1580 and 1700, the United Provinces saw a vast expansion in the number of people (some of them immigrants from the South) who earned their living by teaching the elements of the mathematical arts to whomever wished to pay. Sometimes these practitioners received additional income by selling books and instruments or providing expert advice on request.[25] As in London in the eighteenth century, these mathematical practitioners in Amsterdam were mostly concentrated in parts of the town close to the centres of trade, shipping and finance: the Nieuwendijk, the Zeedijk and the Haarlemmerstraat.[26]

It was a peculiar feature of the Dutch Republic, however, that instruction in practical mathematics to a non-academic audience was in part supplied by institutions of higher learning as well. On the urging of *Stadthouder* and commander-in-chief of the Dutch army Prince Maurice, the

---

[22] E. Muller and K. Zandvliet (eds.), *Admissies als landmeter in Nederland voor 1811* (Alphen aan de Rijn, 1987).

[23] H.R. Reinders, *Modderwerk. Het uitdiepen van de haven van Amsterdam in de tweede helft van de zeventiende eeuw* (Lelystad, 1978).

[24] Meskens, *Wiskunde*, pp. 21–90, 106–74 and chapter 16 by Larry Stewart in this volume.

[25] C.A. Davids, 'Ondernemers in kennis. Het zeevaartkundig onderwijs in de Republiek gedurende de zeventiende eeuw', *De zeventiende eeuw* 7 (1991), pp. 37–48.

[26] C.A. Davids, *Zeewezen en wetenschap. De wetenschap en de ontwikkeling van de navigatietechniek in Nederland tussen 1585 en 1815* (Amsterdam/Dieren, 1986), p. 314; see de Vries and van der Woude, *Nederland 1500–1815*, p. 184.

University of Leiden was in 1600 expanded with a school of engineering, called the 'Duytsche mathematicque'. The curriculum of the institute was drafted by Stevin. Professors of the Duytsche mathematicque, who were paid by the university, lectured in Dutch on surveying, gauging and fortification to whomever wished to attend. At the University of Franeker, professor of mathematics Adriaan Metius received permission in 1600 to lecture in Dutch on navigation, surveying and fortification. The tradition thus established was continued up to the abolition of the university in 1811. At the Athenaeum in Amsterdam, vernacular courses on mathematics and navigation were taught with only brief interruptions from 1635 to 1838.[27]

Perhaps even more impressive than the growth in the number of experts in mathematical knowledge was the expansion of the medical establishment. The number of Dutchmen taking a doctor's degree in medicine at a Dutch or foreign university increased from about 60 in the period 1575–99 to almost 650 in the third quarter of the seventeenth century. The density of *medicinae doctores* in the United Provinces in the course of the period 1600–75 almost trebled, from one doctor per 7,500 inhabitants to one per 2,500. As doctors almost exclusively chose to reside in cities, the figure in urban centres reached even higher levels. In Amsterdam, the growth in the number of doctors of medicine in the middle decades of the century vastly outstripped the rapid expansion of the city itself. Whereas in the early 1640s the density was still only one per 3,160 inhabitants, the figure had risen to one per 1,000 by the middle of the 1670s. It is not unlikely, as Willem Frijhoff suggests, that some of these newcomers were in reality 'underemployed', or even did not practice medicine at all. All of the doctors of medicine had in common that they had received an education at an institution of higher learning, had graduated from a university and in the course of their training had become acquainted with the established traditions of scholarship in both medicine and natural philosophy.[28] As the medical establishment swiftly expanded in size, the pattern of public institutional facilities in the sphere of science underwent a transformation as well. Although the number and status of chairs in mathematics at institutions for higher learning in the later seventeenth century somewhat

---

[27] P.J. van Winter, *Hoger beroepsonderwijs avant-la-lettre. Bemoeiingen met de vorming van landmeters en ingenieurs bij de Nederlandse universiteiten in de 17e en 18e eeuw* (Amsterdam, 1988), pp. 14–36, 46–77; F. Westra, *Nederlandse ingenieurs en de fortificatiewerken in het eerste tijdperk van de Tachtigjarige Oorlog, 1573–1604* (Alphen aan de Rijn, 1992), pp. 82–9; E. Taverne, *In 't land van belofte: in de nieue stadt. Ideaal en werkelijkheid van de stadsuitleg in de Republiek 1580–1680* (Maarssen, 1978), pp. 61–9, 75–81; C.A. Davids, 'Universiteiten, illustre scholen en de verspreiding van technische kennis in Nederland, eind 16e – begin 19e eeuw', *Batavia Academia* 8 (1990), pp. 4–6.

[28] Frijhoff, *La société néerlandaise*, pp. 135, 230–45.

declined, the variety and quantity of institutional facilities for the cultivation of the life sciences (chairs, lectureships, botanical gardens, anatomical theatres) after *c.* 1630 considerably grew.

As the Dutch Republic developed from the late sixteenth century onwards into a leading centre of world trade – forming the hub of a far-flung commercial network embracing northern Europe, the Mediterranean, South America, the Caribbean, the west coast of Africa as well as Arabia, Iran, India, Indonesia, China and Japan – it became increasingly easy moreover for anyone interested in the field of the life sciences to collect specimens of natural objects from all over the world, especially if one happened to live in a port city such as Amsterdam, Enkhuizen, Hoorn, Delft (Delfshaven), Rotterdam, Middelburg or Vlissingen, or in an inland town well connected to merchant elites in the East or West India trades, such as Leiden. The expansion of the collection of the botanical garden in Amsterdam from the 1680s onwards was in fact chiefly due to the excellent relations of the municipal commissioners of the garden with officials and directors of the East and West India Companies.[29] Private collections of curiosities, including exotic *naturalia*, flourished thanks to the growth of trade as well. Most of these private collections were to be found in urban centres in Holland. The total number of collections known in Amsterdam in the period 1585–1730 amounts to no fewer than ninety.[30] The import of natural curiosities from overseas may well have given an additional boost to the growth of interest in the life sciences which became manifest in the Dutch Republic by the second quarter of the seventeenth century.[31]

The extension of public institutional facilities in the field of scientific and useful knowledge in cities of the Dutch Republic was further aided by its particular political structure which took shape in the early phase of the Revolt. The degree of autonomy of cities was strengthened as a result of the Revolt rather than weakened. Indeed, as J.L. Price has written in his study on the 'politics of particularism' in the Republic, 'the powers and privileges of the towns were consistently supported by the [provincial] States because this body was effectively controlled by the votes of the

[29] Wijnands, *Botany*, pp. 3–4.
[30] L. Noordegraaf and T. Wijsenbeek-Olthuis, 'De wereld ontsloten. Aanvoer van rariteiten naar Nederland' in E. Bergvelt and R. Kistemaker (eds.), *De wereld binnen handbereik. Nederlandse kunst- en rariteitenverzamelingen, 1585–1735* (Zwolle, 1992), pp. 39–50; J. van der Veen, 'Dit klain vertrek bevat een weereld vol gewoel. Negentig Amsterdammers en hun kabinetten' in Bergvelt and Kistemaker, *De wereld binnen handbereik*, pp. 236–7.
[31] See also David Freedberg, 'Science, Commerce and Art: Neglected Topics at the Junction of History and Art History' in David Freedberg and Jan de Vries (eds.), *Art in History/History in Art. Studies in Seventeenth-century Dutch Culture* (Santa Monica, 1991), pp. 377–428.

town delegations'.[32] Cooperation at a provincial or federal level was accompanied by persistent tensions and rivalries between individual towns, which found expression in the fields of economic, domestic and foreign policies as well as in the sphere of culture.[33] As long as the costs of buildings, instruments and other material facilities needed for the practice of scholarship were still comparatively low (and in part were borne by scholars themselves), even a medium-sized town could lay claim to a certain independent status in the cultural sphere by maintaining an institute for higher learning, a permanent anatomical theatre, a botanical garden, or a lectureship in botany, surgery or anatomy, provided it took care not to infringe the privileges of other towns. The expenditure on personnel after all amounted to only a few hundred or, at most, a few thousand guilders per year. Rivalries between cities were to some extent the driving force behind the spread of institutional facilities in the Northern Netherlands from the end of the sixteenth century onwards. Cities in the Dutch Republic – and in particular in Holland – vied with each other to get a university, illustrious school or permanent anatomical theatre within their walls. An institute of higher learning or a *theatrum anatomicum* came to be regarded as one of the essential attributes of a city. It was thought to be part of its urban identity.[34]

Among these rival cities in the Northern Netherlands it was, of course, Amsterdam that was able to muster the largest measure of economic and political power at home and abroad. In contrast to Antwerp, Amsterdam aspired from an early stage in its rise to prominence to obtain in the sphere of scholarship a status commensurate to the leading role achieved in other fields of human endeavour. The magistrate of Amsterdam set about building a local network of public institutional facilities in support of science and useful knowledge earlier than any other urban government in the United Provinces, and went to much greater lengths to do so.

First of all, after the city had changed over from the Habsburg to the rebel side in the spring of 1578, the magistrates founded a municipal library consisting of books and manuscripts from confiscated churches, convents and monasteries, which was housed in the (confiscated)

---

[32] J.L. Price, *Holland and the Dutch Republic in the Seventeenth Century* (Oxford, 1994), p. 13.
[33] Ibid., pp. 172–82; Marjolein 't Hart, 'Freedom and Restrictions. State and Economy in the Dutch Republic, 1570–1670' in Karel Davids and Leo Noordegraaf (eds.), *The Dutch Economy in the Golden Age. Nine Studies* (Amsterdam, 1993), pp. 114–18; de Vries and van der Woude, *Nederland 1500–1815*, pp. 215–16.
[34] Willem Frijhoff, 'Hoger onderwijs als inzet van stedelijke naijver in de vroegmoderne tijd' in P.B.M. Blaas and J. van Herwaarden (eds.), *Stedelijke naijver. De betekenis van interstedelijke conflicten in de geschiedenis* (The Hague, 1986), pp. 102–5; Slenders, *Theatrum anatomicum*, p. 13.

Nieuwe Kerk and administered by the churchwardens.[35] Next, in the same year the city government established a public lectureship in anatomy, in 1619 created a permanent anatomical theatre and in 1646 expanded a small *hortus pharmaceuticus*, which had been laid out in 1638 on the instance of the newly founded *collegium medicum* into a larger municipal botanical garden.[36] Finally, in the early 1630s the city fathers began preparations to add yet another basic element of an infrastructure for science: an institute for higher learning. Although the public aim of the new foundation, the Athenaeum Illustre, was ostensibly quite modest (enhancing the knowledge of philosophy and history of pupils in local Latin schools before they entered university, while keeping them under parental control), the scholars who were approached to become its first professors were in no doubt about the underlying purpose. Gerard Johannes Vossius, who was appointed to the chair of history in 1632, noted in one of his letters: 'Desiderium est igitur civitatis, ut quemadmodum longe supra alias urbes caput extulit divitiis, ita etiam literarum laudibus magis et magis fiat inclyta.'[37] Both Vossius and his colleague Caspar Barlaeus, who had immigrated into Holland from Antwerp in 1585, were lured away from their former employer, the University of Leiden, by 'princely wages'. After the founding of the Athenaeum, the municipal library was transferred to the building that housed the newly established school, the Agnietenkapel, and would henceforth serve as the Athenaeum library as well.[38] Between 1635 and 1686, the staff of the new institute was expanded to include chairs of mathematics and astronomy, law, medicine, theology and oriental languages, so that the curriculum offered at the Athenaeum in the later seventeenth century covered almost the entire range of disciplines taught at a full-blown university.[39] When the botanical garden moved in the 1680s to a more spacious location in the newly laid-out *Plantage* and its collection was vastly enriched by fresh shipments from the East and West Indies, the city magistrates again showed their support for science by creating a municipal professorship in botany.[40]

[35] H. de la Fontaine Verwey, *De Stedelijke Bibliotheek van Amsterdam in de Nieuwe Kerk 1578–1632* (Meppel, 1980), pp. 7–8.
[36] Slenders, *Het theatrum anatomicum*, p. 137; Rupp, 'Matters of Life and Death', pp. 263 and 276; van Seters, 'De voorgeschiedenis', pp. 37, 43–4.
[37] 'It is therefore the wish of the city to become more and more famous for its achievements in the field of letters, just as it already excels other cities in wealth', quoted in Chris L. Heesakkers, 'Foundation and Early Development of the Athenaeum Illustre at Amsterdam', *Lias* 9 (1982), p. 4; see also Caspar Barlaeus, *Mercator sapiens, sive oratio de conjungendis mercaturae et philosophiae studiis* (Amsterdam, 1632), pp. 6–7.
[38] A.R.A. Croiset van Uchelen, 'Van Amsterdamse Stadslibrije tot UB', *Spiegel Historiael* 27 (1992), p. 378.   [39] Heesakkers, 'Foundation', pp. 12–14.   [40] Wijnands, *Botany*.

Compared with Antwerp in the sixteenth and early seventeenth centuries, where economic and political power within the city were less intertwined than in Amsterdam during the golden age,[41] the public institutional facilities for science created in Amsterdam were not only more varied in texture – including such provisions as a permanent anatomical theatre and municipal lectureships in anatomy and botany – but also more responsive to practical needs. Antwerp, for instance, did not boast of an institute of higher learning that concerned itself with teaching mathematical arts such as surveying or navigation to a broader audience – not excepting the Jesuit school of mathematics (1617–21).[42] The city fathers of Amsterdam, moreover, went much further than the magistrate of Antwerp in promoting the openness of knowledge. Their encouragement was not confined merely to a policy of practical tolerance for the sake of the prosperity of commerce – though tolerance in matters of conscience and thought, as Henry Méchoulan reminds us, was indeed one of the hallmarks of the culture of Amsterdam in the golden age.[43] They set a high value on the spread of learning itself. It was the view of the ruling elite, perhaps inspired by humanistic ideals, that access to the fruits of scholarship should not remain restricted to a select audience of experts. Both the merchant elite and the civic community at large should have the opportunity to benefit from the store of knowledge concentrated in the institutions for scholarship created within the city walls. Professors at the Athenaeum Illustre were, significantly, instructed to finish their lectures by 11 a.m. in order to enable merchants to be on time for the opening of the Exchange.[44] From the 1650s onwards, the professor of mathematics was even obliged to teach in Dutch on Thursdays and Fridays for those unable to understand Latin.[45] Access to the municipal library, which by the 1620s contained some 1,000 books in Latin, Greek,

[41] See Guido Marnef, *Antwerpen in de tijd van de Reformatie. Ondergronds Protestantisme in een handelsmetropool 1550–1577* (Antwerp/Amsterdam, 1996), pp. 35–46, who points out the dominance of the nobility in the town council and the dependence of the city on the central power in Brussels; and Peter Burke, *Venice and Amsterdam. A Study of Seventeenth-Century Elites* (London, 1974), pp. 58–60, who shows that 'more than half' of the members of the ruling elite of Amsterdam in the period 1578–1719 were 'concerned with trade'. Of the thirty-seven members of the town council in 1652, eighteen were merchants or manufacturers and another eight were directors of the East India or West India Companies (p. 105).   [42] Meskens, *Wiskunde*, pp. 91–105.

[43] Marnef, *Antwerpen*, pp. 43–6, 119; Henry Méchoulan, *Amsterdam au temps de Spinoza* (Paris, 1990). The tolerant atmosphere in Amsterdam was, among other things, exemplified by the foundation of training schools for pastors of two dissenter denominations, the Arminians (in 1634) and the Mennonites (in 1692); Frijhoff, *La société néerlandaise*, p. 14.

[44] C.S.M. Rademakers, 'Het Athenaeum Illustre in the Correspondence of Gerardus Johannes Vossius', *Lias* 9 (1982), p. 33.

[45] Van Domselaer, *Beschrijvinge*, pp. 194–6; Fokkens, *Beschrijvinge*, pp. 241–2.

Hebrew and Arabic as well as French, Italian, German and Dutch, was from the very start free for 'all learned persons and lovers of learning', including people 'very young of age'.[46] A similar policy of openness later applied to the municipal botanical garden.[47]

The role of Amsterdam in the advance of scientific and useful knowledge reached its peak in the second half of the seventeenth century, when all the favourable elements in the urban context were in place: a concentration of experts in the mathematical arts, a high density of doctors of medicine, a large inflow of natural curiosities from all over the world, a well-endowed infrastructure of public facilities for scholarship and a sympathetic attitude by the ruling elite towards the openness of knowledge. This was the period when mathematical practitioners in Amsterdam (Abraham de Graaf and Claes Hendricksz. Gietermaker) facilitated the use of logarithms by common seamen by including tables of logarithms (largely computed by Ezechiël de Decker and Adriaen Vlacq) in their manuals of navigation, published in 1658 and 1660, and when burgomaster Johannes Hudde in collaboration with his old fellow-member of van Schooten's circle in Leiden, Pensionary of Holland Johan de Witt, constructed a life expextancy table on the basis of mortality figures from Amsterdam.[48] This was the time when a doctor of medicine born in Antwerp and graduated from the University of Leuven, Franciscus van den Ende, set up a school of philosophy in Amsterdam and began to teach the young Baruch de Spinoza, who in 1666 would enter into a correspondence on philosophical matters with the same Johannes Hudde.[49] It was the time when another doctor of medicine (who would never set up practice), Jan Swammerdam, learnt from Hudde the technique of making simple microscopes with glass spherules and, thanks to the patronage of another member of the ruling elite, Coenraad van Beuningen, received permission to dissect the bodies of people who had died in the local hospital.[50] It was also the time when Swammerdam, the public lecturer in anatomy Frederik Ruysch and other doctors of medicine – gathered

---

[46] De la Fontaine Verwey, *De Stedelijke Bibliotheek*, pp. 23, 28, 39–43; Rademakers, 'The Athenaeum Illustre', pp. 34–5; Dapper, *Historische beschrijving*, pp. 439–40; Commelin, *Beschrijving*, p. 648; Fokkens, *Beschrijvinge*, p. 241.

[47] Commelin, *Beschrijving*, pp. 655–6.

[48] Davids, *Zeewezen en wetenschap*, pp. 116–17, 155; H.L. Houtzager, 'Johan Hudde en zijn verdiensten voor de actuariële wetenschap', *Maandblad Amstelodamum* 75 (1988), pp. 126–32.

[49] K.O. Meinsma, *Spinoza en zijn kring. Historisch-kritische studiën over Hollandsche vrijgeesten*, 2nd edn (Utrecht, 1980), pp. 124–37, 260–2; Wim Klever, *Mannen rond Spinoza. Presentatie van een emanciperende generatie 1650–1700* (Hilversum, 1997), p. 54; Frijhoff, *La société néerlandaise*, pp. 236, 241.

[50] Edward G. Ruestow, *The Microscope in the Dutch Republic. The Shaping of Discovery* (Cambridge, 1996), pp. 22 and 30; C.W. Roldanus, *Coenraad van Beuningen. Staatsman en libertijn* (The Hague, 1931), p. 147.

around the first professor of medicine at the Athenaeum Illustre, Gerard Blasius, in an informal society called the *collegium privatum Amstelodamense* – engaged in a programme of comparative anatomical research with the help of new techniques such as preparation of bodies by injection of the vessels with fluids.[51] It was, moreover, in this very period that a chemical practitioner emigrating from Germany, Johann Rudolf Glauber, founded a private laboratory for the production of medicines and chemicals, which served as the training ground for the first two professors appointed to the chair of chemistry at the University of Leiden.[52] In this period, too, the government of Amsterdam subsidized the publication (in 1697 and 1701) of a magnificent catalogue of the plants of the municipal botanical garden composed by the professor of botany at the Athenaeum and commissioner of the *hortus*, Jan Commelin, and his grand-nephew Caspar Commelin.[53]

Yet, the liberal support from the city magistrate of Amsterdam for the building of an infrastructure for the cultivation of scientific and useful knowledge could not ensure that Amsterdam would permanently outdo all other cities in the Dutch Republic in the range and quality of its contributions to the advance of scholarship. The Athenaeum Illustre never superseded the University of Leiden as the principal institute of higher learning in the Dutch Republic. The move of Vossius and Barlaeus from Leiden to Amsterdam proved to be the exception rather than the rule. The professor appointed to the chair of mathematics in 1635, Martinus Hortensius, in fact moved in the opposite direction four years later. Normally, Leiden, not Amsterdam, was the climax of an academic career. In numbers of chairs, in the range of facilities (aside from an anatomical theatre and a botanical garden, Leiden in the course of the seventeenth century also acquired an observatory and laboratories for physics and chemistry) and in sheer international standing, the Athenaeum always lagged far behind the first university of the Dutch Republic.

The scheme by the magistrates of Amsterdam to endow their city with the finest facilities in scholarship to be found in the United Provinces was strongly opposed by the university and the town government of the second-largest city in Holland, Leiden. In 1631, fearing a sharp decline in enrolment of students (Amsterdam accounted for many more students than any other city in Holland, let alone other provinces of the

[51] Ruestow, *The Microscope*, pp. 82–7; G.A. Lindeboom (ed.), *Observationes anatomicae collegii privati Amstelodamense. Pars prior (1667) et altera (1673)* (Nieuwkoop, 1975).
[52] J.W. van Spronsen, 'The Beginnings of Chemistry' in Lunsingh Scheurleer and Posthumus Meyjes, *Leiden University*, pp. 337 and 339; they were appointed in 1672 and 1702.   [53] Wijnands, *Botany*; Freedberg, 'Science', p. 386.

Republic),[54] the Senate of the University of Leiden and the Leiden town magistrate disputed the foundation of the Athenaeum before the States of Holland, appealing to the exclusive privilege for the provinces of Holland and Zeeland that had been granted to this University by virtue of its foundation charter of 1575 (after the heroic siege of the city in 1574) at a time when Amsterdam was still on the Habsburg side in the Dutch Revolt.[55] Although the Court of Justice, to which the case had been referred, in the end ruled against any obstruction of Amsterdam's plan to establish professorships in history and philosophy, the qualification was that the new foundation was allowed to function only as a propaedeutic institute.[56] The Athenaeum therefore did not receive the *ius promovendi*. Anyone who wished to take a higher degree in law, medicine, theology or philosophy still had to enrol in Leiden or whatever other institute of university status he chose to attend. It was Leiden, not Amsterdam, which continued to enjoy financial support from provincial sources.

Given the political structure of the Dutch Republic, it was actually impossible for a city as mighty and wealthy as Amsterdam to obtain an overall lead in the field of scientific and useful knowledge. Moreover, by the end of the seventeenth century the upkeep of the public infrastructure for science became beset by problems of a more material nature. Owing to the staggering burden of the expenses of the extension of the city in the 1660s and the war with France in the 1670s, the city government from the 1680s onwards felt obliged to make heavy cuts in public spending, including halving the number of professorships at the Athenaeum. As a consequence, the chairs of history, medicine, mathematics, astronomy and navigation were left vacant in the 1690s once their incumbents had died.[57]

Moreover, the concern for the spread of knowledge to a non-academic audience, which among all the cities in the Dutch Republic received its fullest expression in the public institutions in Amsterdam, did not herald the growth of a movement to make science into a 'public' enterprise. Mathematical practitioners in Amsterdam or in any other town of the Republic did not assume the role of public spokesmen for science. In contrast with their colleagues in London in the late seventeenth and early eighteenth centuries,[58] mathematical practitioners in the United

---

[54] Heesakkers, 'Foundation', p. 7.
[55] P.C. Molhuysen (ed.), *Bronnen tot de geschiedenis der Leidsche universiteit*, 6 vols. (The Hague, 1913–24), vol. II, pp. 159–60, 214*–19*.
[56] Ibid., pp. 286*–9*; Heesakkers, 'Foundation', pp. 6–8, 10.
[57] *Gedenkboek van het Athenaeum*, pp. 34–7, 39–40; Davids, 'Universiteiten, illustre scholen', p. 27.
[58] Larry Stewart, *The Rise of Public Science. Rhetoric, Technology, and Natural Philosophy in Newtonian Britain, 1660–1750* (Cambridge, 1992) and chapter 16 by Stewart in this volume.

Provinces up to the 1740s were not keen on making the utmost use of the potential value of the 'new science' for the world of trade and industry. Nor did they expand their teaching to include natural philosophy. They were not active in seeking to widen the audience for science as a 'useful' enterprise.

This divergence between the Dutch Republic and England, I would suggest, was a result of particular differences in the social contexts in which science evolved. In the context of the seventeenth-century Netherlands, it would have been pointless for mathematical practitioners or scientists themselves to organize a movement to establish the legimitacy of the scientific enterprise by laying stress on its utilitarian value.[59] Science was not in need of a secure political 'niche'. The urban elites who ruled the Republic did not have to be persuaded by utilitarian arguments to take a favourable attitude towards the practice of science; they supported the spread of institutional facilities for scholarship and in Amsterdam actively promoted the openness of knowledge. This was perhaps one of the reasons the Dutch Republic in the golden age lacked a particular kind of institution that emerged in England and other countries of Europe in the course of the seventeenth century: a scientific society. Given the policy of the ruling elites, in contrast with England there was no urge in the Netherlands to create 'a focus through which the public acceptability of science could be enhanced'.[60]

---

[59] On the absence of a 'scientific movement' in the Netherlands before the 1740s, see Davids, *Zeewezen en wetenschap*, pp. 356–61, and C.A. Davids, 'Shifts of Technological Leadership in Early Modern Europe' in K. Davids and J. Lucassen (eds.), *A Miracle Mirrored. The Dutch Republic in European Perspective* (Cambridge, 1995), pp. 357–61; K. van Berkel, 'From Simon Stevin to Robert Boyle: Reflections on the Place of Science in Dutch Culture in the Seventeenth Century' in Simon Groenveld and Michael Wintle (eds.), *Britain and the Netherlands, Vol. XI, Religion, Scholarship and Art in Anglo-Dutch Relations in the 17th Century* (Zutphen, 1994), p. 112, has come round to this view, too.

[60] Michael Hunter, *Establishing the New Science. The Experience of the Early Royal Society* (Woodbridge, 1989), p. 15.

Table 15.1 *Institutional facilities for science in cities of the United Provinces, 1575–1800, with date of foundation*

City	U	I	A	PA	B	PB
				Facility[a]		
Holland						
Amsterdam	–	1632	1619	1578	c.1640	1685
Leiden	1575	–	1593	1587	1594	1587
Delft	–	–	1614	1614	–	–
Dordrecht	–	1636	1634	1634	–	
Rotterdam	–	1681	1642	1642	–	
Haarlem	–		1799	1799	–	–
The Hague	–	–	1628	1637	c.1750	1750
Alkmaar	–	–	1772	1772	–	–
Zeeland						
Middelburg[b]	–	1611/1650/1709	1658	1658	–	–
Zierikzee	–	–	1768	1768	–	–
Goes	–	–	1769	1769	–	–
Friesland						
Franeker	1585	–	1616	1616	1631	1616
Leeuwarden	–	–	1702	1794	–	–
Groningen						
Groningen	1614	–	1615	1615	1642	1628
Overijssel						
Deventer	–	1630	1771	1771	–	–
Gelderland						
Harderwijk	1648[d]	1600	1649	1649	1649	1743
Zutphen	–	1686	–	–	–	–
Nijmegen[c]	1655–79[d]	1653	–	–	–	–
Utrecht						
Utrecht	1636[d]	1634	1621	1621	1639	1638
Staats-Brabant						
Breda[c]	–	1646–69	1646	–	–	–
Den Bosch	–	1636	1662	1662	–	–
Staats-Limburg						
Maastricht	–	1683	–	–	–	–

Notes:
[a] U = university; I = illustrious school; A = permanent anatomical theatre; PA = professorship or praelectorship of anatomy; B = botanical garden; PB = professorship of botany.
[b] The Illustrious School of Middelburg was refounded several times.

Notes to Table 15.1 (*cont.*)
c The University of Nijmegen and the Illustrious School at Breda existed for only twenty-odd years (start- and end dates given)
d Illustrious school elevated to rank of University.
Sources: Boeles, 'Levensschets'; W.B.S. Boeles, *Frieslands Hoogeschool en het Rijksathenaeum te Franeker*, 2 vols. (Leeuwarden, 1878–87); H. Bouman, *Geschiedenis van de voormalige Geldersche hoogeschool en hare hoogleraren*, 2 vols. (Utrecht, 1844–47); Endtz, *Hage-professoren*; Frijhoff, *Société*, pp. 13–18; Jensma, Smit and Westra, *Universiteit te Franeker*; Kernkamp, *Utrechtsche academie*; Lunsingh Scheurleer and Posthumus Meyjes, *Leiden university*; Rupp, 'Matters of Life and Death'; Slenders, *Het theatrum anatomicum*; Wijnands, *Botany*.

16 Philosophers in the counting-houses: commerce, coffee-houses and experiment in early modern London

Larry Stewart

In the early modern world, science was part public spectacle and part private contemplation. Experimental discoveries and their demonstrations were performed before audiences who might bestow their blessing on discovered facts and on hopeful explanation. Science, or natural philosophy as it was then properly called, was never easily limited to a few initiates who might gather together in the arcane rites of experimental practice.[1] During the seventeenth century, the expansion of experimentalism took two forms. Remarkable insights into nature could often open courtly culture to philosophers, giving them access, variously, to the Medici of Florence, Louis XIV or England's Charles II. More importantly, early groups (such as the Royal Society of London for Improving Natural Knowledge) acknowledged, as through Henry Oldenburg's *Philosophical Transactions*, an audience that was at least literate and socially respectable – such as the aristocracy which might in turn grant its patronage, or even a wider society whose reception of the scientific world demanded convincing promises of practical or, possibly, national advantage.[2] England's golden age of science in the late seventeenth and early eighteenth centuries did not emerge completely formed from Robert Boyle's laboratory or from Newton's shuttered rooms in Cambridge. Any definition of Europe's scientific achievement, therefore, is the consequence not only of private genius and solitary innovation but of a collective response to imperial opportunities.

Decades after he had left Trinity College for London's Royal Mint, Sir Isaac Newton contemplated the measure of achievement. Probably shortly before 1725, Newton scribbled on the undated cover of a letter a brief list of those accomplishments he believed belonged 'to ye English'. Included, without individual attribution however, were 'the variation of ye Variation'

---

[1] See William Eamon, *Science and the Secrets of Nature. Books of Secrets in Medieval and Early Modern Culture* (Princeton, N.J.: 1994), esp. ch. 9.

[2] See Steven Shapin, *A Social History of Truth. Civility and Science in Seventeenth-Century England* (Chicago, 1994), esp. ch. 3.

(magnetic declination), probably by Henry Gellibrand and Edmond Halley; the circulation of the blood by William Harvey; telescopic sights and the micrometer variously improved by Richard Townely, Robert Hooke and John Flamsteed; and 'the Libration of the Moon', likely in reference to Newton's own explanation of lunar eccentricity.[3] Surprisingly, Newton makes no mention of those controversial matters, such as the fluxions or the much disputed refraction of light, which he otherwise might have claimed to his own efforts. Even the private lights of solitary genius implied a distinctly broader sense of national accomplishment.

Newton's own nationalist enthusiasm was of long standing. It had taken shape in the cauldron of seventeenth-century imperial conflict and of the Protestant struggle. Inherent in Newton's calculus of philosophical insight was his proposal for 'a Catalogue of the names & excellencys of those men that are most wise learned or esteemed in any nation'.[4] Such at least was one version of scientific achievement where even Newton might stand on the shoulders of giants. In 1669, the young Newton had written to his younger colleague Francis Aston with some hints 'about wt may bee to your advantage in travelling' – something which Bacon had recommended, but which Newton was evidently loath to venture. Among Newton's suggestions for a voyage to foreign parts were proposals 'to observe ye policys wealth & state affairs of nations so far as a solitary Traveller may conveniently doe. 2 Their impositions upon all sorts of People Trades or commoditys yt are remarkeable. 3 Their Laws & Customes how far they differ from ours. 4 Their Trades & Arts wherin they excell or come short of us in England.' There followed a series of queries to be investigated from Holland to Hungary about devices for grinding glasses to the secrets of the transmutation of metals. During a lull in the Dutch Wars, Newton sought practical information to England's advantage. Virtually simultaneously, the Reverend Thomas Sprat made the Royal Society agenda explicit – 'to be the Head of a Philosophical League, above all other Countries in Europe'.[5] This chapter is about the

---

[3] Cambridge University Library, Additional MSS. 3965 (13), f. 479r. I owe this reference to Alan Gabbey who brought it to my attention. See Gabbey, 'Innovation and Continuity in the History of Astronomy: The Case of the Rotating Moon' in Peter Barker and Roger Ariew, *Revolution and Continuity: Essays in the History and Philosophy of Early Modern Science* (Washington, D.C., 1991), pp. 95–129, esp. pp. 95–6.

[4] H.W. Turnbull (ed.), *The Correspondence of Isaac Newton* (Cambridge, 1959), vol. I, pp. 9–13, esp. p. 10, Newton to Aston, 18 May 1669. I wish to thank James MacLachlan for drawing this to my attention and for his comments on an earlier draft of this paper.

[5] Quoted in Mordechai Feingold, 'Reversal of Fortunes: The Displacement of Cultural Hegemony from the Netherlands to England in the Seventeenth and Early Eighteenth Centuries' in Dale Hoak and Mordechai Feingold (eds.), *The World of William and Mary. Anglo-Dutch Perspectives of the Revolution of 1688–89* (Stanford, Calif., 1996), p. 256.

manner by which London's natural philosophers sought to transmute natural knowledge into national achievement.

Much dismay followed the many failed projects of the Restoration, while international competition magnified the urgency of the search for advantage. Inevitable frustrations were reflected in a glaringly obvious divergence of philosophical styles among the earliest Fellows of the Royal Society.[6] While Sprat's *History of the Royal Society* (1667) printed visions of the encouragement of trades – such as William Petty's paper on dyeing, the success of the Society's Committee on Trades was severely limited. Early enthusiasm for the inspection of machines or the examination of proposals to determine the longitude at sea ultimately came to nothing, partly, one suspects, because of the collision of aristocratic elitism with the personal survival of tradespeople and their secrets.[7] Notwithstanding Sprat's assertions of social diversity and of the participation of 'vulgar hands', the activities of the early Royal Society provided ample evidence that the role of mere technicians and the performance of salaried demonstrators were fundamentally problematic.[8]

Newton's career as Master of the Mint suggests that trade, technology and public policy were never far beyond the reach of philosophers. At least since Francis Bacon, this was the problematic agenda of natural philosophy.[9] In the Restoration London of Christopher Wren, Robert Hooke and Jonas Moore, and especially of the Reverend Thomas Sprat, there was promised a kind of practical achievement which the Royal Society found impossible to realize. Sprat's *History of the Royal Society* publicly staked a claim to a utilitarian science; yet, more often disappointment was the end of dreams of useful knowledge.

Royal Society promises were, in reality, constraints. I contend here that the technicians and philosophy demonstrators of Restoration and Augustan London transported natural philosophy from such elevated (if shop-worn) places such as Gresham College into public spaces. The Royal Society self-image was better reflected in the Stuart court than in the promises of commerce. Indeed, the Society's location at Gresham College was inherently difficult – in a place purportedly under the patronage of the Charles II, and yet entirely at odds with the purpose of public

---

[6] See Paul Wood and Michael Hunter, 'Towards Solomon's House: Rival Strategies for Reforming the Early Royal Society' in Michael Hunter, *Establishing the New Science. The Experience of the Early Royal Society* (Woodbridge, Suffolk, 1989), esp. pp. 216–18.

[7] See Michael Hunter, *Science and Society in Restoration England* (Cambridge, 1981), pp. 94–100.

[8] Steven Shapin, 'The House of Experiment in Seventeenth-Century England', *Isis* 79 (1989), esp. pp. 396, 400–2; and Shapin, *A Social History of Truth*, esp. ch. 8.

[9] Eamon, *Science and the Secrets of Nature*, pp. 341–50; Julian Martin, *Francis Bacon, the State, and the Reform of Natural Philosophy* (Cambridge, 1992), pp. 63, 134 ff.

education which had been the Elizabethan objective of Sir Thomas Gresham. Almost in spite of the Royal Society, the later Augustan refashioning of exclusive experimentalism by philosophy and mathematical practitioners created a public natural philosophy that came to dominate the common view of the sciences in pre-industrial England.

We cannot, of course, account for the obvious anglomania of the late seventeenth century out of a Baconian programme of practicality. Rhetorical promotion of trade failed to produce the benefits Sprat or adventurers like William Petty expected. Nor, by the eighteenth century, can we simply identify the triumph of London as Newton's triumph, however much Voltaire might have thought it so. The roots of achievement run far deeper, and perhaps sometimes in contrary directions, than the relatively recent roots of the early eighteenth-century enlightenment.

Images of natural philosophy and of metropolitan commerce that had converged in Restoration rhetoric surfaced once again in the financial 'bubbles' of Revolutionary and Newtonian London. Beyond Newton's own stewardship of the Mint and of the Royal Society, the breadth of British scientific and technical achievement was often linked to commercial survival. In the after-shock of the South Sea Bubble of 1720, his contemporary Daniel Defoe was, like many, desperately seeking to restore his own fortunes. While Newton then mused in Leicester Fields, British achievement was tangled in a web of fear and uncertainty that had likewise undermined the markets of Amsterdam and Paris. In the querulous, vindictive, aftermath of the collapse of joint-stocks in the Bubble and the evaporation of the Mississippi Scheme, devastating aristocratic adventurers on both sides of the Channel, Daniel Defoe sought to affirm the dignity of trade. At this crucial moment, Defoe was convinced that Britain had much more to offer than did its commercial and imperial rivals such as the French and the Dutch. To Defoe, the once obvious ascent to 'prodigious heights, both in wealth and number' of the English gentry had followed directly from the promotion of '*Trade and Learning*'.[10] Notwithstanding that he remarkably numbered among English advantages a 'climate [that] is the most agreeable climate in the world to live in'[!], we might usefully adopt Defoe's promotion of commerce and education.[11]

[10] Daniel Defoe, *The Complete English Tradesman in Familiar Letters*, 2nd edn (London, 1727; reprint, New York, 1969), Letter XXII, 'Of the Dignity of Trade in England More Than Any Other Countries', p. 306; emphasis added.

[11] On Defoe's view of the importance of science and reason, see Simon Schaffer, 'Defoe's Natural Philosophy and the Worlds of Credit' in John Christie and Sally Shuttleworth (eds.), *Nature Transfigured. Science and Literature, 1700–1900* (Manchester, 1989), pp. 13–44, esp. p. 26.

My focus is the convergence of these early modern visions of Newton and Defoe, of private ventures with public understanding. Here we must take into account the interplay of forces that pushed Newton's own apostles into the very alleys where Defoe could trace the mechanisms of trade.[12] By the early eighteenth century, the market-place for natural philosophy implied the intersection of the worlds of Gresham and Sprat, of Defoe and Newton. The assertion of an essential interaction between traders and financiers and the role of scholars and natural philosophers in Restoration and post-Revolutionary London was as important as it was accurate. The issue here is the recognition of London's achievement.

Daniel Defoe's hyperbole contemplated a general set of conditions unique to England and to London in particular. Yet he was nonetheless misguided. Whatever his purpose, Defoe misunderstood that the circumstances that existed in late Stuart and early Hanoverian London had antecedents at least from the sixteenth century in many of the great commercial entrepôts of western Europe. This brings us to recognize the significance of commercial and trading networks that were likewise highly integrated in their financial and credit arrangements. This was as true since the reign of Elizabeth as it would prove to be in that of George I and George II. Connections that had once flourished between the merchants of London and the wool factors of Antwerp, for example, were superseded by similar relations over the seventeenth and early eighteenth centuries involving Amsterdam, London, Stockholm, Hamburg and Paris.[13] These cities were variously centres of an international economy reflected not solely by trade but also in culture, in the arts and as foci for a broad European web of communication vital to trade and finance and fundamental to scholarship – and to the growing networks of natural philosophers cultivated in the Royal Society by its first Secretary, Henry Oldenburg.

Commerce makes companions of us all. Such is a function of the urban concentration of the lines of communication.[14] And ideas, like money,

[12] Schaffer, 'Defoe's Natural Philosophy', and Simon Schaffer, 'A Social History of Plausibility: Country, City and Calculation in Augustan Britain' in Adrian Wilson (ed.), *Rethinking Social History. English Society 1750–1920 and Its Interpretation* (Manchester, 1993), pp. 128–57.

[13] Fernand Braudel, *The Perspective of the World. Civilization and Capitalism, 15th–18th Century*, trans. Sian Reynolds (New York, 1984), pp. 143 ff.; H.G. Roseveare, 'Stockholm–London–Amsterdam: The Triangle of Trade 1660–1680' and K. Newman, 'Anglo-Dutch Commercial Co-operation and the Russia Trade in the Eighteenth Century' in *The Interactions of Amsterdam and Antwerp with the Baltic Region, 1400–1800* (Leiden, 1983), chs 10 and 11; and A.J.G. Cummings, 'The Harburgh Company and Its Lottery, 1716–1723', *Business History* 28 (July 1986), pp. 1–18.

[14] Mary Douglas and Baron Isherwood, *The World of Goods* (New York, 1979), pp. 11–12.

follow the routes of trade. Cities such as Amsterdam or London functioned as clearing houses of information through their increasingly ubiquitous newspapers with lists of goods for sale, of stocks and their trading
prices, and of advertisements for books and infallible cures, for lectures
by quacks as well as by philosophers.[15] As early as the fifteenth century,
from the Adriatic to the Atlantic, printers parleyed the learning of merchants in bookkeeping and accounts into instruments of instruction.[16]
Similarly by the early seventeenth century, in the plurality of major
trading centres such as Antwerp and Amsterdam, schools emerged where
the teaching in the ways of 'the wise merchant' were promoted side by
side with the sciences. Mixed mathematics and astronomy had a place
alongside Cartesian philosophy in Amsterdam's Athenaeum after 1632.
As Karel Davids points out, cities provided the concentrations of industry
and initiative that threw together scholars and tradespeople, cartographers and chemists, lens makers and instrument makers with searchers
for the longitude that made scientific instruction a marketable commodity. Thus, Isaac Beeckman's *collegium mechanicum* included merchants
and millwrights as well as doctors and mathematicians.[17] This provided
one model for the practical vision of Sir William Petty whose notion of a
gymnasium mechanicum intended craftspeople to collaborate so that ultimately 'new Inventions would be more frequent than new fashions of
clothes and household-stuffe'.[18] In Petty's imagination, learning would
reinforce the prosperity of trade, and ideas could compete with goods in
the market-place.

Competition in trade merged the social spaces of the merchant and
the scholar. It has long been recognized that the Elizabethan merchant
Sir Thomas Gresham sought to promote learning in the interests of
trade. The difficulties experienced by Antwerp during the Spanish conflicts provided a perfect opportunity that Gresham exploited to

[15] Clé Lesger, chapter 3 in this volume; Marten Jan Bok, 'The Rise of Amsterdam as a
Cultural Centre: the Market for Paintings, ca. 1580–1680', *Clusters of Achievement*,
unpublished essay (March, 1994), *passim*; A.T. van Deursen, *Plain Lives in a Golden Age.
Popular Culture, Religion and Society in Seventeenth-century Holland*, trans. Marten Ultee
(Cambridge, 1991), pp. 141 ff.
[16] Pierre Jennin, *Merchants of the 16th Century*. trans. Paul Fitingoff (New York/London,
1972), pp. 86 and 97.
[17] Karel Davids, 'Cities and Science in the Dutch Republic, c. 1580–1750', *Clusters of
Achievement*, unpublished essay (March 1994), p. 13; Geert Vanpaemel, 'Science in
Antwerp 1550–1585', *Clusters of Achievement*, unpublished essay (May 1995), pp. 3–5.
On English contacts with Dutch examples, see Karel Davids, 'The Rise of Mathematical
Practitioners in England and the Dutch Republic, 1580–1650', in H. Beukers and P.
Hoftijzer (eds.), *The Scientific Exchange between England and the Continent in the 17th and
18th Centuries* (Rotterdam, 1994).
[18] Quoted in Alex Keller, 'Technological Aspirations and the Motivation of Natural
Philosophy in Seventeenth-Century England', *History of Technology*, 15 (1993), p. 88.

compete with the wool factors of the Antwerp mart. In 1566 he recruited the London livery companies to construct 'a house and place like unto the New Bourse at Antwerp'. Opened by 1568, it was officially commissioned as the Royal Exchange in 1571.[19] Spanish *realpolitik* thus worked to English advantage. When Gresham died in 1579, his will charged the Mercers' Company and the City of London to support seven professorships directly from the revenues of the Royal Exchange.[20] The Exchange was, thus, one focus for the promotion of practical mathematics and of the presumption of the benefits of natural philosophy. Imperial threats to English trade and the frequently terrifying uncertainties of navigation were reason enough for the cultivation of mathematics and astronomy.[21] And the Royal Exchange itself became one of those buildings which helped to define the character of London as much as the bourse of any great European port. This was so much the case that, when it was rebuilt in 1669 after the Great Fire, it was soon regarded as 'the greatest and the finest of the kind in the world', having cost the enormous sum of over £65,000 yet generating great rent from the double row of shops which ringed the structure.[22] In these shops and in the nearby social spaces where merchants congregated in the late seventeenth century, the talk was then as much of inventions and philosophy as of ships and sales.[23]

To focus on elites and their cultivation of mathematics, natural philosophy and even medicine reveals the conditions of clientage and corporate influence which define early modern urban centres. But it also eclipses many of those who made London's achievement possible. The activities of mere empirics, such as those tied to London's Society of Apothecaries, the College of Chemical Physicians or the Royal Society, might challenge the corporate authority of those such as the Royal College of Physicians. Philosophical tensions were also commercial ones, revealed in the recurrent strife between the Royal Charter of the physicians and the guild foundation of the Society of Apothecaries, with its laboratory built in

[19] G.D. Ramsay, *The Queen's Merchants and the Revolt of the Netherlands. The End of the Antwerp Mart, Part II* (Manchester, 1986), pp. 79–80; Braudel, *Perspective of the World*, pp. 153 and 355; Ann Saunders, *The Royal Exchange* (London, 1991), pp. 7–12.

[20] See Christopher Hill, *Intellectual Origins of the English Revolution* (London, 1965), pp. 34 ff.

[21] See Mordechai Feingold, *The Mathematicians' Apprenticeship. Science, Universities and Society in England 1560–1640* (Cambridge, 1984), pp. 180–1, 185–7, and ch. VI on patronage.

[22] Daniel Defoe, *A Tour Through the Whole Island of Great Britain*, ed., Pat Rogers (Harmondsworth, Middx., 1971), Letter 5, p. 302; and Saunders, *The Royal Exchange*, pp. 21–4.

[23] See Robert Iliffe, '"A Bag of Live Boglice": Hooke, Material Culture and Sources of Skill in 1670s London', unpublished paper (1994), esp. pp. 12 ff. I wish to thank Dr Iliffe for allowing me to read this essay.

1671 and its physic garden founded in 1673.[24] In late Stuart London, it is remarkable that conflicts over new cures and personal reputations were often settled in rancorous disputes and pamphlet wars. Significantly, the market in medicine metamorphosed into public display.

Even those sites which evidently reflected London's scientific reputation, such as Gresham College and the Royal Society, did not have a straight-forward social or intellectual trajectory. It is undoubtedly the case that the promotion of science in the Restoration owed much to the remarkable brilliance of such men as Newton and Boyle, just as the Dutch Republic had marked its own achievement through the likes of Isaac Beeckman, Antoni van Leeuwenhoek, Samuel van Musschenbroek or Willem s'-Gravesande. But, by the eighteenth century, individual ventures broke institutional boundaries. Cross-Channel transactions of Dutch *Stadhouders* and European traders were soon followed by engineers and experimentalists such as the Huguenot John Theophilus Desaguliers, who lectured in both England and the Netherlands.[25]

This raises an important question about a historical focus that sees institutions such as the Royal Society as the pre-eminent focus of scientific achievement. That may indeed have been the Restoration agenda. Champions of the Royal Society represented that it was formed 'of all sorts of men, of the Gown, of the Sword, of the Shop, of the Field, of the Court, of the Sea; all mutually assisting each other'. The reality was, however, that the Royal centre could not hold. The Society periodically struggled with secrecy and 'troublesome and prejudicial' visitors who did not meet a proper social standard.[26] While Gresham's Royal Exchange was encouraging the building of bridges, the Royal Society sometimes dug moats.

---

[24] Harold J. Cook, *The Decline of the Old Medical Regime in Stuart London* (Ithaca, N.Y.,1986), pp. 70, 149, 184, 215, 247. John Colbatch, who began as an apothecary's apprentice, campaigned for a new medicine which would curtail bleeding in surgical cases. Colbatch challenged the physicians to experimental tests and was attacked in turn for his cant of experimentalism. He persevered against the pretended powers of the College of Physicians and was knighted by George I. See Harold J. Cook, 'Sir John Colbatch and Augustan Medicine: Experimentalism, Character and Entrepreneurialism', *Annals of Science* 47 (September 1990), pp. 475–505.

[25] See Michael Hunter, 'Science and the English Public' and Willem Hackman, 'Experimental Philosophy and the Dutch Republic', both in Robert P. Maccubbin and Martha Hamilton-Phillips (eds.), *The Age of William II & Mary II. Power, Politics, and Patronage 1688–1702* (Williamsburg, 1989), pp. 165–70 and 171–8.

[26] See Thomas Sprat, *History of the Royal Society* (London, 1667), p. 76; Hunter, *Establishing the New Science*, p. 199. See also Stephen Pumfrey, 'Ideas above His Station: A Social Study of Hooke's Curatorship of Experiments', *History of Science* 29 (March 1991), pp. 1–44; and Stephen Pumfrey, 'Who Did the Work? Experimental Philosophers and Public Demonstrators in Augustan England', *British Journal for the History of Science* 28 (June 1995), pp. 131–56.

Even a glance at the Royal Society during the Restoration reveals a tension between artisans and gentlemen virtuosi. Shifting our gaze from the passions of elites within the Royal Society toward the less gentrified stratum of London's instrument makers and mathematicians reveals the significance of the practitioners.[27] Robert Hooke's Restoration round of the tumult of the coffee-houses and taverns and the meetings of Fellows in Garraway's and Jonathan's near the Exchange anticipate a time when discourse over a bowl of coffee would be transformed into experimental demonstrations before mechanics and merchants.[28] Sir Jonas Moore was one of many, like Hooke, who inhabited both worlds. Moore was a mathematics teacher, but a patronage culture made him a surveyor of the Fens under the Protectorate, and later Surveyor at the Ordnance Office in the Tower during the Stuart Restoration. Yet he never abandoned his interest in the teaching of mathematics. The necessity of adequate instruction was reaffirmed in his provision of a textbook to be employed, along with 'Globes, & Mapps & other Mathematical Instruments', by the Master at the new Royal Mathematical School at Christ's Hospital. Moore knew the needs of such instructors and was a friend of many.[29] The expanded market in natural philosophy books and instruments was one way of evading the exclusivity and control assumed by the Royal Society.[30]

The market for mixed mathematics meant the existence of a community of learned practitioners who were more likely to be found on the London docks than in the common-rooms of Cambridge or at Whitehall.[31] Among London's many centres of mathematical learning, the lectureship at Christ's Hospital Mathematical School in 1673 rested substantially on Samuel Pepys' fear of the inadequacy of navigational

[27] See Hunter, *Science and Society*, pp. 73–9.
[28] Shapin, 'House of Experiment', pp. 393 and 400. On Hooke and his haunts among the coffee-houses, see Iliffe, '"A Bag of Boglice"', pp. 20–5.
[29] Frances Willmoth, '"The Genius of All Arts" and the Use of Instruments: Jonas Moore (1617–1679) as a Mathematician, Surveyor, and Astronomer', *Annals of Science* 48 (July 1991), pp. 355–65, esp. pp. 363–4; and Frances Willmoth, *Sir Jonas Moore. Practical Mathematics and Restoration Science* (Woodbridge, Suffolk, 1993), pp. 195 ff; J.A. Bennett, 'The Mathematicians' Apprenticeship', *British Journal for the History of Science* 18 (July 1985), pp. 212–17.
[30] See Douglas and Isherwood, *The World of Goods*, p. 90
[31] In the past two decades the literature on the world of mathematicians and mechanics has become voluminous. See, for example, Feingold, *The Mathematician's Apprenticeship* (Cambridge, 1984); Bennett, 'The Mathematicians' Apprenticeship'; J.A. Bennett, 'The Mechanics' Philosophy and the Mechanical Philosophy', *History of Science* 24 (1986), pp. 1–28; J.A. Bennett, 'The Longitude and the New Science', *Vistas in Astronomy* 28 (1985), pp. 219–25; J.A. Bennett, 'Geometry and Surveying in Early-Seventeenth-Century England', *Annals of Science* 48 (July 1991), pp. 345–54; Stephen Johnston, 'Mathematical Practitioners and Instruments in Elizabethan England', *Annals of Science* 48 (July 1991), pp. 319–44; Willmoth, '"The Genius of All Arts"'; and Willmoth, *Sir Jonas Moore*, passim.

practice among naval officers. Despite difficult beginnings, especially at the end of the Dutch Wars, Christ's Hospital was competing with other schools in the teaching of navigation and mathematics in order to fit boys to become apprentices to the captains of ships.[32] It was not long before Moore, Pepys and, ultimately, Newton were exerting considerable authority over the choice of masters.[33] Newton's own influence at Christ's eventually extended to the employment of the Nonconformist Humphrey Ditton and, significantly, of James Hodgson, who abandoned the employ of the Astronomer Royal, Flamsteed, for life as a mathematics lecturer.

The networks amongst the mathematicians had an impact far beyond the walls of institutions such as Christ's Hospital or Gresham College. James Hodgson's early career is a particularly important example of this community. It is clear that, whatever ultimately would recommend Hodgson to Newton, it was as much Hodgson's experience as a promoter of natural philosophy as of mathematics. He left Flamsteed late in 1702 to join the elder Francis Hauksbee in public lectures on experimental philosophy. Flamsteed's assistant, Abraham Sharp, was alarmed by this move as 'a great undertaking for one, especially so young a man, to teach all parts of experimental philosophy, and the apparatus or instruments in order thereto which he intimates is now making for him. It will [he warned] be too great a charge for a single purse.' Sharp went on to remark disingenously that he was 'sure ye Royal Society or some generous Members thereof or others, might contribute to so laudable a work, which seems designed on purpose & is like to be very much instrumental to revive that society now in appearance sadly drooping & languishing, the products of their consultations or correspondencys &c. being of late very inconsiderable'.[34] Sharp's reaction barely hinted at a crucial transition of which Hodgson was to become an important agent.

It is to the mathematical practitioners and their schools that we must turn to comprehend the importance of natural philosophy in the emergent British imperium. Assertions by eighteenth-century lecturers of

[32] Nicholas Hans, *New Trends in Education in the Eighteenth Century* (London, 1966), pp. 213–14; Ralph Davis, *The Rise of the English Shipping Industry* (Newton Abbot, Devon, 1972), pp. 124–6; and A.G. Howson, *A History of Mathematics Education in England* (Cambridge, 1982), pp. 35–8.

[33] Willmoth, *Sir Jonas Moore*, pp. 196–200.

[34] Margaret E. Rowbottom, 'The Teaching of Experimental Philosophy in England, 1700–1730', *XIe congres international d'histoire des sciences (1965)*, Actes IV (1968), pp. 48–9; Cambridge University Library, Flamsteed Correspondence, RGO 1/34, f.33, Sharp to Flamsteed, 25 September 1704; also William Cudworth, *Life and Correspondence of Abraham Sharp* (London, 1889), p. 81.

the conquest of nature's bounty complemented the navigational and mercantile interests long promoted in London's mathematics schools. James Hodgson, for one, had ambitions beyond that of an astronomer's calculator. His associations with instrument makers and craftspeople afforded advantages most other mathematics lecturers had failed to exploit. Yet, unlike some chemical promoters, who might charge more than 2 guineas, Hodgson also had the model of mathematics lectures given free of charge. Such lectures certainly existed in London from 1698, having been organized by the brewer Charles Cox for the public good and delivered, *gratis*, by the Newtonian John Harris first in Southwark and later at the Marine Coffee-House near the Royal Exchange. By the spring of 1704, Cox's patronage evidently grew more precarious, thereby repeating a pattern common to early enthusiasts of public knowledge.

It was precisely the uncertainty of the Marine Coffee-House lectures that gave Hodgson his opportunity. In December 1704, Hodgson advertised classes in natural philosophy and astronomy to 'lay the best and surest Foundation for all useful knowledge'. Significantly, Hodgson proposed a course of experiments based on an extensive range of apparatus seldom before seen outside of the Royal Society. This vast array included 'Engines for Raising and Condensing Air with all their Appurtenances, Microscopes of the best Contrivance, Telescopes of a convenient Length, with Micrometers adapted to them, Barometers, Thermometers, and Utensils proper for Hydrostatical Experiments, with such other Instruments as are necessary for the purpose'. The experiments were to be presented at the Hand and Pen bookshop, formerly the Writing School of Col. John Ayres,[35] then operated by Robert More among the booksellers of St Paul's Churchyard.

The Hodgson circle was one of the nodes of a network of mathematicians, writing masters, instrument makers and empirics crucial to the promotion of experimental learning.[36] Within a few weeks, Hodgson proposed the highly contentious prisms be added to his armoury as well as instruments necessary 'to prove the Weight and Elasticity of the Air, its Pressure or Gravitation of Fluids upon each other: Also the new Doctrine of Lights and Colours, and several other matters relating to the same Subjects,' all of which was described as 'so great an Undertaking' as to

---

[35] R.V. and P.J. Wallis, *Index of British Mathematicians. Part III (1701–1800)* (Newcastle upon Tyne, 1993), p. 6.

[36] Alan Morton, 'Public Science in Mid-18th Century London: the King George III Collection at the Science Museum', typescript, (1990), p. 5; Alan Q. Morton and Jane A. Wess, *Public & Private Science. The King George III Collection* (Oxford, 1993), ch. II; see *Daily Courant*, Tuesday, 5 December 1704.

require a subscription of 2 guineas.[37] Instruments magnified the charge. This vast apparatus was an immensely expensive gamble indeed, even with the support of the instrument makers John Rowley and the elder Francis Hauksbee.

It would be misleading to see these experimental ventures as merely an exercise in vulgar entertainment. There had long been similar diversions in the chemistry lectures of Edward Bright off Fleet Street or even in the genteel guise of the Chelsea Physick Garden – both of which were tied to the practical expansion of medical knowledge. Queen Anne's mathematics lecturers went much further. Hodgson in 1704 was not so much testing the elasticity of his purse as exploring the limits of polite experimental society. The venture of mathematical learning, already established by Harris and Cox in the public interest, was now extended to the creation of an experimental space for a broad community unconstrained by the uninspired notions of a private, polite, 'Society of persons of Quality and Honour'.[38] Hodgson claimed new spaces for demonstrations in astronomy, on the weight of air, or of Newton's disputed optical theories.[39] With his immense caravan of apparatus he forced experimental philosophy out of the Royal Society closet.

The effort was an immense success. By 1706 Hodgson was presenting experimental philosophy at the Queen's Head Tavern in Fleet Street with Hauksbee and again at the Marine until 1709 or 1710. In the shadow of the Exchange, the lectures at the Marine were soon adopted by Humphrey Ditton, yet another of Newton's mathematics disciples. Very quickly during Anne's reign, the teaching of natural and experimental philosophy recommended the mathematician to a public whose interest in such subjects was growing rapidly. For example, in 1706 Robert Arnold had followed the lead and was offering astronomy lectures along with mathematics at the Swan Coffee-House in Threadneedle Street, by the Exchange.[40] Such was the rapid proliferation of natural philosophy lecturing that quickly followed in Hodgson's wake.

---

[37] *Daily Courant*, Thursday, 11 January 1705. On the significance of some of these experiments within the natural philosophy community, see Henry Guerlac, 'Francis Hauksbee: Experimentateur au profit de Newton' in Henry Guerlac, *Essays and Papers in the History of Modern Science* (Baltimore, 1977), pp. 107–19; W.D. Hackmann, 'Scientific Instruments: Models of Brass and Aids to Discovery', and Simon Schaffer, 'Glass Works: Newton's Prisms and the Uses of Experiment', both in David Gooding, Trevor Pinch and Simon Schaffer (eds.), *The Uses of Experiment. Studies in the Natural Sciences* (Cambridge, 1989), pp. 49–52, 94 ff.

[38] Quoting Glanvill, in Steven Shapin, '"A Scholar and a Gentleman": The Problematic Identity of the Scientific Practitioner in Early Modern England', *History of Science* 29 (September 1991), p. 297; see also Shapin, 'The House of Experiment', passim.

[39] See Bennett, 'The Mathematicians' Apprenticeship', p. 217; and see Shapin, 'A Scholar and a Gentleman', pp. 311–12.

When James Hodgson brought his apparatus to the Hand and Pen, he transformed the social space in which experimental philosophy was performed. By January 1706, Hodgson and Hauksbee introduced to the Queen's Head Tavern even more dramatic demonstrations of the vacuum pump, including 'several new and surprizing Experiments concerning the production of Light in Vacuo . . . [and] of Fluids Gravitating upon each other'.[41] No mere entertainment, the cutting edge of Hauksbee's Royal Society experiments was immediately found amongst the brokers and the tavern-goers.[42]

Reaching an audience was essential to experimental philosophy. Witnesses as well as gossip and trade were found in the coffee-houses of London. It is the atmosphere of the Marine which must particularly concern us, for even there by candlelight Newton's abstractions would be revealed. Besides its proximity to the Royal Exchange and Gresham College, and to the numerous nearby coffee-houses in Threadneedle Street and Birchin Lane (see figure 16.1), the Marine was significantly well suited to reaching those who might be convinced of the potential for natural philosophical improvements. Certainly, the loss of lives and shipping was one issue that opened the coffee-house doors to the mathematicians; but it was merely the first step in bringing experiments among the merchants.

The Marine Coffee-House was well known in the early eighteenth century as a bustling site of mercantile transactions. It was particularly noted for its auctions, which took place in the afternoons to dispose of large quantities of goods clearing the customs' warehouses or, perhaps, taken by privateers preying on the French and Spanish. Constantly advertising in the London papers, the Marine became one of the most active brokerage pits that ringed the Royal Exchange. Offered for sale 'by the candle' were often large quantities of 'new red French Wines, Pontac, . . . free of all Duties'; or 800 bushels of chestnuts, 14,000 walking-canes and a parcel of white genoa soap, 100 bales of coffee newly landed, hogsheads of tobacco, crepes, broad cloths, serges, shalloons, Popes Head-Alley toys, haberdashers' ware, bags of Spanish wool, and, on one occasion, 80 tons of iron from a Portuguese vessel. There was no limit to the types of commodities that could be made available. Such material madness might easily have overwhelmed the lectures, as these sales occasionally began in

[40] *Daily Courant*, Monday, 29 July 1706. Arnold apparently ran the bookshop called the Hand and Pen in the Barbican. See *Daily Courant*, Wednesday, 3 April 1706. See E.G.R. Taylor, *Mathematical Practitioners of Tudor & Stuart England* (Cambridge, 1954), p. 291; Wallis and Wallis, *Index*, p. 4.
[41] *Daily Courant*, Friday, 4 January 1706.
[42] See Marie Boas Hall, *Promoting Experimental Learning. Experiment and the Royal Society 1660–1727* (Cambridge, 1991), pp. 118–19.

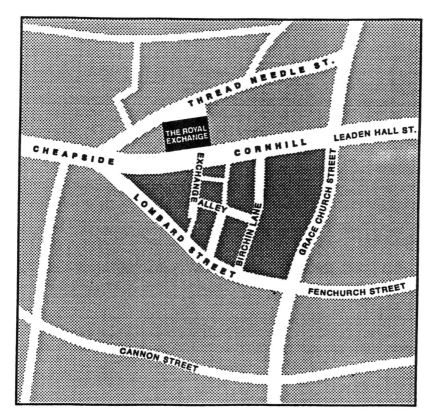

16.1 Map of the area around the Royal Exchange, London

mid-afternoon just before the lectures of John Harris.[43] But the Marine provided the space in which mathematics and experimental philosophy were promoted, just like any other commodity, to the traders of London.

The scientific lectures made Defoe's view of commercial achievement possible. The essential reason was the exchange not merely of commodities but of ideas. Uniquely situated, the Exchange coffee-houses existed where the convergence of commodity and credibility would ultimately produce a dynamic consumer society. Here lay the force of metropolis and mercantilism. The frantic bustle of London's financial revolution produced a hectic market for lecturers, mathematical practitioners and

[43] See *Daily Courant*, Friday, 1 October 1703; Wednesday, 17 January 1705; for Harris, Friday, 19 January 1705; Monday, 30 July 1705; Wednesday, 17 April 1706; Monday, 23 September 1706; Tuesday, 24 September 1706; Wednesday, 6 November 1706; Monday, 16 December 1706.

instrument makers who offered practical and technical knowledge to the many anxious to exploit it. And there was no shortage of such philosophical entrepreneurs amongst the stockjobbing company of Jonathan's or Garraway's, both in Exchange Alley (see figure 16.2).[44] Hodgson, it is clear, knew Hooke's haunts well. In the warrens about the Royal Exchange, the public demand for natural philosophy made real what Thomas Gresham had barely imagined.

The mania for mathematics and natural philosophy in the reign of Anne thus raises interesting questions about the Royal Society and its relation to Gresham's dreams. Long housed in rooms in Gresham College, the Society nonetheless found itself at constant war with the Gresham trustees who, in turn, felt themselves besieged by the Fellows and their political patrons. Hooke and the Royal Society continually obstructed any attempts by the trustees to revise the terms of the legislation which enforced Gresham's will. As the Fellows had a proprietary interest in rooms in Gresham, any effort to demolish the decaying College and to rebuild it elsewhere might seriously affect the Society's position. Amidst these institutional wars Newton drafted a revealing petition in which he told the Queen that 'a seat nearer Westminster would be more convenient for persons of Quality & render ye meetings more numerous & thereby conduce more of the improvement of natural knowledge'.[45] Newton adhered to the proposition that social exclusivity defined the proper audience of natural philosophy.

Newton's cultivation of connection failed to produce effective results for the Royal Society. Indeed, when the continental traveller Zacharias Conrad von Uffenbach visited Gresham College and the Society in 1710, the experience was a shocking disappointment. He sneered at a Royal Society populated by 'all kinds of people of no account' whom he dismissed as 'none but apothecaries or other such people'.[46] Neither the Royal Society nor Gresham College seemed then in any position to promote natural philosophy effectively. It is remarkable, however, that, at about the time von Uffenbach sought out the Society and its Curator,

[44] John Houghton, *A Collection for Improvement of Husbandry and Trade*, no. 2 (Wednesday, 6 April 1692); Bryant Lillywhite, *London Coffee Houses* (London, 1963), pp. 219 and 360; Geoffrey Holmes, *British Politics in the Age of Anne* (London, 1967), p. 154.
[45] Adamson, 'The Royal Society and Gresham College', pp. 10–12; Royal Society, Dom. MSS. V, f. 45, Newton to Queen Anne, a draft, n.d. The issue of persons of proper reputation was central to the image of the Fellows of the Royal Society in the early eighteenth century. Public attacks on the Society in the press were met with a defence based on an account of Royal patronage and 'meetings [that] are ever allmost constantly graced & honoured by the presence of personages of the first Rank & Character'. Dom. MSS. V, f. 23, Roger Gale to the *Daily Post*, a draft, [1731].
[46] W.H. Quarrell and Margaret Mare (eds.), *London in 1710. From the Travels of Zacharias von Uffenbach* (London, 1934), pp. 98–9.

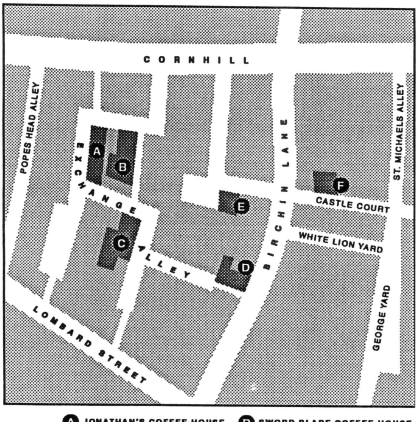

(A) JONATHAN'S COFFEE-HOUSE   (D) SWORD BLADE COFFEE-HOUSE

(B) SWAN COFFEE-HOUSE   (E) FLEECE TAVERN

(C) GARRAWAY'S COFFEE-HOUSE   (F) MARINE COFFEE-HOUSE

16.2 Exchange Alley, London

Francis Hauksbee was conducting public experiments on falling weights in the dome of St Paul's.[47] If the notion of a languishing Society is remotely accurate, it may go some way to explaining the translation of experimental philosophy out of the Royal Society closet. As the merchants and traders repeatedly criticized what Gresham College had to offer, it cannot then be surprising that they also provided an audience for

[47] Hall, *Promoting Experimental Learning*, p. 119; and Henry Guerlac, s.v. Hauksbee, *Dictionary of Scientific Biography* (New Yorks, 1972), vol. VI, pp. 169–75.

those lecturers who sought out a broader public than 'persons of Quality'.

London's breadth of consumption for science meant an increasing demand for philosophers. Gresham's Elizabethan vision of a college as a clearing house of practical knowledge had been transformed. But it had been his construction of an Exchange that magnified the market for philosophers. Hence, we need to understand that the market for philosophical entertainment could not, and need not, have issued from the repository of the Royal Society or full-blown from the head of Newton.

It was undoubtedly because of the continual promises of improved navigation that the world of traders and seamen provided a particular response to the peripatetic philosophers of London. Here Hodgson's credentials could hardly be questioned. His great business in London had included *The Theory of Navigation Demonstrated*, which he had published in 1706, and this, undoubtedly, served to recommend him to Christ's Hospital when he was chosen as mathematics master in 1709. Thus, Hodgson ultimately retreated into a much more structured world than the one into which he had ventured in 1702. Nonetheless, it was the immensely difficult problem of navigation which, as in the time of Elizabeth and Gresham, continued to recommend the mathematicians to the merchants of Bishopsgate and the Exchange.

Navigational improvements, especially of latitude and longitude, were obviously critical to those mercantile circles served by the mathematics teachers. In the late summer of 1714, the lecturer William Whiston waited amid the darkness of Hampstead Heath on the northern edge of London. Whiston was the ideal exponent of public experiment. Like Galileo, with whom he compared himself, he never hid long in the shadows when he could create a more dramatic light. Anticipating the explosion of his rockets above the city, Whiston was actually extending a process of public spectacle increasingly common among the cosmopolitan promoters of early modern science. But Whiston would prove to be more than a demonstrator. In the summer after Parliament established the phenomenal reward of up to £20,000 for the discovery of longitude at sea, few living within sight or sound of Hampstead Heath could have escaped the blast of Whiston's mortars which shattered the evening air late in 1714 and again in the spring of 1715.

Whiston's trials had the potential to attract anyone who read his advertisements in the daily newspapers and who had the instruments and skill to report the sightings. Possibly mistaken for a celebration of the Hanoverian succession, Whiston's bombs burst into the twilight a mile high in an experiment in determining longitude. Intended to test the time between the instantaneous flash of the explosions high over a largely unsuspecting City and the subsequent report of the sound, Whiston's first experiments were the most startlingly public. Beginning on Saturday evenings at 8 o'clock, and continuing intermittently for almost two years, Whiston's rockets burst over Hampstead, Gravesend and – underlining the failures of astronomers – near the Royal Observatory at Greenwich.

The idea supposedly had first come to Whiston when, at Cambridge after the Glorious Revolution, he had heard the distant reports of the guns of the French fleet off Beachy Head in 1690 when they came to the aid of deposed King James. Or perhaps he had been reminded by the flash of the fireworks in the celebrations in 1713 for the Treaty of Utrecht, which had ended the latest war against Louis XIV over the Spanish succession. Whatever the reason, the attempt to measure distance and position clearly had potential. By such means Whiston and Humphrey Ditton thought they might then be able to create an accurate map of Britain and its coastline. Such a method, they thought, would overcome the great difficulties of establishing longitude, especially along the dangerous Channel coast.

Public experiments were the logical end of Oldenburg's *Philosophical Transactions*. Yet, in the early eighteenth century, Newton wanted nothing to do with the outspoken Whiston – indeed, he looked upon Whiston's vulgar pandering with disgust. In this, at least, Newton apparently adopted the common attitudes expressed even by bitter anti-Newtonians. But Newton's universe was in upheaval in ways even he could barely recognize. And he evidently shared some of the distrust of those who, for reasons political, religious or economic, thought their world overturned. In the 1720s Roger North, a one-time solicitor to the Stuart monarchy and since a frustrated Jacobite sympathizer, cast his jaundiced eye over the London of Defoe and Newton. Mixing metaphor with aversion, North commented on the new world of Newtonian mechanics and Robert Walpole's Whig machinations – which Voltaire might celebrate but North continued to deplore: 'If any one sees a vessell in the Thames thrown up by a still tide towards London, would he not say it is conveyed by the stream rather than attracted by that Monstrous City.'[48]

Sustaining the philosophical flux of the Cartesian ether was a minor part of the issue. There were tides in the river on which trade – and philosophy – would depend. Voltaire may have praised a world of active forces, as distinct from a Paris full of Cartesian pressures, but London in the eighteenth century had established an atmosphere where anything seemed possible.[49] However, the ruin caused by the bursting of the South Sea Bubble in 1720 in the alleys of the Exchange provoked profound

---

[48] British Library, Add. MSS. 32548, Works of Roger North, no. 2, fols. 51–2.
[49] Voltaire, *Letters on England*, trans. Leonard Tancock (Harmondsworth, 1980), Letter 14, p. 68.

reactions. The commerce of the Thames had produced a transformation in philosophy and in the metropolis that was left to Jonathan Swift to lament and to others to exploit. North's private but deep dismay was a reaction to the victory of Newtonian natural philosophy that had followed, so he thought, in the wake of Robert Walpole's rapacious Whiggery and a triumphant deism. Like Nicholas Hawksmoor's unfortunate visions, the world had gone to hell.

To look upon London in the aftermath of the South Sea Bubble, and to recognize in the denizens of Birchin Lane and Exchange Alley the promoters of nitre from May-dew that Sprat had once reported or of sunbeams extracted from cucumbers, as Swift soon related, was also to reflect upon what Hogarth then portrayed as the widening gyre of social degeneration. This was profoundly to distrust claims of achievement that were distinctly vulgar and commercial and that left upheaval in their wake. What had begun in the Mississippi debacle in Paris in 1719 and on the Amsterdam bourse had crept across the Channel to destroy fortunes and shatter families in its collapse. Mathematics, in some minds, had gone mad. Thus, Newton's remote and obscure self-fashioning above the vulgar crowd fitted the bill in reinforcing a distance that made the achievement of natural philosophy an exclusive venture of the virtuoso and the scholar.

It is necessary, in my view, to overcome the history of the philosophical hero.[50] Newton could no more control the market in philosophy than he could the laws of gravity. Even the notion of a society of 'Persons of Quality' was overtaken by a more common, commercial and potentially democratic initiative. The very mathematics and experiments which he had helped create were happily exploited by his exponents. His disciples such as Harris and Hodgson, who had appointed themselves his apostles, seized an opportunity and clearly understood the possible expansion of private patronage into a more public world where the market would be moulded to the benefit of philosophers. By the 1730s this public was the mainly anonymous audience of the coffee-houses and those who had witnessed, and puzzled over, the experiments on the mapping of longitude in the nightly burst of William Whiston's mortars over Hampstead Heath.[51]

[50] For one such version see Allan Chapman, 'Edmond Halley's Use of Historical Evidence in the Advancement of Science', *Notes and Records of the Royal Society* 48 (July 1994), pp. 167–91.
[51] Cambridge University Library, RGO.1/34/119, Sharp to Flamsteed, 18 October 1714; Trinity College Library, MS. R.4.42, n. 8, Whiston to Roger Cotes, 26 November 1714; no. 9, Cotes to Whiston, 2 December 1714; no. 11, Whiston to Cotes, 7 April 1715; L. Stewart, *The Rise of Public Science. Rhetoric, Technology, and Natural Philosophy in Newtonian Britain, 1660–1750* (Cambridge, 1992), pp. 190–1; A.J. Turner, 'In the Wake of the Act, but Mainly Before' in William J.H. Andrewes, *The Quest for Longitude* (Cambridge, Mass., 1996), pp. 116–27; Andrea Rusnock, 'Correspondence Networks', unpublished manuscript (1996), pp. 8–10.

In 1742, Whiston was still disturbing the peace, this time beyond Greenwich Observatory from the summit of Shooters Hill.

Like eighteenth-century novelists and painters, the Newtonian lecturers made the image of the solitary, experimental experience one of public exposition. Thus, as Hooke had once undoubtedly known, the coffee-houses tied Fellows of the Royal Society to a commerce that turned scientific principles into commodities – ultimately sold by endless itinerant philosophers in the eighteenth century. The early public performances of the mathematicians of the Marine and of the Hand and Pen represented the transfiguration of the social space of natural philosophy. By the candlelight of Cornhill coffee-houses, Hodgson and Harris asserted the unification of commerce with experiment, of that trade *with* learning which Defoe believed had such consequence. London's dramatic achievement in natural philosophy was not the genteel, and empiric, contemplation of a botanic garden or the prediction of an eclipse to calm simple folk. It was part of a wider national agenda which we might now glimpse in Newton's list of discovery and invention.

Index